POLICE OFFICER

16TH EDITION

DISCARD

Fred M. Rafilson, Ph.D.
I/O Solutions, Inc.
Illinois Fire and Police Recruitment Administration, Inc.

THOMSON

ARCO

Australia • Canada • Mexico • Singapore • Spain • United Kingdom • United States

THOMSON

ARCO

CONTENTS

PART TWO: REVIEW

PART THREE: PRACTICE EXAMINATIONS

PART FOUR: TRAINING

APPENDIX

WHAT THIS BOOK WILL DO FOR YOU

Every city, every town, every county, and every state needs qualified and enthusiastic new police recruits to maintain staffing at full level and to cover all posts. This book was carefully researched and was written to help you through the application and screening process. The information provided will prepare you for the written exam, forewarn about the physical skills you need to concentrate on, and give you valuable tips for your interview and psychological screening.

To make the most of this book, read it carefully. Information about police work itself and the organization of police forces should help psyche you up for the job. Step-by-step descriptions of the screening process give you details about what to expect and will help alleviate any fears or worries you may have about the process. Once you know what to expect, half the battle is won. You can win the other half of the battle by being thoroughly prepared for the written test. You will do this by completing the exercises and practice exams in this book. If you are prepared for both the screening process and your Police Officer exam day, you can feel self-confident, be able to answer questions quickly and decisively, finish the exam, and earn a high score.

HOW TO USE THIS BOOK

The first step is to make a study schedule. Assign yourself a period of time each day to devote to preparation for the police screening process. Choose a quiet, well-lighted spot with as few distractions as possible. Try to arrange not to be interrupted.

Once you have your study plan in place, start reading from the beginning of the book. The first chapters give an overview of the duties of Police Officers and the qualifications that are required. It also gives an overview of the organization and functions within municipal police forces. All of this information will give you a sense of what to expect as a Police Officer and the options you may have in the department to which you are assigned. Don't hesitate to underline points that you consider significant or to make notes in the margins.

The next chapter of the book contains details about each portion of the Police Officer screening process. This includes information about the written and video-based exams, the oral board interview, the medical exam, they psychological evaluation, the background check, and the physical performance tests. Tips are given to help you understand each step of the process. Once you finish reading about the process, you are ready to begin some exercises.

The review sections and exercises in the next chapters cover the three main types of questions that appear on the written police examination. The question types are Practical Judgment, Reading-Based, and Observation and Memory. Many police forces test only in these three areas. Each of these chapters begins with instructions about the topic and the kind of question and gives practical suggestions about how to answer the questions. Read the instructions in each chapter and try the practice questions. Then study the answer explanations. You can learn a great deal from them, and even when you have answered correctly, the explanation may bring out points that had not occurred to you. This will reinforce your understanding of the questions.

When you feel that you are well prepared, move on to the exams. They are sample police examinations and practice exams that were created using questions that have appeared on police exams over the years. We are grateful to the New York Police Department for use of their Test Preparation Kit containing sample exams. Note that many cities have different types of exams; included in this book are samples of various types that you may encounter.

If possible, answer an entire exam in one sitting. If you must divide your time, divide it into no more than two sessions per exam. You need not do the first exam first. The practice exams are somewhat shorter than the actual New York City exams. It might be wise to save the longest exams for a weekend.

When you do take the exams, time yourself accurately and do not peek at the correct answers. Remember, you are taking these for practice; they will not be scored and do not count. So learn from them. Learn to think, learn to reason like a Police Officer, and learn to pace yourself so that you can answer all the questions. Then learn from the explanations. This same suggestion—read *all* the explanations—applies throughout this book, to the exams as well as to the instructional chapters.

Once you have conquered the exams, or if you want to take a break between exams, there is an entire chapter dedicated to the activities of the police academy. It gives information about the type of training to expect and what your classroom experience will be like at the academy.

Lastly, the Appendix of this book gives a sample physical fitness course with a program for women and a program for men. This will help you prepare for your physical performance tests and to reach the fitness level you need for success at the police academy.

The intent is for this book to be an all-inclusive guide for you in that it contains career information and the steps you need to take to launch your career. You will need to do a bit of work on your own to find out about the specifics for the police department in your city since some may have other requirements. But the basics are here, and you will have a better understanding of the Police Officer screening process and the practice you need to score high on your exam.

Congratulations on choosing a career as a Police Officer, and best of luck!

ONE

INTRODUCTION

CHAPTER 1: A CAREER AS A POLICE OFFICER

Why Do People Become Police Officers?

A Police Officer on the beat or in the patrol car is a familiar figure on the American scene. Except among certain criminal elements, the officer is highly respected. Law-abiding citizens are reassured by the presence of police officers whether those officers are directing traffic, discouraging crime by their visible presence, or helping citizens during actual or potential emergencies.

The respect commanded by the Police Officer makes him or her a role model to all young children. Many youngsters entertain the thought of becoming a Police Officer at some point in their lives. In fact, they may retain this career goal into their teen years and take active steps to join a police force as they become young adults.

A combination of factors makes police work attractive. The idealistic young person sees police work as a worthwhile activity. A police officer serves the community. His or her work is absolutely vital to the welfare of the public. Police work provides an opportunity to serve while gaining respect and earning a good living.

The material benefits of police work are very real. Police officers are well-paid public servants. Their salary levels are above average and they receive excellent benefits packages. Police officers also receive health and life insurance coverage along with generous time-off and vacation allotments. They have opportunities for increased responsibility, advancement, promotions, and an early, well-paid retirement.

Another appeal to this career is that a police department never shuts down. This 24-hour, year-round coverage means that police officers sometimes must work nontraditional hours. While the odd working hours may at times interfere with sleep patterns, they offer benefits as well. Family men, in particular, find it a real asset to have some "primetime" hours at home with their children. Police Officers with rotating shifts may have opportunities to share school events or afternoon leisure time with their growing families. Traditional 9-to-5 workers miss these opportunities. Flexible work schedules allow Police Officers to attend to personal business without having to borrow precious vacation days. In addition, local police officers are not required to spend long periods on the road away from their homes and families. Police scheduling is one of the appealing features that draws people into this field and that adds to the competitiveness of entry.

One final aspect of police work that attracts applicants is the potential for excitement. Much police work is routine and monotonous, but the possibility of variety and excitement does exist. The reality is that many desk or production jobs are routine and monotonous with no prospects for interesting relief. Police departments are careful to avoid hiring candidates who seek police work only for the excitement, but they look favorably upon candidates who welcome the challenge of the unexpected.

The popularity of police work makes the field a highly competitive one to enter. There are many more aspiring Police Officers than there are openings on the force. This situation allows police departments to be very selective in the hiring process. Since they have a large applicant pool, they can afford to hire only those applicants who they feel will succeed in their police training and who they expect to become superior Police Officers.

The police department is looking for a combination of positive traits in each prospective Police Officer. The screening process takes each applicant through a series of steps; each are designed to measure a different trait. Recruits must successfully pass through each of these stages. Failure at any stage eliminates a candidate. This leads us to a discussion of the desired traits of police officers and the reasons they are so important to the police force.

Traits of a Police Officer

1. **A Police Officer must be intelligent.** First of all, a recruit must be intelligent enough to make it through the police academy or whatever training program the particular department offers. A recruit must read well to comprehend written materials, must have good listening skills, and must remember what he or she has been taught. A recruit must also be able to learn rules and be able to apply them to hypothetical or actual situations. Remembering information is not enough. The candidate must convince the examiners that he or she can understand, interpret, and apply information in the field. The intelligent Police Officer can separate what is important from what is less important, can make quick judgments, and can express him- or herself well in speech and in writing. Most police departments begin the applicant screening process with a written test. Written tests require a minimum of administrative time. They can be administered to a large number of applicants at one sitting. Applicants who do not score well on the written test are dropped from consideration. There is no reason to spend time administering medical exams, physical performance tests, psychological exams, or interviews to candidates who do not demonstrate the intelligence to learn the job and to serve as effective Police Officers.

2. **A Police Officer must be healthy and physically strong and agile.** Police work is physically taxing. The officer must be able to spend many hours on his or her feet, to move quickly, to see and hear accurately, and to lift, move, or carry as the emergency requires. Obviously, a Police Officer who is often ill or who cannot perform all physical activities adequately is not acceptable. Police departments have strict medical standards so that they hire only recruits in excellent health. A great many medical conditions that are not so severe as to interfere with everyday life nor with most occupations are disqualifying for the Police Officer. Likewise, police departments have carefully devised physical performance tests of strength, speed, and agility. The applicant who cannot qualify on the tests does not show great promise for success as a Police Officer. Medical and physical screening are important hurdles in the selection process.

3. **A Police Officer must be emotionally stable.** A Police Officer carries a gun; anyone who is armed must be even-tempered, well adjusted, and impartial. When it comes to

dealing with firearms, there is no room for error. It is vital that the Police Officer not become excited nor fire too soon. The Police Officer must be able to size up a situation without fear or prejudice, then act appropriately. He or she cannot be ruled by anger; at the same time, the Police Officer cannot hesitate when prompt action is required. Police brutality, insult, and behavior on the basis of preconceived opinions have no place anywhere in the police force. Choosing the most stable recruits from among the applicants is one of the more difficult tasks for those in charge of hiring. Applicants who have done well on the written exam and who have passed a medical examination and physical fitness tests must often submit to psychological exams. Psychological examinations are not always satisfactory, but police departments must rely on them to eliminate those candidates who appear to be less than perfectly adjusted and stable. Because psychological testing tends to be inexact, the test results are often confirmed through interviews. Through a psychological test (often more than one) and interviews, each applicant who has reached this stage of the screening process must demonstrate the emotional stability required for responsible behavior in the police role.

4. **A Police Officer must be self-confident and tactful.** These personality aspects are the final refinements upon which hiring decisions are based. Judgments of these traits are based on interviews. The Police Officer must have the self-confidence to make quick decisions and to stick with them. Unwavering decisions and firm actions are vital in maintaining control. Tactful, gentle, but firm: these are the hallmarks of the effective, successful Police Officer. The interviewer hopes to choose the applicants who best display these qualities in a fine, delicate balance. The judgment cannot be entirely objective, but the interviewer does his or her best. The Police Officer candidate, in turn, can make a conscious effort to impress the interviewer as a tactful, thoughtful person who can communicate and take over effectively under pressure.

Duties of a Police Officer

The fundamental purpose of the police throughout America is crime prevention through law enforcement, and, to most citizens, the most visible representative of this effort is the uniformed Police Officer. There is no more important police function than day-to-day patrol activities, for the effectiveness of police agencies depends on it.

After basic training, most Police Officers are assigned to patrol duty and their specific duties and responsibilities are numerous and varied. Unlike the specialist, Patrol Officers must perform well in a variety of tasks. Regardless of police department size, these officers have two basic responsibilities:

1. To prevent criminal activities.
2. To furnish day-to-day police service to the community.

Patrol Officers protect the public, interpret and enforce the law, control traffic, and perform preliminary investigations. They frequently face situations that require swift yet sound decisions. For example, they must decide whether to refrain from taking action in an incident or to offer advice, and whether to warn or to arrest persons, perhaps using firearms or substantial force. In some situations, they must determine the difference between crime and bizarre behavior, or between disturbing the peace and legitimate dissent by citizens. Regardless of the circumstances, their first duty is protection of constitutional guarantees, and their second duty is enforcement of the law.

Police Officers patrol assigned sectors in motor vehicles or on foot, working alone or with a partner, paying close attention to area conditions and inhabitants. During patrol, Police Officers observe suspicious behavior or conditions and illegal activities in their sector and report incidents by radio to a superior officer prior to taking action. They investigate incidents and question the individuals involved to determine violations of the law. They respond to radio calls sent by police dispatchers or superior officers ordering them to the scene of incidents such as burglaries, bank robberies, homicides, rapes, suicides, assaults, and crimes in progress. They make preliminary investigations, question victims and witnesses, recover stolen property, and take evidence into possession. Where indicated, they arrest suspects at crime scenes or after pursuit and use physical force and firearms to subdue them. When making arrests, they advise suspects of their constitutional rights, as required by law, and transport them in police vehicles to police booking and detention facilities prior to court arraignment. At the time of trial, Police Officers testify in court to provide evidence for prosecuting attorneys.

Traffic control is an essential part of police patrol activities. Police Officers direct and control pedestrian and vehicular traffic in high-density areas to ensure safe and rapid movement, observe parked and moving vehicles for evidence of traffic violations, and issue citations for violations of traffic regulations. Other responsibilities include maintaining order and traffic flow during public gatherings, demonstrations, and emergencies such as riots, fires, explosions, auto accidents, and natural disasters, using crowd control and traffic direction techniques to carry out such assignments. They administer first aid to victims of accidents or crimes and arrange for the dispatch of medical units to the scene. In cases of traffic accidents, they investigate circumstances and causes and record findings for subsequent use by the parties involved and their attorneys.

Assignment to patrol duty requires performance of a number of miscellaneous tasks. Police Officers check entrances and exits of commercial facilities for security during hours of darkness. In some police departments, officers inspect residential buildings for safety and suggest methods of improving security, such as installing special locks, alarms, or improved lighting in entry areas. They inspect premises of public, licensed business establishments to enforce laws, local ordinances, and regulations concerning their operation. Police Officers also provide information and assistance to inquiring citizens, help to settle domestic disputes when called to the scene, and may lend assistance in cases of emergency childbirth. They note conditions that are hazardous to the public such as obstructions, potholes, inoperable street lamps, and defective traffic signals, and report them for appropriate action. At the conclusion of each daily work tour, a Police Officer prepares a written activity report that describes arrests, incidents, and all relevant information gathered and submits it to a superior officer, usually a Police Sergeant.

As noted previously, Police Officers on patrol duty are generalists who perform a number of police functions as well. The chart below lists many of the varied functions they must perform.

LISTING OF ESSENTIAL JOB TASKS PERFORMED BY POLICE OFFICERS

Arrest and Apprehension

Use appropriate level of force

Make judgments about arresting or releasing suspects or offenders

Identify and apprehend offenders

Handcuff suspects or prisoners

Conduct frisk and pat down

Advise persons of constitutional rights

Seize contraband

Use deadly force when necessary

Execute arrest warrants

Fire weapons on duty

Pursue suspects on foot

Execute search warrants

Pursue suspects in vehicle

Obtain and serve protection orders and committals

Investigation

Secure and maintain accident, crime, and disaster scenes

Investigate crimes against persons and property

Investigate suspicious and criminal activity

Interview witnesses

Investigate suspicious persons or vehicles

Collect and preserve evidence

Make judgments about probable cause for warrantless searches

Search crime scene for physical evidence

Investigate complaints of drug law violations

Locate witnesses to crime

Interrogate suspects

Process crime scene, fingerprints, accident scene, etc

Search premises or property

Document chain of custody for evidence

Review information on criminal activity in area

Transport property or evidence

Diagram crime/accident scenes

Check stolen status on property through computer network

Search for missing people

Recover and inventory stolen property

Photograph crime/accident scenes

Investigate nontraffic accidents

Conduct criminal background checks

Examine dead bodies

Collect and maintain intelligence data

Conduct surveillance of locations

Conduct surveillance of individuals

Estimate value of stolen or recovered goods

Trace stolen goods

Patrol

Enforce criminal laws

Respond to calls

Drive motor vehicle under nonemergency conditions

Search persons, vehicles, and places

Drive motor vehicle under emergency conditions

Patrol assigned area in a vehicle

Issue citations for nontraffic offenses

Make checks of various types of premises

Check schools, playgrounds, parks, and recreational centers

Patrol (cont.)

Warn offenders in lieu of arrest or citation

Assist emergency medical officers

Patrol assigned area on foot

Advise vehicle owners to remove abandoned vehicles

Traffic Enforcement

Enforce traffic and parking laws and ordinances

Investigate traffic accidents

Check vehicles for proper registration

Request emergency assistance for accidents

Identify owners of vehicle involved in accidents

Control, regulate, and direct vehicular and pedestrian traffic

Locate witnesses to accidents

Direct traffic using barriers, flares, and hand signals

Administer roadside sobriety tests

Follow suspicious vehicles

Operate breathalyzer test apparatus

Remove hazards from roadways

Arrange for obtaining blood or urine samples for sobriety tests

Collect physical evidence from accident scenes

Aid the injured

Assist stranded motorists

Measure skid marks

Issue parking citations

Communication

Communicate with dispatcher, other police vehicles, and commanding officers by radio

Exchange necessary information with other police officers at a scene

Provide accurate oral descriptions

Interact, communicate, and work with citizens

Participate in briefings/debriefings with other officers

Conduct interrogations/interviews

Mediate domestic disputes

Explain nature of complaints to offenders, witnesses, and victims

Inform other units of major incidents

Contact supervisory personnel to discuss problems or obtain information

Interact, communicate, and work with a diverse group of citizens from various cultural backgrounds

Direct actions of assisting officers or public service personnel

Comfort emotionally upset persons

Advise offenders, witnesses, and victims on legal procedures

Refer persons to agencies providing social services

Facilitate parent-juvenile communications

Request assistance from other agencies

Court Procedures

Testify in criminal and civil court cases

Read and review reports for court testimony

Present evidence in legal proceedings

Confer with judges, attorneys, bailiffs, sheriffs, probation, parole, and correction officers

Obtain search and arrest warrants

Paperwork

Write reports

Write citations and summonses

Write memos

Review and sign reports to ensure completeness and accuracy

Physical Tasks

- Subdue and arrest resisting/attacking individuals
- Encounter armed suspects
- Encounter resistance during an arrest or in an emergency situation
- Sit or stand for long periods of time
- Recover weapon from suspect who gives it up voluntarily
- Perform an evasive maneuver (dodge, duck, block, push, shove, pull, etc.) in order to disarm a suspect
- Subdue and physically restrain an intoxicated individual
- Run fast for a short period of time to apprehend a suspect
- Climb over obstacles such as fences, shrubs, and ditches
- Walk up and down flights of stairs
- Climb over obstacles lower than six feet
- Run a distance under 50 yards
- Force entry into buildings
- Run to persons requiring emergency assistance
- Pull self up over obstacles
- Run a distance over 50 yards
- Jump down from elevated surfaces
- Walk for long periods of time
- Lift, pick up, and/or carry heavy objects or equipment
- Pull self through openings
- Climb through small openings (e.g., windows)
- Drag an injured/deceased person
- Physically push large heavy objects
- Run for long periods of time

Miscellaneous

- Clean and inspect weapons, patrol equipment, and patrol vehicle
- Maintain target practice skills
- Perform special duties as assigned by supervisors
- Transport children and endangered individuals to protective environments
- Evacuate persons from dangerous areas
- Assist elderly or disabled persons
- Transport mental patients to rehabilitation facilities
- Maintain crowd control at special events, etc.
- Respond to and resolve animal complaints

Working Conditions

- Work during night shifts
- Work on or around moving machinery or equipment, including patrol cars
- Work for extended periods of time without breaks or relief
- Work in confined spaces in cramped body positions, including patrol car
- Work in extreme temperatures
- Work when visibility is poor
- Work when visibility is nonexistent
- Avoid and protect against high noise levels when riding in emergency vehicles
- Work in wet areas
- Work in icy areas
- Work in slippery areas
- Work in muddy areas

SPECIALIZED ASSIGNMENTS

Many aspects of modern police service are complex and require use of specialized personnel. The degree of specialization within a police agency varies with the size and resources of the department and needs of the community. Small communities usually require less specialization, while highly populated areas make specialists a necessity. In small police agencies, specialists are generally used on a part-time basis, while the larger departments usually employ full-time specialists. The following are some examples of the various specialized assignments carried out by Police Officers.

Bomb Squad Officers are highly trained police personnel who respond to incidents of bomb threats and report to locations where bombs have been detonated. Sophisticated equipment and specially trained dogs may be used to locate and disarm explosive and incendiary devices; many of them are real while others are cleverly constructed hoaxes.

Community Relations Officers help to develop and maintain contact between the police department and community groups, organizations, and schools in the area. Their objective is to promote understanding of the police role in the community, develop closer working relationships, and keep open the lines of communication between citizens and the police department. These officers meet with members of the community and assist in developing police-sponsored programs to help reduce crime. Other duties include conducting tours of police facilities and addressing student and civic groups on relevant topics such as drug abuse, crime prevention, and traffic safety.

Canine Officers team with specially trained dogs to provide assistance to other police units within the department. For example, they are called to different scenes where their special skills are used to conduct building searches, track suspects in wooded or mountainous terrain, locate lost persons, or help in crowd-control operations. Canine Officers personally train their dogs with the help of professional instructors and are responsible for the animals' general care as well.

Crime Prevention Officers conduct security surveys of multiple-dwelling and commercial establishments and suggest methods of improving security, such as the use of burglar alarms, window gates, and better locking devices. Speaking before civic groups to inform citizens of crime prevention and safety methods and presenting slides and movies that demonstrate various crime prevention programs may be other job duties. In some departments, Crime Prevention Officers analyze information contained in police reports for indications of crime patterns or trends. They then alert police units to potential problem areas and methods of operation used by perpetrators. This often effects a reduction in criminal activities.

Emergency Service Officers are highly trained police personnel who are brought into situations that other Police Officers are not equipped to handle. Examples of problems dealt with range from people threatening to jump from bridges or high buildings to persons trapped in automobile wreckage or threatened by a dangerous animal. Such cases require a special expertise, and these officers have the equipment and training needed to do the job.

In some police agencies, Police Officers are assigned to **Fugitive Search Units,** where they are responsible for conducting investigations to locate and return fugitives for prosecution by criminal justice agencies. Data received from national, regional, and state crime information centers is examined and employers and other law enforcement agencies are contacted to develop leads. Once a fugitive is located, these officers obtain the legal documents necessary for custody and may be required to travel to other criminal justice agencies throughout the country to return prisoners wanted for unlawful flight.

Harbor Patrol is a specialized unit in which Police Officers are responsible for patrolling municipal harbors to detect and apprehend criminals and to aid persons in distress. Patrol is usually in power launches and may involve rescuing drowning victims, recovering bodies, or assisting ships in distress. These officers also cooperate with other law enforcement agencies in an effort to apprehend criminals and prevent smuggling or entry of illegal aliens.

Hostage Negotiation Teams are another area in which some Police Officers may specialize. Members of these units are specially trained officers who have the difficult task of rescuing hostages from their captors without bloodshed or violence. This is hardly easy, because persons holding hostages are often nervous and desperate. Such situations require cool, calm, and logical actions on the part of each officer.

Police Officers in certain police departments are members of **Intelligence Units.** These units gather and compile information about community conditions, potential problems, organized crime, and lawlessness in the form of civil disorder. To obtain this data, officers often work undercover to infiltrate organized crime and terrorist groups or seemingly legitimate businesses used as fronts for criminal activities. They coordinate their activities with other law enforcement agencies, and furnish current information about the location and activities of members of organized crime and subversive groups to local, state, and federal agents.

Police Officers assigned to **Juvenile Units** have the responsibility of conducting juvenile investigations, providing assistance to field officers in matters involving juvenile problems, and coordinating efforts with other agencies such as courts, schools, and social service and counseling agencies. Juvenile Officers investigate not only juvenile offenses but also cases of lost or runaway children to discover their whereabouts and to locate their parents. They take into custody delinquent or neglected children and refer cases involving serious offenses to the juvenile court system. They also patrol neighborhoods where youths gather, investigate reports of large gatherings that might indicate trouble, and enlist the help of the community in preventing potential juvenile problems.

Mounted Police Officers are specially trained officers who patrol their assigned areas on horseback or motorcycle. Officers on horseback perform the basic duties of the Patrol Officer, but their skills are particularly effective in crowd control activities. Through skillful handling of their mounts, these officers preserve order where large crowds congregate, such as at parades and sporting events, and, in cases of riot or civil unrest, disperse unruly crowds. Officers patrolling on motorcycles perform important traffic control duties in congested areas by helping to facilitate the flow of traffic. In many cases, patrol cars are unable to reach the scene of disturbances or accidents, and motorcycle officers, first on the scene, provide assistance to sick or injured persons, direct traffic around fires or explosions, and perform general police work by keeping order and apprehending criminals.

Another specialized assignment that may be available to Police Officers is the **Property Unit.** Property Officers are responsible for property confiscated as evidence, removed from suspects, lost or stolen, or purchased by police department officials. Work also involves keeping detailed records of all properties under their control and, when authorized, releasing property to arresting officers for use as evidence in legal proceedings. They return personal property to suspects being released from custody and contact owners of lost or stolen property to claim articles upon proof of ownership. Property Officers keep extensive records of articles confiscated during arrests, such as narcotics and firearms, and arrange for their transfer to official disposal sites when required by law. Responsibilities may also include receiving and examining property purchased by the department to verify the completeness and satisfactory condition of these purchases against invoices or other records.

Aviation programs in which Police Officers are trained as **Police Pilots** provide another area of police specialization. Because aircraft are not restricted by roads or traffic congestion, larger areas can be patrolled, and aircraft can be used for aerial surveillance missions, high-speed transportation, and police rescue missions. Police pilots may fly helicopters, conventional fixed-wing aircraft, or Short Takeoff and Landing (STOL) aircraft in carrying out their assignments. Helicopters are very effective in urban patrol as part of helicopter-automobile patrol teams. They can shorten response time to crime scenes, hover, or patrol at slow speeds to observe ground activities or illuminate an area at night. Conventional fixed-wing aircraft are very effective in highway speed enforcement as part of air-ground teams and in search and surveillance operations. Unlike the helicopter, however, they cannot hover or cruise at the reduced speeds needed in urban areas. STOL aircraft combine some of the characteristics of the helicopter with those of conventional fixed-wing aircraft. These aircraft can take off and land in shorter distances than those required for other fixed-wing aircraft. Faster than most helicopters, they can cruise at slower speeds than other fixed-wing craft and can stay airborne without refueling twice as long as rotary-wing aircraft. Regardless of the type of aircraft they fly, Police Pilots play a crucial role in law enforcement activities.

In some departments, cases of rape and sexual assault are the responsibility of Police Officers assigned to **Sex Crimes Units**. These crimes create special problems for both victims and the criminal justice system. Fear of harassment or humiliation during police investigations and medical examinations can make victims reluctant to report such crimes and to go through the ordeal of a trial. Sex Crimes Units are staffed with both male and female officers who are specially trained and sensitive to the plight of victims. They can provide needed support during medical examinations, interviews with police and public prosecutors, and subsequent investigations. In some departments, rape victims, if they so desire, can deal exclusively with other women who act both as interviewers and as criminal investigators. These officers can also provide referral to community agencies that give special help to victims of sex crimes.

Anti-Crime or **Street-Crime Units** are a successful innovation being used by many departments throughout the country. Police Officers assigned to these units work in high-crime areas, out of uniform, and pose as unsuspecting citizens from various walks of life. Their objective is to present themselves as targets for assaults and robberies and to apprehend suspects who attempt to commit such crimes. These decoys team with backup units in the area so that a response is made when suspects attempt to carry out crimes against the decoy officers. Members of these units also conduct surveillance activities on stakeouts.

Many police agencies have developed **Tactical Forces**—highly mobile units that can be deployed rapidly against special crime problems. Normally made up of Police Officers from within the police agency, and varying in size from a few officers on small forces to several hundred on larger forces, these units are motorized and assigned to areas where patterns of serious crimes are occurring. The work can be varied and officers may find themselves working in plainclothes on a robbery detail and then be abruptly assigned to work in uniform on a different type of assignment. When no specific crime problems occur in a particular area, these officers are deployed over a wider area and then, if needed, can be called back quickly to work as a unit on a particular case. In some police agencies, these officers are members of specially trained units, such as sniper-suppression teams and Special Weapons Attack Teams (SWAT), which are used during specified emergency situations. The overall purpose of Tactical Forces is to strengthen the regular patrol force and help the line units to meet their goals.

Police Instructors are another example of the varied specializations into which Police Officers may move. These training officers instruct police recruits in basic phases of police work and in the duties and responsibilities of the Police Officer. They conduct lectures, discussions, and demonstrations and use audiovisual materials to teach basic core skills to new personnel. Subject matter of the training sessions includes criminal law, traffic regulations, human relations, criminal investigation, patrol techniques, report writing, firearms, and physical training. In addition to training police recruits, Police Instructors train veteran officers through in-service courses and refresher sessions. Some instructors specialize in one area of training. The educational and background qualifications for this position vary among departments.

Traffic Officers are members of specialized police units whose aim is to produce voluntary compliance with traffic regulations and provide maximum mobility of traffic with a minimum of interruption. These enforcement units operate in preselected locations in which high rates of vehicular and pedestrian accidents, auto thefts, and traffic-law violations occur. Traffic enforcement is closely related to other police activities because, in many instances, persons stopped for traffic violations are found to be involved in criminal activities or are fugitives wanted in another jurisdiction.

SPECIAL-PURPOSE PUBLIC POLICE FORCES

In addition to the Police Officers who work in local and county police agencies, there are others who are employed by special-purpose public police forces in many cities throughout the United States. Some typical examples include park, harbor, airport, sanitation, transit, housing, and port police forces. Some of these agencies have full peace-officer powers within their limited jurisdictions, while others have limited authority.

Housing Authority Officers patrol grounds, cellars, roofs, stairwells, and elevators of public housing projects. Officers are assigned to various housing projects around the clock according to local crime statistics. They conduct investigations of all crimes and disturbances on properties within their jurisdiction and apprehend and arrest suspects, using physical force or firearms if necessary.

Transit Authority Officers enforce the law and provide security services for municipal transit systems. These officers patrol subway stations, trains, and bus terminals, particularly during the high-crime late-night hours. They apprehend and arrest suspects and use physical force and firearms if necessary to carry out their duties. The jurisdiction of Transit Officers is not limited to Transit Authority property. They have full police powers to enforce all local, state, and federal laws anywhere in the city.

Port Authority Police may be employed by an authority created to administer a port that spans more than one city or state. The Port Authority of New York and New Jersey is one example of such a port authority. Port Authority Police are responsible for policing and providing security in bus, rail, and air terminals; tunnels and bridges; and any properties or facilities operated by the Port Authority. Port Authority Officers enforce the law and apprehend and arrest suspects using physical force or firearms if necessary. Other responsibilities include controlling traffic and crowds and handling emergency situations occurring within their jurisdiction.

General Working Conditions

Police Officers work in many locations, which range from boroughs, townships, and counties to urban areas of varying sizes. Working conditions vary considerably according to location, size, organization, and jurisdiction of the police agency. Those who work in small towns and rural communities most certainly face problems different from those met by their counterparts in the inner cities of larger urban areas.

There are definite differences in pace, types of criminal activities encountered, and availability of manpower and services needed to provide adequate police protection to the public. But all Police Officers, regardless of where they work, share certain problems. They constantly deal with human suffering, yet must always maintain self-control and act in a calm, efficient manner. They face danger, difficulty, and frustration, perhaps daily, but can do little to prevent it from happening. They also share the problems of long, irregular hours and, in some communities, a lack of public support for police officers.

As a rule, most Police Officers, while conducting patrols or carrying out other assignments, work outdoors in all types of weather. Some officers on special duty may perform their duties indoors at police facilities. Depending on the size of the department, Police Officers work alone or may have a partner. Because police agencies operate 24 hours a day, officers are usually required to work five-day rotating shifts, including holidays and weekends. Police Officers are on call at all times and, during periods of emergency or manpower shortages, are required to work additional tours of duty.

All Police Officers, regardless of where they work or the size of the employing police agency, *live with the very real threat of physical injury or death*. The apprehension of suspects who may be armed and dangerous, situations involving high-speed chases, or the rescue of individuals attempting suicide are some of the possibilities that make this work *hazardous*. Such hazards should be fully considered by individuals thinking about a police career.

In most police agencies, Police Officers have fringe benefits that include some or all of the following:

- paid vacation
- sick leave
- holidays
- overtime pay
- life, medical, and disability insurance

- uniform allowances
- tuition assistance or refund programs for college studies
- retirement pension

In some departments, officers may retire after 20 years of service if they are from 50 to 55 years of age. In departments with different standards, Police Officers may retire after 20 years of service regardless of age.

Employment Outlook

The tragic events of September 11, 2001 highlighted both the dangers of the law enforcement occupation and the courage of the men and women who are called to the profession. According to the Officer Down Memorial Page, seventy-two law enforcement officers lost their lives that day. However, because of their selfless actions, many more lives were saved. Even though the hazards of the profession have become all too clear, thousands of men and women strongly desire to become police officers and serve their communities. It is a particularly attractive career because of the challenges it presents and the personal responsibility that is bestowed upon every officer. In addition, in many agencies, law enforcement officers are assured financial stability through pension plans that are available after 20 or 25 years of service. This allows many individuals to pursue a second career while still in their 40s.

Due to the relatively attractive salaries and benefits afforded to those with jobs in law enforcement, there are currently more qualified candidates than job openings in federal law enforcement agencies and in most local, state, and special police departments. As a result, hiring standards have become increasingly selective. Competition for law enforcement jobs is particularly intense for higher-paying jobs with state and federal agencies and in police departments that are located in more affluent areas. Accordingly, opportunities for employment are likely to be best in communities whose departments offer relatively low salaries and where the crime rate is relatively high. Candidates with military experience, college training in police science, or both are likely to have the best opportunities.

According to the U.S. Department of Labor's Bureau of Labor Statistics, employment of police and detectives is expected to increase faster than the average for all occupations through 2010. Citizen concern about terrorism and drug-related crimes contributes to the increasing demand for police services. At the local and state levels, growth is likely to continue as long as citizens remain seriously concerned about crime. However, employment at the federal level will depend upon the continuing budgetary constraints faced by many law enforcement agencies.

The level of government spending for those occupations determines the level of employment for law enforcement occupations. Therefore, the number of job opportunities can vary from place to place and from year to year. Layoffs for these occupations are rare, however, because most staffing cuts can be handled through retirement. In addition, those in law enforcement occupations who lose their jobs because of budget cuts rarely have difficulty finding employment with other agencies. Overall, turnover in law enforcement occupations is among the lowest for all occupations. Most job openings come from those who retire, transfer to other occupations, or stop working for other reasons.

Training and Promotion Opportunities

Following the completion of training, new officers are assigned to work under the supervision of a veteran officer. Experienced officers evaluate their work performance from time to time during the probationary period, which may last one year to 18 months. New officers may also team with experienced officers who provide them with practical instruction and field experience. After successfully completing the probationary period, these officers become permanent licensed or certified law enforcement officers; then they are sworn in and awarded a badge.

Once entry into this work is made, promotional prospects are generally good and are usually governed by merit or civil service system regulations. Police Officers as a rule become eligible for promotion after a specified number of years (three to five in most police agencies). Promotions are made according to the officer's position on a promotion list, determined by scores on a competitive written examination as well as ratings of on-the-job performance. The first promotional level for uniformed Police Officers is the position of Sergeant. Thereafter, they are eligible to compete for other positions such as Lieutenant, Captain, or higher command positions the titles of which vary among police agencies throughout the country. A Police Officer might instead opt for lateral promotion into the Detective division. The officer would then begin as a Police Detective, moving up the ranks to Detective Sergeant, Detective Lieutenant, Detective Captain, and even beyond as merited by education, performance, and scores on competitive examinations.

Current Earnings

According to the U.S. Department of Labor Statistics, police and sheriff's patrol officers had median annual earnings of $39,790 in 2000. The middle 50 percent earned between $30,460 and $50,230. The lowest 10 percent earned less than $23,790 and the highest 10 percent earned more than $58,900. Median annual earnings were $44,400 in state government positions, $39,710 in local government positions, and $37,760 in federal government positions.

In 2000, median annual earnings of police and detective supervisors were $57,210. The middle 50 percent earned between $43,630 and $70,680. The lowest 10 percent earned less than $34,660 and the highest 10 percent earned more than $86,060. Median annual earnings were $74,070 in federal government positions, $57,030 in local government positions, and $53,960 in state government positions.

In 2000, median annual earnings of detectives and criminal investigators were $48,870. The middle 50 percent earned between $37,240 and $61,750. The lowest 10 percent earned less than $29,600 and the highest 10 percent earned more than $72,160. Median annual earnings were $61,180 in federal government positions, $46,340 in local government positions, and $43,050 in state government positions.

Federal employees who serve in law enforcement are provided with special salary rates through federal laws. Federal special agents and inspectors also receive law enforcement availability pay (LEAP), which is equal to 25 percent of the agent's grade and step-awarded because of the large amount of overtime that these agents are expected to work. In 2001, FBI agents entered federal services as GS-10 employees on the pay scale at a base salary of $36,621, yet earned about $45,776 a year with availability pay. They can advance to the GS-13 grade level in field nonsupervisory assignments at a base salary of $57,345, which is worth almost $71,681 with availability pay. Salaries were slightly higher in selected areas where the prevailing local pay was higher. Applicants should ask their recruiter for more information regarding the special law enforcement benefits packages available to federal agents.

Due to payments for overtime, total earnings for local, state, and special Police Officers and Detectives frequently exceeds the stated salary. In addition, most law enforcement positions are provided with benefits such as paid vacation, sick leave, medical and life insurance, and special allowances for uniforms.

A Career as a Police Detective

Police Detectives, key members of the police law enforcement team, conduct investigations to prevent crime, protect life and property, and solve criminal cases, which can range from misdemeanors to homicide. As a rule, crimes are initially investigated by uniformed Police Officers who are dispatched to crime scenes to apprehend suspects, question witnesses, and preserve evidence. If arrests are not made or the crime remains unsolved, Detectives take over the criminal investigation.

DUTIES OF THE JOB

Working in plainclothes, Detectives assigned to a case report to the scene, where possible, and determine the nature of the incident, exact location and time of the occurrence, and probable reason for the crime. They obtain reports from uniformed Police Officers; question witnesses, victims, and suspects if they have been apprehended; and arrange for official statements to be given at a police station or headquarters. In addition, they search the area carefully to detect clues and gather evidence for use in the investigation. Detectives then direct Evidence Technicians to examine the scene to locate and lift latent fingerprints and to photograph the scene and any evidence obtained for eventual use in preparing the case for court. In some police departments, Detectives trained in fingerprinting and photography perform these duties themselves.

In seeking solutions to crimes, Detectives use all the resources of the police agency, such as ballistics experts, police chemists, laboratory technicians, computers, and speedy communication systems. Once all of the available information has been compiled, they analyze the results to determine the direction the investigation will take. Detectives study the files and records of suspects, if any; evaluate police laboratory findings; and prepare detailed reports including descriptions of evidence, names and statements of witnesses and victims, circumstances of the crime, and statements made by suspects. In attempts to develop leads, copies of fingerprints found at the crime scene may be transmitted to the State Crime Information Center (S.C.I.C.) and National Crime Information Center (N.C.I.C.) for comparison with those found at scenes in other localities. Information may also be given to police artists in their own departments or state and local law enforcement agencies for use in preparing composite sketches of suspects. Members of police patrol units are advised about crimes occurring in various areas and about the methods of operation used by perpetrators. In many instances, Police Detectives question informants on their knowledge of a crime or on their information about the personal habits, associates, characteristics, and aliases of crime suspects.

As evidence begins to develop, court-approved wire-tapping or electronic surveillance methods may be used to gather data pertinent to the investigation. Detectives conduct surveillance of suspects on foot or in vehicles to uncover illegal activities; they participate in stakeouts at specific locations to gather evidence or prevent commission of crimes. When all investigative efforts have been made, each Detective prepares a written progress report of the case assigned and submits it to the Detective Sergeant or other superior officer for criticism and suggestions. At this point, the Detective usually plans what action is to be taken to resolve the case based on the evidence gathered and the recommendations of supervisory officers. Police Detectives arrest, or participate in the arrest of suspects based on this evidence and as authorized by appropriate legal warrants.

During the process of arrest, Detectives are authorized to use firearms and/or physical force where necessary to subdue suspects. At the time of arrest, they advise suspects of their constitutional rights and escort them to the police station or headquarters for booking, interrogation, and detention. Suspects are turned over to designated police personnel for fingerprinting, photographing, recording of personal effects, and checking of their records by the records section of the department against outstanding warrants in other jurisdictions.

An important responsibility of Police Detectives involves the preparation of criminal cases scheduled for trial. This entails preparing a written summary of facts gathered during the investigation, including evidence obtained and official statements made by witnesses, victims, Police Officers, and defendants. Prior to trial, Detectives usually review the case summary with the prosecutor to detect legal flaws; they may have to supply supplemental data to strengthen the case for the prosecution. Detectives spend many hours in court testifying as arresting officers and appearing as witnesses for the prosecution. In instances of unsolved cases, Detectives usually forward copies of the fingerprints gathered during the investigation to the FBI for comparison with prints that will be recorded during future arrests made nationwide by other law enforcement agencies.

The duties just described are common to Police Detectives in most local, county, and state investigative units. The increasing complexities of police work, however, have caused many agencies to use Detectives as specialists in various types of investigations. The size and resources of the department plus the needs of the community determine the extent of such specialization. Detectives in small police agencies tend to specialize less and are usually generalists who investigate a wide range of crimes. Detectives in large departments in heavily populated urban or suburban areas are more likely to specialize. The following are examples of some of the specialized assignments carried out by Police Detectives.

SPECIALIZED ASSIGNMENTS

Bombing/arson cases are those in which Detectives investigate incidents of suspected arson or the use or presence of explosive devices. Arson is the intentional or attempted destruction, by fire or explosion, of the property of another, or of one's own property, with the intent to defraud. Bombing incidents involve detonation or attempted detonation of an explosive or incendiary device for a criminal purpose or with disregard for the safety and property of others. In some departments, Detectives remove or supervise the removal of suspected explosive devices to safe areas, using special skills and equipment to reduce the risk to police personnel and public safety.

Detectives assigned to **Burglary/Robbery Units** specialize in the investigation of such incidents to solve current criminal cases and to prevent future crimes of this sort. Burglary is the actual or attempted entry of a structure, with or without force, with the intent to steal or commit a felony (serious crime). Robbery is the unlawful taking or attempted taking of property in the immediate possession of another person by force or threat of force, with or without a deadly weapon.

Fraud and Embezzlement Detectives specialize in crimes involving embezzlement, fraud, forgery, and counterfeiting. Embezzlement is the illegal appropriation of entrusted property with the intention of defrauding the legal owner or beneficiary. Fraud involves deceit or intentional misrepresentation with the aim of illegally depriving a person of his or her property or legal rights. Forgery is the creation or alteration of a written or printed document with the intention to defraud by claiming it is the act of an unknown second party. In a check forgery, for example, the forged signature is accepted as being legitimate and the transaction is completed. Counterfeiting involves manufacture of a copy or imitation of a negotiable instrument with value set by law. Examples of counterfeited items include paper currency, coins, postage, food stamps, and bearer bonds. The investigations into these "white-collar crimes" bring Detectives into close association with representatives of banks, brokerage firms, hotels, and retail establishments, as well as law enforcement agencies.

Homicide Detectives investigate criminal homicide cases in which one person is killed by another or other cases where death appears imminent as the result of aggravated assault. Criminal homicides are those that involve the death of another person without justification or excuse and include acts such as murder and voluntary, involuntary, and vehicular man-slaughter.

Detectives assigned to a **Juvenile Section** or **Division** specialize in investigating cases involving juveniles (youths under 18 years of age who are subject to the jurisdiction of a Juvenile Court). These Detectives investigate all cases of juvenile crime. They maintain surveillance in areas where youths gather to keep abreast of happenings and to develop case leads and arrest juveniles suspected of violating the law. Cases involving serious offenses are referred to the Juvenile Court and parents or guardians are notified to advise them of circumstances in the case. Meetings may also be held with parents or guardians of juveniles in detainment, but not arrested or charged, to stress the need for increased supervision to prevent development of delinquent behavior.

Narcotics Detectives conduct specialized investigations to identify and apprehend persons suspected of illegal use or sale of narcotics and other dangerous drugs. Narcotics Detectives examine physicians' and pharmacists' records to determine the legality of sales and to monitor the distribution of narcotics and the quantity of drugs in stock. They must often perform undercover work to investigate known or suspected drug suppliers and handlers who have been identified through surveillance or informants. Detectives purchase narcotics from suspects for use as evidence and arrest individuals identified as distributors, suppliers, and pushers. Narcotics Detectives also work on a cooperative basis with other police agencies involved in narcotics investigations and with federal agencies such as the Drug Enforcement Administration (DEA).

Detectives in some police agencies are part of **Organized Crime Activities Units** and specialize in investigating such activities. They gather data about members of organized criminal groups through the use of informers, surveillance, and infiltration by undercover officers. Not only are cases involving members of organized crime solved by such efforts, but also numerous criminal acts are prevented from occurring at all. Often, participation in the Federal Organized Strike Force Programs and work with members of law enforcement agencies from all levels of government is part of these Detectives' assignments.

Motor Vehicle Theft and Truck Hijacking is another type of investigative specialization. Detectives question salvage and junkyard operators, motor vehicle and motor parts dealers, owners of retail stores, and pawnbrokers to uncover possible leads. They check inventories and records to make certain that stocks are legitimate. They maintain surveillance of known thieves and fences who illegally dispose of stolen property, use informers, and take suspects into custody when sufficient evidence has been gathered. Other duties include identification of stolen property and making arrangements for its return to owners.

Investigation of establishments and persons suspected of violating morality and antivice laws pertaining to liquor, gambling, and prostitution is the concern of **Vice Squad Detectives**. They monitor places where liquor is sold to check on hours of operation, underage patrons, and general adherence to the law. Establishing surveillance of suspects and locations to gather evidence of gambling and/or prostitution activities and working undercover to gain access are also part of the job. When sufficient evidence is gathered, necessary legal warrants are obtained, raids on suspects' "establishments" are conducted, and accused persons are taken into custody.

In addition to those just mentioned, Detectives may, in some police agencies, specialize in the investigation of sex offenses, kidnappings, bank robberies, and missing person cases.

WORKING CONDITIONS

Local, county, and state police agencies employ Detectives. Working conditions differ widely according to the size, location, organization, and jurisdiction of the police agency. During investigations, considerable time is spent performing office work, reviewing files, gathering data, evaluating and preparing reports, meeting with other Police Officers, and making telephone inquiries. A good deal of time is also spent away from Police Officers working in a variety of locations, in all kinds of weather, reporting to crime scenes, questioning suspects and witnesses, conducting surveillance and stakeouts, and making arrests.

Detectives drive unmarked police vehicles. They may work alone or with partners. Their basic work schedule is rotating shifts of five days a week, eight hours a day, including weekends and holidays. At times they work long, irregular hours; a considerable amount of overtime may be necessary during the investigation of certain cases. As with other Police

Officers, Detectives are on call at all times and may be recalled to duty during periods of emergency. *Although detective work is a challenging career, there are times when it is tedious, routine, and frustrating.* Furthermore, *Detectives are often exposed to the risks of bodily injury and death* during the course of criminal investigations.

In most police agencies, Detectives receive fringe benefits including some or all of the following: paid vacation, sick leave, and holidays; overtime pay; life, medical, and disability insurance; tuition assistance or refund programs for college studies; and retirement pension. In some departments, Detectives can retire after 20 years of service if they are in the 50- to 55-year age bracket. Other departments have different standards, and Detectives may retire after 20 years of service regardless of age.

TRAINING AND PROMOTION OPPORTUNITIES

After successfully completing their training, new Detectives remain on probation. They are assigned to work with experienced investigative personnel who provide practical guidance and assistance under actual field conditions. After demonstrating the ability to perform this job on an independent basis, newly hired Detectives are permanently assigned.

Work performance, as well as the personnel practices and size of the agency govern advancement prospects for Detectives. Promotional opportunities are usually good and are made according to merit system or civil service regulations. Detectives are, as a rule, eligible for promotion after satisfactory service for a specified period of time, often two to four years. When skills are developed through training, experience, and further education, it is possible to compete for the position of Sergeant, the first step on the promotion ladder. Subsequently, qualified candidates can compete for such positions as Lieutenant, Captain, and other high-level jobs known in different parts of the country by various titles such as Inspector, Major, Lieutenant Colonel, and Colonel.

CHAPTER 2: POLICE RECRUIT QUALIFICATIONS

General Requirements

Entry requirements for Police Officers vary to a certain degree among police agencies throughout the country. As a rule, the following requirements apply:

- Applicants must be U.S. citizens between the ages of 20 and 35 at the time of appointment to service.
- Time served in the military is usually deducted from a candidate's chronological age in meeting the upper age requirement.
- Most police agencies require completion of high school or its equivalent as the educational minimum.
- Some police agencies insist on completion of a specified number of college credits and, in some instances, a college degree.
- Possession of a valid driver's license is required prior to employment by a police agency.

Note that secondary and postsecondary courses helpful in preparing for police work include government, English, psychology, sociology, American history, physics, and foreign languages. In addition, more than 1,000 junior colleges, colleges, and universities offer programs in police science or criminal justice.

The vast majority of police agencies in the United States operate under civil service systems and select candidates accordingly. Candidates must pass a competitive examination and obtain a qualifying rating on an interview conducted by senior Police Officers. Each applicant must pass a comprehensive medical examination, which in some agencies includes psychological and psychiatric evaluations to determine emotional stability and acceptability for police work. Performance tests designed to gauge strength, agility, and stamina must be passed, and departmental standards with regard to height, weight, and eyesight must also be met. Because good judgment and a sense of responsibility are essential in police work, a thorough background investigation is conducted to assess general character, past history, honesty, and general suitability for this work.

Cadets and Interns

Meeting the preceding requirements is the typical way of beginning a police career. In some localities, however, young high school graduates or law enforcement students in college can enter this field as police cadets or interns. These individuals, hired as paid civilian employees of the police agency, perform non-enforcement duties and attend classes to learn basic police skills. Those who successfully complete this type of program and meet the basic entry requirements for Police Officer may be appointed to the regular force at age 21.

Probationary Period

Newly hired Police Officers enter training on a probationary basis prior to being assigned to duty. Programs vary widely with regard to length and content. In small departments, there is less formal instruction and a greater degree of on-the-job training as a means of developing skills. In large police agencies, formalized programs of instruction are the rule and may last from several weeks to six months, depending on department policy and availability of training facilities. Newly hired officers receive instruction in a variety of subjects including:

- criminal law
- motor vehicle codes
- arrest, search, and seizure procedures
- constitutional law
- civil rights
- methods of patrol, surveillance, and communications
- traffic control
- accident investigation
- laws of evidence
- crime prevention and criminal investigation procedures
- pursuit driving
- armed and unarmed defense tactics
- use of various types of firearms
- physical conditioning
- crowd control
- first aid
- community relations
- preparation of reports
- court procedures
- use of legal warrants
- police ethics
- departmental regulations

Some departments combine this formal training with field experience to reinforce concepts learned in the classroom.

Work Assignments

Following the completion of training, new officers are assigned to work under the supervision of an experienced officer. The experienced officers with whom probationary officers are teamed provide them with practical instruction and field experience and evaluate their work performance from time to time during the probationary period. Probation may last from a year to 18 months, after which the new officer becomes a permanent member of the force.

Promotion Eligibility

Police Officers usually become eligible for promotion after a specified length of service. In a large department, promotion may allow an officer to specialize in one type of police work such as laboratory work, traffic control, communications, or work with juveniles. Promotions to the rank of Sergeant, Lieutenant, and Captain are usually made according to a candidate's position on a promotion list, as determined by scores on a written examination and on-the-job performance.

ADDITIONAL TRAINING

Many types of training help Police Officers improve their performance on the job and prepare for advancement. Through training given at police department academies and colleges, officers keep abreast of crowd control techniques, civil defense, legal developments that affect their work, and advances in law enforcement equipment. Many police departments encourage officers to work toward college degrees, and some pay all or part of the tuition.

IMPORTANT NOTE: If you are a veteran of the United States Armed Forces, be sure to make this fact known. Veterans receive some form of employment preference when they apply for any government position—local, state, or federal. The veteran's preference sometimes takes the form of points added to the examination score. For some positions, the maximum age of entry is raised by the number of years served. Service-connected disability, if it is not disqualifying for the job, can add still more weight to the application. Even if your experience in the Armed Forces was such that it cannot be counted towards the experience requirements of the position, be sure that you get credit for the very fact of that service.

A Typical Notice of Examination

Here is a sample of a typical exam notice an applicant may receive. Note that this is a sample and all references to the job as well as addresses and dates were created for this book.

Police Officer, Exam. No. XXX

JOB DESCRIPTION

To perform general police duties and related work in the New York City Police Department.

Examples of Typical Tasks: Patrols an assigned area on foot or in a vehicle; apprehends crime suspects; intervenes in various situations involving crimes in progress, aided cases, complaints, emotionally disturbed persons, etc.; responds to and investigates vehicular accidents; investigates specific offenses; interacts with prisoners; operates and maintains patrol vehicle; issues summonses; obtains information regarding incidents by interviewing witnesses, victims, and/or complainants; safeguards and vouchers found, seized, or recovered property; provides information to the public; handles situations involving maltreated, abused, or missing children; interacts with juveniles; prepares forms and reports; testifies in court.

Other Job Factors: Listed below are examples of physical activities that Police Officers perform and environmental conditions in which their activities are conducted. This is not a comprehensive listing, only an indication of some of the job factors.

Works outdoors in all kinds of weather; walks and/or stands in an assigned area during a tour; drives or sits in a patrol car during a tour while remaining alert; runs after a fleeing suspect; climbs up stairs; carries an injured adult with assistance; grips persons to prevent escape; restrains a suspect by use of handcuffs; detects odors such as those caused by smoke or gas leaks; engages in hand-to-hand struggles to subdue a suspect resisting arrest; may be physically active for prolonged periods of time; understands verbal communication over the radio with background noise; reads and writes under low light conditions; carries or wears heavy equipment; wears bulletproof vest.

Police Officers are required to work Saturdays, Sundays, holidays, nights, and change tours or work overtime when ordered as permitted by the Collective Bargaining Agreement.

REQUIREMENTS

Candidates must have successfully completed either 60 semester credits from an accredited college or university or two years of full-time U.S. military service.

Character and Background: Proof of good character and satisfactory background will be absolute prerequisites to appointment. The following are among the factors which would ordinarily be cause for disqualification: (a) conviction of an offense, the nature of which indicates lack of good moral character or disposition towards violence or disorder, or which is punishable by one or more years of imprisonment; (b) repeated convictions of an offense, where such convictions indicate a disrespect for the law; (c) discharge from employment, where such discharge indicates poor behavior or inability to adjust to discipline; (d) dishonorable discharge from the Armed Forces; and (e) persons who have been convicted of petit larceny.

In accordance with provisions of law, persons convicted of a felony are not eligible for appointment to the title of Police Officer.

License Requirement: On the date of appointment, possession of a valid unrestricted New York State Driver's License is required. Employees must maintain such license during their employment.

Medical, Psychological, and Physical Standards: Eligibles must pass medical and psychological tests. Eligibles will be rejected for any medical condition which impairs their ability to perform the duties of the position in a reasonable manner, or which may reasonably be expected to render them unfit to continue to perform those duties in a reasonable manner. All employees must be medically, psychologically, and physically fit to perform the full duties of the position and must continue to meet prescribed standards throughout their careers. Periodic testing may be required. Medical Standards are available at the Application Section of the Department of Personnel, 18 Washington Street, New York, NY 10004.

Candidates may be required to pass a qualifying physical test.

Drug Testing: A drug screening test will be conducted as part of a pre-employment screening process. Drug tests will also be administered to all Probationary Police Officers during Academy Training and again as part of the medical examination at the end of probation. All employees may again be drug tested on a random basis after their probationary periods are completed. Any member of the NYC Police Department found in possession of or using illegal drugs will be terminated.

Employees may be drug tested on a random basis as a prerequisite for assignment or promotion.

Minimum Age Requirement: Eligibles must have attained age 22 to be appointed. Candidates who are too young for appointment on the date the lists are terminated will have no further opportunity for appointment from these lists.

Applicants must be at least of age by the last date of the application period to take this examination.

Citizenship Requirement: United States citizenship is required at the time of appointment.

All qualification requirements mentioned above must be met by the date of appointment.

Applicants may be summoned for the test prior to a review of their qualifications.

TEST INFORMATION

Test Description: Written, multiple-choice test, weight 100.

The written test may include questions requiring any of the following abilities: written comprehension, written expression, memorization, problem sensitivity, number facility, deductive reasoning, inductive reasoning, information ordering, spatial orientation, and visualization.

The passing score will be determined after an analysis of the results.

Five points will be added to the written test score of those candidates who qualify for the New York City Residency Credit. To be eligible for the residency credit, a candidate must have achieved a passing score on the written examination and be a resident of New York City: (1) on the date of the written examination; and (2) on the date the eligible list is established. Candidates seeking residency credit must apply by completing the required forms on the date of the written test.

Eligibility for the residency credit will be investigated. As in the case of any intentional misrepresentation of a material fact on an employment application, candidates who claim residency credit and who are determined to have intentionally misrepresented facts concerning City residency shall be disqualified and their names shall be removed from the eligible list.

Selective Certification: The eligible list resulting from this examination may be selectively certified to fill positions which require a working knowledge of both English and another language. Those who pass the written test and are placed on the eligible list may be permitted to take a qualifying oral test to determine ability to speak and understand other languages as needed. Candidates wishing to take such a qualifying test must indicate at the time of the written test the language for which they wish to be tested. Eligibles may be called to the qualifying oral test as needed. Only those eligibles who pass this qualifying oral test will be eligible for such selective certification.

APPOINTMENT INFORMATION

Investigation: Candidates are subject to investigation before appointment. At the time of investigation, candidates will be required to pay a fee for fingerprint screening.

At the time of investigation and at the time of appointment, candidates must present originals or certified copies of all required documents and proof, including but not limited to proof of date and place of birth by transcript of record of the Bureau of Vital Statistics or other satisfactory evidence, naturalization papers if necessary, proof of any military service, and proof of meeting educational requirements.

Any willful misstatement or failure to present any documents required for investigation will be cause for disqualification.

Probationary Period: The probationary period is 24 months. Among other requirements, each appointee will be required to pass the Police Academy firearms, academic, physical performance, and driving tests.

Firearms Qualification: Candidates must qualify and remain qualified for firearms usage as a condition of employment for the duration of their tenure. A firearms qualification test will be administered annually to determine qualification.

Residency Requirement: The New York State Public Officers Law requires that any person employed as a Police Officer in the New York City Police Department must be a resident of the City of New York or of Nassau, Westchester, Suffolk, Orange, Rockland, or Putnam counties.

English Requirement: Candidates must be able to understand and be understood in English. (See General Examination Regulation E.9.)

Proof of Identity: Under the Immigration Reform and Control Act of 1986, you must be able to prove your identity and your right to obtain employment in the United States prior to employment with the City of New York.

Promotion Opportunities: Employees in the title of Police Officer are accorded the opportunity to be promoted to the title of Sergeant and are also accorded an opportunity to be designated Detective.

Currently, educational requirements for appointment to successive ranks are: (1) Sergeant—satisfactory completion of two years (64 credits) of coursework at an accredited college or university; (2) Lieutenant—satisfactory completion of three years (96 credits) of coursework at an accredited college or university; (3) Captain—attainment of a Baccalaureate degree from an accredited college or university. College credits which are earned as a result of satisfactorily completing the Police Academy curriculum can be used towards meeting the educational requirements.

APPLICATION INFORMATION

Application Period: From February 7 through March 26. Application forms may be obtained in person or by mail from the Application Section, New York City Department of Personnel, 18 Washington Street, New York, NY 10004. Properly completed **ORIGINAL** application forms (**NO COPIES**) must be submitted only by mail to the **New York City Department of Personnel, Bowling Green Station, P. O. Box 996, New York, NY 10274-0996.** Applications must be postmarked no later than the last date of the application period.

In addition to the above, applications will also be available at all NYC Police Department precincts.

Application Fee: Payable by money order ONLY. Money orders should be made payable to the New York City Department of Personnel. The social security number of the candidate and the number(s) of the examination(s) for which he or she is applying must be written on the money order. Cash and checks will *not* be accepted. The application fee will be waived for a New York City resident receiving public assistance who submits a clear photocopy of a current Medicaid card along with the application. Applicants should retain their money order receipt as proof of filing until they receive notice of their test results.

Test Date: The multiple-choice test is expected to be held on Saturday, June 15.

Admission Card: Applicants who do not receive an admission card at least 4 days prior to the tentative test date must appear at the Examining Service Division of the Department of Personnel, 2 Washington Street, Manhattan, 17th floor, during normal business hours on one of the 4 days preceding the test date to obtain an admission card.

Accommodations are available for applicants who provide satisfactory proof of disability. Applications for accommodations must be submitted as early as possible and in no event later than 30 working days before the test or part of a test for which accommodation is requested. Consult General Examination Regulation E.10 for further requirements.

The Department of Personnel makes provisions for candidates claiming inability to participate in an examination when originally scheduled because of the candidate's religious beliefs. Such candidates should consult General Examination Regulation E.11.2 for applicable procedures in requesting a special examination. Such requests must be submitted no later than 15 days before the scheduled date of the regular examination.

List Termination: The eligible list will be terminated one year from the date it is established, unless extended by the City Personnel Director.

CHAPTER 3: MUNICIPAL POLICE FORCES

Organization of Municipal Police Departments

The entire criminal justice system in the United States starts with the police, and it is the municipal police officer who is most familiar to the average person. Municipal police departments, in both personnel and management practices, are generally organized along semi-military lines. Police officers wear uniforms, usually blue or brown; they are ranked according to a military system, such as sergeant, lieutenant, captain, colonel; and they are governed by specific, written rules and regulations. Highly trained police officers are found in both large and small cities. Of the more than 17,000 cities in the United States, 55 have populations exceeding a quarter of a million, and these employ about one-third of all police personnel. It is in the cities that American police problems are concentrated, and these problems present the greatest challenges to law enforcement.

All police agencies, large or small, have similar problems and responsibilities. Each engages in common activities that prevent crime and disorder, preserve the peace, and protect individual life and property. Police work is often thought of as a matter of confrontations between police officers and hardened criminals; this frequently is so. In many instances, however, police officers deal with quite different and surprisingly varied situations.

Police activities can be divided into two functions: line and staff. Line functions involve activities that result directly in meeting police service goals; staff activities help administrators organize and manage the police agency. The line functions common to most municipal police departments include patrol, investigation, vice, traffic, juvenile, and crime prevention. Staff functions involve activities that result directly in the management of police agencies.

Line Functions

At the center of police law enforcement is patrol. It involves movement of uniformed police personnel, on foot or in vehicles, through designated areas. In most departments, at least half of all police personnel are assigned to patrol. Officers on patrol have a variety of duties that include:

- interviewing and interrogating suspects
- arresting lawbreakers
- controlling crowds at public gatherings
- enforcing laws regulating public conduct
- intervening in personal, family, and public disputes

- issuing warnings and citations;
- providing miscellaneous services to members of the public.

Although patrol officers spend more time carrying out routine police services than in catching criminals, their importance cannot be underestimated. Because their primary duties are performed on the street, patrol officers are the most visible representatives of local government.

INVESTIGATION ACTIVITIES

Investigation activities come into play when patrol officers are unable to prevent a crime or to arrest a suspect in the act of committing a crime. Investigative specialists, better known as detectives, help to solve crimes by skillful questioning of victims, witnesses, and suspects; by gathering evidence at crime sites; and by tracing stolen property or vehicles connected with crime. Detectives investigate many types of crimes including murder, manslaughter, robbery, rape, aggravated assault, burglary, auto theft, forgery, embezzlement, and weapons violations. They spend considerable time reviewing physical evidence, clues, interviews, and methods used by the criminal that may provide a break in solving a case. In addition, investigations are coordinated by use of information provided by patrol officers, laboratory personnel, records clerks, and concerned citizens. All of these may lead to the arrest of a suspect.

VICE OPERATIONS

Vice operations in the local police agency are aimed at illegal activities that corrupt and destroy the physical, mental, and moral health of the public. Enforcement activities in vice operations are directed principally against illegal gambling, narcotics violations, illegal traffic in liquor, prostitution, pandering, pornography, and obscene conduct. Organized crime is involved in many vice crimes, and vice crimes are directly linked to other types of street crime. For example, gambling is associated with loansharking, and prostitution and drug abuse are linked with robbery. Patrol units have the primary responsibility of enforcing vice laws and can significantly prevent such illegal activities, particularly in high-crime areas. In order for this to be effective, however, there must be a continual exchange of information and coordinated effort between vice units and all other elements of the police department, as well as cooperation with federal law enforcement agencies such as the Drug Enforcement Agency and the Bureau of Alcohol, Tobacco, and Firearms.

TRAFFIC LAW ENFORCEMENT

Traffic law enforcement seeks the voluntary compliance of citizens with traffic regulations to provide maximum movement of traffic with a minimum of interruption. As no shame is associated with most traffic violations, and the public often breaks traffic regulations without realizing it, breaking these laws is made an unpleasant experience by enforcing penalties such as fines, loss of license, or imprisonment. In addition to vehicular traffic enforcement, uniformed police officers also engage in pedestrian control, traffic direction, investigation of accidents, and traffic education. There is an important relationship between traffic law enforcement and other police services. Stopping a motorist for a routine vehicle check or for a traffic violation often results in an arrest for a nontraffic-related reason, such as weapons or drug possession, vehicle theft, or flight to avoid prosecution in another jurisdiction. As in the case of other police assignments, traffic officers give court testimony and are often involved in civil cases because of traffic accident investigations.

JUVENILES

Most municipal police agencies have specific policy guidelines for dealing with juveniles. However, there may be differences in approach or philosophy among various departments depending on the needs of individual communities. In some cases, police officers are given special training and are assigned to juvenile activities on a full-time basis. In other police departments, the training in this area is minimal, and officers rely on the traditional police methods in dealing with juveniles. A juvenile becomes a delinquent by committing an act, which, if he or she were an adult, would be a crime. The police, however, have greater responsibilities in juvenile matters than merely enforcing laws by taking youthful offenders into custody. Police juvenile efforts are aimed at identifying neglected and/or abused children, detecting and preventing predelinquent behavior, finding and investigating delinquency breeding grounds within the community, and proper disposition of juvenile cases.

CRIME PREVENTION

The last of the basic line functions of the municipal police agency involves crime prevention. When citizens are hostile to the police agency in their community, it is as real a threat to peace and order as would be police indifference to the needs of the citizens. Police serve all segments of the community, but they cannot preserve law and order and control crime unless the public cooperates and participates in the law enforcement process. Hostility between citizens and police not only creates explosive situations, but, more important, can promote crime in the community. Crime is both a police and social problem that will continue to grow unless the public becomes more involved. Community relations programs, for example, help to close the gap between citizens and police by making each aware of the other's problems and providing the impetus to settle their differences. In some municipalities, police agencies have introduced crime prevention techniques such as neighborhood security and watch programs. These encourage citizens to take security measures in their homes and businesses and to report any suspicious persons or activities in the neighborhood.

Staff Functions

Staff functions are activities performed by police officers to help administrators organize and manage the police agency. Personnel recruitment (which includes selection and training), planning, finance, employee services, public relations, and use of civilian personnel are examples of staff work.

Staff is the costliest and most important of all the resources committed to the law enforcement process, and a police agency is only as able and effective as its personnel. To varying degrees, every police department engages in recruitment, selection, and training of personnel. It sets qualifications, recruits candidates, tests and screens applicants, and places them in training facilities. The police department also reviews performance during probation and develops salary schedules and lines of promotion for police officers. In addition, staff units are responsible for providing ongoing training to police officers at all levels in the department as a means of keeping them up-to-date on the latest developments in law enforcement. All of these factors are important because the quality of the personnel and their training determine the character of police performance and, in the final analysis, the quality of police leadership.

PLANNING

To be effective, police departments must plan and organize numerous activities that characterize around-the-clock operations. The unpredictable nature of police work, however, and the problems that arise from emergency situations sometimes make planning difficult. Work schedules, paydays, patrol assignments, uniforms, and equipment all require planning; this, in turn, involves administrative staff and line operations, extradepartmental plans, research, and development. Good planning by the police agency produces effective police service in the community.

BUDGETING

Budgeting is an important part of the staff functions of police personnel. These responsibilities include, but are not limited to, fiscal planning and preparation of cost estimates for personnel, equipment, facilities, and programs necessary to meet the established goals of the police department.

EMPLOYEE SERVICES

The staff must also provide employee services to members of the police agency. They must explain benefits and help employees and their families to obtain all the services to which they are entitled. For example, in cases of illness, injury, or death, specialists in employee benefits take care of matters with a minimum of inconvenience to the officers and their families.

PUBLIC RELATIONS

Police personnel also engage in public relations activities. This entails the development of programs that acquaint the community with police goals and help to gain public support for police activities. Duties include providing information to the press and public, maintaining liaison with community representatives, and working with educational organizations to improve relations with youth in the community.

CIVILIAN PERSONNEL

A widespread practice is the use of civilian personnel in certain jobs within police agencies. Civilian personnel are assigned to duties that do not require the exercise of police authority or the application of the skills and knowledge of the professional police officer. Work typically performed by civilians includes clerical or secretarial work, maintenance or sanitation work, prisoner booking, and motor vehicle maintenance. Many civilian employees develop an interest in regular police work, and, if they meet the requirements for sworn status, become potential candidates for the police officer position. Some police departments will help pay for the schooling required for their civilian employees to meet the educational standards of the department. Some offer part-time training to their employees.

Auxiliary Staff Services

Besides the primary staff functions, important auxiliary staff services help line and administrative personnel to meet police objectives. These services include crime laboratory, property and detention, transportation, communications, and information systems. In addition, many police departments have intelligence operations and systems of internal discipline. Brief descriptions of these auxiliary services follow.

CRIME LABORATORY

Because solutions to many crimes are found through the application of the physical and biological sciences, the crime laboratory is of great value to law enforcement officers. In an initial critical phase, police officers or specially trained evidence technicians identify, collect, and preserve physical evidence at scenes of crime. Overlooking, contaminating, or accidentally destroying evidence can hinder the progress of an investigation. After the evidence reaches the crime laboratory, forensic personnel perform qualitative, quantitative, and interpretive analyses. Crime laboratory personnel are responsible for fingerprint operations, ballistics, polygraph tests, blood and alcohol tests, and examination of questioned documents. Owing to the considerable expense involved with operating crime laboratory facilities, not all police agencies have them. Local and regional laboratories have therefore been established in most states to provide services to law enforcement agencies from different jurisdictions.

PROPERTY AND DETENTION

Regardless of their size, locale, or functions, police agencies are responsible for evidence, personal property, and articles of value confiscated when carrying out police business. In addition, they must take inventory and inspect, replace, and maintain departmental property and facilities. Each police department must ensure the safekeeping of all property and evidence and make provisions for its storage, retrieval, and disposition to authorized police personnel.

Detention activities in a police agency involve temporary confinement of persons arrested and awaiting investigation or trial and permanent imprisonment in city or county facilities for those sentenced by the court. Typical activities include booking, searching, fingerprinting, photographing, and feeding prisoners.

TRANSPORTATION

Police mobility is crucial to crime prevention. Police officers must have the capability of moving safely and swiftly to meet their responsibilities. Police transportation activities center on the acquisition, use, maintenance, cost, and safety of a variety of vehicles. These include automobiles (patrol and unmarked), motorcycles, trucks, buses, motor scooters, aircraft (helicopters and planes), watercraft, and horses. By developing and maintaining an efficient transportation program, the police agency increases its effectiveness and ability to enforce the law.

COMMUNICATIONS

Communications in a police agency are the lifeline of the organization. Most police department communications systems have three parts: the telephone communications system, command and control operations, and radio communications. Though communications systems differ among departments throughout the country because of variation in staffing and funding, they generally operate as follows:

Telephone communications systems aim to reduce crime through rapid and accurate communication with the public. The telephone is the primary link between the police and the community, and, in an emergency, the public must be able to contact the police immediately. This is vitally important because rapid police response to an emergency call can mean the difference between life and death or between the capture and escape of suspects.

Command and control means coordinating operations of radio-equipped field units through exchange of information between field units and communications centers. In its simplest form, it is the receipt, processing, and dispatching of information received in telephone complaints to field units for action. This process becomes more complex as calls increase. In large departments, the use of automated command control equipment is widespread. Regardless of department size, rapid and accurate command and control operations are needed to ensure the safety of the community.

Radio communications, an integral part of police operations, involve use of radio frequencies by command control and police officers both to receive and transmit information. The efficiency of radio communications, however, is often impaired because frequency ranges are limited. In recent years, frequency congestion has been the result of increasing use of communication devices by the public and businesses. Efforts to solve this problem are receiving constant attention by law enforcement agencies at all levels. Where possible, in addition to radio-equipped vehicles, police departments provide police officers with specialized equipment such as miniature transceivers, mobile and portable radio units, and walkie-talkies. The object is to provide continuous communication among commanders, supervisors, and field personnel.

POLICE INFORMATION SYSTEMS

Another staff service, the information system, can also significantly affect efforts to reduce crime. Such a system consists of three components: reporting, collection and recording of crime data, and information storage and retrieval.

Reporting means thorough and precise reporting of all crimes that come to the department's attention. Included are telephone and field investigation reports and warrant information received from judicial agencies. Such information can assist criminal investigations and is useful in other parts of the criminal justice system.

Collection and recording of crime data helps evaluate crime conditions and the effectiveness of police operations. The data is obtained from the department's reportable incident files, such as precinct and field unit activity logs, accident reports, and criminal investigation reports, as well as summary dossier files consisting of fingerprints, name indexes to fingerprints, and criminal histories.

Information storage and retrieval, the third part of police information systems, supports police in the field by providing quick and accurate criminal information on request. Field personnel have access, for example, to arrest records, outstanding warrants, stolen vehicles, and serially identified stolen weapons and property. Development of good information systems for police officers contributes significantly to the effectiveness of the police agency.

INTELLIGENCE

Intelligence operations, still another staff service, also contribute to efficient police work. Information is gathered to keep police officials attuned to happenings in their areas of jurisdiction by providing insight into community conditions, potential problem areas, and criminal activities—all essential to law enforcement. This work deals with activities that present a threat to the community. The most common targets of intelligence investigations are organized crime and individuals or groups who cause public disorder. To be effective, intelligence activities must be continuous; the data gathered must be used to plan and carry out crime-fighting programs.

INTERNAL DISCIPLINE

Another auxiliary staff service is internal discipline. Discipline and accountability are vital to any police agency in maintaining its integrity. Internal discipline, also known as internal affairs, involves investigation of complaints related to police department services and personnel. Citizens or police personnel themselves can lodge complaints. Depending on whether the charges are substantiated, complaints can lead to departmental discipline, dismissal, arrest, prosecution, and imprisonment of those found guilty. By protecting the public from police misconduct and corruption and by taking positive action against employees found guilty of misconduct, the department strengthens morale and gains the support of the community it serves.

LARGE VS. SMALL AGENCIES

When all of the line and staff functions performed in police agencies of any size are considered, it is obvious that effective administration is not easily attained. Large agencies tend to use police officers as specialists in specific types of operations, while smaller departments use officers as generalists performing a wide variety of functions. There are merits to both systems, and the needs and composition of the communities in which they are located generally dictate their use.

SPECIAL-PURPOSE PUBLIC POLICE FORCES

In addition to the local police agencies in municipalities, other special-purpose public police forces are found in many cities throughout the United States. Their jurisdictions include parks, harbors, airports, sanitation departments, transit systems, housing facilities, and ports. Some of these agencies have full police officer powers within their jurisdictions, while others have more limited authority.

CHAPTER 4: THE POLICE OFFICER SCREENING PROCESS

The Written Examination

Step one in the screening process is nearly always the written examination. Police departments want to avoid any possible accusation of favoritism or prejudice in hiring, so they invariably use written examinations to screen out unqualified candidates. The written examination is in almost all cases a multiple-choice test. The multiple-choice format assures objectivity in grading. If the questions are well designed, each question has only one right answer. Such exams are easy to score and are generally considered to be fair.

The unique feature of entry-level examinations is that they do not presuppose any knowledge. The applicant taking a Police Officer entry exam is not expected to know police rules, regulations, or procedures. On the other hand, the candidate is expected to reason and even to think like a Police Officer. Questions that evaluate the candidate's thinking and reasoning processes will include all the necessary information from which to reason. This means that Police Officer exams tend to include many lists of rules and procedures. They often include long excerpts from manuals and rulebooks. The test-taker must read and understand the rules that are the basis for each judgment or reasoning question and then must think through the best answer.

READING-BASED QUESTIONS

Much of the measure of police intelligence is based upon how well you read and what you do with that which you read. Reading-based questions include:

- Questions of fact to be extracted directly from reading passages
- Questions of inference from reading passages
- Questions that require a choice of actions based upon rules and a fact situation
- Questions of judgment of the behavior of others, again based upon both rules and a fact situation

Reading-based questions may also probe your ability to interpret and judge from what you read by presenting a series of definitions and descriptions of situations and then asking you to classify the situations based on the fact situations. Since reading-based questions in one form or another constitute the bulk of all police exams, we have devoted Chapter 6 of this book to prepare you for these questions.

PRACTICAL JUDGMENT QUESTIONS

Closely related to reading-based questions are questions of practical police judgment. These are questions that present you with a fact situation and require you to make a spot decision for appropriate action in that situation. The judgment questions do not presuppose knowledge of the proper police action. Your answer should be based upon good judgment and common sense. However, some familiarity with "police thinking" should stand you in good stead with these questions. The good judgment that you demonstrate in police practical judgment questions should predict the same good judgment in actual police situations. Chapter 5, Police Judgment Quizzer, prepares you for police judgment questions and introduces you to "police thinking," which you can then combine with your own common sense in answering the questions. The Judgment Quizzer gives you lots of practice with this important question type, and the answer explanations will contribute to training you to "think right."

OBSERVATION AND MEMORY QUESTIONS

The intelligent Police Officer not only reads well but is also able to choose a course of action on the basis of knowledge from reading and can make good judgments in both emergency and nonemergency situations. He or she must also be a keen observer with a good memory. Observation is totally useless if the details are instantly forgotten. Observation and memory questions, which appear on many, though by no means all, Police Officer exams, serve to identify those recruits who are wide awake and know what to watch for. In a way, they also are a test of judgment, for the test-taker must be able to decide what to focus on. Obviously, no one can notice and remember every detail of a scene or event. The intelligent observer chooses what is most important and commits it to memory. The test situation is not, of course, the same as real life. If your exam does not include this type of question, it is because your police department considers observation and memory questions on a written test to be too artificial to be truly predictive. Since this type of question does appear frequently, we include a chapter for instruction and practice. The information will prove useful whether or not you must answer observation and memory questions on your exam since you will certainly need to sharpen these skills in order to perform your police duties.

GRAMMAR AND EFFECTIVE EXPRESSION QUESTIONS

Another important line of questioning on police entrance exams has to do with grammar and effective expression. The reason for these questions is obvious. A Police Officer must communicate in both speech and in writing; his or her message must come across clearly and accurately. All-important information must be included, and it must be stated in logical order. There must be no opportunity for misinterpretation or misunderstanding. Police recruits should present their best language skills along with their other qualifications. Grammar and effective expression are, of course, also related to reading. The person who has done extensive reading should be aware of ways to best express information in clear and orderly fashion.

We do not attempt to teach grammar; your logical thinking and your eye for what "looks right" will have to see you through. However, we do forewarn you of the following five forms that grammar and effective expression questions may take and how to approach them.

1. Your exam may offer you four sentences and ask you to choose the sentence that is wrong with respect to grammar or English usage. This type of question can prove quite difficult. Often two or even three sentences appear to be wrong. Draw upon your school training. Read the sentences aloud. You may have to weed out the sentences that you are sure are correct, then guess from among the remaining ones.

2. Another approach is to offer you four sentences, often all attempting to give the same information, and to ask you which one is best. This is a little easier. Concentrate on literal reading of each sentence. Be sure that the one you choose says what you think it means.

3. Other exams may ask your advice in rephrasing an awkward sentence or in repositioning a sentence or paragraph for more reasonable presentation.

4. A common effective expression question gives a series of sentences in random order. You must choose the logical progression of steps—what happened first, next, and so on.

5. A final form of this question is one that presents a list of facts then asks you to include all these facts in a statement of one or two sentences. You must take care to include all the facts and to express them in an unambiguous way. Read each choice literally to catch word orders that may make the meaning incorrect or even ridiculous. Check the list of facts often to ensure that all facts are presented clearly and appropriately in the statement.

Related to questions of effective expression are questions of what information is important to include in a statement or report. This type of question relies on judgment as well as on knowing the best way of expressing information. Put yourself in the position of the person receiving and having to act on the information. What would be most useful? What do you need to know? In what order would you find the information most helpful?

READING MAPS

Except in cases of extreme emergency, Police Officers are required to obey all traffic laws. The Police Officer who goes to the scene of an accident by entering a one-way street in the wrong direction is likely to cause another accident. On the other hand, time may be of the essence. A victim may have injuries that require immediate attention and an officer may have to choose the most efficient legal way to get there. Map questions on police exams involve a combination of reading, logical thinking, and common sense. Police candidates can learn how to use maps effectively while undergoing training; however, applicants who come with a well-developed skill will be able to spend more time getting specialized police training.

Be sure to concentrate on the map questions on your exam. Read them carefully. Put yourself in the driver's seat, and follow all instructions. Do not hesitate to turn the test booklet as needed to maintain your sense of direction.

FILLING OUT FORMS

Police Officers must fill out forms. They also must read the forms and follow them. Some police exams include questions based upon a form, instructions for filling out the form, and a fact situation. There is no trick to these questions. Read carefully. Be especially alert to instructions that read "fill in blank 3 only if such and such" or "leave number 7 blank unless this and that both apply." Exclusionary and inclusive words present the keys to answering many form questions.

MISCELLANEOUS QUESTIONS

There are a variety of miscellaneous questions that appear on isolated police qualification exams. Some, all, or none of them may occur on yours. If they are included, they tend not to comprise a significant part of the exam. These questions include arithmetic, synonyms, verbal analogies, spelling, and various types of coding. Read the directions carefully, then do your best.

Oral Board Interviews

The structured oral interview or oral board interview as it is commonly referred to is an integral part of the entry-level hiring process for police officers. It is a highly reliable and valid method of measuring the knowledge, skills and abilities necessary to perform the job. It is also simply an interview before a panel of assessors. A well-constructed oral interview is developed from an in-depth analysis of the job, the requirements of position, and the skills and abilities needed to perform the job (this is known as a job analysis).

Generally, oral interview questions measure important knowledge, skill and ability areas necessary for successful performance in a law enforcement position. For example, a job analysis might indicate that problem-solving ability is critical for success as a police officer. Thus, job-related questions are developed that measure the candidate's problem-solving skill.

The typical performance dimensions covered in the oral board interview include the following:

- Problem-solving
- Judgment and reasoning
- Decision-making
- Teamwork orientation
- Interpersonal skill
- Oral communication and presentation skill
- Honesty and integrity
- Self-motivation/initiative
- Stress tolerance/composure

FORMAT OF ORAL BOARD INTERVIEWS

The term *structured* is used to indicate the nature of the development and administration of the oral board interview. Structured oral interviews are always administered in a fair and consistent manner. For example, the same questions are given to all candidates, presented in the same order. Often the interview is timed such that candidates have a given amount of time to respond to each question individually or a given time to complete the entire interview.

Furthermore, structured oral interviews have structured guidelines to help the assessors rate your performance in a fair, consistent and accurate manner. Often questions have detailed guidelines or scoring criteria that indicate the behaviors one should exhibit (or discuss) when responding.

The assessors used for entry-level structured oral interviews may come from different areas or occupations in your community. Assessors include members of the Board of Fire and Police Commissioners (citizen panel) or the Merit Commission, police personnel, psychologists, and even ordinary trained citizens. Assessors always receive thorough training on the content of the questions, the rating guidelines, the rating process, and the administration of the oral interview. Assessors are capable of making a thorough, fair, and accurate assessment of a candidate's performance.

PREPARATION FOR THE ORAL BOARD INTERVIEW

The oral interview presents an opportunity for you to offer your best ideas and responses to questions that are relevant to serving as a police officer. Here are six steps you can take to prepare yourself for the structured oral interview:

1. Familiarize yourself with the roles and responsibilities of a police officer. This will help you learn as much as you can about the position and what will be expected of you. You may be asked questions regarding the decisions you will make on the job, the interpersonal interactions you will have and your expectations for how you will perform. Therefore, it is important to understand what duties you will be responsible for in this position.

2. You should become familiar with the municipality or agency to which you are applying for employment or you are interested in serving. Knowledge of the agency, village or city has proven valuable in answering structured oral interview questions.

3. You can prepare yourself for the types of questions you will encounter by researching important topics in law-enforcement. Interview questions may ask for your review of relevant themes and how you intend to address these issues should you be selected for employment. Researching areas that could be the basis for interview questions will enable you to formulate well-informed and structured responses.

4. Ask yourself the following questions: How will I handle problematic situations as a police officer? How will I communicate information to others? What do I know about important issues related to law-enforcement? Where do I stand (and what justification do I have for my stance) on critical issues in the field? Do I understand the nature of public service and how this profession is a public service profession? How will I react in stressful and trying circumstances? What are my opinions

regarding the use of deadly force? What is my opinion on customer service with regard to policing (Do you understand that good customer service and positive community relations are critical to serving as an officer)?

5. You can study for the oral interview with a partner. Develop a set of commonly asked questions and practice answering questions with a partner. You can answer questions that your partner developed to make the practice more realistic.

6. If you do not have a study partner you may practice answering questions in the mirror or by audiotaping your responses and playing back the response. When you do this, evaluate your communication skills. Do you pause a great deal when responding? Do you say 'um'? Is your response clear, understandable, and articulate?

TIPS FOR DOING WELL ON THE ORAL BOARD INTERVIEW

When responding to questions in the structured oral board interview there are a few things you should keep in mind. The following presents some helpful information to remember when answering structured interview questions:

- **Take some time to formulate an organized response.** Do not be afraid to pause for some time after listening to a question to carefully consider your answer and to organize it in a way that is meaningful and will ultimately make sense to those individuals who are rating your response. The more organized and well thought out your answers, the more favorably assessors will view them. You will often be provided with paper and a pen if you want to write down your thoughts to better organize them.

- **Answer the question as it is asked.** It is common for interview candidates to answer a question other than the one posed. Interviews are stressful and it is not uncommon for a candidate to misunderstand or misinterpret the question, and then provide an answer that is completely 'off-base'. Be sure to listen carefully to the question and provide an answer for that specific question. Do not go outside the bounds of the question or ramble onto unrelated issues.

- **Answer each and every part of the question posed.** Questions often have multiple parts. If you do not answer all questions asked of you, you may be severely penalized.

- **Read along with the assessor as they read the question.** Questions are often provided to you on paper, so you can then refer back to the question to ensure that you understand what is being asked of you. It also helps to ensure that you have answered all parts of the question.

- **Provide a single comprehensive response to each question.** It is common for a candidate to answer a question and repeat the same answer over and over. Offer an answer that is complete, but do not reiterate your response multiple times. Keep your answer somewhat concise but ensure that you provide a comprehensive response to the question that is posed.

- **Ensure that you answer each question fully within the time limits.** There are often time limits for each question or for the interview as a whole. You may have to monitor your own time on a question so it will be helpful if you wear a watch with a second hand.

- **Speak clearly.** Oral communication skills are obviously paramount in an oral interview. Oral communication is often rated separately from your answers to the questions in the interview. Thus, if you communicate poorly, the assessors will not penalize you on your answers to each question - but you will be penalized on the 'communication and presentation' dimension of the interview rating form. That said, the rating of oral communication and presentation is an important element of the oral assessment and can sometimes be weighted higher than your responses to the actual questions.

- **Convey a professional demeanor by speaking in a clear and articulate manner and demonstrating good posture and appearance.** Ensure that you maintain good eye contact with the assessors and keep your interaction positive. Good communication skills will only accentuate your response to a question.

- **Dress appropriately for the interview.** Remember: this is an interview for a job. You should dress your best and be well groomed to ensure that you will make a good impression on the assessors.

Video-Based Examinations

A new trend in police officer candidate testing is the use of video-based examinations. During these tests, candidates view video simulations on a TV monitor and then either respond to questions in a multiple-choice format or the candidates respond verbally, as if talking to real people in a real situation. Candidates' responses are then immediately scored, or in the case of the role-playing format, the candidates are videotaped, and their responses are scored later by trained professional raters. Video-based examinations attempt to measure interpersonal skills, common sense and judgment and do not assess any job knowledge specifically required of police officers. In other words, you do not need any prior experience as a law enforcement officer to perform well on this kind of test.

This section is intended to introduce you to popular types of video-based examinations that are currently available and used by many departments. It will also provide you with a sample scenario and multiple-choice questions as well as some hints that will help you to perform your best on the test.

THE NATIONAL CRIMINAL JUSTICE OFFICER VIDEO EXAMINATION (NCJOVE)™

The National Criminal Justice Officer Video Examination was developed by I/O Solutions, Inc., and is designed to test basic skills and abilities, such as ethics and integrity, interpersonal skills, situational judgment and assertiveness. These skills and abilities relate to how you would deal with real-life situations that you are likely to encounter as a law enforcement officer. During the test, you will be shown a series of one- or two-minute scenarios. After each scenario, you will be required to answer a series of multiple-choice questions relating to the scene. These questions ask you about your opinions and what you would do in the same situation, i.e. "Which of the following BEST expresses your opinion?" or "Which of the following would be WORST to do in this situation?" The questions will appear on the screen. They will be read aloud, and each question will remain on the screen for 60 seconds. Based on what you have observed in the scenario, choose the most appropriate answer from the choices that you have been given. Choosing the most appropriate answer from the four choices will earn you the highest number of points; choosing a less appropriate answer will earn you fewer points; choosing the least appropriate answer from the four choices will earn you no points. Please note that you are NOT required to have any previous knowledge of state and local laws or departmental policies and procedures. Answer the questions based *only* on what you know from the scenarios.

Sample NCJOVE Video-Based Scenario Script

Trooper Lennox walks into the office of Sergeant Morris. He closes the door behind him and sits down in front of the sergeant's desk.

Trooper Lennox:
They said you wanted to see me, sir?

Sergeant Morris:
Yes, Lennox. I just received a memo that you testified in court recently—for that DUI on US 93 . . . the guy who killed two people?

Officer Lennox:
Mitchell Allen? Yes, I was in court for that last . . . Tuesday.

Sergeant Morris:
Now, Lennox, I know that you've only been on duty for six months, but you know that you're only supposed to take copies of the accident reports to court with you, not the originals, right?

Officer Lennox:
Yes, sir. Did I accidentally take the originals with me?

Sergeant Morris:
You must have. Because we don't have them here. And they can't find them in the courthouse. That means that the original documentation is just gone.

Officer Lennox:
I...I'm sorry, sir. I had no idea. The copies and the originals look alike to me.

Sergeant Morris:
That's no excuse, Lennox. The copies clearly have the word "PHOTOCOPY" stamped right on the top of the page.

Officer Lennox:
I really am sorry, sir. It won't happen again, I promise.

Sergeant Morris:
Well, that doesn't bring our documentation back, does it? I have to say that I'm disappointed, Lennox. I'm sorry, but I'm afraid that I'm going to have to write this up.

Sample Video-Based Question

1. Based on the information provided in the scenario, which of the following would be the BEST way to characterize Officer Lennox's attitude in this scene?
   (A) He is suspicious that someone else is purposely trying to make him look bad.
   (B) He is eager to blame someone else for his mistake.
   (C) He is apologetic and willing to change his behavior in the future.
   (D) He is angry that he is being reprimanded for a trivial oversight.

To answer this question, choose the response that most accurately reflects your interpretation of the scenario.

Tips and Strategies for the NCJOVE

The best way for you to answer these questions is to be honest. Select the response that most closely reflects what you would or would not do in a given situation.

Make sure to watch the short scenarios VERY carefully and pay attention to the details. Also, pay attention to the characters' reactions to the scenario and to each other. Do you agree with what they do? Do their opinions and attitudes match your own? If you were confronted with the same situation, would do you do the same sorts of things that the characters do, or would you react differently? Once you mentally determine the answers to these questions, it will be easier to select the best response.

Think about the kinds of problems that you imagine you would have to face as a law enforcement officer. Think about what steps you would take to solve these problems if you encountered them on the job. Think of several different strategies to solve each problem and then try to imagine the consequences that would arise if you followed each strategy. Enlist a friend or relative to help you act out these problems in a role-playing exercise!

BEHAVIORAL PERSONNEL ASSESSMENT DEVICE (B-PAD)™

Another type of commonly used video-based test is the Behavioral Personnel Assessment Device (B-PAD). According to the test publisher, the B-Pad Group, the "B-PAD measures behavioral competence in handling job-relevant interpersonal challenges: what is called 'interpersonal competence.' B-PAD derives from the basic tenet of 'behavioral consistency'—that the best predictor of performance not yet observed is performance already observed under similar circumstances. B-PAD's focus is narrow: it assesses social (interpersonal) judgment and skill."

During the examination, you will be seated in front of a television and a video camera. You will then watch eight scenarios that portray common situations encountered in law enforcement. During each scenario, you will be prompted to respond, and you will then have 45 seconds to respond to the actors as though you were responding to a real-life situation. Your response will be videotaped and scored by trained raters. Again, this test will not require previous knowledge of local, state and federal laws or departmental policies and procedures.

Tips and Strategies for the B-PAD

It is crucial that you respond to the scenario as though you were actually on the scene. You may not answer questions in the form of "I would do this" or "I would do that." Talk to the characters on the screen as though you were really there.

Relax and be yourself so that you can perform to the best of your ability. You may find it helpful to enlist the aid of a friend or relative to help you act out common scenarios, such as dealing with an angry citizen or a troublesome coworker. If possible, record your role-playing exercises and listen to or watch them afterwards to think about how you can improve your performance.

FRONTLINE™

FrontLine is another common video-based examination. Like the NCJOVE, FrontLine requires candidates to view a scenario and answer multiple-choice questions based on that scenario. According to the examination's official Web site, "FrontLine is a video-based multiple choice test consisting of fifty-four scenarios. Applicants see a typical situation they will face on the job, observe the various elements present, analyze the situation and make a quick judgment about how to respond. To score well on the test, they must evaluate each scenario as an entirely new situation and project the likely outcome of any given action."

The skills measured by FrontLine are as follows:

- Human Interaction
- Responding Calmly to Provocation
- Unbiased Enforcement
- Situational Judgment
- Ethics and Social Maturity
- Handling Authority
- Gaining Cooperation
- Observation and Analysis

Candidates may also encounter complementary FrontLine video-based examinations, measuring report-writing and reading skills.

Tips and Strategies for FrontLine

Because FrontLine and the NCJOVE share a similar format, strategies for these exams are similar. Once again, be sure to pay careful attention to scenarios as they are played for you, making observations about the character's attitudes, actions and reactions. Also be sure to carefully read the questions as they appear. As on many multiple-choice tests, the answer options may be similarly worded to make the question more challenging. Also, carefully consider answer options that contain the words "only," "always," "never," and "all." Make sure to think over the scenario carefully to decide whether an answer option is accurate or an exaggeration. This does not mean that any answer option containing the words listed above is automatically incorrect. Again, you must pay attention to scenarios to determine the validity of an answer option. As with all types of video-based examinations, you will perform your best if you are confident, relaxed and sincere.

Because this type of examination attempts to identify individuals with strong interpersonal skills who have the ability to manage their own emotions as well as the emotions of others, an important point should be emphasized. If you are naturally flexible, caring, confident and assertive, you should do well on this type of test. If such behaviors are not naturally forthcoming, you would do well to learn or practice demonstrating appropriate command presence, confidence and sensitivity under challenging circumstances.

The Medical Examination

The Police Officer's beat must be covered at all times. This means that the assigned officer must show up. Otherwise, the scheduling officer must find a substitute and rearrange the work tours of many other officers. The candidate with a history of frequent illness or one with a chronic ailment that may periodically crop up and interfere with attendance is not an acceptable candidate. Likewise, an applicant with an underlying physical condition that presents no problems in everyday life but that might be aggravated under the stressful activity of a Police Officer is also not an acceptable candidate.

Every applicant under consideration must undergo a thorough medical examination performed by a department physician or by a physician designated by the department. This exam usually occurs after an applicant has passed the written exam and before the test of physical fitness or physical performance. Occasionally, a candidate is required to have a preliminary medical examination by his or her own physician and to present a note attesting to adequate health and fitness for taking the performance test. A medical exam comes before the physical test so that candidates whose health might be jeopardized by the strenuous activity of the physical test are screened out ahead of time. Only the background check may occur either before or after the medical exam. Since both medical exam and background check require an investment of time by police personnel and yet neither depends upon the other, they may be done in either order. Disqualification on the basis of either background check or medical exam stops the screening process and eliminates the candidate from further consideration.

The medical exam resembles an army physical more than a visit to your personal physician. You start by filling out a lengthy questionnaire relating to your medical history. This questionnaire is used by the physician to single out special health areas for consideration. The personal interviewer may also use it when you approach the final step of the screening process.

Do not lie on the medical questionnaire. Your medical history is a matter of record at school, in your service dossier, and in the hospital or clinic files. If you lie, you will be found out. If a medical condition does not disqualify you, your untruthfulness will. On the other hand, there is no need to provide more information than is required. You do not need to expand upon your aches and pains, and you shouldn't make an illness or injury seem more dramatic than it was. Stick to the facts and do not raise any questions. If you have any current concerns, the police department's examining officer is not the person to ask.

The physical examination consists of the following tests. If you have any doubts as to how you will fare with any of these exams, consult your personal physician ahead of time.

You may be able to correct a borderline situation before you appear for the exam.

- Vision
- Hearing
- Blood Tests
- Urinalysis
- Chest X Ray
- Blood Pressure
- Electrocardiogram
- Height and weight measurement
- Actual visual and physical examination by a doctor

Most police departments provide candidates with height-weight standards and with lists of medical requirements before their scheduled medical examinations. If you receive these, look them over carefully. If they present any problems to you, see your doctor. Your worry may be misplaced, or it may be real. You may have to change your career goals. Or, more likely, you can correct the situation, pass the medical exam, and go on to serve on the police force.

Not all police departments have the same standards for medical conditions. Some accept conditions that are absolutely disqualifying in others. The height-weight charts and the list of medical requirements that follow are typical of those of many police departments. They should serve as a general guide at this time. If your own medical position is way out of line, you may need to reconsider or embark on a major health reform campaign right away. Once you get your own department's official set of guidelines, follow those standards rather than the ones printed here.

HEIGHT AND WEIGHT FOR FEMALES

Acceptable Weight in Pounds According to Frame

Height	Small Frame	Medium Frame	Large Frame
	lb.	lb.	lb.
4'10"	92-98	96-107	104-119
4'11"	94-101	98-110	106-122
5'0"	96-104	101-113	109-125
5'1"	99-107	104-116	112-128
5'2"	102-110	107-119	115-131
5'3"	105-113	110-122	118-134
5'4"	108-116	113-126	121-138
5'5"	111-119	116-130	125-142
5'6"	114-123	120-135	129-146
5'7"	118-127	124-139	133-150
5'8"	122-131	128-143	137-154
5'9"	126-135	132-147	141-158
5'10"	130-140	136-151	145-163
5'11"	134-144	140-155	149-168
6'0"	138-148	144-159	153-173
6'1"	142-152	148-163	157-177

BODY FAT PERCENTAGE (MAXIMUM ALLOWED)

Age Group	20-29	30-39
Females	26.1	27.1

HEIGHT AND WEIGHT FOR MALES

Acceptable Weight in Pounds According to Frame

Height	Small Frame	Medium Frame	Large Frame
	lb.	lb.	lb.
5'3"	115-123	121-133	129-144
5'4"	118-126	124-136	132-148
5'5"	121-129	127-139	135-152
5'6"	124-133	130-143	138-156
5'7"	128-137	134-147	142-161
5'8"	132-141	138-152	147-166
5'9"	136-145	142-156	151-170
5'10"	140-150	146-160	155-174
5'11"	144-154	150-165	159-179
6'0"	148-158	154-170	164-184
6'1"	152-162	158-175	168-189
6'2"	156-167	162-180	175-194
6'3"	160-171	167-185	178-199
6'4"	164-175	172-190	182-204
6'5"	168-179	176-194	186-209
6'6"	172-183	180-198	190-214

BODY FAT PERCENTAGE (MAXIMUM ALLOWED)

Age Group	20-29	30-39
Males	18.9	22.0

NOTE: Although the above tables commence at a specified height, no minimum height requirement has been prescribed. This table of height and weight will be adhered to in all instances except where the Civil Service examining physician certifies that weight in excess of that shown in the table (up to a maximum of 20 pounds) is lean body mass and not fat. The examining physician shall make the decision as to frame size of a candidate.

MEDICAL REQUIREMENTS FROM OTHER POLICE DEPARTMENTS

Medical standards vary from department to department, so if you appear to be borderline or even not qualified for one department, it is worthwhile to look into the specifics in another department or jurisdiction. The variations are most notable in standards for vision and hearing. Some Police Officers are permitted to wear glasses or contact lenses; most are not. Some may have limited color blindness. Furthermore, some jurisdictions employ officers who have had their vision surgically corrected by orthokeratology, radial keratotomy, or epikeratoplasty, while in other jurisdictions these procedures are automatically disqualifying. It is worthwhile to do some research before you begin the application process.

While there is variation in the standards of the various police departments, there is more similarity than difference. The greater variation comes in the way the departments state their requirements. Here are formulations from three police jurisdictions.

One Large City's Medical Requirements

Candidates are required to meet the physical and medical requirements stated below and in the announcement at the time of the medical examination, at the time of appointment, and at appropriate intervals thereafter.

1. **Weight.** Candidates should have weight commensurate to frame. Weight should not interfere with candidate's ability to perform the duties of the position of Police Officer.

2. **Vision.** Candidates must have binocular visual acuity not less than 20/20 with or without correction; if correction is required, binocular visual acuity not less than 20/40 without correction. Binocular peripheral vision should not be less than 150 degrees.

3. **Color Vision.** Candidates must be able to distinguish individual basic colors against a favorable background.

4. **Hearing.** Candidates must be able to pass an audiometric test of hearing acuity in each ear. A binaural hearing loss of greater than 15% in the frequency ranges of 500, 1000, 2000 Hz would be considered disqualifying. Hearing appliances should correct the deficiency so the binaural hearing loss in the combined frequency level of 500, 1000, 2000 Hz is no greater than 15%.

5. **Heart.** Candidates must be free of functionally limiting heart disease. Must have a functional cardiac classification of no greater than Class I. This determination is to be made clinically or by cardiac stress test.

6. **Lungs.** The respiratory system must be free of chronic disabling conditions that would interfere with the candidate's performance of required duties.

7. **Diabetes.** Candidates who are diabetic must not require insulin injections or oral hypoglycemic agents for control.

8. **Neurological Health.** Candidates must be free of neurological disorders that may affect job performance. Candidates with epilepsy or seizure disorders must provide evidence of one-year seizure-free history without drug control.

9. **Musculoskeletal Health.** Candidates must be free of musculoskeletal defects, deformities, or disorders that may affect job performance. Functional use of the arms, hands, legs, feet, and back must be demonstrable at the examination. Candidates will be asked to demonstrate physical fitness through tests of strength, agility, flexibility, and endurance.

10. **Hernia.** Candidates must be free of abdominal and inguinal herniae that would interfere with job performance.

11. **Blood/Vascular Health.** Candidates must be free of blood or vascular disorders that interfere with the performance of duties. Candidates with uncontrolled high blood pressure will be disqualified immediately.

12. **Mental Health.** Candidates must be free of mental illness, serious emotional disturbances, or nervous disorders and from alcoholism or drug dependence or abuse.

13. **General Medical Statement.** Candidates must be free of any medical and/or nervous condition that would jeopardize the safety and health of others. Candidates with communicable diseases will be disqualified immediately.

Sample Medical Requirements from a Second Police Department

The duties of these positions involve physical exertion under rigorous environmental conditions; irregular and protracted hours of work; patrol duties on foot, motor vehicle, and aircraft; and participation in physical training. Applicants must be in sound physical condition and of good muscular development.

Vision

- Binocular vision is required and must test 20/40 (Snellen) without corrective lenses,
- Uncorrected vision must test at least 20/70 in each eye,
- Vision in each eye must be corrected to 20/20,
- Near vision, corrected or uncorrected, must be sufficient to read Jaeger Type 2 at 14 inches, and
- Ability to distinguish basic colors by pseudoisochromatic plate test (missing no more than four plates) is required, as is normal peripheral vision.

Hearing

- Without using a hearing aid, the applicant must be able to hear the whispered voice at 15 feet with each ear; or
- Using an audiometer for measurement, there should be no loss of 30 or more decibels in each ear at the 500, 1,000, and 2,000 levels.

Speech

- Diseases or conditions resulting in indistinct speech are disqualifying.

Respiratory System

- Any chronic disease or condition affecting the respiratory system of a nature that would impair the full performance of duties of the position is disqualifying; e.g., conditions that result in reduced pulmonary function, shortness of breath, or painful respiration.

Cardiovascular System

The following conditions are disqualifying:

- Organic heart disease (compensated or not),
- Hypertension with repeated readings which exceed 150 systolic and 90 diastolic without medication, and
- Symptomatic peripheral vascular disease and severe varicose veins.

Gastrointestinal System

- Chronic symptomatic diseases or conditions of the gastrointestinal tract are disqualifying.
- Conditions requiring special diets or medications are disqualifying.

Endocrine System

- Any history of a systemic metabolic disease, such as diabetes or gout, is disqualifying.

Genito-Urinary Disorders

- Chronic, symptomatic diseases or conditions of the genito-urinary tract are disqualifying.

Extremities and Spine

- Any deformity or disease that would interfere with range of motion, or dexterity, or that is severe enough to affect adversely the full performance of the duties of the position is disqualifying.

Hernias

- Inguinal and femoral hernias with or without the use of a truss are disqualifying. Other hernias are disqualifying if they interfere with performance of the duties of the position.

Nervous System

- Applicants must possess emotional and mental stability with no history of a basic personality disorder.
- Applicants with a history of epilepsy or convulsive disorder must have been seizure free for the past two years without medication.
- Any neurological disorder with resulting decreased neurological or muscular function is disqualifying.

Miscellaneous

Though not mentioned specifically above, any other disease or condition that interferes with the full performance of duties is also grounds for medical rejection.

Before entrance on duty, all applicants must undergo a pre-employment medical examination and be medically suitable to perform the full duties of the position efficiently and without hazard to themselves and others. Failure to meet any one of the required medical qualifications will be disqualifying for appointment. These standards are considered minimum standards and will not be waived in any case. Applicants found to have a correctable condition may be restored to any existing list of eligibles for further consideration for appointment when the disqualifying condition has been satisfactorily corrected or eliminated.

Statement of Medical Requirements from a Third Department

> **NOTE:** Candidates are required to meet the physical and medical requirements stated below and in the announcement at the time of the medical examination, at the time of appointment, and at appropriate intervals thereafter.

1. **Height and Weight**—Will not interfere with the candidate's ability to perform the essential functions of the position. All candidates will be evaluated for stamina and vigor to demonstrate their physical fitness through tests of strength, agility, flexibility, and endurance.
2. **Speech**—Must be free of speech pathology that would interfere with the ability to communicate clearly.
3. **Vision**—Distant visual acuity should be correctable to better than, or equal to, 20/30 (Snellen) in each eye; if correction is required, binocular visual acuity not less than 20/70 without correction. Binocular peripheral vision should not be less than 170 degrees.
4. **Color Vision**—Perception of color is deemed acceptable if the candidate correctly reads nine (9) or more of the first thirteen (13) plates of the 24-plate edition of the Ishihara Test. If the candidate's color perception is deemed unacceptable through the use of said test and he/she believes the results to be incorrect, such an individual may at his/her own expense take the Farnsworth-Munsell 100-Hue Test under the following conditions:
   a. The test must be taken under the supervision of an ophthalmologist having the proper equipment and utilizing the standards established by the Municipal Police Training Council.
   b. If the candidate takes and completes the Farnsworth-Munsell 100-Hue Test, the specialist shall certify in writing whether or not the candidate meets the required color perception standards.
   c. Both eyes should be examined together and scored as such.
   d. If a candidate fails the initial test, he/she must, upon request, be immediately retested and the lower total error score used for purposes of qualification. A total error score of not more than 124 is deemed acceptable.

e. The use of any lens by an officer candidate in order to meet the color perception standard is not acceptable.

5. **Hearing**—The average hearing level (HL) for the three (3) test frequencies of 500, 1000, and 2000 Hz will not exceed 25 dB in either ear, and no single hearing level will exceed 30 dB at any of these 3 test frequencies in either ear. Hearing loss at 3000 Hz will not exceed 40 dB HL in either ear. Use of hearing aids is permitted as long as they are self-contained and fit within (auricular) or behind or over (post-auricular) the ear. Candidates with hearing aids, at their own expense, must provide evidence from a licensed audiologist, using functional gain or real ear measurements, that their aid(s) meet the stipulated manufacturer's standards. *Recourse Testing:* If the candidate's pure tone screening test is deemed unacceptable, such candidate may at his/her own expense have an audiological evaluation administered by a NYS licensed audiologist, including:

a. hearing sensitivity
b. speech discrimination in quiet
c. speech discrimination in noise

Testing should be performed in a sound-treated environment meeting the 1969 ANSI or any subsequent standard. The CID W-22 word lists should be presented at 50 dB HL via a calibrated speed audiometer through a single speaker stationed at 0 degrees azimuth with the candidate seated at approximately 1 meter (39 inches) from the speaker. Speech (hearing) discrimination testing in a background of broadband noise should be conducted in the same sound field environment. Again, using a different version of one of the CID W-22 word lists presented at 50 dB HL, a competing noise should be simultaneously presented at 40 dB HL (S/N = + 10) through the same speaker (0 degrees azimuth) as the test words or through a separate speaker located at 180 degrees azimuth. The minimal acceptable standard of speech (hearing) discrimination shall be a score no poorer than 90% in quiet and 70% in noise on two of the pre-recorded versions of the CID W-22 word lists. An open-test response format should be utilized with the candidate responding in writing.

6. **Cardiovascular**—Candidate must have a functional and therapeutic cardiac classification no greater than NYS Class IA. This determination must be made clinically or by cardiac stress test. Candidates with uncontrolled high blood pressure will be restricted pending remediation.

7. **Respiratory System**—The respiratory system must be free of chronically disabling conditions that would interfere with the candidate's ability to perform the essential functions of the position.

8. **Diabetes**—Candidates who are diabetic must provide evidence of satisfactory medical control. Candidates will be evaluated on a case-by-case assessment as to the control of diabetes and presence and severity of symptoms and complications.

9. **Neurological Health**—Candidates must be free of neurological disorders that would interfere with the candidate's ability to perform the essential functions of the position. Candidates with any type of epilepsy or seizure disorders must provide evidence of one-year seizure-free history with or without drug control.

10. **Musculoskeletal Health**—Candidates must have no defects, deformities, or disorders that will interfere with the candidate's ability to perform the essential functions of the position. The use of prostheses or braces is allowed as long as the candidate can perform the full range of duties of the position and no security risk is posed.

11. **General Medical Statement**
    a. Candidates must be free of any medical condition, including alcohol abuse, and/or psychiatric disorder that would jeopardize the safety and health of the public and/or other employees, or would clearly interfere with the ability to perform the essential functions of the position.
    b. Candidates may not have a medical problem that prevents them from working mandatory unscheduled overtime.
    c. Candidates found to be abusing legal drugs or using illegal drugs will be disqualified.

Physical Performance Tests

Almost all police departments require successful candidates to pass some sort of physical test. This physical test will either be called a fitness test or a physical ability (or agility) test. These two types of tests are very different, yet they are both designed to ensure that individuals are able to perform the physically demanding tasks of the Police Officer position.

Fitness tests are designed to measure your level of general fitness through sit-ups, mile-and-a-half runs, bench press repetitions, etc. The fitness test uses different cutoff scores on these components for men and women and for various age groups; however, these cutoff scores are set at the same percentile for everyone. In other words, even if men and women are not required to bench press the same amount of weight, the amount that is required of each can probably be pressed by about three fourths (75%) of the men and three fourths (75%) of the women.

Physical ability (or agility) tests require candidates to perform a series of linked exercises that simulate a Police Officer's job such as pursuing a suspect, climbing over a wall and through a window, and dry-firing a weapon. This type of physical testing is not measuring general fitness; rather, it is measuring your ability to perform essential job tasks. Since the tasks are essential to the job, the same score (i.e., the ability to perform these tasks in a reasonable period of time) is required of all candidates to pass regardless of sex or age. Physical ability (or agility) tests also require a high level of physical fitness in order to perform well.

The physical performance requirements for all law enforcement officers—Police Officers, State Troopers, Corrections Officers, Special Agents—are very similar. All law enforcement officers must be able to:

- jump into action in an instant
- move very quickly
- be strong
- have the stamina to maintain speed and strength for a long time
- continue physically stressful activity at a high level while withstanding discomfort and pain

The ideal law enforcement officer is "Superman." The actual officer does well to approach those qualities.

While all departments have similar physical performance requirements, each tends to measure fitness in its own way. Because physical ability is absolutely vital to the officer's effectiveness and survival on the job, departments place a great deal of emphasis on their physical performance tests. In some jurisdictions, the physical performance test is a competitive test. This means that the test is scored, and the numerical score contributes to the candidate's place on the eligibility list. In other jurisdictions, the physical performance test is qualifying. This means that the candidate must pass the test in order to be hired, but ranking on the list is based on other factors. Either way, you must be well prepared for the performance test.

All tests are not alike. The following selection of tests of physical fitness and agility will introduce you to many different tasks. Read them through and note the variations. Try each out to the extent that you can without the actual testing course. See how you do. You may need to get yourself into a regular bodybuilding routine sometime before you are called for your examination since strength and fitness cannot be developed overnight. You will need to work yourself up to par over a long period. Set up a program and get started right away.

You will not be called for a physical fitness test until after you have passed the written examination and the medical examination. The background check may also be conducted before your physical fitness test. Chances are that you will not be called for a physical fitness test until there is some possibility that your place on the list will soon be reached. The hiring process moves along slowly, but it does move. You have time, but not that much time. Start now. Buy a book, join a gym or a fitness class, design a program of your own, or turn to the appendix of this book. You can pick and choose from among the suggested activities or follow the entire fitness course.

I. Job-Simulation Physical-Ability Test

ORIENTATION AND PREPARATION GUIDE FOR THE NATIONAL CRIMINAL JUSTICE OFFICER PHYSICAL-ABILITY TEST (NCJOPAT)™

Introduction

The National Criminal Justice Officer Physical-Ability Test (NCJOPAT) is an actual job-simulation test that was developed by I/O Solutions, Inc. It is similar or identical to those that may be encountered by police officer candidates during the hiring process.

This section was developed to introduce you to and prepare you for the NCJOPAT. The test consists of a series of job-related tasks designed to ensure that candidates are able to perform the necessary job functions they will face as police officers. Because these simulation exercises were developed to mirror police officers' most critical job tasks, the test is a highly valid and realistic assessment of the physical aspects of the job.

Based on the expert judgment of command-rank personnel, the following five physical-ability test components were identified:

1. Vehicle Exit
2. Stair Climb
3. Fence Obstacle
4. Trigger Pull
5. Dummy Drag

The NCJOPAT is pass/fail based on a cut-off score that equates to the minimum level of physical aptitude necessary to perform the police officer job. When a department chooses to use the NCJOPAT as part of their hiring process, only those candidates who pass the physical-aptitude test will be eligible for employment. The cut-off score should be established by each department through a field-testing process, so it is impossible to tell you the exact amount of time you will have to complete all five events. However, *on average*, you will be required to complete these events between one-and-a-half (1.5) and four (4) minutes. There will be no breaks or rest periods between these events.

In this section, you will learn more about what these components measure, the regulations you must follow when performing these test components and guidelines to help you prepare for this examination. By reading this guide carefully, you will be better prepared for the test and are more likely to perform according to your true potential.

The Components of the Test

The following five events will be timed continuously although you may not complete them in the order that is presented here. You will be given an on-site orientation, and proctors will lead you on a tour of the course before you begin. During the examination, proctors will be there to monitor your progress and to assist you if necessary. The total length of the course will be approximately 200-250 yards in length.

Vehicle Exit

Police officers are often required to address crimes or violent situations in progress, and they must be ready for action as soon as they arrive on the scene. This component of the test will determine how quickly you can exit a vehicle in a seated position while restrained by a seat belt. In this event, you will be seated in a squad car with your seat belt fastened and the driver's side door open. When the proctors start the clock, you will unfasten the seat belt and exit the vehicle. This is a component that you can easily practice at home although obviously you will want to take care if you choose to practice in an area where other traffic may be present!

Stair Climb

Police officers often assist citizens in high-rise buildings, large apartment complexes, multi-story homes, etc., and part of their duties requires climbing stairs. During this event, you will enter the staircase and climb to the second level where you will place both of your feet on a square that is marked on the landing. You will then immediately descend the staircase. You are not required to climb the stairs in any particular fashion, and you may use the railings. And although you need to complete this portion of the test quickly in order to meet the overall time requirement, you must exercise great caution when climbing and descending the stairs.

You can prepare for this component by ascending and descending staircases at home or in multi-story buildings. You should practice climbing two flights of stairs as quickly as possible after you have engaged in other physically taxing activities.

Fence Obstacle

In order to capture fleeing perpetrators and suspects, the police often have to pursue them not only in their squad cars but also on foot, sometimes climbing over walls and fences to eventually make an arrest. Therefore, in this portion of the physical-ability test, you will be required to climb over a six-foot wall. The wall will be fitted with rungs that will assist you as you climb. You may climb over the wall in any way you wish, but keep in mind that in order to pass the test, you must meet the overall time requirement.

You can prepare for this component by climbing over obstacles of various construction types. You may want to start by climbing over four-foot chain-link fences. After you are comfortable with this height, you should practice climbing over five- and six-foot fences. Remember that the fence you climb during the test will have rungs that will help you to ascend to the top. Do not practice climbing structures that are too high or lack structural integrity.

Trigger Pull

It is vital for the safety of officers and citizens that police officers are able to hold their gun in a steady position, ensuring that they will be able to consistently and accurately hit their targets. For this event, you will be required to hold a plastic pistol (a plastic composite mold that simulates a real pistol) in both hands with arms outstretched for 60 seconds. You will not be allowed to drop the pistol below shoulder height. If the pistol does drop below shoulder height, the proctor will give you **one** warning to return the pistol to the required level. The proctor's warning will not affect the timing of this event. If you allow the pistol to drop a second time, the exam will be over, and you will be disqualified.

You can prepare for this component by holding a one-pound weight at shoulder height for periods of one minute or longer. Remember that both hands must be grasping the weight, and your arms should be fully extended. The weight should not fall below shoulder height for the entire 60 seconds. You will be winded by the time you perform this component of the actual physical-ability test, so you should practice with the weight after you have engaged in other aerobic activities.

Dummy Drag

Police officers are sometimes required to pull subjects to the ground in order to restrain them or drag people away from a hazardous scene, such as a fiery automobile accident. This exercise will test your ability to perform both activities. During this event, a 165-pound dummy will be placed in a seated position inside a vehicle. You will be required to pull the dummy out of the vehicle and onto the ground. You will then continue dragging the dummy for a distance of 25 feet from the vehicle. Once both you and the dummy cross the finish line, the clock will be stopped. There are no restrictions on holding the dummy, pausing or adjusting your grip.

You can prepare for this component by dragging a sled or other object weighing approximately 165 pounds by a rope. You should be able to drag the weight on a flat surface for a minimum of 25 feet. You should start with lesser weight and build up to 165 pounds to avoid injury.

Helpful Hints and Strategies

The most important thing to keep in mind when preparing for any physical-ability test is to practice and train well in advance of the examination day. Many candidates have been overheard saying, "I haven't run in a long time" or "I've never lifted this much weight before." Test administrators are not surprised when these candidates quickly fail. Make sure that you are physically fit and can meet all test requirements **before** the examination date. Spend the rest of the time before the test maintaining that level of fitness.

Some of the NCJOPAT exam components may be recreated at home. For example, you can practice climbing stairs or holding your arms at the proper position for the trigger pull event. If you are going to try to practice NCJOPAT events at home, please be sure to take all necessary safety precautions. You will not be able to pass the test if you injure yourself while practicing. Here are some other tips:

- Be sure to get a good night's rest the night before the test so that you wake up refreshed and prepared to do your best.
- You are required to wear athletic shoes to this examination. We also strongly recommend that you wear a short-sleeved shirt and long pants.
- Be prepared to arrive at the examination site early so that you can complete required sign-in procedures and attend mandatory orientation sessions. By arriving early, not only will you display your interest in a career with the department to which you have applied, but you will also prevent your disqualification due to tardiness.

Once again, please use caution when participating in this examination. You may complete the first component or two faster than any other candidate, but you will fail if you injure yourself and cannot complete the rest of the test.

Fitness Program

In this section, you will be provided with general information on health and exercise, a list of health factors that you need to consider before beginning an exercise program, the basic principles of training, and an outline of a basic fitness program you can perform in preparation for this type of examination.

Physical Fitness

Physical fitness enables an individual to perform up to his or her potential. Fitness can be described as a condition that helps us to look, feel, and do our best. The Guidelines for Personal Exercise Programs as developed by the President's Council on Physical Fitness and Sports describes it as, "the ability to perform daily tasks vigorously and alertly, with energy left over for enjoying leisure-time activities and meeting emergency demands. It is the ability to endure, to bear up, to withstand stress, to carry on in circumstances where an unfit person could not continue and is a major basis for good health and well-being."

Physical fitness involves the performance of all major muscle groups in the body. When your body is in shape, you feel better overall and are able to think more clearly. Physical fitness is influenced by many factors, such as age, gender, genetics, personal habits, exercise and eating practices. In general, physical fitness is made up of four components:

1. Cardiorespiratory Endurance—the body's ability to deliver oxygen and nutrients to tissues and to remove wastes over significant periods of time. For example, running and swimming are considered endurance sports.
2. Muscular Strength—a muscle's ability to exert force for a brief period of time. For example, lower-body strength can be measured by various weight-lifting exercises.
3. Muscular Endurance—a muscle's ability to sustain successive contractions or to continue applying force against a fixed object. For example, pull-ups are often used as a test of arm and shoulder muscle endurance.

4. Flexibility—the ability to move joints and use muscles through their full range of motion. For example, a sit-and-reach test measures the flexibility of the lower back and backs of the upper legs.

By becoming more physically fit, you are able to help reduce the possibility of heart disease and some forms of cancer. Fitness can help improve blood cholesterol levels, increase immunity to illness and help to control high blood pressure, osteoporosis, diabetes, arthritis, asthma and other health problems. It also helps to increase one's energy throughout the day, aid in control of one's weight and increase life expectancies. Exercise can also act as a stress reliever and promote sound sleep.

Health Factors to Consider

Typically, if you are under 35 years of age and are in good health, there may be no need to see a doctor before beginning an exercise program. However, the following are health factors that may require the consultation of a physician:

- High blood pressure
- Heart trouble
- Family history of strokes or heart attacks
- Frequent dizzy spells
- Extreme breathlessness after mild exertion
- Arthritis or other bone problems
- Severe muscular, ligament or tendon problems
- Back pain
- Bone or joint pain
- Smoking
- Obesity

Principles of Training

When starting a new fitness program, you should be in good health. A healthy body will ensure a safe and enjoyable exercise experience.

Setting Goals

When beginning an exercising program, set short-term goals that will help you to achieve your long-term goal of overall physical fitness. Specific short-term and long-term goals should be identified. An example of a short-term goal is jogging for 15 minutes, which may help you to achieve your long-term goal of a specific weight by a given date. Short-term goals should be set as a result of long-term goals.

Your short-term goals will be dependent upon your current level of physical fitness and will be a major factor in determining where you will begin your exercise program. If you are starting a running program with some calisthenics, your goals might be to run for 10 minutes and to perform a given number of calisthenics. If you are in better shape, then your goals will be higher. Short-term goals are the building blocks to achieving your long-term goals.

Even if you are in great shape but have not been exercising regularly, you will want to start your program slowly at first and progress at an even pace. If you start the program too quickly, you may become tired, injured or frustrated with the program, and this may cause you to lose motivation to continue with it. It is important to match your activities with your abilities.

Once you have found a comfortable but challenging level of exercise, stay with it for one to two weeks before you increase it. Try to increase your level of activity as it feels comfortable to you and with a smooth progression.

Effective Training

Three factors make up an effective exercise program: frequency, intensity and time.

1. Frequency—this is how often you perform an exercise activity. It is typically suggested that you work out at least three times a week for 20 minutes to increase cardiovascular fitness.

2. Intensity—this is how hard you are working out, which is often measured using your heart rate. To calculate your maximum heart rate, you should subtract your age from 220. This is your estimated maximum heart rate, and you should train at a level of 50 percent to 80 percent of your maximum. Beginners should start at 50 percent and experienced individuals at 80 percent.
   —For a 40-year-old person at 50 percent of his/her maximum:
   (220-40) * 50% = 90
   —For a 40-year-old person at 80 percent of his/her maximum:
   (220-40) * 80% = 144

   Using a percentage of maximum heart rate is the easiest and safest way to regulate intensity.

3. Time—this is the amount of time spent working out. A minimum of 20 minutes is recommended for each exercise session at 50 to 60 percent of your maximum heart rate.

Equipment Needed for Training

One of the benefits of fitness training is that it can be relatively inexpensive. There is no need to spend a great deal of money on equipment. Most activities require the following:

- Shorts
- Tee-shirt
- Sweats
- Socks
- Athletic shoes

There are some activities, such as swimming and racquetball, that require eye-protective goggles. For walking and running, a good pair of athletic shoes is recommended.

The Fitness Program

A fitness program consists of three phases: the warm-up, the training period and the cool-down. Each is outlined below, and exercises are outlined on the following pages.

1. **Warm-up (5-10 minutes)**—the warm-up is the phase just before your training period when you do a few stretches and exercise to raise your body temperature and loosen up your body muscles. This is an important part of your fitness program because it helps to reduce the likelihood of injury. The warm-up exercises are designed not only to get a person physically and mentally ready for a workout but also to help develop flexibility in the joints and muscle groups.

2. **Training Period (20-30 minutes)**—this phase consists of cardiovascular and muscle strength and endurance exercises.

   Cardiovascular Training—cardiovascular training consists of any exercise such as swimming, running or biking, during which your heart is working at an elevated level.

   Strength and Endurance Training—the strength and muscular endurance exercises do not have to be done on the same day or during the same exercise session as the cardiovascular program. Every exercise program should be complemented with a warm-up and cool-down.

   The strength and endurance exercises can be done in one of two ways, depending on the availability of equipment. They can be performed by doing calisthenics, which requires little or no equipment, or by training with weights. Training with weights can be done either by using free weights, such as barbells or by using weight machines. Training for muscular strength is done with high resistance, large amounts of weight and low repetitions (3-5). Training for endurance requires low resistance and a very high number of repetitions (10-20).

   Weekly Log—a weekly log sheet should be kept describing the date, type of activity and amount of time you exercised so that you can keep track of your progress in developing strength, muscular endurance, and cardiovascular fitness.

3. **Cool-Down (5-10 minutes)**—this is the transition from the training period to your body's normal resting state. Your heartbeat should be about 100 beats per minute when you are sufficiently cooled down. Typically, you will want to do a few cool-down exercises, such as walking and stretching, so that your heart rate will steadily decrease until it is at 100 or less.

Establishing a Training Schedule

Establishing a training schedule is important if you want to be successful. Set aside an hour or so every other day at a specific time of day so that you are able to establish a routine. Pick a time that works for your schedule and consider personal preferences, job and family responsibilities, availability of exercise facilities, and weather when thinking about your workout schedule. It is important to schedule your workouts for a time when there is little opportunity for interruption. Also try to avoid exercising during extremely hot, humid weather or within two hours after eating.

It is important to establish a routine and stick with it. As long as this guideline is followed, positive results will be achieved.

> **Note:** The techniques, ideas and suggestions in this section are not intended as medical advice. Consult your physician or health-care professional should you have concerns about your ability to perform these exercises. Any application of the techniques, ideas, and suggestions in this document is at the reader's sole discretion and risk. The authors and publishers make no warranty of any kind in regard to the content of this document, including but not limited to, any implied fitness for any particular purpose. The authors and publisher are not liable or responsible to any person or entity for any special, incidental, or consequential damage caused or alleged to be caused directly or indirectly by the information contained in this section.

Exercises

Warm-up

As stated earlier, the warm-up phase should take approximately 5-10 minutes. This is an important part of your workout because it allows your body to increase blood flow, raise your body temperature, and prevent injury through stretching. Several exercises are listed below and should be done before each workout session. It is not necessary to do all of the exercises listed below, but you should try to cover all muscle groups.

1. Seated Toe Touch (Back and back of leg muscles)—sit down with your legs fully extended in front of you. Hold your hands out and slide them down your legs until you feel a stretch in your back and legs. This should be a comfortable stretch, not painful. Continue to stretch as you approach your feet, always being conscious of your comfort. If there is any pain, you should not stretch beyond that point. Repeat this exercise five times.

2. Toe Pull (Groin and Thigh Muscles)—while in a seated position, pull the toes in with both feet so that your knees bend and are pointed outward. Press the knees down with your elbows. Hold this position for two to three seconds.

3. Pelvic Girdle Stretch (Pelvic muscles)—sit on the floor with your legs comfortably apart and reach through. Keep your head up and chest out, which will keep your back straight. Relax and hold this position for 30 seconds.

4. Stride Stretch (Thigh muscles)—slowly slide your body into a stride position so that your hands are on the ground a shoulder-width apart and your right knee is inline with your shoulders. Your right foot should be almost flat on the floor, and your left leg should be fully extended behind you on your toes. Lean forward while pushing your hips downward and hold this stretch for five seconds. Repeat this stretch for the opposite side.

5. Wall Stretch (Calf muscles)—Facing a wall, stand about three feet from it with your feet slightly apart and place both hands on the wall. Your heels should be firmly planted on the ground. Lean forward, keeping your body straight, and concentrate on the stretch in your calves. Hold this position for 15-20 seconds.

6. Lower Leg Stretch (Leg muscles)—begin by standing arm's length from a wall or doorframe, one foot in front of the other, back straight, shoulders back and chest up. Moving forward, bend your front knee, keeping your back leg straight at the knee and keeping your foot of the back leg flat on the floor. Don't bend forward at the waist; maintain an arch in the small of your back. Move as far forward until you feel the pull in the back of the leg around the knee. Relax and hold for 10 seconds.

7. Continuation of Lower Leg (Leg Muscles)—to continue to the stretch of the lower leg, stand at a doorframe and hold on. Lean back and sit on your back leg with your foot on the floor. Hold for 10 seconds. Repeat this stretch on the opposite side.

8. Side stretch (Torso muscles)—standing with your feet a shoulder-width apart, place one arm on your hip for balance and extend the other over your head. Slowly bend your body so that you are stretching the side with the arm extended overhead. Stretch for a few seconds and return to the starting position. Then repeat this exercise on the opposite side.

9. Side twister (Torso muscles)—standing with your feet a shoulder-width apart and heels planted firmly on the ground, extend your arms so that they are parallel to the ground and even with your shoulders. Turn your palms up and begin the stretch by twisting your torso to one side and then to the other. Repeat this stretch five times on each side.

10. Arm Circles (Chest and shoulder muscles)—standing with your feet a shoulder-width apart, slowly move both arms backward in a full-circle motion five to ten times. Then repeat this exercise in a forward motion.

11. Jumping Jacks (Leg and shoulder muscles)—standing with your feet together and your arms at your sides, jump and spread your feet apart about a shoulder-width while simultaneously swinging your arms over your head. Repeat this exercise 15-25 times.

12. Upper Leg Stretch (Leg muscles)—stand next to a table, chair or rail and cross the closest leg in front of the other leg. Bend at the waist, reaching for the floor with your opposite hand and relax. Hold this stretch for 10 seconds. Repeat this exercise on the opposite side.

Calisthenics

Calisthenics is a common way for an individual to exercise while using their own body weight as the load or resistance to build his/her strength. There are many exercises available to increase muscle strength and endurance. These exercises should be performed several times a week, each for 20-30 minutes.

Each exercise should be performed as many times as possible at a steady pace. These exercises should be repeated for the first week and increased to your maximum potential.

The following is a list of several different calisthenic exercises:

- Push-ups (Shoulder and arm muscles)—while on your hands and knees on a padded surface, spread your hands to the same width of your shoulders and push up while keeping your back straight. Slowly lower yourself to the floor and push up again.

- Narrow Pushup (Chest, shoulders and tricep muscles)—assume a knees-on-the-floor, feet-crossed push-up position but move your hands together so that your thumbs and index fingers touch. The space between your hands should form a triangle. Complete as many push-ups as you can in one minute.

- Chin-ups (Shoulder and arm muscles)—while grasping a bar underhand approximately six feet from the ground, pull up until your chin is over the bar. Slowly lower your body and repeat.

- Leg Lifts (Back, buttocks and hamstring muscles)—on a padded surface, get down on your hands and knees and press your left knee forward. Then slowly extend the leg behind you until it's in line with your back. Lower your leg slowly and again press the knee forward. Do 20 repetitions with each leg.

- Sit-ups (Abdominal muscles and hip flexors)—lie down on your back on a padded surface with your shoulders on the floor and your knees bent at a 45-degree angle. Lace your fingers behind your head and curl up to a sitting position so that you are able to touch your right elbow to your left knee. Now touch your left elbow to your right knee. Repeat this motion but alternate between your left and right elbows.

- Crunch (Abdominal muscles)—start with a basic crunch to work your upper abdominal muscles. Lie on your back, knees bent, feet flat on the floor, hands lightly touching the back of your head, elbows out. Keeping your lower back pressed to the floor, slowly curl your head and shoulders up then lower them back down. Do as many repetitions as you can in one minute.

- Side Leg Lifts (Back and thigh muscles)—lie on a padded surface on your side with your head cradled by your hand and elbow and your legs fully extended. Your other arm should be on the floor in front of your upper body. Lift your top leg, which should be fully extended, about 60 degrees and then return it to the starting position. Continue this exercise using the other leg.

- Squats (Leg muscles)—stand with your feet at about shoulder-width apart. Place your hands on your hips for balance and bend your knees so that your thighs are parallel to the ground. Then return to the starting position. You may alter this exercise by squatting in the center then moving one leg out to the left, squatting, then back to center and then out to the right.

- Squat jumps (Leg muscles)—stand with your hands on your hips for balance and place one foot a step ahead of the other. Squat down by bending your knees in a 90-degree angle and then jump as high as you can so that your knees are no longer bent. Alternate the position of your feet on your return and then repeat the exercise.

- Dips (Arm, shoulder and chest muscles)—grasp the sides of the seat of a chair and allow your legs and feet to slide forward while supporting the weight of your body with your arms. Bend your elbows at a 90-degree angle and then push up back to the starting position.

- Bench Steps (Leg muscles)—place a bench in front of your feet at a height that is comfortable for you. Begin by stepping up on the bench with your left foot and then following with the right. Step down with the left and follow with the right. Continue this exercise for 30 seconds counting the number of times you successfully stepped onto the bench with both feet. Be careful not to perform this exercise too quickly as it is easy to catch your foot on the bench.

- The Superwoman (Lower back)—lie face down on a mat with your arms extended over your head. Raise your right arm and left leg simultaneously until you feel a gentle tension in your lower back. Resist twisting your torso or raising your other hip or shoulder at the same time. Hold for five seconds then slowly lower. Repeat, using your other arm and leg. Complete the series as many times as you can in one minute.

- Running in Place/Jumping Jacks—alternating a few sets of calisthenics with an aerobic interval helps keep your heart rate elevated throughout the routine. For this set of aerobic moves, run in place for 30 seconds then immediately do 15 jumping jacks.

- Reverse Lunge (Butt and leg muscles)—stand straight with your hands on your hips. Keeping your left leg straight, step back with your left foot as far as you can and then lower your left knee until it nearly touches the floor, or as low as you can. Your right knee should automatically bend to a 90-degree angle. Lift yourself back into the starting position, tightening your butt muscles as you go. Repeat 10-15 times with your left leg and then work your right leg.

- One-legged Calf Raise (Calf muscles)—stand with your left forefoot on the edge of a step so that your left heel hangs off the edge. Wrap your right foot around your left ankle and grab a railing or wall for balance. Rise up onto your toes then slowly lower yourself until your heel falls slightly below the step. Repeat 12 to 20 times then switch to work the right leg.

- Shoulder Raise (Shoulder muscles)—stand with your arms straight out from your sides, parallel to the floor. Slowly rotate both arms forward as if you were drawing 6-inch-diameter circles with your fingertips. Continue for 30 seconds then draw backward circles for 30 seconds.

Cool Down

When you have concluded the training period of the workout, it is important that you continue to walk around so that your body becomes adjusted to less movement and a slower heart rate. Exercises from the warm-up phase can be done as a means of stretching out the muscles after the training period.

Weight Control

Exercise plays an important role in weight control by increasing your body's energy output, which uses stored calories for extra fuel. Much of exercise physiology research shows that exercise increases metabolism and causes it to maintain itself at an increased level over time. Weight control can be increased through exercise depending on the amount and type of activity as well as the number of calories you consume. If you consume 100 calories a day more than your body needs, you will gain approximately 10 pounds in a year. You could take that weight off, or keep it off, by doing 30 minutes of moderate exercise daily. The combination of exercise and diet is the best approach to manage your weight.

Note that as you continue to exercise, you may not lose weight as quickly as you would like because muscle weighs more than fat.

What to Expect from Exercise

Exercise has wonderful benefits, but it often takes quite a bit of time to see results. It may be a long and slow process. Exercise will benefit all areas of your body, and improvements will appear as you progress. By keeping a log of your exercise routine, you will be able to see a progression of your improved fitness over time.

Good luck to you on the NCJOPAT or other similar job-simulation physical-ability tests!

II. Another Physical Fitness Test

Medical evidence to allow participation in the Physical Fitness Test may be required, and the Department of Personnel reserves the right to exclude from the physical test any eligibles who, upon examination of such evidence, are apparently medically unfit. Eligibles will take the Physical Fitness Test at their own risk of injury, although efforts will be made to safeguard them.

Candidates must complete the *entire* course consisting of seven events in not more than *65 seconds*.

Candidates who do not successfully complete events 3, 5, and 6 will fail the test.

DESCRIPTION OF EVENTS

1. Run up approximately 40 steps.
2. Run approximately 40 yards, following a designated path including at least four 90-degree turns, to a sandbag.
3. Push the sandbag, weighing approximately 100 pounds, forward a distance of approximately five yards and then back to its original position. (Failure to meet all of the conditions for this event will result in failure of the test as a whole.)
4. Run approximately 10 yards to a dummy, weighing approximately 110 pounds, which is hanging with its lowest point approximately 3 feet above the floor.
5. Raise the dummy so as to lift the attached ring off the metal pipe. Allow the dummy to slide onto the floor or place it on the floor. You must not drop it or throw it down. (Failure to meet all of the conditions for this event will result in failure of the test as a whole.)
6. Step up approximately 18 inches and walk across a 12-foot beam by placing one foot in front of the other until you reach the other end. (You must be in control at all times, and falling off the beam will result in failure of the test as a whole.)
7. Run approximately 10 yards to the finish line.

Candidates who fail the test on their first trial will be allowed a second trial on the same date after a rest period.

Candidates who do not successfully complete all the events in their proper sequence will fail the test.

III. Physical Agility Test

The first part of the test consists of the first seven elements described below, all of which are essential for the satisfactory performance of the duties of the position.

All elements are scored on a pass/fail basis, and candidates must satisfactorily complete each element of the test in order to successfully complete the test. Candidates who fail the test will not be appointed to the position. Unsuccessful candidates will be considered for retesting at a future date.

ELEMENT 1: STAIR CLIMB

This task consists of safely going up and down one flight of stairs.

ELEMENT 2: LADDER ASCENT

The candidate safely climbs to a height of approximately 12 feet, the ladder encased by a standard industrial safety cage with an interior dimension of approximately 30 inches, until the designated rung is touched. The candidate then descends to the floor in a safe manner.

ELEMENT 3: SUSPENDED DUMMY RAISE

A rescue dummy simulating a body weighing 120 pounds is hanging by a rope. The dummy must be raised vertically (3 inches) until the noose pressure is off the neck and held there for a period of five (5) consecutive seconds. The dummy must be raised by facing it and using hands and arms (as in a "bear hug").

ELEMENT 4: BODY TRANSPORT

A 160-pound dummy is placed on a blanket. The candidate must pull the weighted blanket a total distance of 30 feet.

ELEMENT 5: OBSTACLE VAULT

This task consists of getting over a 3-foot-high obstacle in a safe manner. Hurdling or diving is not permitted.

ELEMENT 6: DOOR LOCK AND UNLOCK

This task consists of properly unlocking a standard-use security cell door, using the assigned key, going through the door, and relocking the same door.

ELEMENT 7: LOAD AND UNLOAD

This task consists of properly loading and unloading a weapon, 4-inch revolver, observing all specified safety regulations. Live ammunition will not be used.

ELEMENT 8: THREE-MINUTE STEP TEST

In addition, the agility test includes an element to screen for cardiovascular disease: For 3 minutes, the candidate will lift one foot at a time while stepping on and off a 12-inch bench at a rate of 24 times per minute. The candidate must keep pace with a metronome set at 96 beats per minute. After the 3 minutes of stepping, the candidate will sit down and relax without talking. A 60-second heart count will be taken starting 5 seconds after the completion of stepping. There is no pass/fail on this test. Instead, EHS medical staff will consider the results of this test along with other aspects of the examination to determine if a candidate is capable of performing the essential duties of a Police Officer.

IV. Physical Performance Test

There are six test parts designed to assess: strength to push, pull, drag, and lift; cardiorespiratory endurance for strenuous work and running; abdominal strength and spine flexibility to avoid low back pain, problems of strains, and loss of mobility and agility.

The physical performance test consists of the following:

1. **Push-ups:** This is a standard push-up where the back and legs are kept straight. The event starts in the up position and the count occurs when the applicant returns to the up position after having touched an audible beeper on the mat with his or her chest. The applicant is to do as many push-ups as possible in 60 seconds.

2. **Grip:** Using a hand-grip dynamometer, the applicant squeezes the meter while keeping the arm extended parallel to the leg. Both right and left grips are tested and recorded in kilograms of pressure.

3. **Obstacle Course:** The total distance for this obstacle course is 90 feet and it is run for time. The applicant runs 20 feet, crawls 6 feet through a 2½ simulated tunnel, runs 20 feet, and climbs a 6-foot-6-inch barrier with footholds and handholds. The applicant then runs 20 feet to and around a set of pylons, then back to the barrier, which has footholds and handholds on it. After climbing the barrier a second time, the applicant runs 4 feet to the stop position.

4. **165-Pound Drag:** The applicant drags a 165-pound life-form dummy 30 feet for time. The dummy is gripped in the armpits and dragged backwards.

5. **95-Pound Carry.** The applicant lifts a 95-pound bag, which has handholds, runs with it 30 feet, and places it on a 32-inch platform for time.

6. **Half-Mile Shuttle Run:** The applicant runs between two pylons placed 88 feet apart for a total of 15 round trips for time.

Examinees are encouraged to practice ahead of time for the physical performance test. All physical tests, and especially the half-mile run, are aided by conditioning ahead of time. Physical training for law enforcement positions requires that new hires be physically fit when they are hired.

V. Qualifying Physical Agility Test

> **Note:** The qualifying physical agility test is a series of six sub-tests in four events that take place consecutively. There are only two rest periods permitted, each rest period lasting only 2 minutes. You must pass all six sub-tests; a fail in any one sub-test will cause you to fail the entire test. A pass in one sub-test cannot be used to cover a fail in a different sub-test. You must pass all six sub-tests.

300-Yard Run—Explanation of sub-tests 1, 2, and 3: You will run six continuous laps along an oblong course where you will be timed at the 50-yard point (1 lap), then at the 100-yard point (2 laps), and finally at the 300-yard point (6 laps).

1. **50-yard run:** Run a distance of 50 yards as fast as possible. Maximum allowable time is 13 seconds. You will be timed at the 50-yard point.

2. **100-yard run:** Run a distance of 100 yards as fast as possible. Maximum allowable time is 28 seconds. You will be timed at the 100-yard point.

3. **300-yard run:** Run a distance of 300 yards as fast as possible. Maximum allowable time is 1 minute 20 seconds (80 seconds). You will be timed at the 300-yard point (conclusion of the run).

A 2-MINUTE REST PERIOD IS PERMITTED AT THIS POINT.

4. **Fire extinguisher carry:** Carry a fully loaded fire extinguisher weighing about 25 pounds a distance of 50 feet as fast as possible. Maximum allowable time is 10 seconds.

5. **Stair climb:** Run down three flights of stairs and climb back up three flights of stairs as fast as possible. Maximum allowable time is 45 seconds.

A 2-MINUTE REST PERIOD IS PERMITTED AT THIS POINT.

6. **Deadweight drag:** Drag a bag weighing 50 pounds a distance of 50 feet as fast as possible. Maximum allowable time is 8 seconds.

VI. Physical Assessment

This phase is intended to give an overall measurement of a candidate's physical fitness and preparation for Police Academy training. Blood pressure and vision will be measured, and candidates must fall within required levels to continue in the process, which includes:

- A 1.5-mile run measuring cardiovascular efficiency.
- Push-ups measuring shoulder muscular endurance.
- Sit-ups measuring abdominal and hip flex or muscle strength.
- An agility run measuring quickness, speed, and balance.
- A vertical jump measuring leg muscle strength and explosiveness.
- A sit-and-reach test measuring thigh and back muscle extensiveness.
- A grip test measuring wrist and finger muscle strength.
- A measure of body fat composition.

VII. Physical Fitness Test

The candidates who qualify on the medical examination will be required to pass the qualifying Physical Fitness Test. A total score of 20 is required for passing this test; the scores attained on the five individual tests are added together to obtain your final score.

TEST 1: TRUNK FLEXION TEST (THREE CHANCES)

Candidates will assume a sitting position on the floor with the legs extended at right angles to a line drawn on the floor. The heels should touch the near edge of the line and be 5 inches apart. The candidate should slowly reach with both hands as far forward as possible on a yardstick that is placed between the legs with the 15-inch mark resting on the near edge of the heel line. The score is the most distant point (in inches) reached on the yardstick with fingertips.

Rating	Trunk Flexion (Inches)	Points
Excellent	22 and over	6
Good	20-21	5
Average	14-19	4
Fair	12-13	3
Poor	10-11	2
Very Poor	9 and under	1

TEST 2: HAND GRIP STRENGTH TEST (THREE CHANCES)

The candidate places the dynamometer (hand grip tester) at the side and, without touching the body with any part of the arm, hand, or dynamometer, should grip the dynamometer as hard as possible in one quick movement. The best of the three tries will be recorded.

Rating	Hand Grip in Kg.	Points
Excellent	65 and above	6
Good	57-64	5
Average	45-56	4
Fair	37-44	3
Poor	30-36	2
Very Poor	29 and under	1

TEST 3: STANDING BROAD JUMP (THREE CHANCES)

Candidates will be permitted three chances in consecutive order, and the longest distance will be credited. Candidates will be required to jump from a standing position, both feet together. Distance of jump will be recorded from starting point to back of heels. It is each candidate's responsibility to have a non-skid surface on the soles of his or her sneakers.

Rating	Distance	Points
Excellent	7'10"or better	6
Good	7'0" to 7'9"	5
Average	6'1" to 6'11"	4
Fair	5'6" to 6'0"	3
Poor	5'0" to 5'5"	2
Very Poor	Less than 5'	1

TEST 4: ONE-MINUTE SIT-UP TEST

The candidate will start by lying on the back with the knees bent so that the heels are about 18 inches away from the buttocks. An examiner will hold the ankles to give support. The candidate will then perform as many correct sit-ups (elbows alternately touching the opposite knee) as possible within a 1-minute period. The candidate should return to the starting position (back to floor) between sit-ups.

Rating	Sit-Ups in 1 Minute	Points
Excellent	35	6
Good	30-34	5
Average	20-29	4
Fair	15-19	3
Poor	10-14	2
Very Poor	9 and under	1

TEST 5: THREE-MINUTE STEP TEST

The candidate will step for three minutes on a 1-inch bench at a rate of 24 steps per minute. The time will be maintained by a metronome. Immediately after the 3 minutes of stepping, the subject will sit down and relax without talking. A 60-second heart-rate count is taken starting 5 seconds after the completion of stepping.

Rating	Pulse	Points
Excellent	75-84	6
Good	85-94	5
Average	95-119	4
Fair	120-129	3
Poor	130-139	2
Very Poor	Over 140	1

SLIDING SCALE STANDARDS

The Americans with Disabilities Act requires that age not be a consideration in hiring except where youth, or maturity, is a bona fide qualification for performance of the job. The federal government has established 37 as the highest age at which persons can and may effectively enter certain federal law enforcement positions. In order to establish an age-based hiring limit, each jurisdiction must justify the age it has chosen. At this time, not all guidelines are clear. Each jurisdiction makes its own interpretation of the requirements of the Americans with Disabilities Act, and its interpretation remains in effect until challenged and overturned by a court of law. Some states have chosen to take the Act at face value and have done away with upper age limits altogether.

When states, or jurisdictions within those states, discard upper age limits, they open themselves to new complications. According to the U.S. Justice Department, physical fitness standards that are the same for everyone violate the Americans with Disabilities Act. In response to this determination, many jurisdictions have relaxed the physical fitness requirements for their Police Officers. These last two are recently announced Physical Fitness Screening Tests that take into consideration both age and sex.

VIII. Physical Fitness Screening Test

Candidate will go from Stations I through IV in order. Each station is pass/fail. Candidate must pass each station in order to proceed to the next station. Candidate will be allowed up to 3 minutes' rest between stations. Once a station is started, it must be completed according to protocol. See the chart below:

Station 1: Sit-up—Candidate lies flat on the back, knees bent, heels flat on the floor, fingers interlaced behind the head. Monitor holds the feet down firmly. In the up position, candidate should touch elbows to knees and return with shoulder blades touching floor. To pass this component, candidate must complete the requisite number of correct sit-ups in 1 minute.

Station 2: Flex—Candidate removes shoes and places feet squarely against box with feet no wider than 8 inches apart. Toes are pointed directly toward ceiling; knees remain extended throughout test. With hands placed one on top of the other, candidate leans forward without lunging or bobbing and reaches as far down the yardstick as possible. The hands must stay together and the stretch must be held for 1 second. Three attempts are allowed, with the best of three recorded to the nearest ¼ inch to determine whether the candidate passed/failed.

Station 3: Bench—Monitor loads weights to ½ of candidate required weight. Candidate is permitted to "press" this weight once. Monitor increases weight to ⅔ of candidate's required weight. Candidate is permitted to "press" this weight once. The required test weight is then loaded. The candidate has up to four (4) attempts to "press" required (maximum) weight. In order to pass, buttocks must remain on the bench. Candidate will be allowed up to 2 minutes' rest between each "press." (Universal Bench Press Equipment)

Station 4: 1.5-Mile Run—Candidate must be successful on Stations 1, 2, and 3 in order to participate in Station 4. It will be administered on a track. Candidate will be informed of his/her lap time during the test.

SCORING CHART

Age/Sex	Test			
Male	Sit-up	Flex	Bench	1.5-Mi Run
20-29	38	16.5	99	12.51
30-39	35	15.5	88	13.36
40-49	29	14.3	80	14.29
50-59	24	13.3	71	15.26
60+	19	12.5	66	16.43
Female				
20-29	32	19.3	59	15.26
30-39	25	18.3	53	15.57
40-49	20	17.3	50	16.58
50-59	14	16.8	44	17.54
60+	6	15.5	43	18.44

IX. Physical Ability Test

The Physical Ability Test is designed to assess the following fitness components:

- **Flexibility**—the ability of muscles and joints to operate through a normal range of motion without injury.
- **Dynamic Strength**—the ability of the muscles to generate force to perform repeated tasks over an extended period of time.
- **Cardiovascular Endurance**—the ability of the heart and vascular system to transport and utilize oxygen for sustained activity involving stamina.

The Physical Ability Test for candidates consists of four (4) subtests scored in a pass/fail manner. The minimum performance score on each and every subtest must be met in order to continue through the selection process. A schedule of minimum physical fitness standards is included on a chart following the description of the subtests.

SUBTEST 1—SIT-UPS

The candidate shall start in the supine position with knees bent, heels flat on the floor, and fingers interlaced and placed behind the head. The candidate's feet will be held down at the ankle. The candidate shall raise the upper body touching the elbows to the knees, and then return down until the shoulder blades touch the floor. The candidate may rest in the up position only. *The candidate must perform at least the minimum required number of correct sit-ups in 1 minute. Only sit-ups that are performed correctly will be counted.*

SUBTEST 2—FLEXIBILITY—SIT AND REACH

The candidate shall sit on the floor, remove shoes, and place feet squarely against a measuring box. The candidate's feet shall be no wider than 8 inches apart. Knees shall remain extended throughout the test. The candidate's hands are placed exactly together, one on top of the other, fingers extended. A yardstick is placed on top of the box such that the 15-inch mark is flush with the edge of the box at the candidate's feet. The zero end of the yardstick is extended toward the candidate's upper body. The candidate will lean forward without lunging or bobbing and must reach as far down the yardstick as possible. The hands must stay together and even. Exhaling on the reach is recommended. Three reaches are allowed, if needed, and recorded to the nearest ¼ inch. *The candidate must reach the minimum required distance in inches as listed.*

SUBTEST 3—PUSH-UPS

An administrator will hold a three (3)-inch measuring device directly between and in line with the candidate's hands on the floor under the candidate performing the push-up. The candidate will start with his/her hands placed approximately shoulder-width apart on the floor and elbows fully extended. The back and remainder of the body should be kept straight at all times. From this full extension, known as the "up" position, the candidate will lower the body toward the floor until the sternum touches the device being held by the administrator. The candidate then returns to the fully extended "up" position. This completes one repetition. The candidate may rest in the up position only. *The candidate must perform at least the minimum required number of correct push-ups. Only push-ups that are performed correctly will be counted.*

SUBTEST 4—1.5 MILE RUN

Candidates should refrain from smoking or eating for 2 hours preceding the test. Adequate time will be allowed for stretching and warm-up prior to the test. The candidate will run six laps on a 440-yard (¼-mile) track to complete the 1.5-mile run as fast as possible. *The candidate must perform the 1.5-mile run within the required time limit.* Time will be allowed for stretching and cool-down following the test.

MINIMUM PHYSICAL FITNESS STANDARDS FOR ENTRY TO THE TRAINING ACADEMY

Female Candidates		
Age Group	20-29	30-39
Sit-ups (1 minute)	35	27
Sit & Reach (inches)	20	19
Push-ups	18	14
1.5-Mile Run (minutes)	14:55	15:26
Male Candidates		
Age Group	20-29	30-39
Sit-ups (one minute)	40	36
Sit & Reach (inches)	17.5	16.5
Push-ups	33	27
1.5-Mile Run (minutes)	12:18	12:51

Academy Physical Training—The Physical Training course design is based upon the Physical Ability Test Standards candidates were required to meet in order to enter the Academy. In order to graduate, recruits will be expected to perform the same exercises. However, minimum graduation standards reflect the improvement gained from training.

PHYSICAL FITNESS LEVELS (GRADUATION STANDARD)

Female Recruits		
Age Group	20-29	30-39
Sit-ups (1 minute)	41	32
Sit & Reach (inches)	21.5	20.5
Push-ups	23	18
1.5-Mile Run (minutes)	13:53	14:24
Male Recruits		
Age Group	20-29	30-39
Sit-ups (1 minute)	45	41
Sit & Reach (inches)	19.5	18.5
Push-ups	41	34
1.5-Mile Run (minutes)	10:47	11:34

The Background Check

The Police Officer is in a position of public trust. He or she must be deserving of that trust. The police department must feel very certain that the Police Officer will not use his or her position for personal gain, will not use it to harass individuals or groups that he or she dislikes, will not be easily corrupted, and will not take advantage of privileged knowledge.

The standard predictor of future behavior is past behavior. The police department must find out how you have behaved in the past. It will do this by first having you fill out a questionnaire. As with the medical questionnaire, there is no point in lying or cheating. You will be found out and disqualified. State the facts clearly. Explain fully and factually.

If you have a totally clean record and face no problems in your personal or family life, then you need have no concern about the background check. Fill in the blanks. List references, and inform those people whose names you have given so that they are not upset when the police contacts them.

Most people have something in their background that can spark more inquiry, such as the following:

- The problem may be financial: If you are strapped for money, the police department may fear that you might be corruptible.
- The problem may be marital: The police department may worry that you will be distracted by relationship problems at home.
- The problem may be one of frequent job changes: The police department questions your stability and the value of investing in your training.
- The problem may be one of poor credit: Are you responsible and reliable?
- The problem may be one of a brush with the law, minor or major. Most minor infractions can be explained at an interview; reassure the interviewer that these were youthful indiscretions unlikely to recur. Arrests for felonies, and, worse still, convictions present greater obstacles. It may be wise to consult an attorney who specializes in expunging criminal records to see what can be done to clear your name. Some offenses are absolutely disqualifying.

You may as well know about disqualifying factors ahead of time and take all possible steps to make yourself employable by the police department. A felony record needs the services of an attorney. So might multiple misdemeanor convictions. You can help yourself in many other situations. If you have a poor credit rating, pay up and have your rating upgraded. If you are behind on alimony payments, catch up. If you have an unanswered summons, go to court and answer it. Pay your parking tickets. Even if these past problems turn up in the background check, your positive action in clearing them up will be in your favor.

Be sure that you are able to document any claims you make with reference to diplomas, degrees, and honors. You may have to produce these at an interview. Likewise, be certain that you understand the nature and gravity of the problems in your background. Be prepared to admit that you misbehaved and to reassure the examiners that you have matured into a responsible citizen.

The Psychological Evaluation

Some jurisdictions subject all Police Officer candidates to a psychological evaluation before appointment; others, because of the expense involved, limit psychological evaluations to those cases where there are signs that one might be necessary. In all cases, the sole purpose of a psychological evaluation is to determine the candidate's mental fitness for performing the specific duties of a Police Officer. The evaluation is not concerned with other aspects of mental well-being. In fact, because of this exclusive focus on police work, a candidate might be judged psychologically unfit to be a Police Officer even if he or she is perfectly suited for other types of employment.

What makes police work so different from other occupations? Soon after orientation and the usual training at the police academy, the Police Officer begins functioning more or less independently. Although the officer functions under supervision, that supervision is present only periodically; and although the officer should be guided by the department's rules of procedure, many times he or she will be thrust into situations where immediate action is required to save lives or protect property. For example, the officer who answers the call of a pregnant woman about to give birth must take decisive action at once. In such situations, there is no time to consult the rules of procedure. The officer must do whatever is necessary right away.

Another crucial difference is that the Police Officer carries a gun as part of the job. Prudent use of this weapon requires not only conformance to the rules of procedure but also a good sense of police judgment. The officer who must decide in an emergency whether to use that gun must have a very high degree of psychological stability.

Psychological evaluations of Police Officer candidates are usually conducted by a psychologist or psychiatrist who is trained to detect signs of deficiencies that could interfere with the proper performance of police work. The job is two-fold: to look for signs of potential trouble and to evaluate the sincerity of the candidate. For example, consider the possible responses when the psychologist asks, "Why do you want to become a Police Officer?" A proper response would be, "I want a career in the public service, and I feel that effective law enforcement will make for a better society for my children and eventually for my grandchildren." There is nothing wrong with this response. The only thing to be judged is the sincerity of the candidate. Now look at the following response to the same question: "I have always liked uniforms. They bring respect and admiration, and they permit you to perform your duties without interference." Something is wrong here. Or consider this response: "I hate criminals. They take advantage of the weak and elderly. They are cowards, and I want to do everything I can to eliminate them." This intense hatred may indicate the need for further investigation of this candidate's psychological stability.

TYPICAL EVALUATION QUESTIONS

The questions that you will be asked will, for the most part, be quite predictable. The majority of them will be based on your responses to application forms and other papers that you have been required to file. The psychologist will ask you to amplify or to explain the personal data that you listed on those papers. Sometimes you will be asked to describe your feelings about events that happened to you. Also, as a way of encouraging you to talk, you may be asked more open-ended questions about your personal likes, dislikes, or emotions.

You may also be asked what you might do in a hypothetical police work situation, but such questions are unlikely to form the bulk of the evaluation. In this case, the psychologist is not testing your knowledge of police procedures, but only your ability to make reasoned judgments and to avoid rash behavior. Because most of the questions you will be asked are predictable, it is relatively easy to prepare answers for them. Begin your preparation by looking over the application forms that you filled out and any other papers that you were required to file. You should be able to pick out the points that a psychologist will want you to clarify or explain.

Typical questions you might encounter include the following:

- Why did you choose your area of concentration in school?
- What particularly interests you about that subject?
- Why did you transfer from school *x* to school *y*?
- How did you get the job with _____?
- Which of the duties described in your second job did you like best? Which least? Why?
- What did you do during the nine months between your second and third jobs?
- Explain the circumstances of your leaving a particular job.
- Please clarify: armed forces service, arrest record, hospitalization record, etc., as applicable.

Other questions are much like those asked at a routine job interview. They can be anticipated and prepared for as well.

- Why do you want to leave the kind of work you are doing now?
- Why do you want to be a Police Officer?
- How does your family feel about your becoming a Police Officer?
- What do you do in your leisure time?
- Do you have any hobbies? What are they? What do you particularly like about _____?
- What is your favorite sport? Would you rather play or watch?
- How do you react to criticism? If you think the criticism is reasonable? If you consider the criticism unwarranted?
- What is your pet peeve?
- What are your greatest strengths? Weaknesses?
- What could make you lose your temper?
- Of what accomplishment in your life are you most proud?
- What act do you most regret?
- If you could start over, what would you do differently?
- What traits do you value most in a co-worker? In a friend?
- What makes you think you would make a good Police Officer?

Still other questions may be more specific to police work. You should have prepared answers to:

- How much sleep do you need?
- Are you afraid of heights?
- What is your attitude toward irregular hours?
- Do you prefer working alone or on a team?
- Are you afraid of dying?
- What would you do with the rest of your life if your legs were crippled in an injury?
- How do you deal with panic? Your own? That of others'?
- What is your attitude toward smoking? Drinking? Drugs? *Playboy* magazine? Gambling?
- What is your favorite TV program? How do you feel about watching news? Sports? Classical drama? Rock music? Opera? Game shows?

Now make a list of your own. The variety of evaluation questions is endless, but most can be answered with ease. Preparation makes the whole process much more pleasant and less frightening.

There is one question that strikes terror into the heart of nearly every candidate for Police Officer or any other job. This question is likely to be the first and, unless you are prepared for it, may well throw you off your guard. The question is: "Tell me about yourself." For this question you should have a script prepared in your head. Think well ahead of time about what you want to tell. What could the psychologist be interested in? This question is not seeking information about your birthweight nor about your food preferences. The psychologist wants you to talk about yourself with relation to your interest in and qualifications for police work. Think of how to describe yourself with this goal in mind. What information puts you in a good light with reference to the work for which you are applying? Organize your presentation. Then analyze what you plan to say. What is a psychologist likely to pick up on? To what questions will your speech lead? You must prepare to answer any questions to which you have opened yourself.

Toward the end of the evaluation, the psychologist will most likely ask if you have any questions. You undoubtedly will have had some beforehand and should have come prepared to ask them. If all of your questions have been answered in the course of the evaluation, tell this to the psychologist. If not, or if the evaluation has raised new questions in your mind, by all means ask them. The evaluation should serve for your benefit; it is not just to serve the purposes of the police department.

The invitation of your questions tends to be the signal that the evaluation is nearly over. The psychologist is satisfied that he or she has gathered enough information. The time allotted to you is up. Be alert to the cues. Do not spoil the good impression you have made by trying to prolong the evaluation.

Should You Reveal Personal Opinions and Feelings?

The psychologist does not expect candidates to be devoid of personal feelings. After all, everyone has likes and dislikes. However, the mature, psychologically stable person is able to keep those feelings from interfering with the performance of job duties. The Police

Officer will encounter a very wide variety of people on the job. Some the officer may find personally likeable; others may be unlikable, even downright unpleasant. However, whatever the officer's true feelings about the persons encountered, he or she must service those individuals in an effective manner or serious repercussions—even loss of life—may result. This type of behavior takes mental maturity and stability, qualities every officer must possess. It is these qualities that the psychologist is looking for at the evaluation, not an absence of personal feelings. The successful candidate does not have to like everyone he or she meets. What is important is the ability to control personal feelings in order to function effectively.

Sometimes during an evaluation a candidate will express "extreme" views on certain subjects. Unlike more typical opinions or feelings, these may indeed be cause for disqualification. An obvious example is a display of unreasoning dislike for people from a particular ethnic or religious background. To the psychologist, this is a sure sign of trouble. The candidate who says, "People from ethnic group *x* are always the ones who commit the violent crimes" will never be appointed a Police Officer.

Should You Volunteer Information?

One very important point to remember at the evaluation is to limit your responses to what is asked. An evaluation session of this type is one of the very few opportunities most people have to reveal their true inner selves to others. The psychologist knows this and often encourages the person being evaluated to talk freely and openly about personal matters and opinions. An unthinking candidate may use this opportunity to bring up matters that ordinarily he or she would never discuss. A talkative candidate might even know that he or she is getting in too deep but may be unable to refrain from continuing. The psychologist encourages this type of individual to talk at length in order to reveal personal matters that will indicate the level of the candidate's psychological stability.

One device that psychologists use to make candidates keep talking is to assume a facial expression that indicates that further explanation is expected. It is very important not to respond to this suggestion. If you do, you are likely to say things that can only be harmful to you. Try to be satisfied with your original response, and have the maturity to stand by it no matter what expression you see on the psychologist's face. Display a sense of self-assurance that convinces the psychologist that you are satisfied with your answers.

How to Explain Problem Incidents in Your Past

One concern of many Police Officer candidates is how to handle questions about problem incidents in their past. More than a few candidates have at some time—usually in their youth—gotten into trouble in some incident involving property damage or even personal injury to others. Such incidents almost always come to light during the candidate's background check, often through school, court, or military records. If you have such an incident in your past and are questioned about it by the psychologist, the wisest course is to accept full responsibility for it and to attribute it to your youthful immaturity at the time. Claiming that the record is false or giving excuses for your bad behavior is not likely to be regarded favorably. The psychologist is much more apt to respond positively if you accept responsibility and—just as important—you attribute any such incident to an immature outlook that you have now outgrown. One mistake of this type will not necessarily disqualify you if you can convince the psychologist that you have become a fully responsible adult and will never do anything of the kind again.

"Pencil-and-Paper" Evaluations

As part of the psychological evaluation, some jurisdictions use standardized personality tests that you answer by marking a sheet of paper. These tests may contain a hundred or more questions. Your responses help the psychologist determine your specific personality traits. Your answer to any one question by itself usually means very little, but your answers to a group of questions, taken together, will have significance to the psychologist. Your wisest course when taking one of these written personality tests is to give truthful answers. Any attempt to make yourself appear different from the way you really are is not likely to be successful.

KEEP A POSITIVE ATTITUDE

One final word of advice: It is important to approach all psychological evaluations with a positive attitude. Think of the evaluation not as an ordeal that you must endure, but rather as an opportunity to prove that you are qualified to become a Police Officer. In truth, the psychologist will be looking for traits that qualify you, not ones that disqualify you. And if disqualifying evidence exists, it is the psychologist's responsibility to consider every factor before making a negative recommendation. So go into the evaluation with confidence and be prepared to "sell" yourself to the psychologist. You will be given every chance to prove your worth.

EVALUATION CHECKLIST

Here are some valuable points to remember as you prepare for the psychological evaluation.

1. Get a good night's sleep the night before the evaluation.
2. Do not take any medication beforehand to calm yourself. You may be tested for drugs before the evaluation.
3. Dress neatly and conservatively.
4. Be polite to the psychologist or psychiatrist.
5. Respond to all questions honestly and forthrightly.

TWO

REVIEW

CHAPTER 5: POLICE JUDGMENT QUIZZER

About the Police Judgment Quizzer

Early Police Officer examinations were a strange mixture of questions covering municipal government, municipal geography, spelling, grammar, first aid—everything, in fact, that every person should know something about, but very little that was specific to measuring the ability of future Police Officers to do their job well. As testing methods matured and examiners gained experience in mass testing, they determined that the best measure of a good Police Officer is a measure of his or her judgment in actual police situations. So the emphasis shifted from factual to actual exams. "Let the questions supply the facts," the examiners reasoned, "and let the aspiring Police Officers display their judgment in choosing the correct answers."

WHAT WOULD YOU DO IF...

This is the essential form of the practical question on Police Officer exams. Assume you are a Police Officer. Here is a given situation. How would you respond to it? This is a very subtle and efficient method of testing. Questions are often based on actual patrol situations. What would you do if you saw a woman walking down the street dressed only in a sheet and leading a doe on a leash? Arrest her? On what charge? Take the doe to an animal shelter? Take the woman to a doctor? Ask her for her phone number? It actually happened. What would *you* do?

Test-Taking Strategies for the Police Judgment Quizzer

Police applicants are placed in a peculiar position by practical judgment questions in that the correct answers for these questions are influenced by actual police department procedures. As an applicant taking the exam, you are not expected to know the police department's policies or procedures. Yet test-makers often assume that police departmental policies or procedures are just common sense. To do really well on practical judgment questions, you need something more than common sense. You need a good understanding of ordinary police department policies and procedures as they apply to routine patrol situations. This is the reason why close relatives of Police Officers tend to earn high scores on the Police

Officer exam. Their familiarity with "police language" and "police thinking" stands them in good stead when they must choose the correct answers to police practical judgment questions.

This chapter familiarizes you with many of the "common sense" ideas that underlie police practical judgment questions. The chapter will serve as "your brother the Police Officer," teaching you to think like a patrol officer. By the time you have finished studying this material, you will be thinking like a patrol officer. You will then be prepared to score high on your Police Officer exam.

THE POLICE ROLE

To start with, you must understand the role of a Police Officer. This role varies according to the size, location, and philosophy of the police department. State police find that their role encompasses major problems like traffic pileups and serious accidents, as well as the more routine problems of stranded motorists. Small-town police find that they have a broad role in maintaining public safety and assuring law and order. Big-city police tend to have a more narrow role because in big cities other agencies take on primary responsibility for certain tasks: medics handle health situations beyond emergency first aid; traffic department personnel deal with many traffic situations; social workers handle many crises concerning the elderly, children, and the mentally ill. Part of your preparation for your own exam should be acquiring some familiarity with the ordinary role of Police Officers in the department to which you are applying.

With this information in mind, you must follow one basic rule when answering police practical judgment questions: fulfill the police role and only the police role. This means:

1. Be professional. Avoid emotional responses, show of bias, or incurring any kind of indebtedness to persons on your beat.

2. Avoid all roles other than the police role, e.g., parent, physician, tradesman, private security, etc. Sometimes you may find it hard to draw the line, such as that between emergency first aid and the role of the medic. In an emergency where time is pressing, the Police Officer must provide assistance to people to the full extent of his or her competence. Where more time is available, leave doubtful roles to others.

3. Fulfill the police role of assisting endangered people 24 hours a day. Be prepared to assist in keeping the peace at any time and to take the initiative in urgent situations. Fulfilling the police role does not necessarily mean making arrests when there is no great need to do so. In practical judgment questions, think of the police role as one of keeping the peace rather than one of making arrests, especially in an off-duty situation.

4. Avoid even the slightest appearance of corruption. Maintain police integrity. Avoid all partiality. Do not accept any gifts or favors. Do not refer business to any particular businessman, company, or professional person.

POLICE PRIORITIES

A *hierarchy* is an arrangement of things according to their importance. Something near the top of a hierarchy is more important than something near the bottom. Basically, a hierarchy is an arrangement of things or activities according to their priority.

There are five basic functions in police work. These have a definite hierarchical order. If an officer finds him- or herself in a situation in which several of these functions must be completed, the officer should consider the hierarchical order, or order of priorities, and act in accordance with the position of each function in that order.

1. *Assist endangered people.* Essentially this means assisting:
   a. seriously injured persons.
   b. physically endangered persons (e.g., victims of a crime in progress, drowning persons, etc.).
2. *Keep the peace.* Calm any major disorder. Prevent tumult, aggression, or destruction of property.
3. *Enforce the law.* Where no actual harm to persons or property is threatened, peace-keeping and maintaining order may be adequate. Where there is unlawful injury or loss, arrest may be necessary in addition to the restoring of order.
4. *Assist people who are not immediately endangered but who need help.* This means assisting:
   a. physically or mentally needy persons: children, the elderly, the handicapped, the homeless, and persons who appear to be sick, mentally ill, or intoxicated.
   b. crime victims, lost persons, and stranded persons.
5. *Maintain order on the beat.* This involves:
   a. Investigating suspicious persons or circumstances. Something is suspicious if it is unusual for the time or the place or the persons involved.
   b. Regulating the use of streets and sidewalks for safety and for the efficient flow of traffic.
   c. Knowing the beat. You must be familiar with the physical features of the beat, you must be aware of routine events, and you must develop positive contacts with the people on the beat.
   d. Making recommendations that will improve safety or flow of traffic in the area. Remember to stay "professional" by recommending only activities, not particular products or businesses.

THE PRINCIPAL OF USE OF MINIMUM NECESSARY FORCE

Many police practical judgment questions concern the possible use of force. Police officers are empowered to use force, even deadly force, under certain circumstances. In general, common sense should rule judgments about the use of force. There are some basic principles that are part of "common sense."

Police Officers should always handle problems with the *minimum amount of force necessary* to resolve the problem. Never use more force than the problem deserves. Obviously, a Police Officer should not shoot somebody for failing to show identification, even if the person is unreasonably stubborn. A Police Officer's action should not cause greater harm than the problem the officer is trying to resolve. In other words, a problem should not be handled in such a way as to create an even bigger problem.

When a Police Officer is evaluating the gravity of a situation to determine how much force is necessary (or when a candidate is making this choice in an examination), the officer must consider the physical setting, the actual actions and the apparent intentions of the people involved, and the intent of the law. Differences in physical settings require differences in policies and regulations. Big-city police departments, for example, practically never permit Police Officers to fire warning shots, to shoot at moving vehicles, or to shoot at people on public streets. It is assumed that such shooting would endanger innocent bystanders. On the other hand, state police departments often do allow warning shots, shooting at moving vehicles, and even shooting at people on the road because they assume a highway setting without any innocent bystanders in the line of fire.

THE VALUE HIERARCHY

Occasionally a Police Officer has to make a quick decision in a situation that involves value conflicts. For example, it may be necessary to choose between risking serious injury to a hostage or letting a dangerous criminal escape. Such a decision involves a value judgment. An officer makes the decision based on the order of priorities.

If a police department's hierarchy of values is spelled out clearly, officers are assisted in making rapid and proper judgments. Police exam candidates can rely on the same list of priorities. The list below is the value hierarchy that has been the basis for practical judgment questions on Police Officer exams for many years. In order of priority:

1. Protection of life and limb.
2. Obeying orders in an emergency situation.
3. Protection of property.
4. Obeying orders in a nonemergency situation.
5. Maintaining the assigned role.
6. Efficiency in getting the job done.
7. Avoiding blame or earning praise or respect.

Use the hierarchy of values in making decisions. If a situation presents a conflict of values, always choose the value that is highest on the list. Here are three examples:

Example 1. You are assigned to stay in a particular spot during an emergency situation, but by leaving that spot you will save a life. You are justified in choosing to save a life (1) rather than obeying orders (2). The understanding is, of course, that leaving your spot will not result in other lives being lost. "Protecting life and limb" is your number-one priority, the highest value in the police hierarchy of values.

Example 2. You are assigned to watch a prisoner, and a fellow officer is assigned to write up the arrest report. Stay in your own role even if you are more skilled than the other officer at writing up arrest reports. The conflict is between carrying out an assigned duty (5) and getting a job done efficiently (6). Choose the higher priority.

Example 3. You are patrolling alone at night, and you come across a business that has been burglarized with the front door smashed in. At this hour you are expected to be making a routine check of illegal parking on a certain street. Residents might criticize the police department if the illegal parking is not acted on, but the store is likely to be further burglarized if you leave this spot. Stay where you are and protect the property (3) rather than carrying out your assigned illegal parking patrol (5) or concerning yourself with criticism of the department (7). Always choose the highest value.

Please note that no value is given to the officer's personal gains or benefits or reputation. Personal consideration is *never* a good reason for doing anything so far as a civil service exam question is concerned.

As the hierarchy of values suggests, the best reason for any action is the protection of life and limb. If safety is a real issue in the fact pattern of the question, then safety is the number-one priority in choosing the answer. Sometimes there is no real issue of safety. In such a case, the next value assumes the greatest importance. If there is an emergency situation and you have been given specific orders, your priority is to carry out those orders. If not, the next priority is the protection of property. Property includes public property and police department property as well as private property. If there are no threats to property, you are expected to carry out routine, non-emergency orders and to fulfill your assigned duties. Doing what you were told to do and carrying out your routine assignments as a police officer take priority over efficiency. A police force is a highly organized bureaucracy. The organization will function best as a whole if each person does just his or her own assigned job.

Read each question carefully. Is there really something in the question situation to indicate that there is an issue of life and limb at stake? Would a proposed answer based on efficiency really be possible and efficient? Be realistic. Unless told otherwise, assume that the officer is an ordinary Police Officer and not a sharpshooter or a trained firefighter.

When all other reasoning fails you, answer to the Chief. In other words, the Chief of Police is testing you for your job. If you are faced with a difficult choice in making a decision, imagine that the Chief of Police is asking you the question personally. Give the answer the Chief would want you to give.

Sample Police Quizzer

The following police quizzer contains questions that have actually appeared on examinations for entry-level law enforcement positions conducted over a considerable number of years. The questions have been carefully screened for current relevancy.

Answering these questions will accomplish much in preparing you to do your best on the examination. Ideally, you can consider yourself well prepared if on the day of the examination you are thinking like a Police Officer. This quizzer will help you get in that frame of mind. Most of the questions found here concern incidents that a Police Officer may encounter on a daily basis.

The position of Police Officer is unique in that, although it is an entry-level position, it involves a great deal of responsibility and requires the ability to make reliable on-the-spot decisions. Therefore, accurate judgment is perhaps the most important qualification of the Police Officer. In order to make accurate police decisions, the officer must thoroughly understand the duties of the position and the Police Officer's role in society.

By the time you finish the Police Judgment Quizzer, you no doubt will be thinking like a Police Officer, and you will be well on your way towards earning that high examination score.

Directions: *Choose from among the four suggested answers the best answer to each question. Write the letter of your answer choice beside the corresponding question number. An answer key appears at the end of the quizzer. Following the answer key are full answer explanations of the police reasoning behind each correct answer choice.*

---

1. A 70-year-old man calls the police and informs them that his wife of 45 years, who had been ill and bedridden for some time, has died in her sleep at home. The man, who had been his wife's sole caretaker during her period of illness, is very distraught. The couple's adult children are estranged from their parents; the man does not anticipate their returning for their mother's funeral. The man makes a comment about wanting to join his wife. Which of the following would be BEST for the police to do in this situation?
   (A) The police should leave the man alone so that he can deal with his feelings of grief.
   (B) The police should do all that they can to locate the couple's children.
   (C) The police should make sure that either a neighbor, relative, friend or social worker is present to keep the man from acting on any suicidal impulses.
   (D) The police should take steps to ensure that the man's medical needs are taken care of, since his sole caretaker has unexpectedly passed away.

2. You are on duty when you receive a call that a minor has been seen walking along a busy highway late at night. You locate the minor, a 15-year-old girl. She explains that she has run away from her family, but she refuses to explain why. Which of the following is the most likely reason that the girl ran away from home?
   (A) The girl is acting irresponsibly as a form of youthful rebellion.
   (B) The girl is being abused by her parents.
   (C) The girl does not receive enough attention from her parents.
   (D) There is too little information to determine the reason that the girl ran away.

3. You've noticed that your coworker appears to be very tense lately. She loses her temper more often than usual and seems to make more simple mistakes than usual. She does, however, have an excellent attendance record and often applies for overtime. She has also requested permission from your department to work a second part-time job. Although she claims that everything is fine at home, you have overheard her on a couple of occasions engaging in an argument with her husband, who was recently laid off. Based on this information, which of the following is most likely to be your coworker's problem?
   (A) Marital problems
   (B) Financial problems
   (C) Drug or alcohol abuse
   (D) Psychological problems

4. You have just graduated from the police academy, and now you are patrolling under the supervision of a field-training officer. Together you pull over a motorist for a minor traffic violation. Your field-training officer orders you to search the woman's car. Based on what you have learned in the academy, you believe that under these circumstances, a search of her car would be unethical and illegal. Which of the following would be best for you to do first in this situation?
   (A) Ask your supervisor to clarify his order.
   (B) Refuse to comply with the order because you believe that it is unethical and illegal.
   (C) Comply with the order because your field-training officer has more experience than you do.
   (D) Comply with the order but speak with your field-training officer's immediate supervisor after the incident.

5. An off-duty Police Officer was seated in a restaurant when two men entered, drew guns, and robbed the cashier. The officer made no attempt to prevent the robbery or apprehend the criminals. Later he justified his conduct by stating that an officer, when off duty, is a private citizen with the same duties and rights of all private citizens. The officer's conduct was
   (A) wrong; a Police Officer must act to prevent crimes and apprehend criminals at all times.
   (B) right; the Police Officer was out of uniform at the time of the robbery.
   (C) wrong; he should have obtained the necessary information and descriptions after the robbers left.
   (D) right; it would have been foolhardy for him to intervene when outnumbered by armed robbers.

6. While you are on traffic duty, a middle-aged man crossing the street cries out in pain, presses his hand to his chest, and stands perfectly still. You suspect that he may have suffered a heart attack. You should
   (A) help him to cross the street quickly in order to prevent his being hit by moving traffic.
   (B) permit him to lie down flat in the street while you divert traffic.
   (C) ask him for the name of his doctor so that you can summon him.
   (D) request a cab to take him to the nearest hospital for immediate treatment.

7. Assume that you have been assigned to a traffic post at a busy intersection. A car bearing out-of-state license plates is about to turn into a one-way street going in the opposite direction. You should blow your whistle and stop the car. You should then
   (A) hand out a summons to the driver in order to make an example of him, since out-of-town drivers notoriously disregard our traffic regulations.
   (B) pay no attention to him and let him continue in the proper direction.
   (C) ask him to pull over to the curb and advise him to get a copy of the latest New York City traffic regulations.
   (D) call his attention to the fact that he was violating a traffic regulation and permit him to continue in the proper direction.

8. You have been assigned to a patrol post in the park during the winter months. You hear the cries of a boy who has fallen through the ice. The first thing you should do is to
   (A) rush to the nearest telephone and call an ambulance.
   (B) call upon a passerby to summon additional Police Officers.
   (C) rush to the spot from which the cries came and try to save the boy.
   (D) rush to the spot from which the cries came and question the boy concerning his identity so that you can summon his parents.

9. While you are patrolling your post, you find a flashlight and a screwdriver lying near a closed bar and grill. You also notice some jimmy marks on the door. You should
   (A) continue patrolling your post after noting in your memorandum book what you have seen.
   (B) arrest any persons standing in the vicinity.
   (C) determine whether the bar has been robbed.
   (D) telephone the owner of the bar and grill to relate what you have seen outside the door.

10. You are on your way to report for an assignment when you see two men fighting on the street. For you to attempt to stop the fight would be
   (A) unjustified; it is none of your business.
   (B) justified; a fight between individuals may turn into a riot.
   (C) unjustified; you may get hurt with the result that you will not be able to report for duty.
   (D) justified; as a police officer, it is your duty to see that the public peace is kept.

11. Suppose a Police Officer's tour of duty extends from 12:00 midnight to 8:00 a.m. While on the first round of her tour, she notices that the night light in the front of a small candy store is out. In the past, the proprietor has always left the light on. The door to the store is locked. Of the following, the most appropriate action for the officer to take *first* is to
    (A) use her flashlight to light the store interior so that she may inspect it for unusual conditions.
    (B) continue on her beat, since the light probably burned out.
    (C) break open the door lock to conduct a thorough search of the store.
    (D) call the storekeeper to say that the night light is out.

12. You arrive at the scene of a traffic accident, which took place at an intersection with a four-way stop sign. Before you speak to the drivers involved or any witnesses, you notice that one car involved in the accident, a gray Honda Accord, has incurred damage to the front of the passenger side of the car. The other car involved in the accident, a red Hyundai Tiburon, has a damaged front bumper and hood. Based on this information, which of the following scenarios is the most likely explanation for the accident?
    (A) The driver of the Hyundai was waiting at the stop sign to proceed and was rear-ended by the driver of the Honda.
    (B) The driver of the Honda was facing west when she collided with the driver of the Hyundai, who was facing north.
    (C) The driver of the Honda was facing south when she collided with the driver of the Hyundai, who was facing east.
    (D) The driver of the Honda was waiting at the stop sign to proceed and was rear-ended by the driver of the Hyundai.

13. While patrolling a post late Saturday night, a Police Officer notices a well-dressed man break a car window with a rock, open the front door, and enter the car. He is followed into the car by a female companion. Of the following, the most essential action for the officer to take is to
    (A) point a gun at the car, enter the car, and order the man to drive to the station house to explain his actions.
    (B) approach the car and ask the man why it was necessary to break the car window.
    (C) take down the license number of the car and note the description of both the man and the woman in the event that the car is later reported as stolen.
    (D) request proof of ownership of the car from the man.

14. Assume that a Police Officer is assigned to duty in a radio patrol car. The situation in which it would be *least* advisable for the officer to use the siren to help clear traffic when answering a call is when a report has come in that
    (A) a man is involved in an argument with a cleaning store proprietor.
    (B) a man is holding up a liquor store.
    (C) two cars have crashed, resulting in loss of life.
    (D) two gangs of juveniles are engaged in a street fight.

15. You notice that a man is limping hurriedly, leaving a trail of blood behind him. You question him and his explanation is that he was hurt accidentally while he was watching a man clean a gun. You should
    (A) let him go, as you have no proof that his story is not true.
    (B) have him sent to the nearest city hospital under police escort so that he may be questioned further after treatment.
    (C) ask him whether the man has a license for his gun.
    (D) ask him to lead you to the man who cleaned his gun so that you may question him further about the accident.

16. At 10 a.m. on a regular school day, a Police Officer notices a boy about 11 years old wandering in the street. When asked why he is not in school, the boy replies that he attends school in the neighborhood, but that he felt sick that morning. The officer then takes the boy to the principal of the school. This method of handling the situation was
    (A) bad; the officer should have obtained verification of the boy's illness.
    (B) good; the school authorities are best equipped to deal with the problem.
    (C) bad; the officer should have obtained the boy's name and address and reported the incident to the attendance officer.
    (D) good; seeing the truant boy escorted by a Police Officer will deter other children from truancy.

17. "A Police Officer should know the occupations and habits of the people on his or her beat. In heavily populated districts, however, it is too much to ask that the officer know all the people on the beat." If this statement is correct, which of the following would be the most practical course for a Police Officer to follow?
    (A) Concentrate on becoming acquainted with the oldest residents on his or her beat.
    (B) Limit his or her attention to people who work as well as live in the district.
    (C) Limit his or her attention to people with criminal records.
    (D) Concentrate on becoming acquainted with key people such as janitors and local merchants.

18. Police Officers are instructed to pay particular attention to anyone apparently making repairs to an auto parked in the street. The most important reason for this rule is that
    (A) the person making the repairs may be stealing the auto.
    (B) the person making the repairs may be obstructing traffic.
    (C) working on autos is prohibited on certain streets.
    (D) many people injure themselves while working on autos.

19. A Police Officer, walking his beat at 3 a.m., notices heavy smoke coming out of a top-floor window of a large apartment house. Of the following, the action the officer should take *first* is to
    (A) make certain that there really is a fire.
    (B) enter the building and warn all the occupants of the apartment house.
    (C) attempt to extinguish the fire before it gets out of control.
    (D) call the fire department.

20. Inspections of critical points on a post are purposely made at irregular intervals to
    (A) permit leaving the post when arrests are necessary.
    (B) make it difficult for wrongdoers to anticipate the inspections.
    (C) allow for delays due to unusual occurrences at other points.
    (D) simplify the scheduling of lunch reliefs and rest periods.

21. Your department receives a phone call from a local drugstore. Managers have caught three teenage boys attempting to steal large numbers of items, including vitamins, over-the-counter cold medications, pantyhose, makeup, etc. You are familiar with these boys, who have been previously arrested for drug possession. Based on this information, which of the following is the most likely reason that the boys were stealing these items?
    (A) They were stealing them as a prank.
    (B) They were stealing these items for their own use or for their friends.
    (C) They were planning to sell these items to get money for drugs.
    (D) They were stealing these items because their families probably could not afford to purchase them.

22. For the third time this month, Mrs. Peterson has called the police department, and each time, she calls due to concerns that someone may be attempting to break into her home. On this occasion, she claims to have seen someone strange walking across her backyard. When the police arrive, no one is in the backyard. Mrs. Peterson offers the officers a cup of coffee while she explains that she is a widow and that her adult children currently live out of state. She apologizes for troubling them but expresses her concerns for her safety. Which of the following would be BEST for the officers to do in this situation?
    (A) They should refer her to a senior citizen police academy, where she can learn to defend herself against crime, or perhaps another senior citizen organization, where she can meet new people in her age group.
    (B) They should gently explain to her that she is wasting department time and resources with her repeated calls.
    (C) They should encourage her to relocate closer to her children.
    (D) They should leave but encourage her to continue to contact the department when she has any concerns.

23. "The woman approached the Police Officer with the tearful request that he call her at home in order to put the fear of the law into her 11-year-old son. The boy, she said, was associating with a group of wild, older youths who were leading the boy astray." The officer should have
    (A) complied with the woman's request.
    (B) obtained further information before committing himself to any cooperative relations with the woman.
    (C) cooperated with the woman in whatever manner seemed appropriate, provided that the boy's history has been reported accurately by his mother.
    (D) denied the woman's request.

24. Suppose that, at 11 a.m., while you are patrolling your post, a young girl runs up to you, saying that a man has just dropped dead on the street a block away. Of the following, your *first* action under the circumstances should be to
    (A) request the young girl to describe the man who is said to be dead.
    (B) approach furtively the scene of the alleged death in order to investigate all the circumstances fully.
    (C) proceed immediately to the place where the man is alleged to have dropped dead.
    (D) request the young girl to identify herself.

25. A group of boys about 17 years of age is standing on a street corner, talking loudly, shouting, and, in general, making a good deal of noise in a residential district in the early hours of the morning. A Police Officer who comes upon this scene should attempt to
    (A) arrest the boy who appears to be the leader.
    (B) arrest the entire group.
    (C) disperse the group.
    (D) summon assistance.

26. Suppose that, in the course of your duties, you are called to the scene of a disturbance in which some seven or eight people are involved. Of the following, the action most likely to end the disturbance quickly and effectively is for you to
    (A) divide the disorderly group immediately into three approximately equal sections.
    (B) take the nearest person promptly into custody and remove that person from the scene.
    (C) announce your authority and call for order in a firm and decisive manner.
    (D) question a bystander in detail about the reasons for the disorder.

27. A newly appointed officer of a uniformed force may *least* reasonably expect an immediate supervising officer to
    (A) help him or her avoid errors.
    (B) give him or her specific instructions.
    (C) check on the progress he or she is making.
    (D) make all necessary decisions for him or her.

28. You are dispatched to the scene of a fatal car accident. A minivan, carrying a husband, wife and their three children, crashed head-on into a telephone pole at approximately 3:35 a.m. Sadly, the wife was not wearing her seatbelt and was killed instantly. One of the children also was not wearing a seatbelt at the time and is critically injured. The husband, who was driving at the time, and the other two children have suffered only minor bruises and cuts. The husband explained that he and his family were driving across the country on their vacation, and he had been driving since approximately 5:00 p.m. the evening before. He does not remember much of what occurred before the accident; one minute, everything was fine, and the next minute, the van slammed into the telephone pole. The driver previously had a clean driving record. Which of the following is most likely to be the cause of the accident?

(A) The husband was fatigued.

(B) The husband was under the influence of drugs or alcohol.

(C) The husband was distracted by his family.

(D) The husband was not familiar with the area.

29. You hear that your neighbor, a 34-year-old mother of two small children, has been arrested for shoplifting clothes from an expensive department store. Other people in your neighborhood inform you that this woman is quite wealthy and has closets full of designer clothes. Which of the following would be the most likely reason that this woman would shoplift?

(A) She and her family must be going through financial difficulties that other people in the neighborhood are unaware of.

(B) She plans to give this clothing away to people she knows who may not be able to afford it on their own.

(C) She and her husband may be involved in some kind of organized crime.

(D) She is shoplifting for the thrill of the experience.

30. The primary function of a police department is

(A) the prevention of crime.

(B) the efficiency and discipline of its members.

(C) to preserve property values.

(D) to minimize conflicts.

31. Law enforcement officials receive badges with numbers on them so that

(A) their personalities may be submerged.

(B) they may be more easily identified.

(C) they may be spied upon.

(D) their movements may be kept under constant control.

32. The best attitude for an officer to take is to

(A) be constantly on the alert.

(B) be hostile.

(C) vary watchfulness with the apparent necessity for it.

(D) regard tact as the most effective weapon for handling any degree of disorder.

33. Ten percent of the inmates released from a certain prison are arrested as parole violators. It follows that
    (A) 90 percent have reformed.
    (B) 10 percent have reformed.
    (C) none has reformed.
    (D) none of the foregoing is necessarily true.

34. A certain committee found that over 90 percent of the murders in the United States are committed by use of pistols. It follows that
    (A) almost all murders are caused by the possession of pistols.
    (B) 90 percent of all murders can be eliminated by eliminating the sale and use of pistols.
    (C) the pistol is a mechanical aid to crime.
    (D) no information is available with regard to the way murders happen.

35. A group of teenagers has been involved in a serious car accident. The driver, a 16-year-old girl, had just received her license and was driving with a group of her friends to the mall. They had gotten food from the drive-thru of a local fast-food restaurant. The fast-food restaurant was situated on a busy road, but there was no stoplight or stop sign at the exit of the drive-thru. As they were preparing to exit, the driver received a call from her boyfriend on her cell phone. They were hit as they turned left out of the drive-thru by a car driven by an elderly couple. Several of the people involved in the accident went to the hospital for a check-up and treatment of minor injuries; one of the teenagers suffered a concussion and briefly lost consciousness. Although the injuries were mostly minor, the cars were severely damaged, and the elderly couple's car was eventually totaled. Which of the following is most likely to be the reason for the accident?
    (A) The elderly driver was not paying attention when the girls turned left out of the drive-thru.
    (B) The elderly driver does not have good enough reflexes due to his advanced age.
    (C) The teenage driver has not had enough training in the rules of the road.
    (D) The teenage driver was distracted by her friends, food and phone call.

36. You pull over a motorist for speeding on a busy highway. As you ask the driver for his license and identification, he displays his badge, signifying that he is a police officer for a neighboring department. He apologizes for speeding but explains that he is on his way to work and is running late. Which of the following would be best for you to do in this situation?
    (A) You should give the police officer either a warning or a citation for this offense.
    (B) You should let the officer proceed to work without further delay.
    (C) You should avoid giving him a traffic citation, but you should continue to follow him to ensure that he drives at a slower, safer speed.
    (D) You should speak with a commanding officer of his department in regards to his off-duty behavior on the road.

37. An officer receives instructions from his supervisor that he does not fully understand. For the officer to ask for a further explanation would be
   (A) good, chiefly because his supervisor will be impressed with his interest in his work.
   (B) poor, chiefly because the supervisor's time will be needlessly wasted.
   (C) good, chiefly because proper performance depends on full understanding of the work to be done.
   (D) poor, chiefly because officers should be able to think for themselves.

38. Which of the following statements concerning the behavior of law enforcement officers is most accurate?
   (A) A show of confident assurance on the part of a law enforcement officer will make it possible to cover a shortage of knowledge in any given duty.
   (B) In ordinary cases, when a newly appointed officer does not know what to do, it is always better to do too much than to do too little.
   (C) It is not advisable that officers recommend the employment of certain attorneys for individuals taken into custody.
   (D) A prisoner who is morose and refuses to talk will need less watching by an officer than one who is suicidal.

39. In dealing with children, a law enforcement officer should always
   (A) treat them the same as adults.
   (B) instill in them a fear of the law.
   (C) secure their confidence.
   (D) impress them with the right of the law to punish them for their wrongdoings.

40. You are sent to an apartment where neighbors have complained that a man and his live-in girlfriend have been engaging in a loud argument. When you knock on the door, the girlfriend answers. She explains that she did have a fight with her boyfriend, and he briefly left the apartment complex, possibly to go to his favorite bar and see his friends. She suggests that her neighbors are simply being nosy and wish to cause her trouble. She does not appear to have any visible physical injuries although she looks disheveled and upset. She nervously asks you to leave before her boyfriend returns. Which of the following would be best for you to do in this situation?
   (A) Immediately arrest the boyfriend.
   (B) Encourage the woman to seek help from a battered women's shelter or other counseling program if needed.
   (C) Warn the neighbors against making any further false reports.
   (D) Leave the woman immediately as she has requested.

41. Increased police vigilance would probably be *least* successful in preventing
   (A) murder.
   (B) burglary.
   (C) prostitution.
   (D) auto theft.

42. It frequently happens that a major crime of an unusual nature is followed almost immediately by an epidemic of several crimes, in widely scattered locations, with elements similar to the first crime. Of the following, the most likely explanation for this situation is that
    (A) the same criminal is likely to commit the same type of crime.
    (B) a gang of criminals will operate in several areas simultaneously.
    (C) newspaper publicity on a major crime is apt to influence other would-be criminals.
    (D) the same causes which are responsible for the first crime are also responsible for the others.

43. Sarah Cunningham is a special-needs child. Her teacher has contacted your department and the local child-welfare agency because she has seen multiple, severe bruises on the child's arms and legs; Sarah was unwilling to discuss these injuries with her teacher. Sarah's parents are divorced; they share joint custody of her and her two older siblings. Sarah lives with her mother during the week and spends every other weekend with her father and his new girlfriend. Of the following, which individuals are most likely to be abusing Sarah?
    (A) The father
    (B) The mother
    (C) The father's new girlfriend
    (D) There is not enough information to determine who may be abusing Sarah.

44. Just before you go on duty, you overhear Officer Jury saying to several coworkers, "I try to pull over as many Mexican drivers as possible. I mean, they're speeding or whatever to begin with, so I have every right to pull them over. But if they're illegal immigrants, I can always get them not just for speeding but for driving without a license, not having insurance, and so on." What would be the best thing for you to do in this situation?
    (A) Avoid becoming involved in the situation.
    (B) Contact members of the media to inform them of the problem.
    (C) Speak to your fellow officers about the problem.
    (D) Immediately talk with Officer Jury's immediate supervisor.

45. A female coworker and friend complains to you that her immediate supervisor, Sergeant Wilcox, keeps making unwanted romantic advances. Although her refusal of these advances hasn't seemed to affect their working relationship as of yet, she is worried that he will eventually write her a poor and unfair performance appraisal or will make her working environment a miserable one if she continues to refuse dates with him. Which of the following would be best for your coworker to do FIRST?
    (A) She should speak with Sergeant Wilcox's immediate supervisor.
    (B) She should ask Sergeant Wilcox to cease his offensive behavior.
    (C) She should contact members of the press about this harassment.
    (D) She should warn other female members of the department about Sergeant Wilcox's harassment.

46. When arrested, boys under 16 years of age are not brought to the same place of detention as older men. The reason for this separation is most likely to
    (A) keep them with others of their own age.
    (B) protect them from rough police methods.
    (C) help them get sound legal aid.
    (D) keep them from contact with hardened criminals.

47. Many criminals dress well and look intelligent but have no regard for a human life if it stands in their way. A reasonable conclusion from this statement is that
    (A) it is almost certain death to combat a criminal.
    (B) criminals are frequently intelligent.
    (C) even some intelligent people have no regard for human life.
    (D) a well-dressed person may be a criminal.

48. A Police Officer stationed along the route of a parade has been ordered not to allow cars to cross the route while the parade is in progress. An ambulance driver on an emergency run attempts to drive an ambulance across the route while the parade is passing. Under these circumstances, the officer should
    (A) ask the driver to wait while the officer calls headquarters and obtains a decision.
    (B) stop the parade long enough to permit the ambulance to cross the street.
    (C) direct the ambulance driver to the shortest detour available, which will add at least ten minutes to the run.
    (D) hold up the ambulance in accordance with the order.

49. An off-duty Police Officer in civilian clothes riding in the rear of a bus notices two teenage boys tampering with the rear emergency door. The most appropriate action for the officer to take is to
    (A) tell the boys to discontinue their tampering, pointing out the dangers to life that their actions create.
    (B) report the boys' actions to the bus operator and let the bus operator take whatever action is deemed best.
    (C) signal the bus operator to stop, show the boys the police badge, and then order them off the bus.
    (D) show the boys the police badge, order them to stop their actions, and take down their names and addresses.

50. Assume that you are on your way home late at night. You notice smoke pouring out of one of the windows of a house in which several families reside. Your first consideration under these circumstances should be to
    (A) determine the cause of the smoke.
    (B) arouse all the residents in the house.
    (C) carry out to safety any persons overcome by smoke.
    (D) call the fire department to the scene.

51. Your department has a policy that states that when you are responding to a bomb threat, you may not communicate with your coworkers and supervisors over your radio and cellular phone within 500 yards of the location of the threat. Which of the following is the most likely reason that your department has this policy?
    (A) In case the person who placed the bomb is on the scene, you do not want him or her to know the department's strategies for dealing with this threat.
    (B) You do not want to cause panic in the area; communication with your fellow officers and superiors should be subtle, quiet and coded.
    (C) Cellular phones and radio devices could possibly detonate the bomb.
    (D) Cellular phones and radio devices are not the most reliable means of communication; communication is vital when dealing with this type of situation, and these devices tend to malfunction.

52. You notice something unusual on your post. You should immediately
    (A) report the matter in writing to your superior.
    (B) look up the rules on the matter.
    (C) investigate the matter.
    (D) wait for a time to see whether anything will happen.

53. A Police Officer is summoned into a subway station where a man has collapsed and is lying unconscious on the floor. His breath smells strongly of alcohol. For the officer to summon medical aid immediately is
    (A) undesirable; the man is merely intoxicated and can be handled by the Police Officer alone.
    (B) desirable; the man's unconsciousness may have a medical cause.
    (C) undesirable; the commotion caused by the incident will be aggravated by the appearance of an ambulance.
    (D) desirable; medical aid is necessary to help him regain consciousness in any event.

54. A Police Officer notices a two-year-old child standing by himself in front of a supermarket and crying. Which of the following actions should the officer take *first*?
    (A) Call the precinct to find out if the child has been reported missing.
    (B) Look for possible identification on the child's clothing.
    (C) Take the child to the police precinct until he is claimed.
    (D) Inquire in the supermarket in an attempt to find his parent.

55. At a crowded bus stop, a Police Officer notices that a child about seven years old has been pushed out of the bus involuntarily. The crowd piling into the bus is so thick that the child is unable to get back into it. After the bus has gone, the officer learns from the child that her mother was on the bus but was probably unable to get out because of the crowd pushing in. The child knows her own address, a considerable distance away, and in an opposite direction from the one in which she was traveling. Of the following, the best action for the officer to take *first* is to

(A) take the child home.

(B) explain to the child how to go home and let her go alone.

(C) leave the child with instructions to wait until her mother returns.

(D) wait at the stop with the child long enough to give the mother a chance to return from the next stop.

56. Which of the following is the most accurate statement concerning the proper attitude of a Police Officer towards persons in his or her custody?

(A) Ignore any serious problems of those in custody, if they have no bearing on the charges preferred.

(B) Do not inform the person who has been arrested of the reason for the arrest.

(C) Do not permit a person in custody to give vent to feelings at any time.

(D) Watch a brooding or silent person more carefully than one who loudly threatens suicide.

57. Two rival youth gangs have been involved in several minor clashes. The officer working in the area believes that a serious clash will occur if steps are not taken to prevent it. Of the following, the *least* desirable action for the officer to take in the effort to head off trouble is to

(A) arrest the leaders of both gangs as a warning.

(B) warn the parents of the dangerous situation.

(C) obtain the cooperation of religious and civic leaders in the community.

(D) report the situation to a superior.

58. If, while you are on traffic duty at a busy intersection, a pedestrian asks you for directions to a particular place, the best course of conduct is for you to

(A) ignore the question and continue directing traffic.

(B) tell the pedestrian to ask an officer on foot patrol.

(C) answer the question in a brief, courteous manner.

(D) leave your traffic post only long enough to give clear and adequate directions.

59. Suppose that, while you are patrolling your post, a middle-aged woman informs you that three men are holding up a nearby bank. You rush immediately to the scene of the holdup. While you are still about 75 feet away, you see the three men, revolvers in their hands, emerge from the bank and run towards what is apparently their getaway car, which is pointed in the opposite direction. Of the following, your *first* consideration in this situation should be to

(A) enter the bank in order to find out what the men have taken.

(B) maneuver quickly so as to get the getaway car between you and the bank

(C) make a mental note of the descriptions of the escaping men for immediate alarm.

(D) draw your gun and shout for the men to surrender.

60. A storekeeper has complained to you that every day at noon several peddlers congregate outside his store in order to sell their merchandise. You should

(A) inform him that such complaints must be made directly to the Police Commissioner.

(B) inform him that peddlers have a right to earn their living too.

(C) make it your business to patrol that part of your post around noon.

(D) pay no attention to him, as this storekeeper is probably a crank inasmuch as nobody else has complained.

61. A Police Officer is approached by an obviously upset woman who reports that her husband is missing. The *first* thing the officer should do is to

(A) check with the hospitals and the police station.

(B) tell the woman to wait a few hours and call the police station if her husband has not returned.

(C) obtain a description of the missing man so that an alarm can be broadcast.

(D) ask the woman why she thinks her husband is missing.

62. When approaching a suspect to make an arrest, it is *least* important for the Police Officer to guard against the possibility that the suspect may

(A) be diseased.

(B) have a gun.

(C) use physical force.

(D) run away.

63. An acceptable proof of the present address of the person to whom a Police Officer is issuing a summons would logically be

(A) a recent photograph.

(B) society membership cards.

(C) recently postmarked letters addressed to that person.

(D) the deed to a house.

64. "In any uniformed service, strict discipline is essential." Of the following, the best justification for requiring that subordinates follow the orders of superior officers without delay is that
    (A) not all orders can be carried out quickly.
    (B) it is more important that an order be obeyed accurately than promptly.
    (C) prompt obedience makes for efficient action in emergencies.
    (D) some superior officers are too strict.

65. The local high school receives the third bomb threat in six months. The other two threats proved to be hoaxes, and it is believed that the same individual was responsible for the other two threats although he/she was not identified. How should your department respond to this newest threat?
    (A) The department should respond to this threat as though it were not a hoax-as quickly as possible and taking every precaution.
    (B) The department should respond to this threat but should focus primarily on identifying the individual responsible for the hoaxes.
    (C) The department should send a single officer to positively determine that there is no bomb and should leave the school to identify and discipline the individual responsible for the hoax.
    (D) The department cannot continue to respond to every bomb threat, especially if they occur more and more frequently in the future. They should encourage the school to investigate the situation further before contacting the department in the future.

66. As a Police Officer, if you think of an idea for improving the police protection in certain areas, your best procedure would be to
    (A) get the opinions of all the people working in those areas.
    (B) suggest it to your superiors immediately.
    (C) forget it, because the department has experts thinking about such problems all the time.
    (D) consider the idea carefully before suggesting it.

67. A person is making a complaint to an officer which seems unreasonable and of little importance. Of the following, the best action for the officer to take is to
    (A) criticize the person making the complaint for taking up valuable time.
    (B) laugh over the matter to show that the complaint is minor and silly.
    (C) tell the person that anyone responsible for the grievance will be arrested.
    (D) listen to the person making the complaint and tell him or her that the matter will be investigated.

68. When reporting a robbery to headquarters over the police telephone system, a Police Officer should make the report as brief as possible so as to avoid
    (A) long entries in the record book.
    (B) confusing the listener.
    (C) errors in fact.
    (D) tying up the line.

69. Police Officers are instructed to confer with the Assistant District Attorney before preparing a formal written complaint. The most probable reason is to
(A) keep it brief.
(B) agree on the facts of the case.
(C) avoid legal errors.
(D) assure a conviction.

70. In submitting a report of an unusual arrest or other unusual occurrence, the first paragraph of the report should contain
(A) a brief outline of what occurred.
(B) your conclusions and recommendations.
(C) the authority and reason for the investigation of the arrest or occurrence.
(D) complete and accurate answers to the questions who?, what?, where?, when?, why?, and how?

71. "If an officer is not relieved at the expiration of a tour of duty, he or she shall not abandon the post, but shall communicate with the desk officer or control sergeant and comply with the instructions received." Of the following, the best reason for this rule is that
(A) it gives the officer definite control over all earned overtime.
(B) the service given to an officer's relief may be repaid at another time when he or she is late.
(C) it gives the officer a chance to make up time which he or she may owe due to previous lateness.
(D) it is necessary for the safety of the public that a post be manned at all times.

72. A factory manager asks a Police Officer to escort the payroll clerk to and from the local bank when payroll money is withdrawn. The Police Officer knows that it is against departmental policy to provide payroll escort service. The officer should
(A) refuse and explain why he or she cannot do what is requested.
(B) refer the manager to the precinct commander.
(C) tell the manager that Police Officers have more important tasks to perform.
(D) advise the manager that he or she will provide this service if other duties do not interfere.

73. A Police Officer in civilian clothes appearing as a witness in a court must wear his or her shield over the left breast. This procedure
(A) helps the officer in reporting for duty promptly if called.
(B) impresses the judge.
(C) identifies the witness as a Police Officer.
(D) preserves order.

74. A married couple informs you that they have witnessed their neighbor's young son abusing a stray cat. What would be the most serious consequence if nothing were to be done about this situation?

(A) The neighbors are likely to get into fights over the boy's behavior.

(B) The boy will have learning disabilities and other developmental problems.

(C) The boy may begin to abuse other people.

(D) The consequences are negligible. The boy is likely to grow out of this immature behavior.

75. You are expected to report for duty at 6:00 a.m. You wake up, look at the clock and realize in a panic that it reads 5:50 a.m. You forgot to set the alarm! There is no way that you will be able to get dressed and ready and drive to work before 6:00 a.m. Which of the following would be best for you to do in this situation?

(A) Get ready as quickly as possible and immediately drive to work.

(B) Call your supervisor and explain that you suddenly became violently ill and won't be able to come in for at least half the day.

(C) Call your supervisor and tell him/her about the situation, explaining that you will be late this morning.

(D) Get ready as normal because you will be in trouble whether you're five minutes late or half an hour late.

76. Certain orders and instructions are transmitted by means of bulletins posted on the precinct bulletin boards. Such a bulletin order would most likely be rescinded if it

(A) conflicted with another order that was issued later.

(B) was not readily understood by the entire force.

(C) had been in force for a long time.

(D) was frequently violated.

77. You have not been getting along with another member of your shift. What started as mean-spirited off-hand comments and jokes on his part has now turned into confrontations before and after your shifts. You have tried to ignore this problem in the past; you are well-liked among other members of your shift, and your adversary is not. However, as the conflict continues, you find yourself arguing back, and you are worried that the verbal arguments will escalate into physical arguments. Which of the following would be best for you to do first in this situation?

(A) You should try to de-escalate the situation by ignoring your coworker's comments.

(B) You should request to change shifts.

(C) You should ask other coworkers to speak to him and persuade him to leave you alone.

(D) You should speak with your immediate supervisor about this situation.

78. According to the police manual, when circumstances permit, not more than one prisoner shall be confined in a cell. Of the following, the most important reason for this regulation is to
    (A) ensure reasonable privacy for the prisoners.
    (B) minimize the development of troublesome situations.
    (C) protect the civil rights of the prisoners.
    (D) separate the hardened from the less hardened criminals.

79. "Parking is prohibited here," the Police Officer said. "You'll have to move farther down." The driver then informed the Police Officer that he was a good friend of an important local political figure and indicated that the officer should attend to other, more significant matters. Of the following courses of action, the one that the officer ought to select is to
    (A) permit the driver to park there for a brief time.
    (B) request the name of the alleged important political figure.
    (C) insist that the car be parked elsewhere.
    (D) attract the attention of bystanders to the incident in order to demonstrate police impartiality.

80. You and several other officers have been dispatched to the scene of a multicar traffic collision. You can tell that your coworker, Officer Reist, is extremely frustrated by this situation. This accident occurred close to the end of the shift, and you will all have to work several hours of overtime, which means that Officer Reist will most likely have to cancel the plans he had for his wife's birthday. As you and the other officers investigate the accident and tend to the needs of the wounded, you see Officer Reist in a heated discussion with a young woman, whom most witnesses agreed is at fault for the accident. Officer Reist is speaking to her in a manner that you think is rude and unprofessional, and you find this behavior surprising since Officer Reist is usually the person you can count on to calm down a tense situation. Which of the following would be best for you to do FIRST in this situation?
    (A) It would be best to leave him alone and not interfere with his discussion with the woman.
    (B) You should immediately speak with Officer Reist's supervisor about his conduct in this situation.
    (C) You should attempt to intervene in the conversation and calm both Officer Reist and the woman down.
    (D) You should immediately confront Officer Reist about the manner in which he is speaking to the woman.

81. You have just worked three hours of overtime and you are finally on your way home when you are flagged down by an elderly man who recognizes you as a local police officer. He explains that his wife has just fallen down while they were working in the garden, and she needs assistance getting up. The man explains that he has a bad back and cannot pick her up. He was just about to go in the house and call 911 when he saw you driving by. Which of the following would be best for you to do in this situation?

    (A) You should assist her as much as you can and contact other emergency personnel to give her a check-up, if desired.

    (B) You should explain to the man that you are no longer on-duty and that he needs to call 911.

    (C) You should pick the woman up and get her in a comfortable position and then leave.

    (D) You should immediately call for emergency assistance for the woman.

82. At 3:00 a.m. while on his tour of duty, a Police Officer notices a traffic light at an intersection is not operating. There is little traffic at night at this intersection. Under these circumstances, the most appropriate action for the Police Officer to take is to

    (A) report this matter to a superior at the end of his tour of duty.

    (B) station himself at the intersection to direct traffic until the appearance of daylight reduces the hazard of a collision.

    (C) report this matter immediately to the precinct.

    (D) post a sign at the intersection stating that the traffic light is not operating.

83. You are visiting your sister's family for the holidays. Your nephew, like most teenagers, has taken to going out at nights with his friends and returning as late as possible. One evening when he returns, he takes off his coat and drops drug paraphernalia that was hidden inside. Your sister is aghast and asks you to speak with him since you are a law enforcement officer. Which of the following would be best for you to do in this situation?

    (A) You should decline to become involved in the situation due to your status as a law enforcement officer.

    (B) You should speak with the boy about the potential physical and legal consequences of his actions.

    (C) You should contact local police to investigate the situation.

    (D) You should order the boy to immediately dispose of the materials.

84. "Driver 1 claimed that the collision occurred because, as he approached the intersection, Driver 2 started to make a left turn suddenly and at a high speed, even though the light had been red for 15 to 20 seconds." Suppose that you have been assigned to make a report on this accident. The position of the vehicles after the accident is indicated in the diagram below. The point in each case indicates the front of the vehicle. On the basis of this diagram, the best reason for concluding that Driver 1's statement is false is that

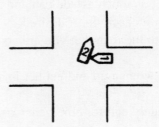

(A) Driver 2's car is beyond the center of the intersection.
(B) Driver 2's car is making the turn on the proper side of the road.
(C) Driver 1's car is beyond the sidewalk line.
(D) Driver 1's car is on the right-hand side of the road.

85. While patrolling a bridge approach road alone in a radio car, you are signaled to stop by a private car traveling in the opposite direction. The driver tells you that he was robbed by two men in a sedan ahead of him. Your car cannot cross the concrete safety-strip to get into the other lane. Of the following, the best course of action for you to take is to
(A) tell the driver you cannot cross to his lane and ask him to report the matter.
(B) leave your car where it is, cross over to the private car, and use it to pursue the suspects.
(C) notify headquarters over your radio.
(D) make a U-turn in your car and chase the suspect vehicle on the wrong side of the parkway.

86. "A courteous warning by an officer to a vehicle operator who has committed a minor traffic violation is usually more effective than a summons." Of the following statements, the one that best supports this point of view is:
(A) An officer should issue a summons whenever one is called for and never show favoritism.
(B) A warning should always be issued for a first offense.
(C) The inconvenience and expense of a summons will keep most motorists from repeating the offense.
(D) The operator who receives a warning for a minor violation will try to avoid repeating the offense.

87. A Police Officer using hand signals is directing traffic at a congested intersection. It is *least* important that
    (A) the officer be visible.
    (B) the officer be accessible.
    (C) the signs used by the officer be uniform.
    (D) the signs used by the officer be simple.

88. It is suggested that an officer should keep all persons away from the area of an accident until an investigation has been completed. This suggested procedure is
    (A) good; witnesses will be more likely to agree on a single story.
    (B) bad; such action blocks traffic flow and causes congestion.
    (C) good; objects of possible use as evidence will be protected from damage or loss.
    (D) bad; the flow of normal pedestrian traffic provides an opportunity for an investigator to determine the cause of the accident.

89. Before permitting automobiles involved in an accident to depart, a Police Officer should take certain measures. Of the following, it is *least* important that the officer make certain that
    (A) both drivers are properly licensed.
    (B) the automobiles are in safe operating condition.
    (C) the drivers have exchanged names and license numbers.
    (D) he or she obtains the names and addresses of drivers and witnesses.

90. A radio motor patrol team arrives on the scene a few minutes after a pedestrian has been killed by a hit-and-run driver. After obtaining a description of the car, the first action the officer should take is to
    (A) radio a description of the fleeing car to precinct headquarters.
    (B) try to overtake the fleeing car.
    (C) obtain complete statements from everyone at the scene.
    (D) inspect the site of the accident for clues.

91. The most effective method of crime prevention is, in general,
    (A) severe punishment of malefactors.
    (B) probation.
    (C) parole.
    (D) eradication of causal factors.

92. Officer Consuelo was dispatched to a reported burglary at a local coffeeshop. She took the burglary report and was kind and supportive to the distraught owner. The next day, the owner stopped by the police station and gave Officer Consuelo a gift certificate for free coffee. It is against her department's policy to accept such token gifts for police services. Which of the following would be best for Officer Consuelo to do in this situation?
    (A) She should quietly accept the gift certificate so that the coffeeshop owner isn't offended.
    (B) She should explain the department's policy to the coffeeshop owner, and if he insists that she accept the gift, she should sternly remind him that his offer is out of line.
    (C) She should explain the department's policy to the coffeeshop owner, and if he insists that she accept the gift, she should immediately turn it in to her supervisor.
    (D) She should advise the coffeeshop owner to give the gift certificate to a member of her family so that she could enjoy the free coffee but not get in trouble at work.

93. It has been claimed that a person who commits a crime sometimes has an unconscious wish to be punished, which is caused by strong unconscious feelings of guilt. Of the following actions by a criminal, the one which may be partly due to an unconscious desire for punishment is
    (A) claiming that he or she doesn't know anything about the crime when questioned by the police.
    (B) running away from the state where the crime was committed.
    (C) revisiting the place where the crime was committed.
    (D) taking care not to leave any clues at the scene of the crime.

94. Which of the following statements about fingerprints is *least* accurate?
    (A) The value of fingerprints left at the scene of the crime does not vary with the distinctness of the fingerprint impressions.
    (B) It is of value to fingerprint a person with an abnormal number of fingers.
    (C) Fingerprints of different persons have never been found to be alike.
    (D) The prime value of fingerprints lies in their effectiveness in identifying people.

95. According to a police manual, the delivery for laboratory examination of any article required as evidence must be made by the member of the force finding or coming into the possession of such evidence. Of the following, the most likely reason for this procedure is that it
    (A) assists in the establishment of the authenticity of the evidence.
    (B) encourages a more careful search of the crime scene for all physical evidence that may be related to the crime.
    (C) ensures that the evidence will be properly marked or tagged for future identification.
    (D) prevents the undue delay that might result from a delivery through official channels.

96. You are getting the description of a lost diamond bracelet. Of the following, the most important piece of information, in addition to knowing that the missing item is a diamond bracelet, is
    (A) value: $10,000.
    (B) design: two intertwining snakes.
    (C) diamonds: many small and several large diamonds.
    (D) owner: Mrs. H. Jones.

97. You are watching a great number of people leave a ball game. Of the persons who are described below, the one whom it would be easiest to spot would be
    (A) female; age 15; height 5'6"; weight 130 lbs.; long straight black hair.
    (B) male; age 50; height 5'8"; weight 150 lbs.; missing toe on right foot.
    (C) male; age 60; height 5'7"; weight 170 lbs.; all false teeth.
    (D) male; age 25; height 6'3"; weight 220 lbs.; pockmarked.

98. You are preparing a description of a woman to be broadcast. Of the following characteristics, the one that would be of most value to an officer driving a squad car is
    (A) wanted for murder.
    (B) age 45 years.
    (C) height 6'1".
    (D) smokes very heavily.

99. A local trailer park will close down soon, and while you are patrolling the area, you see a group of men tearing the trailers apart. You ask them what they are doing, and they explained that they received permission from the owner of the trailer park to tear apart the trailers and sell the scrap metal. Which of the following would be best for you to do in this situation?
    (A) You should let the men go about their business.
    (B) You should contact the owner of the trailer park to verify that they have permission to tear apart the trailers.
    (C) You should let them go about their business, but you should warn them that if you receive any complaints about the situation, they could be arrested.
    (D) You should immediately bring the men back to the station for questioning.

100. You are watching a great number of people leave a sports arena after a boxing match. Of the characteristics listed below, the one that would be of greatest value to you in spotting a man wanted by the department is
    (A) height: 5'3"; weight: 200 lbs.
    (B) eyes: brown; hair: black, wavy; complexion: sallow.
    (C) that he frequents bars and grills and customarily associates with females.
    (D) scars: thin scar on left upper lip; tattoos: on right forearm—"Pinto."

101. "Social Security cards are not acceptable proof of identification for police purposes." Of the following, the most important reason for this rule is that the Social Security card
    (A) is easily obtained.
    (B) states on its face "for Social Security purposes—not for identification."
    (C) is frequently lost.
    (D) does not contain a photograph, description, or fingerprints of the person.

102. "Photographs of suspected persons should not be shown to the witness if the suspect himself can be arrested and placed on view for identification." This recommendation is
    (A) inadvisable; this procedure might subject the witness to future retribution by the suspect.
    (B) advisable; a photograph cannot be used for identification purposes with the same degree of certainty as the suspect in person.
    (C) inadvisable; the appearance of the suspect may have changed since the commission of the crime.
    (D) advisable; photography as an art has not achieved an acceptable degree of perfection.

103. Stationed at a busy intersection, you are given the description of a vehicle that has been stolen. Of the following characteristics, the one which will permit you to eliminate most easily a large number of vehicles is
    (A) no spare tire.
    (B) make: Buick, two-door sedan, 1976.
    (C) color: black.
    (D) tires: 750 × 16, white-walled.

104. If a sick or injured woman, to whom a male Police Officer is rendering aid, is unknown and the officer has reason to believe that her clothing contains means of identification, he should
    (A) immediately search the clothing for such identification and remove any identification found therein.
    (B) send for a female officer to search the clothing before the woman is sent to a hospital.
    (C) ask any female present to search the clothing for such identification.
    (D) accompany her to the hospital and there seek the necessary information from the hospital authorities.

105. Which of the following means of avoiding identification would be most likely to meet with success?
    (A) Growing a beard
    (B) Shaving off the beard if there was one originally
    (C) Burning the fingers so as to remove the fingerprints
    (D) Changing the features by facial surgery

106. In asking a witness of a crime to identify a suspect, it is a common practice to place the suspect with a group of persons and ask the witness to pick out the person in question. Of the following, the best reason for this practice is that it will
(A) make the identification more reliable than if the witness were shown the suspect alone.
(B) protect the witness against reprisals.
(C) make sure that the witness is telling the truth.
(D) help select other participants in the crime at the same time.

107. Suppose that a Police Officer observes an individual acting suspiciously while in a department store. Of the following, the most desirable procedure for her to follow is to
(A) arrest the person.
(B) warn the salespeople that this person may be a thief.
(C) continue to observe this person until sufficient data is present for the formulation of a final decision.
(D) telephone headquarters for assistance as there may soon be a disturbance.

108. A Police Officer who is off duty observes a woman busily engaged in examining fabrics at a counter in a large store. The woman's handbag is open. A number of other persons are at this counter also engaged in examining fabrics. Of the following, the best procedure for the officer to follow *first* is to
(A) tell the woman that her handbag is open.
(B) keep the woman under close observation.
(C) direct a clerk to inform the woman that her handbag is open.
(D) approach the woman and engage her in conversation, by asking a question like, "Do you have the time? My watch seems to have stopped."

109. "The four witnesses to the bank robbery, including the bank president and the cashier, were left together for one hour in the president's office at the bank before they were questioned." This kind of procedure is
(A) desirable and considerate, as there is no point in treating respectable citizens as criminals.
(B) unwise, as it permits undue pressure to be brought upon some of the witnesses.
(C) unwise, as it permits an exchange of actual and imagined details that may result in invalid testimony.
(D) wise, as it keeps the witnesses all in one place.

110. Assume that you are questioning a victim in order to obtain a description of a mugger. Of the following, the best example of the type of question to be avoided is:
(A) Did you notice any scars or unusual features?
(B) Did he wear a brown or black coat?
(C) What color were his shoes?
(D) Approximately how tall was he?

111. Suppose that you are questioning witnesses to a hit-and-run accident. Of the following, the information that will probably be *least* valuable for the purpose of sending out an alarm for the hit-and-run automobile is the
    (A) direction which the automobile took after the accident.
    (B) number of occupants in the automobile at the time of the accident.
    (C) speed at which the automobile was moving when it struck the victim.
    (D) part of the automobile that struck the victim of the accident.

112. The marks left on a bullet by a gun barrel are different from those left by any other gun barrel. This fact is most useful in directly identifying the
    (A) direction from which a shot was fired.
    (B) person who fired a particular gun.
    (C) gun from which a bullet was fired.
    (D) bullet that caused a fatal wound.

113. Uniformed officers are constantly urged to consider every revolver loaded until proven otherwise. Of the following, the best justification for this recommendation is that
    (A) no time is lost when use of the revolver is required.
    (B) there are many accidents involving apparently empty revolvers.
    (C) less danger is involved when facing armed criminals.
    (D) ammunition deteriorates unless replaced periodically.

114. Of the following, the best method to use in shooting a revolver is to keep
    (A) both eyes closed.
    (B) both eyes open.
    (C) the right eye open.
    (D) the left eye open.

115. The Police Officer must inform the person arrested of his or her authority and of the cause of arrest *except* when the
    (A) crime charged is a felony.
    (B) person arrested is a habitual offender.
    (C) officer is in uniform so that authority is apparent.
    (D) person is arrested in the actual commission of the crime.

116. "A woman about 30 years of age accosted a Police Officer with the complaint that her husband had just attacked her with a pair of scissors. 'My husband nearly gouged my eyes out,' the woman said. 'He poked me in the face not once but four or five times. He cut my face into ribbons. He's a dangerous man and I want him arrested. I have five or six witnesses to the attack.' The officer saw no marks on the woman's face." On the basis of these data, the officer may most reasonably take the position that
    (A) the husband ought to be taken into custody immediately.
    (B) the woman's story is at least partially inaccurate.
    (C) no scissors were involved in the accident.
    (D) the incident occurred some time ago.

117. "Generally, before making an arrest for a serious crime, the Police Officer must have facts to provide a reasonable basis for believing the person to be guilty." The best reason for this rule is to
(A) reduce the number of arrests.
(B) protect himself or herself against being charged with false arrest.
(C) safeguard the rights of citizens against improper arrest.
(D) place the burden of disproving the charges upon accused.

118. Suppose that a Police Officer arrests a man accused of molesting a young girl. In an instance of this type, the officer should
(A) behave toward the accused in the same manner as toward any other individual accused of a crime.
(B) be a little rough in handling the man.
(C) inform the man in no uncertain terms that the act of which he is accused is most contemptible.
(D) assume that the man is psychopathic and rightfully a case for institutionalization.

119. Suppose that a Police Officer is summoned by a Mr. Smith, who accuses a Mr. Jones of having aided a Mr. Brown to do an injury to Mr. Smith. The nature of the claimed injury is not such as to give the officer the right to make an arrest. The officer should *first*
(A) prove to Mr. Smith that there is insufficient merit in his case.
(B) refer Mr. Smith to the captain of the precinct.
(C) explain to Mr. Smith the reason why an arrest cannot be made.
(D) refer Mr. Smith to the nearest court.

120. When sent to make an arrest, a Police Officer should be sure he or she is arresting the correct person in order to avoid
(A) publicity.
(B) detaining an innocent person.
(C) having to use force.
(D) having to appear in court.

121. If a Police Officer is called upon to eject a disorderly person from a bus station, the most important consideration must necessarily be to
(A) avoid damaging transit system property.
(B) earn good public opinion.
(C) avoid endangering other passengers.
(D) get the person off the property.

122. "When making arrests, the Police Officer should treat all suspects in the same manner." This suggested rule is
    (A) undesirable; the specific problems presented should govern the officer's actions.
    (B) desirable; this is the only democratic solution to the problem.
    (C) undesirable; persons who are only suspected are not criminals and should not be treated as such.
    (D) desirable; only by setting up fixed and rigid rules can officers know what is expected of them.

123. A Police Officer observes a young man who is obviously very excited, walking unusually fast, and repeatedly halting to look behind him. Upon stopping the young man, the officer finds that he is carrying a gun and has just held up a liquor store a few blocks away. This incident illustrates that
    (A) circumstances that are not suspicious in themselves frequently provide clues for the solution of crimes.
    (B) an experienced officer can pick the criminal type out of a crowd by alert observation.
    (C) action is always to be preferred to thought.
    (D) a police officer should investigate suspicious circumstances.

124. A Police Officer positively recognizes a woman on a busy street as one wanted for passing bad checks. Of the following, the most appropriate action for the officer to take is to
    (A) approach and then arrest the woman.
    (B) follow the woman until a place is reached where there are few people, then take out a gun, and arrest the woman.
    (C) immediately take out a gun, stop the woman, and search her.
    (D) follow the woman, as she may lead the way to associates.

125. A woman has her husband arrested for severely beating their five-year-old son. A crowd of angry neighbors has gathered around the husband. In making the arrest, the arresting officer should
    (A) treat the husband like any other person accused of breaking the law.
    (B) deal with the husband sympathetically, since the man may be mentally ill.
    (C) handle the husband harshly, since his crime is a despicable one.
    (D) treat the husband roughly only if he shows no remorse for his actions.

126. The purpose of a raid is to
    (A) apprehend criminals.
    (B) disclose the members of a certain criminal group.
    (C) secure the probable cause required for the issuance of a search warrant.
    (D) know the fields of observation from a suspected place.

127. There has been a series of burglaries in a residential area consisting of one-family houses. You have been assigned to select a house in this area in which detectives can wait secretly for an attempted burglary of that house so that the burglars can be apprehended in the act. Which of the following would be the best house to select for this purpose?
   (A) The house that was recently burglarized and from which several thousand dollars worth of clothing and personal property were taken.
   (B) The house whose owner reports that several times the telephone has rung, but the person making the call hung up as soon as the telephone was answered.
   (C) The house that is smaller and looks much less pretentious than other houses in the same area.
   (D) The house that is occupied by a widower who works long hours but who lives with an invalid mother requiring constant nursing service.

128. Suppose that a Police Officer observes a young girl picking up small articles of merchandise as she passes from one counter to another of a large department store. The girl does not stop to pay for any of the articles. For the officer to wait until the girl is about to leave the store before apprehending her is
   (A) inadvisable; she may escape.
   (B) advisable; evidence is thereby more firmly established.
   (C) inadvisable if she has an accomplice waiting outside.
   (D) advisable if the Police Officer has a witness to confirm the observations.

129. Jones is accused of having assaulted Smith at a particular time and place. Police investigation disclosed that Jones was present at the time and place where the alleged assault took place. This information makes admissible the conclusion that
   (A) Jones assaulted Smith.
   (B) Smith assaulted Jones.
   (C) Jones may have assaulted Smith.
   (D) Smith may have assaulted Jones.

130. Suppose that a lawyer is attacked in a washroom by a man who delivered several blows from behind with a carpenter's mallet. From this information only, it is safe to infer
   (A) that the attacker is young and strong.
   (B) that the mallet was either recently purchased or stolen.
   (C) that the washroom is located in an office building.
   (D) none of the foregoing.

131. During a quarrel on a crowded city street, one man stabs another and flees. A Police Officer arriving at the scene a short time later finds the victim unconscious, calls for an ambulance, and orders the crowd to leave. The officer's action is
   (A) bad; there may have been witnesses to the assault among the crowd.
   (B) good; it is proper first aid procedure to give an injured person room and air.
   (C) bad; the assailant is probably among the crowd.
   (D) good; a crowd may destroy needed evidence.

132. Green is accused on apparently good evidence of having stolen a radio from Brown at 8:30 p.m., January 18. If Green is able to prove that at 10:00 p.m. of the same day he was not in possession of any radio, Green has

(A) proved his innocence.

(B) yet to establish his innocence.

(C) implied his guilt, since evidence for the period 8:30 p.m. to 10:00 p.m. is absent.

(D) proved that Brown is mistaken or lying.

133. Clothes valued at $800 as well as $1,000 in cash were stolen from the home of one of the residents of a Police Officer's post. The officer learns that Albert Jones, a man 27 years old and not known ever to possess more than a few dollars at one time, has, shortly after the occasion of the robbery, displayed what seemed to be a large roll of bills. The officer may most profitably take, as the basis for first action, the position that

(A) a large roll of bills is sometimes obtained as the result of a burglary.

(B) despite the fact that the clothing is valued at $800, a considerably smaller sum is likely to be realized when the clothing is sold to a second-hand dealer.

(C) Albert Jones may recently have gotten a job.

(D) reputation must be distinguished from character.

134. A resident on your post informs you that a valuable diamond ring has been stolen from her apartment. About two weeks later, a boy gives you what appears to be a diamond ring that he says he found on the street. Of the following, the question that would be *least* significant in this situation is:

(A) Did the boy actually find the ring on the street?

(B) Is this the same ring the resident mentioned?

(C) Was the ring really stolen?

(D) Did the resident wait for more or less than two hours before reporting the theft of the ring?

135. "Goods valued at $75,000 were reported burglarized from a loft. Investigation proved conclusively that it was impossible for burglars either to have entered or left the loft building without having been detected." On the basis of these data, the Police Officer may most reasonably deduce that

(A) more than $75,000 worth of goods were stolen.

(B) the burglary was committed by a person unfamiliar with the habits of the people in the loft where the crime occurred.

(C) what was reported to be a burglary is actually an assault.

(D) the alleged crime did not occur.

136. Suppose that a Police Officer observes that a certain company on his post pays out a large sum in cash weekly in payroll. If the officer were asked to suggest the best method for eliminating the possibility of a successful payroll robbery in this company, he would suggest

(A) the hiring of several armed guards.

(B) that payday occur at irregular intervals.

(C) that payment be made at a place other than at the offices of the company.

(D) payment by check.

137. "Many thieves conceal themselves in a building during business hours, and, when they have accomplished their purpose, escape through a rear door or window." The reason for such concealment in the building is most probably that after business hours

(A) without a key, locked doors are sometimes difficult to open.

(B) poor lighting is conducive to undetected criminal activity.

(C) to accomplish a purpose, one must have a goal.

(D) rear doors ordinarily serve as exits.

138. "When investigating a burglary, a Police Officer should obtain as complete descriptions as possible of articles of value that were stolen, but should list, without describing, stolen articles that are relatively valueless." This suggested procedure is

(A) poor; what is valueless to one person may be of great value to another.

(B) good; it enables the police to concentrate on recovering the most valuable articles.

(C) poor; articles of little value frequently provide the only evidence connecting the suspect to the crime.

(D) good; the listing of the inexpensive items is probably incomplete.

139. Looking through the window of a jewelry store, a Police Officer sees a man take a watch from the counter and drop it into his pocket while the jeweler is busy talking to someone else. The man looks around the store and then walks out. The officer should

(A) stop the man and bring him back into the store so that both he and the jeweler can be questioned.

(B) ignore the incident: if the man were performing an illegal act, the jeweler would have called for help.

(C) arrest the man, take him to the station house, and then return to obtain the jeweler's statement.

(D) ignore the incident; if the man were a thief, the jeweler would not have left the watches unattended.

140. A Police Officer who responded at 2 a.m. to a radio call that a burglary had been committed in an apartment heard the sound of clashing tools coming from the adjoining apartment. For the officer to investigate the noise would be
  (A) undesirable; the officer may not search without a warrant.
  (B) desirable; the thief may be found.
  (C) undesirable; unusual noises in apartments are common.
  (D) desirable; the victim would tend to be impressed by the concern shown.

141. Assume that you are driving a police car, equipped with a two-way radio, along an isolated section of the parkway at 3 a.m. You note that the headlights of a car pulled to the side of the road are blinking rapidly. When you stop to investigate, the driver of the car informs you that he was just forced to the side of the road by two men in a green station wagon, who robbed him of a large amount of cash and jewelry at gunpoint and then sped away. Your *first* consideration in this situation should be to
  (A) drive rapidly along the parkway in the direction taken by the criminals in an effort to apprehend them before they escape.
  (B) question the driver carefully, looking for inconsistencies indicating that he made up the whole story.
  (C) obtain a complete listing and identification of all materials lost.
  (D) notify your superior to have the parkway exits watched for a car answering the description of the getaway car.

142. A Police Officer finds a man dying in one of the city parks. There are several stab wounds in the man's chest and his skull is fractured. Just before dying, the man manages to say that he was the victim of an assault and robbery. Upon investigation by the officer, a bloodstained shoemaker's awl is found nearby. Of the following, the most useful assumption to make *first* in attempting to solve the crime is that
  (A) for some reason the man lied, so tentatively, his statement ought to be disregarded.
  (B) there were no witnesses to the possible crime.
  (C) the awl was deliberately placed near the scene of the crime to mislead the police.
  (D) the murderer had access to shoemaker's tools.

143. "At 2 a.m., while patrolling your post, you find the body of a man lying on the street. A knife is protruding from the man's back." On the basis of these data only, it is *least* likely that the man was lying
  (A) on his left side.
  (B) face downward.
  (C) on his back.
  (D) on his right side.

144. In a recent case of suicide, the body was found slumped in a chair and no revolver, knife, or razor was found in the room. Of the following, the most reasonable hypothesis from the data given is that
(A) the person had taken some poison.
(B) the person had hanged himself.
(C) the person had died as a result of a heart attack.
(D) the murderer had taken the weapon.

145. Suppose that while patrolling your post in an unfrequented area at 1:00 a.m., you find a man sprawled on the ground in an alley. The man's throat has been cut and he is dead. There is considerable blood on the ground, but the man does not appear to be bleeding. Of the following, the *first* step you should take is to
(A) straighten the man out so he is resting comfortably.
(B) telephone your precinct.
(C) investigate to determine whether the blood on the ground is the blood of the dead man.
(D) carry the man out to the street.

146. Suppose that A, the proprietor of a fur business, is found dead at his place of business at 8:00 a.m. His death appears to have occurred as a result of the fact that he is hanging from a rope tied to a water pipe. In the pockets of A's trousers are a number of pawn tickets for furs and a lapsed insurance policy for $10,000. On the basis of this information only, the best inference is that
(A) A committed suicide because of business difficulties.
(B) A had been working late and was murdered by thieves.
(C) A's death is the consequence of an accident.
(D) it is safe only to declare that A probably did not commit suicide. The fact that so few articles were found in his pockets is a substantial basis for extended additional investigation.

147. When the bodies of two women were found stabbed in an inner room of an apartment, it was first believed that it was a case of mutual homicide. Of the following clues found at the scene, the one that indicates that it was more likely a case of murder by a third party is the fact that
(A) the door to the apartment was found locked.
(B) there were bloodstains on the outer door of the apartment.
(C) there was a switchblade knife in each body.
(D) no money could be found in the room where the bodies were.

148. "The questioning of witnesses is often much less truth-revealing than are physical clues found at the scene of the crime." Of the following, the chief justification for this statement is that
(A) most witnesses rarely tell the truth.
(B) physical clues are always present if examination is thorough.
(C) questioning of witnesses must be supported by other evidence.
(D) the memory of witnesses is often unreliable.

149. Jones, who is suspected of having committed a crime of homicide at 8:30 p.m. in the building where he lives, claims that he could not have committed the act because he worked overtime until 8:00 p.m. In order to prove that Jones actually could not have committed the act in question, it is most important to know
    (A) how long it takes to get from Jones' building to Jones' place of work.
    (B) if there are any witnesses to the fact that Jones worked overtime.
    (C) Jones' reputation in the community.
    (D) what kind of work Jones does.

150. A Police Officer on a post hears a cry for help from a woman in a car with two men. He approaches the car and is told by the woman that the men are kidnapping her. The men claim to be the woman's husband and doctor, and they state that they are taking her to a private mental hospital in Westchester County. Of the following, the officer should
    (A) take all of them to the station house for further questioning.
    (B) permit the car to depart on the basis of the explanation.
    (C) call for an ambulance to take the woman to the nearest city mental hospital.
    (D) accompany the car to the private mental hospital.

151. Suppose that a seven-year-old boy has been kidnapped as he was returning home from a playground at dusk. The following day, his parents received an anonymous letter that told them the child was well and designated a close friend of the family, who was known to be very fond of the boy, as an intermediary to arrange payment of a ransom. On the basis of these data only, we may most reasonably assume that
    (A) the friend kidnapped the boy.
    (B) the friend was probably an accessory in the kidnapping.
    (C) further investigation is necessary to determine the identity of the kidnapper.
    (D) the boy is dead.

152. The most frequent cause among the following for making a person a criminal is
    (A) mental retardation.
    (B) good education.
    (C) bad environmental conditions.
    (D) superior ability in a trade.

153. A view widely held among criminologists is that the severity of laws dealing with criminals is not so effective a deterrent to crime as is
    (A) the enactment of less severe laws, coupled with lenient administration.
    (B) a well-organized parole system for even the most hardened criminals.
    (C) psychiatric treatment, as most crimes are committed by persons with emotional and mental difficulties.
    (D) certainty that the criminal will be apprehended and sentenced properly.

154. A representative group of young criminals in a certain state were found to be normal in intelligence, but 86 percent were behind from one to six grades in school. The best inference from these data is that
- **(A)** lack of intelligence is highly correlated with delinquency.
- **(B)** criminals should be removed from the school system.
- **(C)** educational maladjustments are closely associated with delinquency.
- **(D)** the usual rate at which criminals progress educationally represents the limit of their learning powers.

155. "One study shows that boys' clubs and similar programs aimed at the prevention of crime and the rehabilitation of the juvenile delinquent tend to attract the good boys, while the bad boys stay away." This quotation implies most directly that the number of instances in which juvenile delinquents are rehabilitated through such programs as boys' clubs is
- **(A)** relatively large.
- **(B)** relatively small.
- **(C)** a quantity the size of which cannot be estimated even loosely and approximately.
- **(D)** greater for good boys than for bad boys.

156. Two Police Officers patrolling the downtown business streets at 1:00 a.m. observe a young girl dressed in a manner to attract attention, walking slowly down the street. The girl approaches a young man, who disregards her. After a short time, she approaches another man, who also disregards her. The officers should
- **(A)** follow the girl until they are in a position to make a double arrest.
- **(B)** ignore the situation, since the girl is obviously not a professional prostitute.
- **(C)** approach and question the men as well as the girl, since they may give evidence to prove solicitation.
- **(D)** separate, one continuing to observe the girl, the other calling the Missing Persons Bureau to check up on descriptions of missing girls.

157. "Where a satisfactory adjustment can be made without arresting the delinquent minor, it is done. Court action is only taken where it seems best for the minor or the community." Of the following, the best justification for this procedure is that
- **(A)** court cases are costly to the community.
- **(B)** rehabilitation of the delinquent minor is of primary importance.
- **(C)** arresting minors may become a source of inconvenience if not discouraged.
- **(D)** juvenile delinquency can increase if juvenile delinquents are not arrested.

158. Suppose that, while on patrol late at night, you find a woman lying in the street, apparently a victim of a hit-and-run accident. She seems to be injured seriously, but you wish to ask her one or two questions in order to help apprehend the driver of the hit-and-run car. Of the following, the first question to ask is:
   (A) Which direction did the car go?
   (B) What time did it happen?
   (C) What kind of car was it?
   (D) How many persons were in the car?

159. Of the following, the information that would be *least* helpful to the Police Officer assigned to the case of a 14-year-old girl who has been reported by her mother as a runaway is
   (A) the possible cause for her running away.
   (B) a detailed description of her clothing.
   (C) a detailed description of her scholastic abilities.
   (D) a detailed description of her features.

160. A violin is reported as missing from the home of Mrs. Brown. It would be *least* important to the police, before making a routine check of pawn shops, to know that this violin
   (A) is of a certain unusual shade of red.
   (B) has one tuning key with a chip mark on it in the shape of a triangle.
   (C) has a well-known manufacturer's label stamped inside the violin.
   (D) has a hidden number given to the police by the owner.

161. Merely looking at a criminal is enough to tell an intelligent officer
   (A) how educated the person is.
   (B) whether the person will be a troublemaker.
   (C) whether the person is truly a criminal.
   (D) little or nothing.

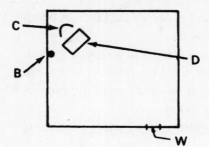

162. Assume that you are investigating a case of reported suicide. You find the deceased sitting in a chair, sprawled over his desk, a revolver still clutched in his right hand. In your examination of the room, you find that the window is partly open. Only one bullet has been fired from the revolver. The bullet has lodged in the wall. Assume that the diagram above is a scale drawing of the scene. D indicates the desk, C indicates the chair, W indicates the window, and B indicates the bullet. Of the following, which indicates most strongly the deceased did not commit suicide?
    (A) The distance between the desk and the bullet hole.
    (B) The relative position of the bullet hole and the chair.
    (C) The fact that the window was partly open.
    (D) The relative position of the desk and the window.

163. As the Police Officer approaches a lighted delicatessen late at night, two men emerge and walk rapidly in the opposite direction. Suspicious of the behavior of these men, the officer looks through the window into the store. Of the following, the circumstances tending most strongly to confirm his suspicions are
    (A) several persons are waiting to be served inside the store.
    (B) the clerk is standing at the counter with his back to the officer.
    (C) the clerk and a customer are engaged in a conversation.
    (D) no one at all is visible inside the store.

164. About 9:00 p.m., a Police Officer observed two men loitering near a neighborhood movie theater. He had not seen either man in the neighborhood before. The agent for the theater usually deposited the night receipts in the local bank's night deposit vault between 9:00 and 9:15 p.m. The most appropriate action for the officer to take was to
    (A) station himself so that he could observe their actions until the theater's money had been deposited.
    (B) demand that they tell him their place of residence and the reason for their presence near the theater.
    (C) pay no further attention, since they were obviously waiting for someone in the theater.
    (D) enter the theater by the side entrance and warn the manager to be prepared for a possible robbery attempt.

165. The proprietor of a tavern summons a Police Officer and turns over a loaded revolver that was found in one of the tavern's booths. The *least* appropriate action for the officer to take is to
    (A) unload the gun and place it in an inside pocket.
    (B) determine exactly when the revolver was found.
    (C) obtain the names or descriptions of the persons who occupied the booth before the revolver was found.
    (D) question the proprietor very closely concerning the matter.

166. Assume that you have stopped a 1978 Dodge four-door sedan, which you suspect is a car reported as stolen the day before. The items of information that would be *most* useful in determining whether or not this is the stolen car is that
    (A) the stolen car's license number was QA2356; this car's license number is U21375.
    (B) the stolen car's engine number was AB6231; this car's engine number is CS2315.
    (C) the windshield of the stolen car was not cracked; this car's windshield is cracked.
    (D) the stolen car had whitewall tires; this car does not have whitewall tires.

167. Crime statistics indicate that property crimes such as larceny, burglary, and robbery are more numerous during winter months than in summer. The explanation that most adequately accounts for this situation is that
    (A) human needs, such as clothing, food, heat, and shelter, are greater in summer.
    (B) criminal tendencies are generally aggravated by climatic changes.
    (C) there are more hours of darkness in winter and such crimes are usually committed under cover of darkness.
    (D) urban areas are more densely populated during winter months, affording greater opportunity for such crimes.

168. Blackmail is an especially troublesome problem for the police. The best justification for this statement is that the
    (A) victim of a blackmail plot usually hesitates to cooperate with the police for fear of publicity.
    (B) blackmailer is usually a hardened criminal who will not hesitate to murder the victim.
    (C) facts constituting the subject matter of a blackmail are seldom known to the victim.
    (D) victim of a blackmail plot is usually anxious to expose all details to the police.

169. In some states, statutes forbid the payment of ransom to kidnappers. Such statutes are
  (A) actually in violation of the due process of law clause of the federal constitution.
  (B) necessary to encourage kidnappers to return the kidnapped person unharmed.
  (C) harmful because kidnapping is encouraged by such legislation.
  (D) examples of laws that protect society although sometimes working hardships on individuals.

170. Any change in insurance coverage immediately prior to a fire should be investigated. Strange as it may seem, most such changes made by convicted arsonists are made to a smaller amount. The most probable reason for such changes is that the arsonist
  (A) was trying to divert suspicion.
  (B) decided to set the fire after the change was made.
  (C) did not have enough money to pay for the full amount.
  (D) reduced the insurance to the amount he or she expected to be lost in the fire.

Answer Key

This answer key is provided so that you can check your answers quickly and easily. Be sure to continue and study all the answer explanations that follow. The explanations point out the police reasoning and judgment involved in the correct answer choices.

1. (C)	35. (D)	69. (C)	103. (C)	137. (A)
2. (D)	36. (A)	70. (A)	104. (D)	138. (C)
3. (B)	37. (C)	71. (D)	105. (D)	139. (A)
4. (A)	38. (C)	72. (A)	106. (A)	140. (B)
5. (A)	39. (C)	73. (C)	107. (C)	141. (D)
6. (A)	40. (B)	74. (C)	108. (A)	142. (D)
7. (D)	41. (A)	75. (C)	109. (C)	143. (C)
8. (C)	42. (C)	76. (A)	110. (B)	144. (A)
9. (C)	43. (D)	77. (D)	111. (C)	145. (B)
10. (D)	44. (D)	78. (B)	112. (C)	146. (A)
11. (A)	45. (B)	79. (C)	113. (B)	147. (B)
12. (C)	46. (D)	80. (C)	114. (B)	148. (D)
13. (D)	47. (D)	81. (A)	115. (D)	149. (A)
14. (A)	48. (B)	82. (C)	116. (B)	150. (A)
15. (B)	49. (A)	83. (B)	117. (C)	151. (C)
16. (B)	50. (D)	84. (A)	118. (A)	152. (C)
17. (D)	51. (C)	85. (C)	119. (C)	153. (D)
18. (A)	52. (C)	86. (D)	120. (B)	154. (C)
19. (D)	53. (B)	87. (B)	121. (C)	155. (B)
20. (B)	54. (D)	88. (C)	122. (A)	156. (C)
21. (C)	55. (D)	89. (C)	123. (D)	157. (B)
22. (A)	56. (D)	90. (A)	124. (A)	158. (C)
23. (D)	57. (A)	91. (D)	125. (A)	159. (C)
24. (C)	58. (C)	92. (C)	126. (A)	160. (C)
25. (C)	59. (C)	93. (C)	127. (B)	161. (D)
26. (C)	60. (C)	94. (A)	128. (B)	162. (B)
27. (D)	61. (D)	95. (A)	129. (C)	163. (D)
28. (A)	62. (A)	96. (B)	130. (D)	164. (A)
29. (D)	63. (C)	97. (D)	131. (A)	165. (A)
30. (A)	64. (C)	98. (C)	132. (B)	166. (B)
31. (B)	65. (A)	99. (B)	133. (A)	167. (C)
32. (A)	66. (D)	100. (A)	134. (D)	168. (A)
33. (D)	67. (D)	101. (D)	135. (D)	169. (D)
34. (C)	68. (D)	102. (B)	136. (D)	170. (A)

Answer Explanations

1. **The correct answer is (C).** Because the man is elderly and because he made a comment about his desire to "join" his wife, the police should be concerned about a suicide attempt; therefore, he should not be left alone at this time, and somebody— whether that is a friend, relative or social worker—should be there to help him deal with his grief. That is the most important concern in this situation.

2. **The correct answer is (D).** Any of the above reasons could be valid explanations for the girl's running away. There is too little information to suggest that she is being abused or neglected or that she is simply being rebellious.

3. **The correct answer is (B).** Because the coworker seems eager to make extra money through overtime and a second job and because her husband is currently unemployed, this suggests that financial problems are the reason for her tension.

4. **The correct answer is (A).** You should not follow orders that you know to be unethical or illegal; however, because you are a new officer in this situation, your field-training officer is likely to have more legal knowledge and experience than you. The best step to take first is to ask your supervisor to clarify his order. With this additional knowledge, you would then be able to make an informed choice as to whether you should comply with this order or not.

5. **The correct answer is (A).** A Police Officer is always a Police Officer, even when not officially on duty. Off-duty status does not relieve a Police Officer from fulfilling the police role.

6. **The correct answer is (A).** The first thing to do is to protect the man's life by escorting him out of danger. Securing medical assistance should follow.

7. **The correct answer is (D).** Obviously, going the wrong way on a one-way street creates a dangerous situation for many people. By stopping the driver, you have averted the danger. The out-of-towner has not actually committed a violation, he was just about to. It would be wise to point out to him exactly how one-way streets are marked in your town.

8. **The correct answer is (C).** Drowning occurs very quickly. Try to rescue the boy.

9. **The correct answer is (C).** Anything unusual should be investigated as soon as possible. The first thing to do is to determine whether or not a burglary has occurred. Then the premises should be secured and the owner notified. If the premises were not entered, they should be kept under surveillance in case the burglar returns.

10. **The correct answer is (D).** Stopping fights is part of keeping the peace and of maintaining order on your beat.

11. **The correct answer is (A).** A burglar may be inside and have turned off the light to escape detection. If there is no evidence of intruders, the storekeeper should be called to turn on the light or to replace the burned-out bulb. This question illustrates the need for a Police Officer to be observant and to remember how things usually appear on the beat.

12. **The correct answer is (C).** Based on the information provided in the scenario, the only possible answer is (C). Because there is no damage to the rear of either car, a rear-end collision did not occur, eliminating choices (A) and (D). If the Honda was facing west and the Hyundai was facing north, then the Hyundai would have collided with the driver's side of the car, not the passenger's side. It may help you to make a diagram when figuring out the answer to this type of question.

13. **The correct answer is (D).** You can assume that these people are up to no good. The quickest way to find this out is to ask for registration papers, for proof of ownership. If the keys were simply locked inside the car, the owner should readily clear up your suspicion. If ownership cannot be proved, arrest is indicated.

14. **The correct answer is (A).** An argument in a cleaning store is not an emergency situation. There is no need to disrupt traffic nor to create alarm. On the other hand, the situation could lead to blows, so the officer should step in to try to calm tempers.

15. **The correct answer is (B).** Your first consideration must be protection of life and limb. Get the man to the hospital for medical attention but have him escorted for further questioning. Gunshot wounds always should be investigated.

16. **The correct answer is (B).** Absolutely. Schools are prepared to deal with unauthorized absences and with children's illness.

17. **The correct answer is (D).** Janitors and local merchants tend to be out on the street often and are very aware of what is happening in the neighborhood. These people also would prefer to avoid having any trouble in the area and, if on friendly terms with a trusted Police Officer, are likely to alert the officer to situations they feel the officer should know about.

18. **The correct answer is (A).** The owner may indeed be caring for his or her car, in which case the owner can prove ownership. An open hood can also be a sign of car theft by means of jump start or of battery theft in progress.

19. **The correct answer is (D).** A Police Officer is a Police Officer, not a firefighter. It is the job of firefighters to ascertain whether or not there really is a fire and to put it out. Fires spread rapidly. The practical move is to call the fire department rather than trying to run through the building alone trying to rouse all occupants.

20. **The correct answer is (B).** A pattern of regular inspections gives fair notice to prospective wrongdoers as to when no one will be looking.

21. **The correct answer is (C).** Because the boys had previously run into trouble with the law due to drug possession and because the boys were stealing large quantities of the items (which makes it slightly more unlikely that they would steal these items as a prank or for their own personal use), the most likely reason for the theft is that they were planning to sell the items for drug money. Drug users often steal items to sell at flea markets and the like to get the money they need to purchase more drugs.

22. **The correct answer is (A).** Mrs. Peterson's frequent calls to the police, the lack of evidence to support the suggestion that someone wants to break into her home, as well as her talkative and friendly behavior when the police arrive suggest that her main problem is loneliness and a fear of crime. The police department should not dismiss her concerns, as in choices (B) or (C), but department resources would be better served if officers did not have to be dispatched frequently to her home for false alarms. Therefore, the best answer to this question would be choice (A) because a senior citizen police academy could provide Mrs. Peterson with valuable information as to how to prevent crime, and a senior citizen organization will help to curb some of her loneliness.

23. **The correct answer is (D).** The Police Officer must maintain the role of Police Officer. He may not assume the role of parent. Rather than simply turning the woman down, he might suggest that she contact the proper social agency.

24. **The correct answer is (C).** Rush to the scene. The girl may have misjudged the situation and the man may be in need of emergency medical assistance. If the man is indeed dead, his body should not lie in the street unattended.

25. **The correct answer is (C).** Dispersing a noisy group of teenagers is generally sufficient to quiet things down.

26. **The correct answer is (C).** Seven or eight people do not constitute an unruly crowd. The appearance of a person of authority demanding order should end the disturbance.

27. **The correct answer is (D).** A newly appointed officer assumes some responsibility immediately. The supervising officer will give guidance but will not make all decisions.

28. **The correct answer is (A).** Because the husband had been driving with his family for approximately 10 hours and 35 minutes and because he does not remember what led to the crash, this suggests that the husband had fallen asleep at the wheel, which caused the tragic accident.

29. **The correct answer is (D).** Because the woman is known to be wealthy and has plenty of designer clothes and because there is no evidence to suggest that she is having financial problems or is involved in any other sort of crime, the *most* likely reason is that she is stealing for the thrill of the experience. According to Theft Talk Counseling Service (www.thefttalk.com), "Common cultural thinking errors are that theft offenders are victims of poverty, poor parenting, hunger, alcohol and drugs, ADHD, peer pressure, etc. The fact is, most people who steal from stores are none of the above..."

30. **The correct answer is (A).** You have four choices. Of these, crime prevention is the primary function of a police department.

31. **The correct answer is (B).** Police badges serve as identification of the Police Officers.

32. **The correct answer is (A).** The Police Officer must be alert at all times.

33. **The correct answer is (D).** If 10 percent of the inmates released from a prison are arrested as parole violators, the one conclusion that may be drawn is that 10 percent have violated parole and have been caught. The statement gives no basis for any other conclusions.

34. **The correct answer is (C).** Murders are not caused by pistols; pistols are often used in the commission of murders. Clearly the pistol is a mechanical aid to crime, and some crimes might be avoided if pistols were unavailable, but there is no one-to-one correspondence between pistols and murders.

35. **The correct answer is (D).** Because there was no traffic device at the drive-thru exit, this suggests that the teenage driver was responsible for yielding to oncoming traffic. With her food, friends and then a phone call, the most likely reason for the accident was that the young driver was too distracted to look for oncoming traffic.

36. **The correct answer is (A).** When pulling a fellow police officer over for a traffic violation, you should treat him/her no differently than you would another citizen. This means that you should give him/her a warning or a violation at your discretion rather than being more lenient (letting him go without a citation) or being more strict (getting him in trouble with his boss!).

37. **The correct answer is (C).** The officer must understand what he or she is to do in order to do it. Watch out for distracting answers like that offered by choice (A). Self-interest is never the reason for doing anything when taking a civil service exam.

38. **The correct answer is (C).** Remember not to step out of the Police Officer's role. The Police Officer must never recommend individuals, not even a choice of individuals. The most the Police Officer may do is recommend that the individual contact the local bar association or consult directories in a library.

39. **The correct answer is (C).** In police exams, older children are generally referred to as juveniles. "Children" means young children. In dealing with children, whether protecting them or arresting them, the Police Officer must secure their confidence to get maximum cooperation.

40. **The correct answer is (B).** Because the woman has no visible physical injuries and because she insists that nothing is wrong, you do not have enough evidence to justify the arrest of the boyfriend. After all, she and her boyfriend could have had a loud argument that left her emotionally upset but did not end in physical violence. However, her nervousness at your presence and the neighbors' complaints do not mean that you should dismiss this problem or warn the neighbors against calling the police in the future. Instead, you should provide the woman with information that she may need if there is a potential for domestic violence in this relationship.

41. **The correct answer is (A).** Since murder is often a crime of passion, the police may have little means to foresee or prevent it. Burglary, prostitution, and auto theft are premeditated and, to some extent, visible. Police vigilance can help prevent opportunities for such crimes to occur.

42. **The correct answer is (C).** This phenomenon is called "copycat crime." It is an unfortunate but unavoidable consequence of a free press.

43. **The correct answer is (D).** There is enough evidence (the multiple, severe bruises) to justify an investigation into this situation; however, based solely upon the information provided, there is not enough evidence to suggest that any of the individuals listed is most likely to be abusing the girl. Her mother, father, and the father's new girlfriend are all at this point equally capable of abusing her.

44. **The correct answer is (D).** By making a point to pull over Hispanic or Latino motorists, Officer Jury is engaging in racial profiling. Racial profiling is extremely damaging to a police department's relationship with the community and is discriminatory to the motorists who face expensive fines and the loss of their valuable time (if not worse) solely because of the color of their skin. Racial profiling is a serious issue that cannot be ignored, and the most effective way to deal with this situation would be to speak with Officer Jury's immediate supervisor so that he can take any necessary disciplinary action and hopefully alleviate the situation.

45. **The correct answer is (B).** Because there is no evidence to suggest that the female coworker has confronted Sergeant Wilcox yet, she should first attempt to solve the problem informally and ask Sergeant Wilcox to stop the offending behavior. If it persists, then the most effective way of handling the situation would be to speak with Sergeant Wilcox's immediate supervisor so that any necessary disciplinary action can be taken. Some victims of sexual harassment feel uncomfortable confronting their harassers; many choose to solve the problem formally first. However, there is a possibility that Sergeant Wilcox would stop the offending behavior if asked, which makes choice (B) a better answer than choice (A).

46. **The correct answer is (D).** Boys under 16 are very impressionable and learn readily. Society's interests are best served by not allowing them contact with hardened criminals.

47. **The correct answer is (D).** According to the statement, it is certainly true that a well-dressed person may be a criminal. Choice (C) is on its face also true, but the statement speaks only of criminals who *look* intelligent, not of criminals who *are* intelligent.

48. **The correct answer is (B).** The Police Officer's first priority is to save lives. An ambulance on an emergency run is on a mission to save a life. Lifesaving supersedes all other orders.

49. **The correct answer is (A).** Even though in civilian clothes and off duty, the Police Officer has the duty to save lives. By educating the youngsters in the dangers of their actions, the Police Officer may be saving their lives and possibly the lives of other passengers on very crowded buses. One must hope that this instruction will also restrain them from tampering with emergency doors in future bus rides.

50. **The correct answer is (D).** Even when the fire is in a house rather than an apartment building, your first duty is to summon firefighters. They most likely can save more lives than you can alone by attempting to rouse residents.

51. **The correct answer is (C).** Because there is no prohibition on other kinds of communication (i.e., voice communication and hand gestures and the use of ground-line telephones), the reason that the policy is in place is not to prohibit communication between members at the scene for fear of causing panic or alerting the bomber to police activity. Also radio devices are not known to be especially unreliable; therefore, the best answer to this question is choice (C), that cellular phones and radio devices could possibly cause the bomb to detonate, leading to the department prohibiting their use within 500 yards of the bomb's location.

52. **The correct answer is (C).** Your job is to investigate anything unusual along your beat and to deal with threats to persons or property.

53. **The correct answer is (B).** Remain in the police role. A Police Officer is a Police Officer, not a paramedic. Send for professional assistance and leave medical decisions to medical personnel.

54. **The correct answer is (D).** This is a true common-sense question. An inquiry over the supermarket's public address system is most likely to produce a parent who had not yet missed the child. If not, proceed with other actions.

55. **The correct answer is (D).** Again, this is common sense. The mother is most likely to return to the spot at which she became separated from the youngster.

56. **The correct answer is (D).** If you do not really know the answer to this question, you can reach it by a process of elimination. Choice (A) is incorrect because a medical problem cannot be ignored; choice (B) is incorrect because the person must be informed of the reason for arrest; and choice (C) is incorrect because the person is certainly allowed to speak and to express feelings. Choice (D) is your best choice. While all suicide threats must be taken seriously, the person newly taken into custody may well be blustering. Suicide in custody is a serious problem. The silent, brooding, distressed prisoner must be carefully watched.

57. **The correct answer is (A).** Note the word *least*. Arresting the leaders who have not been involved in criminal activity would be illegal and foolhardy. Gang members are very loyal to their own, and you could start a riot. All the other choices represent potentially positive steps.

58. **The correct answer is (C).** The Police Officer is the department's representative to the public. The officer should be as helpful as possible without neglecting assigned duties.

59. **The correct answer is (C).** Your first consideration is public safety. You are outnumbered by armed men who are desperate to escape, if you shout, they are likely to shoot, thereby endangering bystanders in the intervening 75 feet. Do your best to identify the men so that officers better positioned to apprehend them can be alerted by alarm.

60. **The correct answer is (C).** Police presence is often sufficient to discourage prohibited activity. The Police Officer should always attempt to accomplish his or her purpose with the least aggressive action.

61. **The correct answer is (D).** The woman is upset, but you must not act too hastily. Ascertain that the husband is really missing before you spend time getting a description and searching for the man.

62. **The correct answer is (A).** Even in this age of AIDS, the officer must be *least* concerned with diseases the suspect may carry. The officer must be more concerned with the possibility that the suspect will use a gun or physical force to resist arrest or that he or she will try to flee.

63. **The correct answer is (C).** Of course, a person may be having mail directed to an address from which he or she has recently moved or even where he or she has never lived; however, it is most likely that mail delivered to an address is meant for persons who reside there. Of the choices, this is clearly the best.

64. **The correct answer is (C).** Your superiors have the advantage of years of training and experience. Their judgment is quicker, and they must be obeyed without question at the site of an emergency.

65. **The correct answer is (A).** Every terrorist or bomb threat should be taken seriously-even if there were hoax threats in the past. The danger of ignoring a bomb threat is too great; therefore, the department should respond as quickly as possible and take every precaution, even if it is likely that the threat is not real.

66. **The correct answer is (D).** Of course there are experts trying to improve the police system, so you should not rush to present every idea. On the other hand, as an active Police Officer you are in daily contact with the special demands of your work. If you have a good idea, consider it carefully, then present it to your superiors.

67. **The correct answer is (D).** Public relations is important, and a little tact can work wonders. You can be polite and noncommittal and satisfy the complainant.

68. **The correct answer is (D).** Obviously, the police emergency telephone lines must be kept open to receive emergency calls. Further, the less time spent talking, the sooner there will be action.

69. **The correct answer is (C).** The police role is to perform police work. The Police Officer is not a lawyer and is not expected to understand the fine points of preparation of legal documents. An Assistant District Attorney is equipped to give proper legal advice.

70. **The correct answer is (A).** An introductory statement describing the occurrence establishes the framework on which to hang details and conclusions.

71. **The correct answer is (D).** Both common sense and proper police practice require that a Police Officer's post be covered at all times. In answering questions on a civil service exam, personal gain is *never* the correct answer.

72. **The correct answer is (A).** A Police Officer must adhere to rules and regulations and so cannot provide a prohibited service. On the other hand, it is easy to be polite and caring. Explain to the manager the reason for your refusal.

73. **The correct answer is (C).** The police badge is an identifying emblem. The Police Officer who serves as a witness must be identified as such.

74. **The correct answer is (C).** It is important not to dismiss cases of animal abuse because many individuals who abuse animals later begin to abuse people. According to Frank R. Ascione in the September 2001 issue of the *OJJDP Juvenile Justice Bulletin*, "studies suggest that animal abuse may be characteristic of the developmental histories of between one in four and nearly two in three violent adult offenders."

75. **The correct answer is (C).** Your supervisor certainly would not appreciate dishonesty, a lack of an explanation or dilly-dallying! Therefore, the best way to deal with this situation would be to let your supervisor know about the situation as soon as possible so that he/she can be prepared for any situations and difficulties that may arise due to your tardiness.

76. **The correct answer is (A).** Two conflicting orders cannot remain in effect at the same time. If a new order is issued and conflicts with a previously issued order, the previous order is thereby rescinded.

77. **The correct answer is (D).** Speaking to your supervisor would be the best way of dealing with this situation because your supervisor may be able to intervene and solve the conflict. Ignoring your aggressive coworker did not work in the past and probably won't solve the problem now. Changing shifts may not be to the department's benefit or to yours. And involving your fellow coworkers will probably only spread the conflict to other individuals. Your supervisor, on the other hand, may hold enough power and status to persuade your coworker to live and let live.

78. **The correct answer is (B).** Pure common sense. Overcrowding leads to friction. Furthermore, convicts in constant close proximity have more opportunity to plan trouble together.

79. **The correct answer is (C).** A Police Officer must never bow to political pressure nor give the appearance of doing so. The officer must politely but firmly insist upon obedience to the law.

80. **The correct answer is (C).** Officer Reist appears to be under some stress, and although it is unusual for him to behave in an unprofessional or rude manner, his discussion with the woman may soon get out of hand. To ignore the situation means that the conflict may escalate; to confront Officer Reist immediately may only make him angrier; to speak to his supervisor may get him in trouble when he's probably only having a bad day. Therefore, the best strategy to try first would be to intervene in the discussion to calm both parties down.

81. **The correct answer is (A).** As before, you are still a police officer even when you are off-duty. It is your responsibility to help this woman to the best of your ability and ensure that she receives further attention if needed by calling the paramedics or other emergency personnel. It would not be good for department-community relations if you were to help the woman half-heartedly or not at all. (It would probably only take a few minutes of your time, anyway).

82. **The correct answer is (C).** Since there is not much danger of traffic accidents caused by the malfunctioning light at this hour, report the matter immediately to allow maximum opportunity for the light's repair before morning traffic. Then post a temporary sign to alert traffic until the light is repaired. If the light cannot be repaired in time, your prompt report to the precinct allows time for a special officer to be assigned to direct traffic in the morning.

83. **The correct answer is (B).** To keep the family peace and to encourage your nephew to stop his drug use, the best answer in this situation is most likely (B). To refuse to become involved would be shirking your responsibility as a law enforcement officer and a caring uncle. To order the boy to simply dispose of the illegal materials will probably not deter him from using them in the future. And to get the local police involved will probably only cause resentment within your family and also probably not deter the boy from using drugs in the future. In this situation, a gentle talk with your nephew about the personal and legal consequences of his actions may be most effective.

84. **The correct answer is (A).** You do not need to have had training in investigation of traffic accidents to recognize from the diagram that car 2 is too far beyond the center of the intersection to have been attempting a left turn. Driver 1 is trying to cover himself with a false statement about driver 2.

85. **The correct answer is (C).** You have a radio. Use it. The alleged robbers should be pursued promptly and safely.

86. **The correct answer is (D).** The vast majority of people wish to be law-abiding citizens. A summons must be issued for a major offense, even if it is a first offense, but a courteous warning may be sufficient for a minor offense that the operator may not even have recognized as an offense.

87. **The correct answer is (B).** The Police Officer directing traffic at a congested intersection must be visible, must use simply understood signals, and must consistently use the same signals. It is *least* important that the officer be physically accessible to motorists or to pedestrians.

88. **The correct answer is (C).** Access to the area of an accident should be limited to those who are attending to the injured. Beyond lifesaving, the first priority is to preserve evidence. Inconvenience to the public is a later consideration.

89. **The correct answer is (C).** The police role at the scene of a property-damage accident is to be certain that both drivers are licensed drivers and are authorized to drive the vehicles, that the automobiles are safe to operate on the public roadway, and that information has been obtained for police files as to those involved in the accident and witnesses. It is not the role of the Police Officer to be concerned with the parties' arrangements to collect damages from one another.

90. **The correct answer is (A).** A hit-and-run driver must be pursued and apprehended as quickly as possible. The efficient way to intercept the hit-and-run car is to radio a description of the car to precinct headquarters for instant broadcast to patrol cars in the vicinity.

91. **The correct answer is (D).** The accepted answer is that eradication of the cause of crime should be the most effective means of crime prevention.

92. **The correct answer is (C).** Under no circumstances should Officer Consuelo violate the department policy and accept the gift, especially in an underhanded way, as in choice (D). Is a free cup of coffee worth that kind of trouble? Besides, were the police to regularly accept gifts and perks from the community, these extra benefits could unduly influence the way police enforce the law. Rather than offending the insistent coffee shop owner with a stern rebuke, as in choice (B), the best option in this situation would be to turn in the gift certificate to her supervisor.

93. **The correct answer is (C).** The person with an unconscious wish to be punished, also known as a "death wish," will draw attention to him- or herself with respect to the crime. Revisiting the crime scene is a common means of doing this. The other choices represent efforts to avoid detection and punishment.

94. **The correct answer is (A).** Read carefully. *The least accurate* format of the question makes it tricky to answer. Choices (B), (C), and (D) make correct, positive statements. Choice (A) makes a wrong statement. The value of fingerprints left at the scene of the crime *does* vary with the distinctness of the fingerprint impressions. Clearer fingerprints are more valuable.

95. **The correct answer is (A).** In general, the fewer people who handle a piece of evidence, the fewer things can go wrong. Personal delivery of the evidence makes for less hearsay. Choice (C) is incorrect because of the strong word "ensures." Evidence can be mismarked even with personal delivery and initially correct information.

96. **The correct answer is (B).** The description that focuses on the unique character of a missing item is most useful for search and recovery.

97. **The correct answer is (D).** Choices (B) and (C) are of no use whatsoever. Watching people leave a ball game, you have no way of knowing who is missing a toe nor who has false teeth. Choice (A) describes a very typical girl. Choice (D) is a big man who stands out in a crowd, and his pockmarked face is further visible identification.

98. **The correct answer is (C).** Common sense. How many 6'1" women do you see roaming the streets?

99. **The correct answer is (B).** The best way to handle this situation is neither to assume the men's guilt or innocence without first verifying their story with the owner of the trailer park.

100. **The correct answer is (A).** A 5'3" man weighing 200 lbs. is obese and very short. He should be relatively easy to spot if you are alerted to watch for him. All these identification judgment questions are meant to test your judgment as to what you would report if other officers needed to search on the basis of your descriptions.

101. **The correct answer is (D).** A Social Security card is not acceptable proof of identification for any purpose because it does not identify. The Social Security card contains no picture and no descriptive text of any sort.

102. **The correct answer is (B).** One picture may be worth a thousand words, but a good look at the person in the flesh leads to greater ease and accuracy of identification than does studying photographs.

103. **The correct answer is (C).** On a busy highway, tire size and spare would be impossible to determine. Make of car is also difficult to screen quickly. Color is obvious, and many cars are not black.

104. **The correct answer is (D).** The key is that the woman is sick or injured and needs medical attention. The first step is to get her to the hospital. Identification is secondary.

105. **The correct answer is (D).** Surgery would be most successful. Few criminals resort to surgery to avoid identification because of the time and pain involved and the need to find a competent person to perform the operation confidentially.

106. **The correct answer is (A).** Identification from a lineup is more reliable. The witness cannot simply say "yes" or "no."

107. **The correct answer is (C).** Citizens have rights that may not be abridged unless they commit some infraction. Suspicious actions are no grounds for arrest, alarm, or embarrassment of the person. The Police Officer who considers behavior suspicious is, in effect, facing an unusual situation on the post. Continued observation is called for.

108. **The correct answer is (A).** An open handbag is a danger to the woman's property. By all means bring the open handbag to the woman's attention.

109. **The correct answer is (C).** You want the personal recollection of each individual witness, not the consensus of a committee.

110. **The correct answer is (B).** Questions should be of the open sort, such as, "Was the mugger wearing an outer garment?" Giving an either-or choice limits the answer and may miss important descriptive information.

111. **The correct answer is (C).** The speed at which an automobile was traveling when it hit a victim may affect the extent of damage to the vehicle, but it is the *least* valuable information from among the choices. The direction in which the automobile fled can direct the chase; the number of occupants helps with identification; the part of the automobile that struck the victim may be distinctively damaged.

112. **The correct answer is (C).** Markings on a bullet left by a gun barrel serve the same purpose as fingerprints. Since barrel markings are unique, they effectively identify the gun from which the bullet was fired.

113. **The correct answer is (B).** Common sense. Read the newspapers for confirmation.

114. **The correct answer is (B).** You need proper depth vision to shoot accurately. Depth vision is achieved with both eyes open.

115. **The correct answer is (D).** A person who is in the physical process of committing a crime is fully aware of that fact. When arresting such a person, it is unnecessary to tell the person that he or she is being arrested because he or she is in the process of committing a crime.

116. **The correct answer is (B).** The woman's intact, scarless face must certainly lead the Police Officer to question her story. The correct answer choice is generous in giving the benefit of some credence to the woman. The situation bears investigation for the sake of the woman who might likely require psychiatric attention.

117. **The correct answer is (C).** Our Constitution protects the rights of the individual. A Police Officer must learn to recognize reasonable basis for arrest so as to protect the rights of the innocent while taking into custody those who, on the basis of evidence, appear to be guilty.

118. **The correct answer is (A).** Professionalism requires that a Police Officer not allow personal prejudices nor emotions to interfere with the manner in which he or she performs duties. In giving the reason for arrest, the officer must state the facts without commentary.

119. **The correct answer is (C).** Much of the work of a Police Officer falls into the realm of public relations. The officer must be patient and tactful in explaining action or inaction on the specific complaint.

120. **The correct answer is (B).** The civil rights of the innocent citizen must be protected. The possibility of personal embarrassment or embarrassment of the police force are not the paramount considerations.

121. **The correct answer is (C).** The number-one priority is the safety of the general public.

122. **The correct answer is (A).** This is not an attitude question; it is an action question. Situations vary greatly. Procedures differ on the basis of circumstances such as: Is the suspect armed? Is the suspect injured and in need of immediate medical attention? Is the suspect in the midst of a crowd? Does the suspect hold hostages? Is the suspect at home in bed?

123. **The correct answer is (D).** Do not read extra meaning into a straightforward question. The young man was acting suspiciously, and the officer correctly investigated his suspicious behavior. The fact that the man had indeed committed a crime confirms that investigation of suspicious incidents is worthwhile and may produce results.

124. **The correct answer is (A).** Where a Police Officer is positive of his or her identification and where immediate arrest threatens no danger, he or she should inform the suspect of the reason for the arrest and should take the suspect into custody.

125. **The correct answer is (A).** Once again, professionalism is the key to the answer. The Police Officer must not let any personal feelings intrude upon performance of duties.

126. **The correct answer is (A).** The ultimate purpose of a raid upon premises, with legal search warrant already in hand, is to secure evidence that leads to the apprehension of criminals or to apprehend the criminals themselves.

127. **The correct answer is (B).** Eliminate choice (A). The burglars know there is nothing more to steal in that house. Eliminate choice (C). Burglars tend to hit houses that look as if the takings would be more worthwhile. Eliminate choice (D). This house is never unoccupied so would be difficult to burglarize. Chances are that the party that calls the house in choice (B) and hangs up when the phone is answered is waiting for a time when the phone is not answered and the house is presumably unattended as an opportunity to burglarize.

128. **The correct answer is (B).** The Police Officer must continue to observe the girl but cannot apprehend her until she signals intent to steal the merchandise by leaving the store without paying. Merely carrying merchandise around in the store is not a prohibited activity.

129. **The correct answer is (C).** You must not jump to conclusions. The fact that Jones was present at the time and place of the assault does not mean that he actually committed the assault. On the other hand, the possibility cannot be ruled out, since he was there. If it had been proven that Jones had been elsewhere at the time of the assault, then it could have been positively stated that Jones did not assault Smith.

130. **The correct answer is (D).** From this fact statement, we know only that the lawyer was attacked from behind in a washroom by a male who had access to the washroom and to a carpenter's mallet. No conclusions can be drawn.

131. **The correct answer is (A).** The officer's immediate sending for an ambulance is correct. However, once the injured is medically cared for, the officer's next responsibility is to learn what happened. Among the bystanders, a witness or several witnesses may be able to describe the circumstances of the stabbing and possibly to identify or at least to describe the assailant.

132. **The correct answer is (B).** Green must prove that he did not steal the radio. One-and-one-half hours is ample time to fence a radio, so nonpossession is not automatic proof of innocence.

133. **The correct answer is (A).** Note that the question merely suggests the given facts as a basis for first action, not that Jones should be assumed guilty. Much police investigative work is based upon reasonable assumptions.

134. **The correct answer is (D).** The length of time that the resident waited before reporting the theft of the ring is totally irrelevant. All the other questions are valid ones.

135. **The correct answer is (D).** If burglary was physically impossible at this site and time, then, from among the choices, we must assume that the crime of burglary did not occur and that the report is a false one. Beyond the scope of the question, an investigator might reasonably suspect an internal theft with the claim of burglary as coverup.

136. **The correct answer is (D).** Since the question has to do with protection of property, the Police Officer is within the scope of the police role to make a suggestion. The suggestion, without reference to a specific bank or payroll service, is entirely proper.

137. **The correct answer is (A).** The thief who is already inside the premises to be burglarized avoids the risk of attracting attention by the act of forcing entrance.

138. **The correct answer is (C).** Thieves are likely to be careful with items of value but to pay less attention to articles they consider worthless. This carelessness combined with care taken by Police Officers can lead to apprehension of the thieves.

139. **The correct answer is (A).** Immediate confrontation will ascertain that the watch was indeed taken from the given jewelry store. If, by chance, the man was authorized to take the watch (if, for example it had been repaired for him), then the matter will be readily clarified. If the Police Officer has indeed observed the man in the process of stealing the watch, this prompt action will make for a neat case.

140. **The correct answer is (B).** A Police Officer must investigate unusual occurrences. The sound of clashing tools at 2 a.m. is certainly worth investigating, especially in an apartment next door to one in which there had just been a burglary.

141. **The correct answer is (D).** You can't catch the robbers yourself; they have already gone too far. On the other hand, you must not allow them to exit the parkway while you are questioning the victim. Radio to have the exits monitored. A limited-access parkway offers possibilities for interception of thieves that are absent on city streets.

142. **The correct answer is (D).** The only immediate assumption is that the murderer had access to shoemaker's tools. This is a useful piece of knowledge. If no shoe repair shop has reported a theft, the field of suspects can be reasonably narrowed.

143. **The correct answer is (C).** Common sense. For the knife to be protruding from his back, the man is unlikely to be lying on his back.

144. **The correct answer is (A).** Read carefully. The question describes a suicide, thereby eliminating choices (C) and (D). A body slumped in a chair is not consistent with hanging.

145. **The correct answer is (B).** The man is dead; there is nothing you can do for him now. On the other hand, there is a body on the ground. Phone your precinct at once. Investigation of circumstances of death will follow.

146. **The correct answer is (A).** The pawn tickets serve as a very good clue. A man in the fur business should sell furs, not pawn them. Obviously, this man was in deep financial trouble. The lapsed insurance policy is further indication of desperation. No businessman willingly allows insurance of property or self (the question does not specify which) to lapse.

147. **The correct answer is (B).** The blood on the door bears investigation. It was likely left by the murderer upon exit.

148. **The correct answer is (D).** Unfortunately, observation is often incomplete and memory may fill in the gaps or even distort the facts.

149. **The correct answer is (A).** The first question to be raised is the amount of time taken to travel from Jones' place of work to his home. If it is determined that it does indeed take longer than one half hour, then Jones must supply proof that he really was working at 8 p.m. If the distance can be covered in less than a half hour, whether or not Jones was really working at 8 p.m. is irrelevant.

150. **The correct answer is (A).** This is an unusual situation that bears investigation. Admission to a private mental hospital is not an emergency situation, especially since the alleged patient will be under observation at the station house, so by all means bring the whole party in for questioning.

151. **The correct answer is (C).** With these facts, the only certainty is that further investigation is warranted on an urgent basis.

152. **The correct answer is (C).** Bad environmental conditions—poverty, poor housing, lack of opportunity, immoral companions—combine to create criminals.

153. **The correct answer is (D).** It is generally assumed that the best deterrent to crime is the expectation that one will be caught and swiftly punished.

154. **The correct answer is (C).** A person who is normal in intelligence but is below grade level in school is educationally maladjusted. The fact that 86 percent of delinquents appear to be normally intelligent but below grade level points to a close association of educational maladjustment with delinquency. With this information, we can describe a correlation but not a causal relationship. The data do not indicate that educational maladjustment causes delinquency nor that delinquency leads to educational maladjustment, only that they are related.

155. **The correct answer is (B).** Unfortunately, the boys who might be most helped by boys' clubs do not join.

156. **The correct answer is (C).** A man who has responded to a prostitute is unlikely to cooperate with the police, but a man who has spurned her advances will probably answer your questions. Both the girl and one or two men should be questioned, for the girl will undoubtedly deny that she is soliciting. Indeed, it may be that she is not, and, if Police Officers approach her, she may ask for needed instructions or assistance. You must not assume guilt without first investigating.

157. **The correct answer is (B).** The expectation and hope is that minors are not incorrigible; that is, their behavior can be corrected and improved. If this can be accomplished without arrest, so much the better.

158. **The correct answer is (C).** The most important information when seeking a hit-and-run vehicle is the appearance of the car. Of the choices, "What kind of car was it?" is by far the most useful.

159. **The correct answer is (C).** One of the last things a runaway is likely to do is to enroll in a school. Therefore, knowledge of her scholastic abilities would not be very helpful in the search for the girl. Detailed description of her features would be most helpful.

160. **The correct answer is (C).** The label of the well-known manufacturer is found in many violins. It does not distinguish this violin from many other violins. All the other choices would help in making a positive identification.

161. **The correct answer is (D).** This is a probe of your prejudices. Looks tell nothing about intelligence, personality, or character.

162. **The correct answer is (B).** For the deceased to have committed suicide with the bullet lodged as indicated, the shot would have had to come from a revolver in his left hand. The revolver is in his right hand.

163.   **The correct answer is (D).** It is most unlikely that a lighted delicatessen is left unattended late at night. The officer should confirm suspicions further by entering the delicatessen to search for foul play with reference to the proprietor or employees.

164.   **The correct answer is (A).** Loitering just before theater deposits are about to be made could be either a coincidence or a plan for robbery. People do loiter around theaters waiting for others or just passing the time away. You must be prepared, but you can take no action unless some crime is committed. The best action is to keep the men under observation until the money has been safely deposited.

165.   **The correct answer is (A).** This is unintelligent handling of evidence. Fingerprints and ballistics evidence may be destroyed. It would be wise to close off the booth to the public so as to safeguard possible clues such as match covers, bits of paper with notes on them, and fingerprints on drinking glasses.

166.   **The correct answer is (B).** Comparison of engine numbers is usually the determining factor in establishing whether or not a car is indeed the stolen one in question. Engine numbers are changed only with great difficulty; it is most unlikely that this would be accomplished in one day. This 1978 Dodge is probably not the car that was reported stolen. License plates and tires are easily changed and cannot serve as positive identification of stolen cars. A stolen car can easily acquire a cracked windshield.

167.   **The correct answer is (C).** Statistical studies show that crimes against property reach a maximum in winter months when human needs are greatest. During winter months, crimes such as larceny, burglary, and robbery show a decided increase for the further reason that longer periods of darkness reduce probability of detection. Crimes against persons and morals (assaults, rapes, homicides, etc.) show an increase during the warm months when the contacts between persons are more frequent.

168.   **The correct answer is (A).** The very subject matter of the blackmail is precisely the reason the victim is unlikely to cooperate with the police. The victim of a blackmail plot usually has some secret that he or she does not wish to reveal to the public by way of the police. It may concern some event, scandalous or otherwise, that occurred in the past and that if revealed may hold him or her up to public ridicule. Because of this, victims are reluctant to cooperate with the police in the prosecution of blackmailers.

169. **The correct answer is (D).** This is a situation in which individual interests must be subverted for the common good. The individual family wants its kidnapped member back at any price. However, allowing kidnappers to profit from kidnapping encourages other kidnappers. The principle is the same as the principle of not negotiating with terrorists. Wrongdoers must not achieve their goals through their wrongdoing. Hopefully, prospective kidnappers who know that they will fail in their attempt to collect ransom will be discouraged from kidnapping.

170. **The correct answer is (A).** As strange as it may seem, intent to defraud the insurer may not always be manifested by increasing insurance just before the commission of the crime. There have been many instances in which the insurance was deliberately reduced in order to divert suspicion.

CHAPTER 6: READING-BASED QUESTIONS

Test-Taking Strategies for Reading-Based Questions

A recent survey of Police Officer examinations given nationwide indicates that there is wide variation in the subject matter of these exams. The single topic that is common to all exams is reading. Some exams include classic reading comprehension questions that present a passage and then ask questions on the details of the passage and, perhaps, on its meaning. Other exams require candidates to indicate proper behavior based on their reading of printed procedures and regulations. Still another type of reading-based question requires candidates to reason and choose next steps on the basis of information presented in a reading passage. There are, of course, nearly as many variations of the reading-based question as there are test makers. In fact, reading skill enters into form-completion questions, arithmetic problems based on fact situations, and police judgment questions as well.

Before you begin to devote attention to strategies for dealing with reading-based questions, give some thought to your reading habits and skills. Of course, you already know how to read. But how well do you read? Do you concentrate? Do you get the point on your first reading? Do you notice details?

Between now and the test day, you must work to improve your reading concentration and comprehension. Your daily newspaper provides excellent material to improve your reading. Try the following routine when you read the newspaper. As you repeat this process day after day, you will find that your reading will become more efficient. You will read with greater understanding, and will get more from your newspaper.

- Make a point of reading all the way through any article that you begin. Do not be satisfied with the first paragraph or two.
- Read with a pencil in hand. Underscore details and ideas that seem to be crucial to the meaning of the article.
- Notice points of view, arguments, and supporting information.
- When you have finished the article, summarize it for yourself. Do you know the purpose of the article? The main idea presented? The attitude of the writer? The points over which there is controversy? Did you find certain information lacking?
- As you answer the questions above, skim back over your underlinings. Did you focus on important words and ideas? Did you read with comprehension?

One aspect of your daily reading that deserves special attention is vocabulary building. The effective reader has a rich, extensive vocabulary. As you read, make a list of unfamiliar words. Include in your list words that you understand within the context of the article, but that you cannot really define. In addition, mark words that you do not understand at all. When you put aside your newspaper, go to the dictionary and look up *every* new and unfamiliar word. Write the word and its definition in a special notebook. Writing the words and their definitions helps seal them in your memory far better than just reading them, and the notebook serves as a handy reference for your own use. A sensitivity to the meanings of words and an understanding of more words will make reading easier and more enjoyable even if none of the words you learn in this way crops up on your exam. In fact, the habit of vocabulary building is a good lifetime habit to develop.

Success with reading questions depends on more than reading comprehension. You must also know how to draw the answers from the reading selection, and be able to distinguish the *best* answer from a number of answers that all seem to be good ones, or from a number of answers that all seem to be wrong.

CHOOSING THE RIGHT ANSWER

Strange as it may seem, it's a good idea to approach reading comprehension questions by reading the questions-not the answer choices, just the questions themselves—before you read the selection. The questions will alert you to look for certain details, ideas, and points of view. Use your pencil. Underscore key words in the questions. These will help direct your attention as you read.

Next, skim the selection very rapidly to get an idea of its subject matter and its organization. If key words or ideas pop out at you, underline them, but do not consciously search out details in the preliminary skimming.

Now read the selection carefully with comprehension as your main goal. Underscore the important words as you have been doing in your newspaper reading.

Finally, return to the questions. Read each question carefully. Be sure you know what it asks. Misreading of questions is a major cause of error on reading comprehension tests. Read *all* the answer choices. Eliminate the obviously incorrect answers. You may be left with only one possible answer. If you find yourself with more than one possible answer, reread the question. Then skim the passage once more, focusing on the underlined segments. By now you should be able to conclude which answer is *best*.

QUESTION FORMATS

Reading-based questions may take a number of different forms. In general, five of the most common forms are as follows:

1. **Question of fact or detail.** You may have to mentally rephrase or rearrange, but you should find the answer stated in the body of the selection.
2. **Best title or main idea.** The answer may be obvious, but the incorrect choices to the "main idea" question are often half-truths that are easily confused with the main idea. They may misstate the idea, omit part of the idea, or even offer a supporting idea quoted directly from the text. The correct answer is the one that covers the largest part of the selection.

3. **Interpretation.** This type of question asks you what the selection means, not just what it says. On police exams, the questions based upon definitions of crimes, for example, fall into this category.

4. **Inference.** This is the most difficult type of reading comprehension question. It asks you to go beyond what the selection says, and to predict what might happen next. You might have to choose the best course of action to take, based upon given procedures and a fact situation, or you may have to judge the actions of others. Your answer must be based upon the information in the selection and your own common sense, but not upon any other information you may have about the subject. A variation of the interference question might be stated as, "The author would expect that. . . ." To answer this question, you must understand the author's point of view, and then make an inference from that viewpoint based upon the information in the selection.

5. **Vocabulary.** Some police reading sections, directly or indirectly, ask the meanings of certain words as used in the selection.

Sample Questions

Let's now work together on some typical reading comprehension selections and questions.

SELECTION FOR QUESTIONS 1 TO 4

Relief printing is the oldest method of printmaking. Traditionally, relief printing has involved cutting away portions of the surface of a wood block so that the desired image remains as a printing surface. Artists typically prefer to use soft woods such as pine when creating the print because harder woods are more difficult to carve. The artist begins by painting or drawing the image on the surface of the wood block. The wood is then cut away between the drawn lines so that only the drawn image is left standing on the surface of the block. The carved surface must then be hardened by treating it with shellac so that the block can withstand the pressure of a press.

Once the printing block has been prepared, it may be used to make any number of prints. The block is first inked by rolling an ink-covered roller completely over the surface of the block. The block and a highly absorbent paper such as rice paper may then be run through a press. The pressure of the press transfers the image to the paper. The print is then pulled by carefully lifting a corner of the paper and peeling it off the printing block. If a color print is desired, separate blocks are used, with one block for each color.

1. The best title for the preceding paragraph is
   (A) "How to Use an Ink-Covered Roller."
   (B) "The Best Type of Wood for Carving."
   (C) "The Process of Relief Printing."
   (D) "How to Create a Wood Carving."

1. Ⓐ Ⓑ Ⓒ Ⓓ

2. According to the preceding paragraph, pine wood is used because   2. Ⓐ Ⓑ Ⓒ Ⓓ
    (A) harder woods are more difficult to carve.
    (B) pine is a highly absorbent type of wood.
    (C) pine is easily peeled off the printing block.
    (D) it can be used for only one print.

3. According to the preceding paragraph, what is the purpose of the   3. Ⓐ Ⓑ Ⓒ Ⓓ
    shellac?
    (A) It makes the drawings permanent.
    (B) It makes the wood more absorbent.
    (C) It makes the color stand out.
    (D) It makes the carved surface stronger.

4. For color prints, each color is applied   4. Ⓐ Ⓑ Ⓒ Ⓓ
    (A) to the corner of the paper.
    (B) to a separate printing block.
    (C) to the same printing block.
    (D) to a separate sheet of paper.

Begin by skimming the questions and underscoring key words. Your underscored questions should look more or less like this:

1. The <u>best title</u> for the preceding paragraph is
2. According to the preceding paragraph, <u>pine wood</u> is used because
3. According to the preceding paragraph, what is the purpose of the <u>shellac</u>?
4. For <u>color prints</u>, each color is applied

Now skim the selection. This quick reading should give you an idea of the structure of the selection and of its overall meaning.

Next read the selection carefully and underscore words that seem important or that you think hold keys to the question answers. Your underscored selection should look something like this:

<u>Relief printing</u> is the oldest method of printmaking. Traditionally, <u>relief printing</u> has involved cutting away portions of the surface of a wood block so that the desired image remains as a printing surface. Artists typically <u>prefer to use soft woods such as pine</u> when creating the print <u>because harder woods are more difficult to carve</u>. The artist begins by painting or drawing the image on the surface of the wood block. The wood is then cut away between the drawn lines so that only the drawn image is left standing on the surface of the block. The <u>carved surface</u> must then be <u>hardened by treating it with shellac</u> so that the <u>block can withstand the pressure of a press</u>.

     Once the printing block has been prepared, it may be used to make any number of prints. The block is first inked by rolling an ink-covered roller completely over the surface of the block. The block and a highly absorbent paper such as rice paper may then be run through a press. The pressure of the press transfers the image to the paper. The print is then pulled by carefully lifting a corner of the paper and peeling it off the printing block. If a color print is desired, separate blocks are used, with one block for each color.

Finally, read the questions and answer choices, and try to choose the correct answer for each question.

The correct answers are: 1. **(C)**, 2. **(A)**, 3. **(D)**, 4. **(B)**. Did you get them all right? Whether you made any errors or not, read these explanations.

1. **The correct answer is (C).** The best title for any selection is the one that takes in all of the ideas presented without being too broad or too narrow. Choice (C) provides the most inclusive title for this passage. A look at the other choices shows you why. The first sentence of the second paragraph briefly describes how to use an ink-covered roller to make a print. However, the rest of the selection does not discuss this particular aspect of the printing process, so choice (A) can be eliminated. The first paragraph briefly mentions that artists prefer to use pine, but the rest of the selection clearly indicates that this is not the main idea of the selection, so choice (B) can be eliminated. The selection does mention that the print is created with a wood carving, but this is not the main focus of the selection, so choice (D) can also be eliminated.

2. **The correct answer is (A).** The first paragraph states that artists prefer to use soft woods such as pine because harder woods are more difficult to carve, so choice (A) is the best answer. The second paragraph states that a highly absorbent paper is desirable, but says nothing about how absorbent pine wood is, so choice (B) can be eliminated. The second paragraph discusses peeling the paper, not pine wood, from the printing block, so choice (C) can be eliminated. The first sentence of the second paragraph states that a printing block may be used to make any number of prints, so choice (D) can also be eliminated.

3. **The correct answer is (D).** The last sentence of the first paragraph states that the carved surface must be hardened by treating it with shellac so the block can withstand the pressure of a press, so choice (D) is the best answer. This sentence is the only one in the selection that mentions treating the carved surface with shellac, so all other choices can be eliminated.

4. **The correct answer is (B).** The last sentence of the selection states that if a color print is desired, separate blocks are used, with one block for each color. Therefore, choice (B) is the best answer. This sentence is the only one in the selection that mentions color prints, so all other choices can be eliminated.

SELECTION FOR QUESTIONS 5 TO 9

Instructions and Indications for Taking Medication XYZ

WHEN YOU SHOULD NOT TAKE THIS MEDICATION:

Do not take medication XYZ if you have had an allergic reaction to it. Do not take this medication in any form on an empty stomach.

HOW TO TAKE AND STORE THIS MEDICATION:

Your doctor's prescription will tell you how much to take and how often. Keep this and all medication out of the reach of children.

XYZ Liquid:
- Take with food.
- Shake well before using.
- Carefully measure the dose using a dropper, marked measuring spoon, or medicine cup.
- Store at room temperature, away from heat, light, and moisture. Do not freeze.

XYZ Tablets/Capsules:
- Take with food and a glass of water.
- Store at room temperature, away from heat, light, and moisture.

XYZ Chewable Tablets:
- Take with food and a glass of water.
- Chew or crush tablet before swallowing.
- Store at room temperature, away from heat, light, and moisture.

5. It is most accurate to state that the author in the preceding selection presents

    5. Ⓐ Ⓑ Ⓒ Ⓓ

    (A) facts, but reaches no conclusion concerning the value of the medication.
    (B) a conclusion concerning the value of the medication unsupported by facts.
    (C) neither facts nor conclusions, but merely describes reasons for taking the medication.
    (D) a conclusion concerning the value of the medication and facts to support that conclusion.

6. Which of the following would NOT be an acceptable place to store   6.   Ⓐ Ⓑ Ⓒ Ⓓ
   XYZ Liquid medication?
   (A) At room temperature in a dark and dry cupboard
   (B) In a dark and dry freezer
   (C) In a dark and dry medicine cabinet at room temperature
   (D) At room temperature on a dark and dry shelf

7. Which form of XYZ medication requires that it be chewed or   7.   Ⓐ Ⓑ Ⓒ Ⓓ
   crushed before swallowing?
   (A) XYZ Liquid
   (B) XYZ Tablets
   (C) XYZ Capsules
   (D) XYZ Chewable Tablets

8. Who should NOT take XYZ medication?   8.   Ⓐ Ⓑ Ⓒ Ⓓ
   (A) Someone who has recently eaten a large meal
   (B) Someone who has had an allergic reaction to it
   (C) Someone who has just had a glass of water
   (D) Someone who has a doctor's prescription for it

9. Which form of XYZ medication allows it to be measured with a   9.   Ⓐ Ⓑ Ⓒ Ⓓ
   medicine cup?
   (A) XYZ Liquid
   (B) XYZ Tablets
   (C) XYZ Capsules
   (D) XYZ Chewable Tablets

Skim the questions and underscore the words that you consider to be key. The questions should look something like this:

5. It is most accurate to state that the author in the preceding selection <u>presents</u>

6. Which of the following would <u>NOT</u> be an <u>acceptable place to store</u> XYZ Liquid medication?

7. Which <u>form of XYZ</u> medication requires that it be <u>chewed or crushed</u> before swallowing?

8. Who should <u>NOT take XYZ</u> medication?

9. Which <u>form of XYZ</u> medication allows it to be measured with a <u>medicine cup</u>?

Skim the reading selection. Get an idea of the subject matter of the selection and of how it is organized.

Now read the selection carefully and underscore the words that you think are especially important. This fact-filled selection might be underlined like this:

Instructions and Indications for Taking Medication XYZ

WHEN YOU SHOULD NOT TAKE THIS MEDICATION:

<u>Do not take</u> medication XYZ if you have had an <u>allergic reaction</u> to it. <u>Do not take</u> this medication in any form <u>on an empty stomach</u>.

HOW TO TAKE AND STORE THIS MEDICATION:

Your doctor's prescription will tell you <u>how much</u> to take and <u>how often</u>. Keep this and all medication out of the reach of children.

XYZ Liquid:

- Take <u>with food</u>.
- <u>Shake well</u> before using.
- Carefully <u>measure</u> the dose using a <u>dropper, marked measuring spoon or medicine cup</u>.
- Store at room temperature, away from heat, light, and moisture. Do not freeze.

XYZ Tablets/Capsules:

- Take with food and a glass of water.
- Store at room temperature, away from heat, light, and moisture.

Chewable tablets:

- Take with food and a glass of water.
- Chew or crush tablet before swallowing.
- Store at room temperature, away from heat, light, and moisture.

Now read each question and all its answer choices, and try to choose the correct answer for each question.

The correct answers are: 5. **(A)**, 6. **(B)**, 7. **(D)**, 8. **(B)**, 9. **(A)**. How did you do on these? Read the explanations.

5. **The correct answer is (A).** This is a combination main idea and interpretation question. If you cannot answer this question readily, reread the selection. The author of this section sticks to the facts concerning medication XYZ but does not discuss the value of this particular medication.

6. **The correct answer is (B).** The last point listed under XYZ Liquid storage instructions states that when the medication is in liquid form it should not be frozen. Choice (B) is therefore the correct answer.

7. **The correct answer is (D).** The second point listed under the instructions for XYZ Chewable Tablets states that when the medication is in this form it should be chewed or crushed before swallowing. Choice (D) is therefore the correct answer.

8. **The correct answer is (B).** The first section of the instructions for taking medication XYZ states that anyone who has had an allergic reaction to this medication should not take it. Choice (**B**) is therefore the correct answer.

9. **The correct answer is (A).** The third point listed under the instructions for XYZ Liquid states that when the medication is in liquid form it may be measured with a medicine cup. This is the only form of the medication that allows it to be measured in this manner. Choice (A) is therefore the correct answer.

You should be getting better at reading and at answering questions. Try this next selection on your own. Read and underline the questions. Skim the selection. Read and underline the selection. Read the questions and answer choices and mark your answers. Then check your answers against the answers and explanations that follow the selection.

SELECTION FOR QUESTIONS 10 TO 12

Students learning to read and write need to begin by developing a functional command of what is commonly called phonics. Students should start by gaining an understanding of the alphabetic principle, or the relationship between letter patterns and sound patterns in English. The next step is to internalize relationships between letter and sound patterns. Eventually the students will develop phonemic awareness, or an awareness of the "separate" sounds in words. Despite the importance of gaining a basic understanding of phonics, it is important that students learn these principles in some literary context rather than as separate rules of language. Research has shown that teaching children the concept of phonics in the context of reading and writing is more effective than teaching strictly through phonics exercises.

10. According to the preceding paragraph, the alphabetic principle involves the relationship between   10. Ⓐ Ⓑ Ⓒ Ⓓ
    (A) phonics and language.
    (B) phonics and "separate" sounds.
    (C) letter and sound patterns.
    (D) context and rules of language.

11. In the preceding paragraph, the author is primarily concerned with   11. Ⓐ Ⓑ Ⓒ Ⓓ
    (A) the importance of the alphabetic principle.
    (B) how to use language exercises.
    (C) the importance of understanding phonics.
    (D) internalizing the alphabetic principle.

12. According to the preceding paragraph, the concept of phonics should be taught   **12.**   Ⓐ Ⓑ Ⓒ Ⓓ
   (A) in the context of reading and writing.
   (B) before the alphabetic principle.
   (C) strictly through phonics exercises.
   (D) as separate rules of language.

The correct answers are: 10. **(C)**, 11. **(C)**, 12. **(A)**.

10. **The correct answer is (C).** The second sentence states that the alphabetic principle involves the relationship between letter patterns and sound patterns. Choice (C) is therefore the correct answer.

11. **The correct answer is (C).** The purpose of this selection should be clear as you read through the paragraph. If you were unsure of the answer, you can easily work backwards by eliminating the wrong answers.

12. **The correct answer is (A).** The last part of the selection states that phonics should be taught in the context of reading and writing rather than strictly through phonics exercises. Choice (A) is therefore the correct answer.

Now try this reading selection and its questions. Once more, explanations follow the correct answers. Follow the procedure you have learned, and be sure to read the explanations even if you have a perfect score.

SELECTION FOR QUESTIONS 13 TO 18

A programming language is an artificial language used by computer programmers to create a sequence of instructions that tell a computer to execute different tasks. Programming languages are similar to natural languages in that they have a vocabulary, grammar, and syntax. However, programming languages are better suited for computer programming because they lack the ambiguities that are inherent in natural languages. For example, many English words can have multiple meanings, making some statements or commands unclear. Programming languages, on the other hand, are free from such ambiguities so that each command corresponds with one single action.

Programming languages vary greatly in their complexity and in the number of applications for which they may be used. Some languages are written to solve a particular kind of computing problem or are created for use with a specific computer system. For instance, language ML was written for scientific applications, while language MP was written for business applications. Other languages, such as machine languages, can be as specific as to be designed for use with one specific computer for certain research applications. Despite the fact that these programming languages are typically written in response to particular computing problems, they are also very useful for solving a wide range of other problems as well. The most commonly used programming languages, such as KN and FS, are highly portable and can be used to effectively solve diverse types of computing problems.

13. Which of the following is the best title for the preceding selection? 13. Ⓐ Ⓑ Ⓒ Ⓓ
    (A) "The Benefits of ML for Scientific Programming Applications"
    (B) "The Grammar of Programming Languages"
    (C) "English as an Effective Programming Language"
    (D) "Characteristics and Applications of Programming Languages"

14. According to the preceding selection, programming languages are 14. Ⓐ Ⓑ Ⓒ Ⓓ
    better suited for computer programming than natural languages
    because
    (A) programming languages do not have grammar.
    (B) programming languages are ambiguous.
    (C) programming languages do not have syntax.
    (D) programming languages are not ambiguous.

15. According to the preceding selection, programming language 15. Ⓐ Ⓑ Ⓒ Ⓓ
    MP was written for
    (A) scientific applications.
    (B) diverse computing problems.
    (C) business applications.
    (D) multiple problem applications.

16. According to the preceding selection, an example of a programming language that may be designed for use with one specific computer for research applications is

    16. Ⓐ Ⓑ Ⓒ Ⓓ

    (A) language ML.
    (B) a machine language.
    (C) language MP.
    (D) languages KN or FS.

17. According to the preceding selection, the most commonly used programming languages are

    17. Ⓐ Ⓑ Ⓒ Ⓓ

    (A) KN and FS.
    (B) MP and FS.
    (C) ML and MP.
    (D) ML and KN.

18. According to the preceding selection, which of the following is NOT a programming language?

    18. Ⓐ Ⓑ Ⓒ Ⓓ

    (A) English
    (B) ML
    (C) KN
    (D) MP

The correct answers are: 13. (D), 14. (D), 15. (C), 16. (B), 17. (A), 18. (A).

13. **The correct answer is (D).** While ML was mentioned as a programming language that is used for scientific applications, its benefits were not mentioned in the passage, so choice (A) can be eliminated. In the same way, the grammar of programming languages was briefly mentioned, but was not the main point of the selection, so choice (B) can be eliminated. English was mentioned as an example of a natural language that could not be used for programming, so choice (C) can be eliminated.

14. **The correct answer is (D).** The first paragraph discusses the advantage of using a programming language rather than a natural language. The main advantage discussed is the lack of ambiguity in programming languages.

15. **The correct answer is (C).** The second paragraph states that the programming language MP was written for business applications.

16. **The correct answer is (B).** The second paragraph discusses machine languages as an example of a programming language that may be used with one specific computer for research applications.

17. **The correct answer is (A).** The last sentence of the second paragraph states that the most commonly used programming languages are KN and FS.

18. **The correct answer is (A).** The first paragraph points out that the English language would not be an effective programming language because of its many ambiguities.

On police exams, many reading passages relate to legal definitions, laws, and police procedures. When reading these passages, you must pay special attention to details relating to exceptions, special preconditions, combinations of activities, choices of actions, and prescribed time sequences. Sometimes the printed procedure specifies that certain actions are to be taken only when there is a combination of factors such as that a person actually breaks a window *and* has a gun. At other times, the procedures give choices of action under certain circumstances. You must read carefully to determine whether the passage requires a combination of factors or gives a choice, then make the appropriate judgment. And when a time sequence is specified, be certain to follow that sequence in the prescribed order.

The remaining selections in this chapter are based on police-type questions. Beyond requiring reading comprehension skills, they require the special police exam emphasis just discussed.

SELECTION FOR QUESTIONS 19 TO 23

The job of Police Officer is a complicated occupation that consists of some activities that are highly visible to the public and other "behind the scenes" activities that most of the public does not think of when they envision the role of a Police Officer. Typically, the job of Police Officer is thought of as involving the highly visible activities that are often portrayed in the media. Particularly in movies and television programs, a Police Officer's daily routine is portrayed as consisting mainly of making arrests, preventing crimes, and participating in the prosecution of those charged with crimes. However, a Police Officer's role is more complicated than the media would make it seem. In reality, the activities listed above typically occupy only 15 to 20 percent of an officer's time. The majority of a Police Officer's time is actually directed towards less glamorous public service activities. Some of these activities may include providing directions to pedestrians, educating children about crime prevention, assisting firefighting personnel at the scene of an emergency, and directing citizens that may be mentally disturbed to social service organizations that have been established to assist them.

19. According to the passage, the majority of a Police Officer's time is spent   19. Ⓐ Ⓑ Ⓒ Ⓓ
    (A) making arrests.
    (B) preventing crimes.
    (C) in highly visible activities.
    (D) "behind the scenes."

20. According to the passage, the highly visible police activities that are often portrayed by the media

    20. Ⓐ Ⓑ Ⓒ Ⓓ

    (A) occupy most of an officer's time.

    (B) occupy 15 to 20 percent of an officer's time.

    (C) are not known by much of the public.

    (D) are not considered very glamorous.

21. According to the passage, educating children about crime prevention

    21. Ⓐ Ⓑ Ⓒ Ⓓ

    (A) is a highly visible part of an officer's job.

    (B) is often portrayed by the media as a part of an officer's job.

    (C) is a "behind the scenes" part of an officer's job.

    (D) occupies 15 to 20 percent of an officer's time.

22. According to the passage, the scene that would most typically be portrayed by the media would be

    22. Ⓐ Ⓑ Ⓒ Ⓓ

    (A) a Police Officer giving directions to a person on the street.

    (B) a Police Officer arresting a shoplifter.

    (C) a Police Officer teaching children not to talk to strangers.

    (D) a Police Officer directing traffic away from a fire scene.

23. Of the following, which best describes the central thought of this passage and would be most suitable as a title?

    23. Ⓐ Ⓑ Ⓒ Ⓓ

    (A) "A Police Officer's Job Is More than What the Media Portrays"

    (B) "The Job of Police Officer: Arrests and Crime Prevention"

    (C) "A Police Officer's Job Is Not as Complicated as It May Seem"

    (D) "How to Become a Behind-the-Scenes Police Officer"

The correct answers are: 19. **(D)**, 20. **(B)**, 21. **(C)**, 22. **(B)**, 23. **(A)**.

19. **The correct answer is (D).** The main point of this passage is that the majority of a Police Officer's time is spent conducting "behind the scenes" activities. The public may be more aware of highly visible activities such as making arrests and preventing crimes; however, these activities only occupy about 15 to 20 percent of an officer's time.

20. **The correct answer is (B).** The passage states that the activities portrayed by the media as typical activities for a Police Officer occupy 15 to 20 percent of an officer's time. This is only a small portion of an officer's time, so choice (A) can be eliminated. However, these activities are known by the public and are generally considered to be the glamorous part of a Police Officer's job, so choices (C) and (D) can be eliminated.

21. **The correct answer is (C).** The passage states that most of a Police Officer's time is spent conducting "behind the scenes" activities. Educating children about crime prevention is listed as one of these activities.

22. **The correct answer is (B).** The beginning of the passage states that an officer's daily routine is typically portrayed by the media as consisting of activities such as making arrests.

23. **The correct answer is (A).** The main idea of this passage is that the media typically portrays the occupation of Police Officer as consisting mainly of things such as making arrests and preventing crimes. However, the passage also points out that these activities make up only a small part of a Police Officer's job. In other words, a Police Officer's job is more than what the media portrays.

SELECTION FOR QUESTIONS 24 TO 26

In recent years, many police departments have shifted from a traditional policing approach to a community policing approach. The basic difference between these two strategies is that traditional policing approaches focus on detecting crimes, while community policing approaches focus more on crime prevention. The basic argument against traditional policing strategies is that they focus on responding to calls that take place after a crime has already occurred. This type of strategy may effectively detect crimes, but does little to prevent them. Research has shown that with a traditional strategy, even increasing the total number of officers on duty does not lower the crime rate or increase the proportion of solved crimes.

Community policing strategies, on the other hand, attempt to increase the quality of service that Police Officers provide by actively involving the community in preventing crime. With this strategy, Police Officers develop close ties to the community in an effort to understand their needs and concerns. This allows officers to customize their service to meet the needs of their particular community, which leads to greater efficiency and helps to build the community's trust in the police.

24. According to the passage, the main difference between traditional and community policing strategies is   24.   Ⓐ Ⓑ Ⓒ Ⓓ
    (A) community strategies focus more on crime detection.
    (B) traditional strategies focus more on crime prevention.
    (C) community strategies focus more on crime prevention.
    (D) traditional strategies lead to more solved crimes.

25. According to the passage, police departments are starting to   25. Ⓐ Ⓑ Ⓒ Ⓓ
    shift toward community policing strategies because
    (A) these strategies lead to greater crime detection.
    (B) these strategies lead to greater crime prevention.
    (C) they are no longer concerned with the community's trust.
    (D) they want to increase the number of Police Officers.

26. According to the passage, the most effective way to prevent   26. Ⓐ Ⓑ Ⓒ Ⓓ
    crime is to
    (A) hire more Police Officers.
    (B) change to a traditional approach.
    (C) focus on crime detection.
    (D) get involved with the community.

The correct answers are: 24. **(C)**, 25. **(B)**, 26. **(D)**.

24. **The correct answer is (C).** The passage states that the main difference between
    traditional and community policing strategies is that community strategies focus
    more on crime prevention, whereas traditional strategies focus more on crime
    detection.

25. **The correct answer is (B).** The main idea of this passage is that many police
    departments are shifting to a community policing approach because it leads to
    greater crime prevention. It is explained that preventing crime is more beneficial
    than merely detecting crimes after they have occurred.

26. **The correct answer is (D).** The passage states that the reason many departments
    are switching to a community policing approach is because this approach leads to
    greater crime prevention. Therefore, the best way to prevent crime is to get involved
    with the community so their needs and concerns can be addressed.

SELECTION FOR QUESTION 27

It is unlawful for the operator of any vehicle, having knowledge that he or she has been directed to stop such vehicle by a duly authorized law enforcement officer, willfully to refuse or fail to stop the vehicle in compliance with such directive or, having stopped in knowing compliance with the directive, willfully to flee in an attempt to elude the officer, and a person who violates this subsection shall, upon conviction, be punished by imprisonment in the county jail for a period not to exceed 1 year, or by fine not to exceed $1,000, or by both such fine and imprisonment.

27. According to the traffic law printed above, a person who stops his car after being directed to do so by a Police Officer   27. Ⓐ Ⓑ Ⓒ Ⓓ
   (A) may be fined $1,500.
   (B) is not in violation of this law.
   (C) may be fined $1,000.
   (D) may be imprisoned for 6 months.

27. **The correct answer is (B).** The language used to explain this law may make it difficult to understand the details of it. However, you should be able to understand that this law is basically directed at those who do not stop their vehicles when a Police Officer requests that they do so. Therefore, a person who stops his car after being directed to do so by a Police Officer is not in violation of this law, so choice (B) is the correct answer.

SELECTION FOR QUESTIONS 28 TO 29

Part of a Police Supervisor's job is to discipline officers who are found to be engaging in misconduct. When misconduct is suspected, supervisors should follow these procedures in the order given:
   1. Review the performance of the employee.
   2. Identify and recognize employee offenses against department policies and procedures.
   3. Select and document appropriate corrective disciplinary measures.
   4. Forward proposed disciplinary actions to the department director and the Personnel Director for review.
   5. After the department director's and the Personnel Director's clearance is provided, carry out the appropriate disciplinary actions.

28. A Police Supervisor just witnessed an employee drinking on the job. What should the supervisor do next?

28. Ⓐ Ⓑ Ⓒ Ⓓ

(A) Review the employee's performance
(B) Identify the offenses that are against department policy
(C) Select and document the appropriate disciplinary measures
(D) Carry out the appropriate disciplinary actions

29. Police Sergeant Smith just witnessed an officer engaging in misconduct. Before disciplining the officer, Police Chief Smith reviewed the officer's performance, identified the offenses that were against department policy, selected and documented the appropriate disciplinary measures, and then carried out the appropriate disciplinary actions. Police Sergeant Smith is acting

29. Ⓐ Ⓑ Ⓒ Ⓓ

(A) correctly; he followed the department's procedures for disciplinary action.
(B) incorrectly; he did not document the appropriate disciplinary measures.
(C) incorrectly; he did not forward the proposed disciplinary actions to the director.
(D) incorrectly; he did not review the officer's performance.

The correct answers are: 28. **(A)**, 29. **(C)**.

28. **The correct answer is (A).** The selection states that part of a Police Supervisor's job is to discipline officers who are found to be engaging in misconduct. The procedures are to be followed in order and the first step is to review the employee's performance, so choice (A) is correct.

29. **The correct answer is (C).** Sergeant Smith followed all of the procedures but failed to forward the proposed disciplinary actions to the department director and the Personnel Director for review, so choice (C) is correct.

SELECTION FOR QUESTIONS 30 TO 31

Researchers have discovered that crimes tend to take place in certain patterns. Police Officer Johnson has noticed that in the beat that she is assigned to, drug-related crimes tend to take place on Larson Road while prostitution-related crimes tend to take place on Kenmore Street. Assaults tend to take place on Kimball Street and most burglaries take place on Main Street. Most assaults occur between 9 p.m. and 3 a.m., drug-related crimes occur between 11 p.m. and 4 a.m., burglaries tend to occur between 10 a.m. and 3 p.m., and prostitution-related crimes occur between 10 p.m. and 2 a.m. Burglaries tend to occur on Monday, Tuesday, and Wednesday. Drug-related crimes usually take place from Thursday night through Sunday night. Assaults tend to happen on Thursday, Friday, and Saturday.

30. Police Officer Johnson would reduce the incidence of what   30. Ⓐ Ⓑ Ⓒ Ⓓ
    type of crime by concentrating her patrol on Larson Road from
    9 p.m. to 5 a.m.?
    (A) Assault
    (B) Prostitution-related crime
    (C) Drug-related crime
    (D) Burglary

31. Burglary has been one of the biggest problems on Officer   31. Ⓐ Ⓑ Ⓒ Ⓓ
    Johnson's beat. How should she concentrate her patrol to curb
    the number of burglaries on her beat?
    (A) Thursday through Sunday from 11 p.m. to 4 a.m.
    (B) Monday through Wednesday from 10 a.m. to 3 p.m.
    (C) Thursday through Saturday from 9 p.m. to 3 a.m.
    (D) Friday through Sunday from 10 p.m. to 2 a.m.

The correct answers are: 30. **(C)**, 31. **(B)**.

30. **The correct answer is (C).** The great number of details in this question can make it particularly difficult. The best way to approach this type of problem is to read the question first. Question 30 mentions Larson Road and the time period from 9 p.m. to 5 a.m. With these facts in mind, you can read through the selection paying particular attention to the street and time period mentioned in the question. This should lead you to conclude that drug-related crimes are most likely to occur on Larson Road from 9 p.m. to 5 a.m.

31. **The correct answer is (B).** Once again, you should benefit from reading the question and then rereading the selection. By looking through the selection for information about burglaries, you should be able to conclude that burglaries tend to take place on Monday through Wednesday and from 10 a.m. to 3 p.m.

SELECTION FOR QUESTION 32

Exploitation occurs when a person is the acting caregiver of a disabled adult or an elderly person and knowingly, by deception, obtains or uses a disabled adult's or an elderly person's funds, assets, or property with the intent to temporarily or permanently deprive a disabled adult or an elderly person of the use or possession of the funds, assets, or property for the benefit of someone other than the disabled adult or elderly person.

Intimidation occurs when a person is the acting caregiver of a disabled adult or an elderly person and communicates by word or act to a disabled adult or an elderly person that that person will be deprived of food, nutrition, clothing, shelter, supervision, medicine, medical services, money, or financial support or will suffer physical violence.

Neglect occurs when a person is the acting caregiver of a disabled adult or an elderly person and fails to provide the care, supervision, and services necessary to maintain the physical and mental health of a disabled adult or an elderly person, including, but not limited to, food, clothing, medicine, shelter, supervision, and medical services.

32. David is the acting caregiver of Mrs. Jordan, who is a disabled woman in her mid-50s. For about 30 hours per week David helps Mrs. Jordan with her everyday activities such as shopping for food and going to the bank. Mrs. Jordan places a great deal of trust in David and even allows him to have access to all of her bank cards and passwords. Recently David has been a little low on cash and has been taking money from Mrs. Jordan's account. She is a very wealthy woman and would never notice that the money is missing. David should be charged with
   (A) nothing; he committed no crime.
   (B) exploitation.
   (C) intimidation.
   (D) neglect.

   32. Ⓐ Ⓑ Ⓒ Ⓓ

32. **The correct answer is (B).** Mrs. Jordan is not even aware of David's activities and certainly does not feel threatened, so choice (C) can be eliminated. Despite his actions, David is not depriving Mrs. Jordan of any of her basic needs, so choice (D) can be eliminated. However, David is deceiving Mrs. Jordan and taking her funds for his own use, so choice (A) can be eliminated. Choice (B) is the correct response.

Use the skills and techniques you have just developed to practice with the traditional-style reading comprehension questions in the following chapter. Then apply your new expertise to the exams in this book and to your Police Officer exam.

Before you begin the exercises, review this list of hints for scoring high on reading comprehension questions.

1. Read the questions and underline key words.

2. Skim the selection to get a general idea of the subject matter, the point that is being made, and the organization of the material.

3. Reread the selection, giving attention to details and point of view. Underscore key words and phrases.

4. If the author has quoted material from another source, be sure that you understand the purpose of the quote. Does the author agree or disagree?

5. Carefully read each question or incomplete statement. Determine exactly what is being asked. Watch for negatives or all-inclusive words such as *always*, *never*, *all*, *only*, *every*, *absolutely*, *completely*, *none*, *entirely*, and *no*.

6. Read all the answer choices. Eliminate those choices that are obviously incorrect. Reread the remaining choices and refer to the selection, if necessary, to determine the *best* answer.

7. Avoid inserting your own judgments into your answers. Even if you disagree with the author or even if you spot a factual error in the selection, you must answer on the basis of what is stated or implied in the selection.

8. Do not allow yourself to spend too much time on any one question. If looking back at the selection does not help you to find or figure out the answer, choose from among the answers remaining after you eliminate the obviously wrong answers, mark the question in the test booklet, and go on. If you have time at the end of the exam or portion of the exam, reread the selection and the question. Often a fresh look provides new insights.

CHAPTER 7: PRACTICE WITH READING-BASED QUESTIONS

> **Directions:** Choose from among the four suggested answers the best *answer to each question.*

1. "The force reconciling and coordinating all human conflicts and directing people in the harmonious accomplishment of their work is the supervisor. To deal with people successfully, the first one a supervisor must learn to work with is himself or herself." According to the quotation, which of the following conclusions is most accurate?
   (A) Human conflicts are the result of harmonious accomplishment.
   (B) A supervisor should attempt to reconcile all the different views subordinates may have.
   (C) A supervisor who understands himself or herself is in a good position to deal with others successfully.
   (D) The reconciling force in human conflicts is the ability to deal with people successfully.

2. "Law must be stable and yet it cannot stand still" means most nearly that
   (A) law is a fixed body of subject matter.
   (B) law must adapt itself to changing conditions.
   (C) law is a poor substitute for justice.
   (D) the true administration of justice is the firmest pillar of good government.

3. "The treatment to be given the offender cannot alter the fact of the offense; but we can take measures to reduce the chance of similar acts occurring in the future. We should banish the criminal, not in order to exact revenge nor directly to encourage reform, but to deter that person and others from further illegal attacks on society." According to the quotation, prisoners should be punished in order to
   (A) alter the nature of their offenses.
   (B) banish them from society.
   (C) deter them and others from similar illegal attacks on society.
   (D) directly encourage reform.

4. "On the other hand, the treatment of prisoners on a basis of direct reform is foredoomed to failure. Neither honest persons nor criminals will tolerate a bald proposition from anyone to alter their characters or habits, least of all if we attempt to gain such a change by a system of coercion." According to this quotation, criminals
   (A) are incorrigible.
   (B) are incapable of being coerced.
   (C) are not likely to turn into law-abiding citizens.
   (D) possess very firm characters.

5. "While much thought has been devoted to the question of how to build walls high enough to keep persons temporarily in prison, we have devoted very little attention to the treatment necessary to enable them to come out permanently cured, inclined to be friends rather than enemies of their law-abiding fellow citizens." According to this quotation, much thought has been devoted to the problem of prisons as
   (A) vengeful agencies.
   (B) efficient custodial agencies.
   (C) efficient sanatoria.
   (D) places from which society's friends might issue.

6. "Community organization most often includes persons whose behavior is unconventional in relation to generally accepted social definition, if such persons wield substantial influence with the residents." The inference one can most validly draw from this statement is that
   (A) influential persons are often likely to be unconventional.
   (B) the success of a community organization depends largely on the democratic processes employed by it.
   (C) a gang leader may sometimes be an acceptable recruit for a community organization.
   (D) the unconventional behavior of a local barkeeper may often become acceptable to the community.

7. "The safeguard of democracy is education. The education of youth during a limited period of more or less compulsory attendance at school does not suffice. The educative process is a lifelong one." Which of the following statements is most consistent with this quotation?
   (A) The school is not the only institution that can contribute to the education of the population.
   (B) All democratic peoples are educated.
   (C) The entire population should be required to go to school throughout life.
   (D) If compulsory education were not required, the educative process would be more effective.

8. "The Police Officer's art consists in applying and enforcing a multitude of laws and ordinances in such degree or proportion and in such manner that the greatest degree of social protection will be secured. The degree of enforcement and the method of application will vary with each neighborhood and community." According to this statement,
- **(A)** each neighborhood or community must judge for itself to what extent the law is to be enforced.
- **(B)** a Police Officer should enforce only those laws that are designed to give the greatest degree of social protection.
- **(C)** the manner and intensity of law enforcement is not necessarily the same in all communities.
- **(D)** all laws and ordinances must be enforced in a community with the same degree of intensity.

9. "As a rule, Police Officers, through service and experience, are familiar with the duties and the methods and means required to perform them. Yet, left to themselves, their aggregate effort would disintegrate and the vital work of preserving the peace would never be accomplished." According to this statement, which of the following conclusions is most accurate?
- **(A)** Police Officers are sufficiently familiar with their duties as to need no supervision.
- **(B)** Working together for a common purpose is not efficient without supervision.
- **(C)** Police Officers are familiar with the methods of performing their duties because of rules.
- **(D)** Preserving the peace is so vital that it can never be said to be completed.

Answer questions 10 through 12 on the basis of the information given in the following passage.

Criminal science is largely the science of identification. Progress in this field has been marked and sometimes very spectacular because new techniques, instruments, and facts flow continuously from the scientists. But the crime laboratories are understaffed; trade secrets still prevail; and inaccurate conclusions are often the result. However, modern gadgets cannot substitute for the skilled intelligent investigator; he or she must be their master.

10. According to this passage, criminal science
- **(A)** excludes the field of investigation.
- **(B)** is primarily interested in establishing identity.
- **(C)** is based on the equipment used in crime laboratories.
- **(D)** uses techniques different from those used in other sciences.

11. Advances in criminal science have been, according to the passage,
    (A) extremely limited.
    (B) slow but steady.
    (C) unusually reliable.
    (D) outstanding.

12. A problem that has not been overcome completely in crime work is, according to the passage,
    (A) unskilled investigators.
    (B) the expense of new equipment and techniques.
    (C) an insufficient number of personnel in crime laboratories.
    (D) inaccurate equipment used in laboratories.

13. "While the safe burglar can ply his or her trade the year round, the loft burglar has more seasonal activities, since only at certain periods of the year is a substantial amount of valuable merchandise stored in lofts." The generalization that this statement best illustrates is that
    (A) nothing is ever completely safe from a thief.
    (B) there are safe burglars and loft burglars.
    (C) some types of burglary are seasonal.
    (D) the safe burglar considers safecracking a trade.

Answer questions 14 through 17 on the basis of the information given in the following passage.

When a vehicle has been disabled in a tunnel, the officer on patrol in this zone shall press the emergency truck light button. In the fast lane, red lights will go on throughout the tunnel; in the slow lane, amber lights will go on throughout the tunnel. The yellow zone light will go on at each signal control station throughout the tunnel and will flash the number of the zone in which the stoppage has occurred. A red flashing pilot light will appear only at the signal control station at which the emergency truck button was pressed. The emergency garage will receive an audible and visual signal indicating the signal control station at which the emergency truck button was pressed. The garage officer shall acknowledge receipt of the signal by pressing the acknowledgment button. This will cause the pilot light at the operated signal control station in the tunnel to cease flashing and to remain steady. It is an answer to the officer at the operated signal control station that the emergency truck is responding to the call.

14. According to this passage, when the emergency truck light button is pressed,
    (A) amber lights will go on in every lane throughout the tunnel.
    (B) emergency signal lights will go on only in the lane in which the disabled vehicle is located.
    (C) red lights will go on in the fast lane throughout the tunnel.
    (D) pilot lights at all signal control stations will turn amber.

15. According to this passage, the number of the zone in which the stoppage has occurred is flashed
   (A) immediately after all the lights in the tunnel turn red.
   (B) by the yellow zone light at each signal control station.
   (C) by the emergency truck at the point of stoppage.
   (D) by the emergency garage.

16. According to the passage, an officer near the disabled vehicle will know that the emergency tow truck is coming when
   (A) the pilot light at the operated signal control station appears and flashes red.
   (B) an audible signal is heard in the tunnel.
   (C) the zone light at the operated signal control station turns red.
   (D) the pilot light at the operated signal control station becomes steady.

17. Under the system described in the passage, it would be correct to come to the conclusion that
   (A) officers at all signal control stations are expected to acknowledge that they have received the stoppage signal.
   (B) officers at all signal control stations will know where the stoppage has occurred.
   (C) all traffic in both lanes of that side of the tunnel in which the stoppage has occurred must stop until the emergency truck has arrived.
   (D) there are two emergency garages, each able to respond to stoppages in traffic going in one particular direction.

Answer questions 18 through 20 on the basis of the information given in the following passage.

   The use of a roadblock is simply an adaptation of the military practice of encirclement by the police. Successful operation of a roadblock plan depends almost entirely on the amount of advance study and planning given to such operations. A thorough and detailed examination of the roads and terrain under the jurisdiction of a given police agency should be made with the locations of the roadblocks pinpointed in advance. The first principle to be borne in mind in the location of each roadblock is the time element. Its location must be at a point beyond which the fugitive could not have possibly traveled in the time elapsed from the commission of the crime to the arrival of the officers at the roadblock.

18. According to the passage,
   (A) military operations have made extensive use of roadblocks.
   (B) the military practice of encirclement is an adaptation of police use of roadblocks.
   (C) the technique of encirclement has been widely used by military forces.
   (D) a roadblock is generally more effective than encirclement.

19. According to the passage,
    (A) advance study and planning are of minor importance in the success of roadblock operations.
    (B) a thorough and detailed examination of all roads within a radius of 50 miles should precede the determination of a roadblock location.
    (C) consideration of terrain features is important in planning the location of roadblocks.
    (D) a roadblock operation can seldom be successfully undertaken by a single police agency.

20. According to the passage,
    (A) the factor of time is the sole consideration in the location of a roadblock.
    (B) the maximum speed possible in the method of escape is of major importance in roadblock location.
    (C) the time the officers arrive at the site of a proposed roadblock is of little importance.
    (D) a roadblock should be sited as close to the scene of the crime as the terrain will permit.

Answer questions 21 and 22 on the basis of the information given in the following passage.

A number of crimes, such as robbery, assault, rape, certain forms of theft, and burglary, are high-visibility crimes in that it is apparent to all concerned that they are criminal acts prior to or at the time they are committed. In contrast to these, check forgeries, especially those committed by first offenders, have low visibility. There is little in the criminal act or in the interaction between the check passer and the person cashing the check to identify it as a crime. Closely related to this special quality of the forgery crime is the fact that, while it is formally defined and treated as a felonious or "infamous" crime, it is informally held by the legally untrained public to be a relatively harmless form of crime.

21. According to the passage, crimes of "high visibility"
    (A) are immediately recognized as crime by the victims.
    (B) take place in public view.
    (C) always involve violence or the threat of violence.
    (D) are usually committed after dark.

22. According to the passage,
    (A) the public regards check forgery as a minor crime.
    (B) the law regards check forgery as a minor crime.
    (C) the law distinguishes between check forgery and other forgery.
    (D) it is easier to spot inexperienced check forgers than other criminals.

Answer questions 23 and 24 on the basis of the information given in the following passage.

The racketeer is primarily concerned with business affairs, legitimate or otherwise, and preferably those that are close to the margin of legitimacy. The racketeer gets the best opportunities from business organizations that meet the need of large sections of the public for goods or services that are defined as illegitimate by the same public, such as prostitution, gambling, illicit drugs, or liquor. In contrast to the thief, the racketeer and the establishments controlled deliver goods and services for money received.

23. It can be deduced from the passage that suppression of racketeers is difficult because
    (A) victims of racketeers are not guilty of violating the law.
    (B) racketeers are generally engaged in fully legitimate enterprises.
    (C) many people want services that are not obtainable through legitimate sources.
    (D) laws prohibiting gambling and prostitution are unenforceable.

24. According to the passage, racketeering, unlike theft, involves
    (A) objects of value.
    (B) payment for goods received.
    (C) organized gangs.
    (D) unlawful activities.

25. "In examining the scene of a homicide, one should not only look for the usual, standard traces—fingerprints, footprints, etc.—but should also have eyes open for details that at first glance may not seem to have any connection with the crime." The most logical inference to be drawn from this statement is that
    (A) in general, standard traces are not important.
    (B) sometimes one should not look for footprints.
    (C) usually only the standard traces are important.
    (D) one cannot tell in advance what will be important.

Answer questions 26 and 27 on the basis of the information given in the following passage.

If a motor vehicle fails to pass inspection, the owner will be given a rejection notice by the inspection station. Repairs must be made within ten days after this notice is issued. It is not necessary to have the required adjustment or repairs made at the station where the inspection occurred. The vehicle may be taken to any other garage. Reinspection after repairs may be made at any official inspection station, not necessarily the same station that made the initial inspection. The registration of any motor vehicle for which an inspection sticker has not been obtained as required, or which is not repaired and inspected within ten days after inspection indicates defects, is subject to suspension. A vehicle cannot be used on public highways while its registration is under suspension.

26. According to the passage, the owner of a car that does not pass inspection must
    (A) have repairs made at the same station that rejected the car.
    (B) take the car to another station and have it reinspected.
    (C) have repairs made anywhere and then have the car reinspected.
    (D) not use the car on a public highway until the necessary repairs have been made.

27. According to the passage, the one of the following that may be cause for suspension of the registration of a vehicle is that
    (A) an inspection sticker was issued before the rejection notice had been in force for ten days.
    (B) it was not reinspected by the station that rejected it originally.
    (C) it was not reinspected either by the station that rejected it originally or by the garage that made the repairs.
    (D) it has not had defective parts repaired within ten days after inspection.

28. A statute states: "A person who steals an article worth less than $100 where no aggravating circumstances accompany the act is guilty of petit larceny. If the article is worth $100 or more, it may be larceny second degree." If all you know is that Edward Smith stole an article worth $100, it may reasonably be said that
    (A) Smith is guilty of petit larceny.
    (B) Smith is guilty of larceny second degree.
    (C) Smith is guilty of neither petit larceny nor larceny second degree.
    (D) precisely what charge will be placed against Smith is uncertain.

Answer questions 29 and 30 on the basis of the information given in the following passage.

The City Police Department will accept for investigation no report of a person missing from his residence if such residence is located outside of the city. The person reporting same will be advised to report such fact to the police department of the locality where the missing person lives, which will, if necessary, communicate officially with the City Police Department. A report will be accepted of a person who is missing from a temporary residence in the city, but the person making the report will be instructed to make a report also to the police department of the locality where the missing person lives.

29. According to the passage, a report to the City Police Department of a missing person whose permanent residence is outside of the city will
    (A) always be investigated provided that a report is also made to local police authorities.
    (B) never be investigated unless requested officially by local police authorities.
    (C) be investigated in cases of temporary residence in the city, but a report should always be made to local police authorities.
    (D) always be investigated and a report will be made to the local police authorities by the City Police Department.

30. Mr. Smith of Oldtown and Mr. Jones of Newtown have an appointment in the city, but Mr. Jones doesn't appear. Mr. Smith, after trying repeatedly to phone Mr. Jones the next day, believes that something has happened to him. According to the passage, Mr. Smith should apply to the police of
(A) Oldtown.
(B) Newtown.
(C) Newtown and the city.
(D) Oldtown and the city.

31. A police department rule reads as follows: "A Deputy Commissioner acting as Police Commissioner shall carry out the orders of the Police Commissioner, previously given, and such orders shall not, except in cases of extreme emergency, be countermanded." This means most nearly that, except in cases of extreme emergency,
(A) the orders given by a Deputy Commissioner acting as Police Commissioner may not be revoked.
(B) a Deputy Commissioner acting as Police Commissioner should not revoke orders previously given by the Police Commissioner.
(C) a Deputy Commissioner acting as Police Commissioner is vested with the same authority to issue orders as the Police Commissioner.
(D) only a Deputy Commissioner acting as Police Commissioner may issue orders in the absence of the Police Commissioner.

32. "A 'crime' is an act committed or omitted in violation of a public law either forbidding or commanding it." This statement implies most nearly that
(A) crimes can be omitted.
(B) a forbidding act, if omitted, is a crime.
(C) an act of omission may be criminal.
(D) to commit an act not commanded is criminal.

33. "He who by command, counsel, or assistance procures another to commit a crime is, in morals and in law, as culpable as the visible actor himself, for the reason that the criminal act, whichever it may be, is imputable to the person who conceived it and set the forces in motion for its actual accomplishment." Of the following, the most accurate inference from this statement is that
(A) a criminal act does not have to be committed for a crime to be committed.
(B) acting as counselor for a criminal is a crime.
(C) the mere counseling of a criminal act can never be a crime if no criminal act is committed.
(D) a person acting only as an adviser may be guilty of committing a criminal act.

34. "A 'felony' is a crime punishable by death or imprisonment in a state prison, and any other crime is a 'misdemeanor.'" According to this quotation, the decisive distinction between "felony" and "misdemeanor" is the
    (A) degree of criminality.
    (B) type of crime.
    (C) place of incarceration.
    (D) judicial jurisdiction.

Question 35 is to be answered on the basis of the information given in the following passage.

If the second or third felony is such that, upon a first conviction, the offender would be punishable by imprisonment for any term less than his or her natural life, then such person must be sentenced to imprisonment for an indeterminate term, the minimum of which shall be not less than one-half of the longest term prescribed upon a first conviction, and the maximum of which shall be not longer than twice such longest term; provided, however, that the minimum sentence imposed hereunder upon such second or third felony offender shall in no case be less than five years; except that where the maximum punishment for a second or third felony offender hereunder is five years or less, the minimum sentence must be not less than two years.

35. According to this passage, a person who has a second felony conviction shall receive as a sentence for that second felony an indeterminate term
    (A) not less than twice the minimum term prescribed upon a first conviction as a maximum.
    (B) not less than one-half the maximum term of the first conviction as a minimum.
    (C) not more than twice the minimum term prescribed upon a first conviction as a minimum.
    (D) with a maximum of not more than twice the longest term prescribed for a first conviction for this crime.

Answer Key

1. **(C)**	8. **(C)**	15. **(B)**	22. **(A)**	29. **(C)**
2. **(B)**	9. **(B)**	16. **(D)**	23. **(C)**	30. **(B)**
3. **(C)**	10. **(B)**	17. **(B)**	24. **(B)**	31. **(B)**
4. **(C)**	11. **(D)**	18. **(C)**	25. **(D)**	32. **(C)**
5. **(B)**	12. **(C)**	19. **(C)**	26. **(C)**	33. **(D)**
6. **(C)**	13. **(C)**	20. **(B)**	27. **(D)**	34. **(C)**
7. **(A)**	14. **(C)**	21. **(A)**	28. **(D)**	35. **(D)**

Answer Explanations

1. **The correct answer is (C).** Before understanding and working with others, one must first understand one's own motivation and working habits. The supervisor with good self-understanding is an effective supervisor.

2. **The correct answer is (B).** Adaptation is changing in response to changing conditions without a total change of substance.

3. **The correct answer is (C).** This quotation expresses the philosophy that the purpose of punishment is neither to make the offender "pay for his/her crime" nor to reform the offender, but rather to protect society from the specific criminal and to serve, by example, as a deterrent to others.

4. **The correct answer is (C).** The philosophy expressed here is "Once a criminal, always a criminal." Attempts at reform and rehabilitation are futile. (Remember: Answer questions based on reading passages on the information in the passages. You may disagree; you may even know that the information is incorrect. However, your answer must be based on the passage, not upon your opinions or your knowledge.)

5. **The correct answer is (B).** This question deals with a philosophy contrary to those expressed in the previous two questions. It states that we have devoted attention to means of making prisons secure places in which to keep offenders but have not given much thought to rehabilitation.

6. **The correct answer is (C).** You may find this principle difficult to accept, but it does represent accepted practice in many quarters. The concept is that if the person with leadership qualities—even if with antisocial behaviors—is drawn into the mainstream, that person can learn to accept certain norms of the majority and transmit these more acceptable attitudes and behaviors to the group that respects him or her. The term used to describe the drawing into the inner circle of the unconventional leader is "co-opting."

7. **The correct answer is (A).** Since education continues throughout life, yet schooling is of limited duration, obviously education occurs in places other than schools.

8. **The correct answer is (C).** The needs and desires of communities vary; therefore degree and manner of enforcement of different laws in different communities will also vary.

9. **The correct answer is (B).** The meaning of this quotation is that good intentions and thorough knowledge of duties are not sufficient. Organization and supervision are vital to efficient operation of the police function.

10. **The correct answer is (B).** The science of identification is primarily interested in establishing identity.

11. **The correct answer is (D).** Marked and spectacular progress is outstanding.

12. **The correct answer is (C).** Understaffed laboratories have insufficient personnel.

13. **The correct answer is (C).** The concept may be novel to you, but the question itself is an easy one. The answer is stated directly in the paragraph.

14. **The correct answer is (C).** See the second sentence. When a reading passage is crammed with details, most of the questions will be strictly factual.

15. **The correct answer is (B).** See the third sentence.

16. **The correct answer is (D).** See the last two sentences.

17. **The correct answer is (B).** The yellow zone light goes on at each signal control station and flashes the number of the zone in which the stoppage has occurred, so all officers receive this information.

18. **The correct answer is (C).** If the military practice of encirclement was adapted for use by the police, we may assume that it was widely and successfully used. Choice (B) reverses the order of the adaptation.

19. **The correct answer is (C).** This is the clear implication of the third sentence.

20. **The correct answer is (B).** The roadblock must be placed beyond the point that the fugitive could have reached, so maximum speed of escape is vitally important in the establishment of a roadblock.

21. **The correct answer is (A).** See the first sentence.

22. **The correct answer is (A).** See the last sentence.

23. **The correct answer is (C).** The racketeer provides goods and services that are officially illegal but that are desired by otherwise respectable members of the general public. Since the public wants these services, active effort to suppress the providers is unlikely.

24. **The correct answer is (B).** See the last sentence.

25. **The correct answer is (D).** The Police Officer must always be observant and alert to both abnormalities and routine details in the environment. This useful quality in a Police Officer is the reason many Police Officer exams include a section testing powers of observation and memory.

26. **The correct answer is (C).** The state is not concerned with who makes repairs nor with who does the inspection, only that these be accomplished.

27. **The correct answer is (D).** See the next-to-last sentence.

28. **The correct answer is (D).** Beware of qualifying words and definite statements. If the article is worth $100 or more, it *may* be larceny second degree, but not necessarily.

29. **The correct answer is (C).** See the last sentence.

30. **The correct answer is (B).** Mr. Jones is a resident of Newtown, so the missing person report must be filed with the Newtown police. The meeting of Smith and Jones was to have taken place in the city, but Jones was not a temporary resident of the city, so the city police are not involved in this case.

31. **The correct answer is (B).** The word *countermand* means "revoke." The Deputy Commissioner carries out the orders of the Police Commissioner and revokes them only in cases of extreme emergency.

32. **The correct answer is (C).** An act of omission, if it is in violation of a public law commanding said act, is a crime. The act of omission is not a crime if it is not in violation of a public law.

33. **The correct answer is (D).** The person who conceives and sets in motion the forces for the accomplishment of a crime—in other words, the adviser who convinced another to commit a criminal act—may well be deemed guilty of committing the criminal act.

34. **The correct answer is (C).** Imprisonment in a state prison is incarceration in the state prison. Imprisonment or incarceration in any other institution is the punishment for a misdemeanor. Crimes are defined by the place of incarceration or imprisonment.

35. **The correct answer is (D).** You may have to do some very careful reading and rereading to find the answer to this question. You will find it in the last clause before the first semicolon.

CHAPTER 8: OBSERVATION AND MEMORY

To function effectively, a Police Officer must possess a keen memory for details. He or she must be on constant alert for physical characteristics that will help identify key people, places, or things, thereby leading to the apprehension of a criminal or the solution of a criminal investigation.

Most people have distinguishing features that are difficult to disguise: the contour of the face; the size, shape, and position of the ears; the shape of the mouth. Any of these may be sufficient for an officer to detect someone wanted for criminal activities. On the other hand, the color or style of an individual's hair or the first impression of his or her face can change drastically with the addition of a wig, mustache, or beard. Eye color can be altered with tinted contact lenses. Therefore, a Police Officer must focus attention on those physical features that cannot be easily changed and could serve as the basis of a positive identification of that person at some time in the future.

Observation is not limited to the act of seeing. An officer must also learn to recognize and recall distinctive features of people, places, and things. An official record in a memorandum book can serve as a refresher for the facts stored in the officer's mental record. The officer should be aware of the people who frequent his or her post, and of the surrounding buildings on that post in order to recall the details when necessary for a case. An officer without a keen sense of recall cannot perform his or her duties effectively.

Since police departments all over the country recognize the importance of a good memory for details and a good sense of recall in an officer's job, examinations for the position frequently contain sections that evaluate these skills. To sharpen your memory and sense of recall, practice using these skills. Walk around your neighborhood and observe. Keep your eyes open to everything you see. Later, try to recall details of buildings or people that you saw. Keep in mind that your environment is your study aid. Virtually any place you go, you can practice observing and recalling details.

Police Observation of Persons, Places, and Things

Police Officers must be thoroughly observant at all times. A nonobservant officer is soon found out by the criminals who will take advantage of their nonobservance to commit crimes on the officer's post. Good observation is a matter of training and knowledge. A Police Officer may have perfect eyesight yet be blind when it comes to observing matters calling for police action.

Many dangerous criminals have been arrested by virtue of a Police Officer's keen observation. An officer should observe the customary activities on his or her post as well as the people who live in or frequent it, so that the officer can quickly spot a stranger or an unusual activity. Some places call for more observation than others: banks, jewelry stores, taverns, service stations, and any place where crime is likely to occur or where the criminal element may gather.

An essential element in observation is the ability to remember details. Officers should practice observation by giving themselves tests, such as describing a man or a woman encountered casually or trying to remember details on a billboard. The identification of persons, places, and things depends on accurate observation. Many witnesses testify inaccurately in court because they failed to observe properly at the time of the incident's occurrence. A failure of this kind is *inexcusable* on the part of an officer.

Memory is a very individualized skill. Some people remember details of what they see and hear while others remember only the most obvious facts. Some people memorize easily or may remember things forever while others find memorizing very difficult or forget in a short time. For some, memorizing is done in a systematic manner while others memorize in a haphazard way or have no method at all. Systematic observation tends to lead to more efficient memorization. Some sort of meaningful grouping of people and activities helps officers recall the descriptions, the activities, and the interactions in their mind. Whether the material is pictorial or narrative, try to organize it in some meaningful way.

Observation and Memory Exercises

We really cannot tell you how to memorize. We can, however, teach you how to look at pictures and point out the details on which you should concentrate. This chapter includes exercises to improve your powers of observation. It points out what to look for and how to look for it. The exercises also direct your attention to details and help you focus your concentration the same way you need to focus when taking your Police Officer exam and when serving as a Police Officer.

Take your time with the exercises. Try to anticipate the questions that might be asked about each photo or drawing. If you train yourself to notice the details in these exercises, you will feel more confident when faced with memory and observation questions on your exam.

Photograph for Exercise 1—Car Repair

Exercise 1

Let us begin by looking at the photograph "Car Repair."

Start With the People

1. How many people are in the photograph?
2. How many men? How many women?
3. What do the people appear to be doing?
4. What is the man holding in his hands?
5. Note the clothing. Both are wearing light colored shirts, the man is wearing shorts. Are any shoes visible in the photograph? Is the woman wearing any jewelry?
6. Note hair. Does the woman have light or dark hair? How would you describe her hairstyle? Does the man have a mustache or beard?
7. Note the expressions: Is the woman looking at the man? What is she looking at? How would you describe her expression?

Observe the Action

8. What part of the car is visible?
9. What does the man have in his right hand? What is he probably doing? What does he hold in his left hand?
10. What might be the relationship of the man to the woman?
11. Are both people under the hood of the car, or is just the man?

Note the Background

12. What time of day is it?
13. What season could it be?
14. Is there anything visible in the background? Can you remember every detail of this setting?

An observant question writer could easily develop ten questions based upon these observations. Would you have noticed everything and made note not only about what was there, but also what was not there?

In looking at a photograph, focus first on the people. Notice their clothing, physical features, and activities. Count, but also make note of which person or persons are wearing what, doing what, interacting with whom, and so on. Then notice the prominent objects. Next, turn your attention to the background, any visible activity or action. Finally, start at the left side of the photograph and move your eyes very slowly to the right, noticing special details such as hairstyles, expression, and any unidentified objects. If you work very hard at noticing, you are likely to remember what you noticed, at least for the duration of the exam.

Photograph for Exercise 2—Refreshments

Exercise 2

Let us look at the photograph "Refreshments."

1. The people in the picture are . . . number, gender, and age.
2. The people are wearing . . . notice the pattern of the man's shirt, and the woman's sweater. (Also notice that she is wearing layered clothing). What are the girls wearing?
3. Notice hair color, type (curly or straight), and length and style.
4. Note that no shoes are visible. Is anyone wearing glasses, a watch, or a hat? Does the woman wear a necklace or ring?
5. What is the woman holding in her hands?
6. Who is standing? Who sitting? On what?
7. What is the design of the tablecloth?
8. What else is on the table? Notice beverages, bread, condiments, and other items.
9. What is on the ground? Snow? Sand? Gravel? Lawn? Rocks? Flowers? Wild grasses?
10. The day is . . . cold? warm? rainy? cloudy? sunny? Where is the sun in the picture?
11. In the background are (is) . . . mountains? trees? water? boats? tents? more grass? other people? animals?

12. Is the sky visible? What else is there on the land?

13. What is the shape of the table? Squared off? Rounded? Other?

14. Is the family likely sitting on chairs or a bench?

15. How many beverage cans or bottles?

16. Is there any activity in the background?

17. Describe the food on the table. Is anyone eating? Who is interacting with whom?

How did you do with this photograph? Are you developing skill at noticing everything?

Photograph for Exercise 3—A Family Camping

Exercise 3

Study the photograph titled "A Family Camping." On a plain piece of paper, make as comprehensive a list as you can. Try to notice every detail on which you could possibly be quizzed. When you have completed your list, compare it with ours that follows. If you noticed everything that we did, you are becoming very observant. Perhaps you found details that we missed. If so, congratulate yourself and keep up the good work.

On the actual exam, you will not be permitted to write any notes. You will have to make observations and hold them as mental notes only. This exercise, however, will be more effective if you jot down everything you see.

Here is our list:

1. There are five people in the photograph, two adults and three children.
2. Two people are sitting in chairs, a woman and a child.
3. The man on the bike has his right foot on the pedal and his left on the ground.
4. The child on the chair has a Band-Aid on his knee.
5. The man on the bike has dark hair; the other four people have light-colored hair.
6. The child on the chair is wearing sandals; the others are wearing sneakers.
7. The little girl has her right hand on the wheel of the bike.
8. Both the seated woman and the seated child are wearing denim overalls.
9. In the foreground is a light-colored dome tent with a canopy over the entrance.
10. The tent faces the cliff.
11. The girl leaning on the chair is wearing a striped, sleeveless shirt.
12. There are three chairs in the picture.
13. All five people are wearing light-colored socks.
14. The man on the bike has his right hand on the handle bars and his left hand is not visible.
15. There is no grass in the background; the ground is dirt.
16. The little girl and the man on the bike are both wearing denim shorts and white shirts.
17. Not visible: sky, trees, other people, animals, cars.

By now you should be getting pretty good at this activity.

Photograph for Exercise 4—Classroom

Exercise 4

Study the final photograph of the classroom. Make this exercise an observation and memory exercise rather than just an observation exercise. Study the photograph for five minutes. Make mental notes of as many details as you can, but do not do any writing at this time. Close the book and write as many details as you can remember. When you have written all that you can remember, draw a line on your paper and reopen the book. Add to the list details that you forgot or previously overlooked. Then compare your list with ours.

1. The scene is a classroom. The students are men and women; the instructor is a woman.

2. The students are all seated; the teacher is standing.

3. The teacher has short, dark hair. She wears a dress, a jacket, and dark shoes.

4. The teacher wears a watch on her left wrist. She has papers in her right hand.

5. The teacher is not wearing glasses. She is facing the class and her mouth is open as if she is speaking to the class.

6. Seven students are visible.

7. One student is wearing white overalls. That student is a woman with short, dark hair.

8. The students are seated on chairs with attached desks. One student is holding her right hand up near her face. That student is closest to the camera. She has her notebook open on her desk, wears some of her hair back in a barrette, is wearing blue jeans and white sneakers, and is wearing glasses.

9. The students all appear to be very attentive.

10. While some students are holding a pen or pencil, none appears to be writing.

11. The room lighting is not visible.

12. The floor is made of square tiles.

13. On the wall beside the teacher is a chalkboard. There is writing on the chalkboard and a box around some of the writing.

14. There is an eraser and a piece of chalk on the ledge of the chalkboard.

15. In the background are open windows.

16. Outside the windows is a tree and a grassy area.

17. There is an empty chair in the far left corner of the room.

18. The floor tiles are in dark and light squares and in a grid-like pattern.

19. There is a shelf beneath each of the desks.

20. One student is wearing sandals.

Exercise 5: Observation and Recognition of Faces

This exercise measures your ability to recognize the basic differences and similarities in the faces of people. Many alleged criminals being sought by the police disguise their facial features to make it difficult for the police to apprehend them. Aside from surgery, there are many things that the wanted person can do to make recognition difficult. The addition and removal of beards and mustaches, and even change in hair color or hair style, are relatively easy to accomplish. As noted previously, tinted contact lenses, now very common, can alter the color of eyes. However, there are some features that an individual cannot change easily. These are the features on which a Police Officer should concentrate when attempting to identify wanted persons: the size, shape, and position of the ears; the shape of the jaw. The shape of the nose and the jaw are difficult to change without surgery. The Police Officer should also recognize that the wanted male with a distinctive jaw would likely try to disguise that feature by growing a beard.

> **Directions:** Answer the following 10 questions by selecting the face, labeled (A), (B), (C), or (D), that is most likely to be the same as that of the suspect on the left. You are to assume that no surgery has taken place since the sketch of the suspect was made. Only observation and recognition are factors in this exercise. Do not try to memorize features of these faces. Circle the letter of the face you choose. Explanations follow the last question.

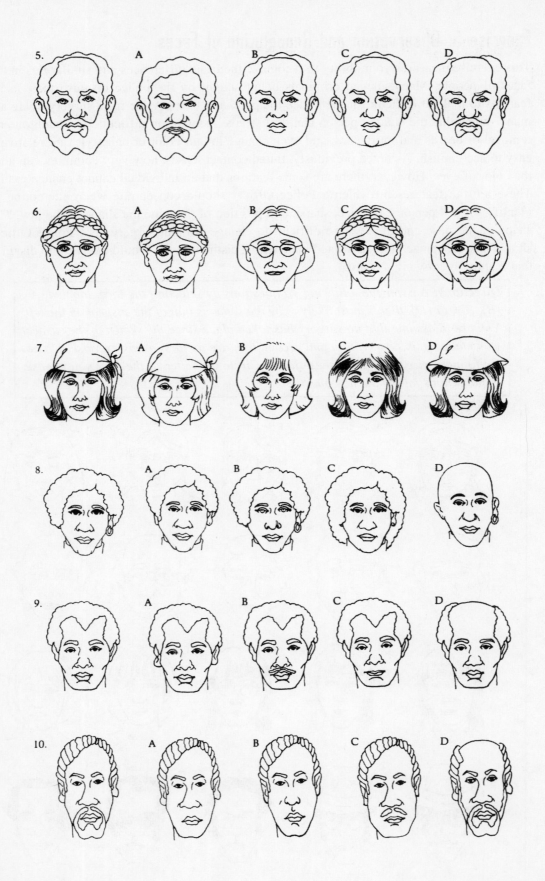

Answer Key for Exercise 5

1. **(D)**	6. **(D)**
2. **(B)**	7. **(B)**
3. **(C)**	8. **(A)**
4. **(D)**	9. **(B)**
5. **(C)**	10. **(A)**

Answer Explanations for Exercise 5

1. **The correct answer is (D).** Choice (A) has a different nose; choices (B) and (C) have different chins.

2. **The correct answer is (B).** Choice (A) has a longer face; choice (C) has a fuller face with different chin; and choice (D) has a different nose.

3. **The correct answer is (C).** Choice (A) has a longer face; choice (B) has dark eyes; and choice (D) has much fuller lips.

4. **The correct answer is (D).** Choice (A) has thinner lips; choice (B) has a different nose; and choice (C) has different ears.

5. **The correct answer is (C).** Choice (A) has a different mouth; choice (B) has a different nose; and choice (D) has different eyes.

THREE

PRACTICE EXAMINATIONS

ANSWER SHEET: PRACTICE EXAMINATION 1

Exercise 1

1. (A) (B) (C) (D)
2. (A) (B) (C) (D)
3. (A) (B) (C) (D)
4. (A) (B) (C) (D)
5. (A) (B) (C) (D)
6. (A) (B) (C) (D)
7. (A) (B) (C) (D)

8. (A) (B) (C) (D)
9. (A) (B) (C) (D)
10. (A) (B) (C) (D)
11. (A) (B) (C) (D)
12. (A) (B) (C) (D)
13. (A) (B) (C) (D)
14. (A) (B) (C) (D)

15. (A) (B) (C) (D)
16. (A) (B) (C) (D)
17. (A) (B) (C) (D)
18. (A) (B) (C) (D)
19. (A) (B) (C) (D)
20. (A) (B) (C) (D)

21. (A) (B) (C) (D)
22. (A) (B) (C) (D)
23. (A) (B) (C) (D)
24. (A) (B) (C) (D)
25. (A) (B) (C) (D)
26. (A) (B) (C) (D)

Exercise 2

1. (A) (B) (C) (D)
2. (A) (B) (C) (D)
3. (A) (B) (C) (D)
4. (A) (B) (C) (D)
5. (A) (B) (C) (D)
6. (A) (B) (C) (D)
7. (A) (B) (C) (D)
8. (A) (B) (C) (D)
9. (A) (B) (C) (D)
10. (A) (B) (C) (D)
11. (A) (B) (C) (D)

12. (A) (B) (C) (D)
13. (A) (B) (C) (D)
14. (A) (B) (C) (D)
15. (A) (B) (C) (D)
16. (A) (B) (C) (D)
17. (A) (B) (C) (D)
18. (A) (B) (C) (D)
19. (A) (B) (C) (D)
20. (A) (B) (C) (D)
21. (A) (B) (C) (D)
22. (A) (B) (C) (D)

23. (A) (B) (C) (D)
24. (A) (B) (C) (D)
25. (A) (B) (C) (D)
26. (A) (B) (C) (D)
27. (A) (B) (C) (D)
28. (A) (B) (C) (D)
29. (A) (B) (C) (D)
30. (A) (B) (C) (D)
31. (A) (B) (C) (D)
32. (A) (B) (C) (D)
33. (A) (B) (C) (D)

34. (A) (B) (C) (D)
35. (A) (B) (C) (D)
36. (A) (B) (C) (D)
37. (A) (B) (C) (D)
38. (A) (B) (C) (D)
39. (A) (B) (C) (D)
40. (A) (B) (C) (D)
41. (A) (B) (C) (D)
42. (A) (B) (C) (D)
43. (A) (B) (C) (D)
44. (A) (B) (C) (D)

CHAPTER 9: PRACTICE EXAMINATION 1

NYPD Test Preparation Kit

The NYPD Test Preparation Kit on the following pages is reprinted with permission of the New York Police Department from their Web site. Note that the New York City Department of Personnel makes no commitment, and no inference is to be drawn, regarding the content, style, or format of any future examination for the position of Police Officer. For more information about NYPD requirements, call (212) RECRUIT or (800) 550-3836.

INTRODUCTION

This Candidate Test Preparation Kit has been distributed by the NYPD to assist you in preparing for the upcoming New York City Police Officer's Examination.

This Test Preparation Kit is provided as a review of standard test-taking techniques and questions commonly used in some law enforcement civil service examinations.

<u>To get the most from this Test Preparation Kit, it is suggested that you:</u>

- Study uninterrupted for at least 30 minutes at a time
- Review each of the eleven (11) ability areas until you are comfortable with the definition and concept.
- Complete sample problems (allow only 3 minutes per question)
- Review incorrect answers
- When you are comfortable with one ability area, move onto the next.
- Do not look over the practice exam (part 2) until you have reviewed all eleven (11) ability areas.
- When you take the practice exams follow all directions provided.

New York's FINEST needs ALL of New York's finest

DIRECTIONS

PART I: ABILITY AREAS

The first part of the Test Preparation Kit contains definitions and examples pertaining to the eleven (11) ability areas. Potential candidates should review the ability area definitions until they are comfortable with the material. Example questions in each ability area are provided for candidates to practice prior to taking the practice examination in part II.

PART II: PRACTICE EXAMINATION

The second part of the Test Preparation Kit contains two practice examinations covering all (11) eleven ability areas. As mentioned previously, the first is a ten (10) minute memorization test, the second covers the ten (10) remaining ability areas. The Practice Examinations are based on examinations commonly used in civil service testing.

Included in the instructions are certain *time restraints*. Be sure and take the practice exams in a test like setting using only the allotted amount of time.

New York's FINEST needs ALL of New York's finest

NOTE

All potential candidates should note that the New York City Department of Citywide Administrative Services (DCAS), a separate agency from the NYPD, administers the entry-level police officer examination, not the NYPD.

This Test Preparation Kit was prepared to assist you in scoring to the best of your ability on the upcoming Police Officer examination.

The material included is based on types of questions used in previous exams. There are no assurances that all of these areas will be covered or that additional areas will not be added.

This kit is not all-inclusive and many candidates find studying additional material such as reading comprehension passages, math problems, and so forth, beneficial to achieve the best score possible.

New York's FINEST needs ALL of New York's finest

Exercise 1

NYPD - TEST PREPARATION KIT

MEMORIZATION - This ability involves remembering information, such as words, numbers, pictures and procedures. Pieces of information can be remembered by themselves or with other pieces of information. Some samples of question formats using this ability follow:

Candidates are given a picture to study for a given amount of time, and then are asked questions concerning the content. The picture might be a photograph or a drawing.

Candidates are given a set of "mug shots," which may be photographs or drawings, accompanied by descriptions and related information. Candidates must study these for a given amount of time, then are asked questions concerning the content.

Candidates are given information (e.g., directions for travel to a location, procedures to follow, operation of equipment, description of a suspect) to study for a given amount of time, then are asked questions concerning the content.

DIRECTIONS – Using a timer or your watch, carefully study the pictures and descriptions on the following page for 5 minutes. Then turn the page away from you and answer the 3 questions based solely on the material you were given.

REMEMBER – You should allow approximately 3 minutes per question, for a total of nine (9) minutes.

NYPD - TEST PREPARATION KIT

WANTED	DRUG SALE
NAME	JAMES WILKINSON
AGE	21
RACE	WHITE
HEIGHT	6'2"
WEIGHT	227lbs.
HAIR	BLACK
EYES	BROWN
COMPLEXION	MEDIUM
SCARS / MARKS	Tattoo on back of neck of a

"BOWLING PIN." Scar on left arm.

WANTED FOR FELONY SALE OF COCAINE. OFTEN FREQUENTS BOWLING ALLEYS CARRIES DRUGS IN BOWLING BAG.

WANTED	ROBBERY
NAME	CARMELLA DIAZ
AGE	28 - 32
RACE	HISPANIC
HEIGHT	5'3"
WEIGHT	125lbs.
HAIR	BROWN
EYES	BROWN
COMPLEXION	FAIR
SCARS / MARKS	Usually wears dark glasses.

Tattoo on left arm with initials, "D.J." IN A HEART.

WANTED FOR MULTIPLE ROBBERIES. THREATENS VICTIMS WITH AN UZI MACHINE GUN. OFTEN ACCOMPANIED BY A YOUNG MALE BLACK WHO GOES BY THE NICKNAME "MONEY".

NYPD - TEST PREPARATION KIT

YOU MAY <u>NOT</u> LOOK BACK AT THE SKETCHES

Answer questions 1 through 3 on the basis of the sketches.

1.   With regard to the person wanted for robbery, which one of the following choices is correct?

    A)   The person has a tattoo on the back of the neck.
    B)   The person has a scar on the left arm.
    C)   The person has a tattoo on the left arm.
    D)   The person has a scar on the back of the neck.

2.   With regard to the person wanted for drug sale, which one of the following choices is correct?

    A)   The person is armed with an Uzi.
    B)   The person uses the nickname "Money."
    C)   The person has a scar on the back of the neck.
    D)   The person often frequents bowling alleys.

3.   With regard to the person wanted for drug sale, which one of the following choices is correct?

    A)   The person is wearing a baseball cap.
    B)   The person has a mustache.
    C)   The person is wearing earrings.
    D)   The person is wearing sunglasses.

NYPD - TEST PREPARATION KIT

SPATIAL ORIENTATION - This ability involves determining where you are in relation to the location of some object or to tell where the object is in relation to you. Another Spatial Orientation format provides the candidates with a map (e.g., of a patrol sector). This map may include one-way streets or streets that are obstructed or unusable for some reason. The candidates are asked to identify the most efficient route to drive from one location to another, given the constraints of the situation.

4.   In a classroom simulation exercise, you are practicing questioning a fellow who is playing the role of a crime victim. You are told "He pulled out a gun, and told me to hand over my wallet. Then he ran out the door of my office, and made a left turn, going north down the corridor, and then made a right turn, and ran down the stairwell. I crossed the corridor, and looked straight ahead out the window, and saw him running away from me, with his back to me, running down the street. He then made a left turn at the corner."

According to this information, you would be most correct to radio that the perpetrator was last seen traveling:

        A) North   B) South   C) East   D) West

NYPD - TEST PREPARATION KIT

VISUALIZATION - This ability involves imagining how something would look when it is moved around or when its parts are moved or rearranged. It requires forming mental images of how patterns or objects would look after certain changes, such as unfolding or rotation. One has to predict how an object, set of objects, or patterns will appear after the changes have been carried out. Some samples of questions using this ability follow:

Another Visualization format presents the candidates with a diagram or floor plan, which may be a mirror image or some other variant of an area officers must enter (see page 6). For instance:

(Scenario)

    Recruit officers are participating in a simulation exercise in which they are responding to the scene of a barricaded emotionally disturbed person in an artist's studio. The barricaded person is a performance artist who has a history of drug use and paranoid schizophrenia. He has broken into the studio of a rival artist, Suite 23C, and is threatening to kill both himself and the other artist in order to "save the world from the commercialization of art." The landlord has been able to provide a diagram of Apt. 13D, which she says is a mirror-image of Apt 23C, on the other side of the hallway corridor. Study the diagram and answer the questions.

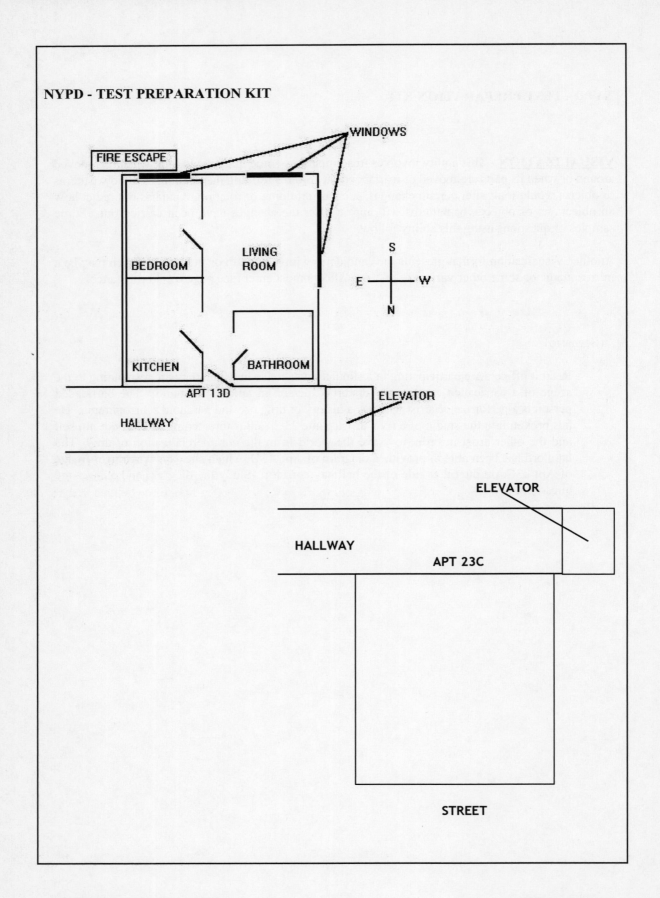

NYPD - TEST PREPARATION KIT

5.   Based on this diagram, if an officer were to climb down the small fire escape and enter Apt. 23C through the bedroom window, the bedroom door would be:

   A)   Straight ahead
   B)   On the right
   C)   On the left
   D)   Behind the officer

6.   Based on this diagram, if an officer were to enter Apt. 23C through the hallway door, the living room would be:

   A)   Ahead, off the right of the officer
   B)   Ahead to the right of the officer
   C)   Ahead to the left of the officer
   D)   Behind the officer

7.   The officers have the emotionally disturbed artist talking to them on the telephone. He says that he can see the officers and emergency vehicles parked in front of the building on the street from the window where he is standing. This would give you reason to believe that he is located near which wall of the building?

   A)   North
   B)   South
   C)   East
   D)   West

NYPD - TEST PREPARATION KIT

WRITTEN COMPREHENSION - This ability involves understanding written sentences and paragraphs. Some examples of questions testing this ability follow:

Answer questions 8 through 10 solely on the basis of the following information:

Police Officer Tom Riggins and John Landry were patrolling in their police car in the 65th Precinct at 10:15 A.M. on December 3, 1992. They came upon the scene of a traffic accident at Avenue C and 30th Street, which had occurred five minutes earlier. Officer Landry called the Police Radio Dispatcher at 10:20 A.M. and reported that he and his partner in police car #65B were handling a traffic accident involving a van and an auto at that location. Officer Landry further reported to the dispatcher that there were no personal injuries to the van driver, or to the driver of the auto, or her two children. However, the two vehicles were damaged.

The officers checked each driver's license, vehicle registration certificate and vehicle insurance identification card. The van driver was John Hudson, age 36, residing at 1102 South Elliot Blvd., Cranford, N.J. He was driving a white 1977 GMC van, N.Y. license plate 9723GH, owned by his employer, Zenith Trucking Corp. of 257 West 63rd St., New York, N.Y. Mr. Hudson's N.J. driver's license identification number is H1385 69774 58612 and the expiration date is December 31, 1992.

The driver of the auto was Mrs. Anne Cloris, age 38, residing at 49 Christopher Avenue, Queens, New York. She had two children with her, Charles Cloris Jr., age 10, and Anita Cloris, age 8. Mrs. Cloris' auto was a red 1989 Chevrolet 4-door station wagon, NY license plate #319GAZ. Mrs. Cloris' NY driver's license identification number is 121 921 661 and the expiration date is May 31, 1994.

The officers examined both vehicles for damage from the accident and found that the van had a dented rear panel on its left side and that the auto had a dented right front fender. The officers completed a Vehicle Accident Report at 10:45 A.M. The report number was 06598004359.

NYPD - TEST PREPARATION KIT

8. Which one of the following is the correct license plate number and description of Mrs. Cloris' vehicle?

   A. NY plate #319GAZ, white 1987 Chevrolet van
   B. NY plate #319GZA, red 1989 GMC station wagon
   C. NY plate #319GAZ, red 1989 Chevrolet station wagon
   D. NY plate #319GAZ, white 1989 Chevrolet van

9. At what time did the traffic accident occur?

   A. Before 10:00 A.M.   C. 10:15 A.M.
   B. 10:10 A.M.   D. 10:20 A.M.

10. How many personal injuries resulted from the traffic accident?

   A. 0   B. 1   C. 2   D. 3

NYPD - TEST PREPARATION KIT

WRITTEN EXPRESSION - This ability involves using English words or sentences in writing so that others will understand. Some samples of questions using this ability follow:

11.   While on patrol, Officer Wilson responds to a traffic accident. The following details were obtained at the scene:

Place of Accident: Intersection of 13th Avenue and 83rd Street
Time of Accident: 6:30 P.M.
Vehicle Involved: 1993 Buick
Driver: Elizabeth Pollock
Damage: Vehicle struck a guardrail causing a dented front fender.

Officer Wilson is completing a report of the incident. Which one of the following expresses the above information <u>most clearly, accurately and completely</u>?

A)   At 6:30 P.M. Elizabeth Pollock was at the intersection of 13th Ave. and 83rd Street. A 1993 Buick was involved in an accident when it struck a guardrail causing a dented front fender.
B)   A car was involved in an accident at the intersection of 13th Ave. and 83rd St. at 6:30 P.M. It struck a guardrail causing a dented front fender. Elizabeth Pollock has a 1993 Buick.
C)   A 1993 Buick driven by Elizabeth Pollock struck a guardrail at the intersection of 13th Ave. and 83rd St. at 6:30 P.M., causing a dented front fender.
D)   A 1993 Buick struck Elizabeth Pollock causing a dented front fender at the intersection of 13th Ave. and 83rd St. at 6:30 P.M.

NYPD - TEST PREPARATION KIT

A student officer is preparing a report on the specialized Bureaus within the NYPD as a homework assignment. She reviews the rough draft of her report, which contains the following two sentences:

1. The Operations Unit the Department's information gathering, storing, and disseminating unit for a wide variety of incidents including spontaneous and ongoing situations.

2. To carry out its mission, it is necessary that the Operations Unit receive status reports concerning ongoing incidents from all Department commands.

12. Which of the following best describes the above sentences?

A) Only sentence #1 is grammatically correct.
B) Only sentence #2 is grammatically correct.
C) Neither sentence #1 nor sentence #2 is grammatically correct.
D) Both sentence #1 and sentence #2 are grammatically correct.

NYPD - TEST PREPARATION KIT

INFORMATION ORDERING - This ability involves following correctly a rule or set of rules or actions in a certain order. The rule or set of rules used must be given. The things or actions to be put in order can include numbers, letters, words, pictures, procedures, sentences, and mathematical or logical operations. Some samples of questions using this ability follow:

Recruit officers in the Academy are told that if they are in a situation in which persons are being held hostage or barricaded persons will not voluntarily surrender, they should do the following in the order given:

1. Notify the Communications Division of the situation, so they can notify the patrol supervisor, Emergency Service Unit, and Operations Unit.

2. Verify that the patrol supervisor and Emergency Service Unit are responding.

3. Attempt to confine and isolate the subjects involved, pending arrival of the patrol supervisor and Emergency Service Unit.

4. Maintain firearms control and establish police lines.

5. Maintain continuous surveillance of the location, if possible. Detain witnesses for later debriefing.

13. In a role-play exercise in class, the recruit officers are given a situation in which officers respond to a barricaded person situation. They have notified the Communications Division, and have verified that the patrol supervisor and the Emergency Service Unit are responding. The next step they should take is to:

A) Direct the Operations Unit to respond.
B) Attempt to confine and isolate the subjects involved.
C) Maintain firearms control and establish police lines.
D) Detain witnesses for later debriefing.

NYPD - TEST PREPARATION KIT

The instructor tells the Police Science class that when officers stop a vehicle and discover that the operator is driving with a revoked or suspended license, the following steps should be taken in the order given:

1. Confiscate the driver's license.

2. Prepare a Seized Driver's License Receipt/Report.

3. Give the driver the receipt for the license.

4. Make sure the vehicle is parked legally until the registered owner of the vehicle can arrange to have the vehicle removed by a licensed operator.

5. If the driver has two or more unrelated suspensions or his license has been revoked for any reason, arrest and transport the driver to the precinct.

14. The instructor gives the class the following example: Officers who observed a motorist driving erratically stopped him and asked to see his license and registration. The license has been revoked, although the car's registration appeared valid. What should the officers do next?

A) Confiscate the driver's license.
B) Prepare a Seized Driver's License Receipt/Report.
C) Arrest the driver and transport him to the precinct.
D) Direct the driver to park the vehicle in a legal space.

NYPD - TEST PREPARATION KIT

INDUCTIVE REASONING - This ability involves combining separate pieces of information, or specific answers to problems, to form general rules or conclusions. It involves the ability to think of possible reasons for why things go together. Some samples of questions using this ability follow:

During a simulation exercise, recruits at the Academy learn that as officers, they may have cause to investigate suspected drug laboratories. In this instance, an immediate notification must be made to the desk officer of the precinct of occurrence, so that the Police Laboratory can send a chemist to the scene. Certain substances in a laboratory are highly volatile, therefore, ALL members of the service will follow these safety guidelines:

1. Ventilate the laboratory by opening doors and windows.
2. DO NOT turn on lights or use flashlights until the area is well ventilated. If necessary to enter prior to the room being ventilated, a flashlight should be turned on BEFORE entering the area.
3. DO NOT smoke at the scene.
4. Use your nose. If vapors are very strong or there is any odor of bitter almonds, remain outside and await arrival of the laboratory chemist.
5. DO NOT use department radios while inside the laboratory.
6. DO NOT disturb flasks or containers that are being heated or cooled. Direct the attention of the chemist to such items.
7. DO NOT allow acid and cyanide to be mixed or come together. The fumes from this mixture can cause death.

15. Based on this information, it would be most correct for the recruits to conclude that the primary concern behind these guidelines is:

A) Proper control of evidence at a possible crime scene until a search warrant can be obtained.
B) Safety of the officers concerning possible explosions or exposure to fumes.
C) Keeping officers from accidental or intentional exposure to controlled substances (e.g. narcotics).
D) Preservation of confidentiality concerning the nature of the situation.

NYPD - TEST PREPARATION KIT

Answer question 16 based solely on the following information:

In a Law class in the Academy, recruit officers learn about the different types and classes of offenses covered in the Penal Law. The class is given the following information:

TYPE OF OFFENSE	CLASS OF OFFENSE	DESCRIPTION OF OFFENSE
Petit Larceny	"A" Misdemeanor	Stealing property worth up to $1,000
Grand Larceny - 4th Degree	"E" Felony	Stealing property worth more than $1,000
Grand Larceny - 3rd Degree	"D" Felony	Stealing property worth more than $3,000
Grand Larceny - 2nd Degree	"C" Felony	Stealing property worth any amount of money while making a person fear injury or damage to property
Assault - 3rd Degree	"A" Misdemeanor	Injuring a person
Assault - 2nd Degree	"D" Felony	1. Seriously injuring a person; or 2. Injuring an officer of the law
Assault - 1st Degree	"B" Felony	Seriously injuring a person using a deadly or dangerous weapon
Aggravated Assault Upon Officer of the Law	"B" Felony	Using a firearm to seriously injure an officer of the law
Menacing - 3rd Degree	"B" Misdemeanor	Making a person fear immediate serious injury
Disorderly Conduct	Violation	Making unreasonable noise

NYPD - TEST PREPARATION KIT

Robbery - 3rd Degree	"D" Felony	Stealing property by force
Robbery - 2nd Degree	"C" Felony	1. Stealing property by force with the help of another person; or 2. Stealing property by force and injuring a person
Robbery - 1st Degree	"B" Felony	Stealing property by force and serious injuring the owner of the property

16.   After reviewing the above table, it would be most correct for a recruit officer to conclude that:

   A)   The higher the alphabetic designation of an offense (e.g. "D" instead of "A"), the more serious it is.
   B)   The higher the degree of an offense (e.g. 3 instead of 1), the more serious it is.
   C)   Injuring a person causes a crime to automatically become a felony.
   D)   Offenses include violations, misdemeanors and felonies.

17.   Student officers are participating in a simulation of exercise in which they have responded to the scene of a mugging. The victim is unconscious, but several witnesses give varying accounts of the incident. Which one of the following is most likely to be correct?

   A) "A male Asian, about 6' 2", 200 lbs, wearing a black jogging suit, approached the victim and began a conversation. He pointed to the telephone, handed her one dollar, and she reached into her pocketbook and took out her change purse. He then struck her in the face, and took both the change purse and her pocketbook, and fled down the stairs to the subway platform and boarded a southbound A train."

   B) "A male Asian, about 6' 2", 200 lbs., wearing a blue jogging suit, approached the victim and began a conversation. He pointed to the telephone, handed her one dollar and she reached into her pocketbook and took out her change purse. He then struck her in the face, and took both the change purse and her pocketbook, and fled down the stairs to the subway platform and boarded a northbound A train."

NYPD - TEST PREPARATION KIT

C) "A male Asian, about 6' 5", 200 lbs., wearing a blue jogging suit, approached the victim and began a conversation. He pointed to the telephone, handed her one dollar, and she reached into her pocketbook and took out her change purse. He then struck her in the stomach, and took both the change purse and her pocketbook, and fled down the stairs to the subway platform and boarded a northbound A train."

D) "A male Asian, about 6' 2", 200 lbs., wearing a blue jogging suit, approached the victim and began a conversation. He pointed to the telephone, handed her one dollar, and she reached into her pocketbook and took out her change purse. He then struck her in the face, and took both the change purse and her necklace, and fled down the stairs to the subway platform and boarded a northbound #3 train."

18. Four witnesses give different accounts of the license plate of a vehicle involved in a hit-and-run accident. Which one of the following is most likely to be correct?

    A)   237AJX
    B)   231AJX
    C)   281AJX
    D)   231AIX

NYPD - TEST PREPARATION

DEDUCTIVE REASONING - This ability involves applying general rules to specific problems and coming up with logical answers. It involves deciding if an answer makes sense. Some samples of questions using this ability follow:

The instructor in the Academy is preparing the class for a role-playing exercise concerning Family Offenses and domestic violence. As such problems require special treatment, it is important that officers be able to recognize these situations. The instructor provides the following information:

As defined in the Family Court Act, a family or household includes persons who:

* Are related by blood (consanguinity)
* Are legally married to one another
* Were formally legally married to one another
* Are related by marriage (affinity)
* Have a child in common regardless of whether such persons have been married or have lived together at any time

An expanded definition of family or household includes the above, as well as persons who:

* Are not legally married, but are currently living together in a family-type relationship
* Are not legally married, but formerly lived together in a family-type relationship

A family/household thus includes "common-law" marriages, same sex couples, different generation of the same family, siblings and in-laws.

A family offense is any act which may constitute disorderly conduct (including acts amounting to disorderly conduct <u>not</u> committed in a public place), harassment, menacing, reckless endangerment, assault 2nd or 3rd degree, or attempted assault between members of the same family/household, as defined in the Family Court Act. If the offense is other than one of the foregoing, and/or the family/household relationship is NOT one defined in the Family Court Act, the offense is NOT A FAMILY OFFENSE and must be processed in Criminal Court.

NYPD - TEST PREPARATION KIT

19. The student officers are now asked to enact a role-play situation involving a family offense. According to the above information, which one of the following would be considered a family offense?

    A) Joey assaults another member of the college football team when he discovers that he "borrowed" both his car and girlfriend for the weekend.

    B) Samantha believes that her ex-husband is not really the father of their oldest child, but has still requested that he pay child support.

    C) Leigh makes a series of harassing midnight calls to her daughter-in-law, accusing her of being an unfit mother.

    D) Roger brings a lawsuit against Susan, his ex-live-in-girlfriend and business partner, for patent infringement.

NYPD - TEST PREPARATION KIT

PROBLEM SENSITIVITY - This ability involves being able to tell when something is wrong or is likely to go wrong. It includes being able to identify the whole problem as well as elements of the problem. Some samples of questions using this ability follow:

20.   During field training, Recruit Officer Washington is assisting at the scene of an explosion. She has been assigned to crowd control while firefighters and emergency medical personnel are at work. Several persons try to move forward past the perimeter line she has established and must maintain. When she asks them to step back, they say that as citizens, it is their duty to help in civic emergencies. Which one of the following things would be best for her to say to avoid problems?

    A)   "If you don't get out of here immediately, I am going to arrest all of you."
    B)   "Deadly asbestos and gasses are in this area. Get out quickly. NOW!"
    C)   "Help me by moving back, and telling the other people to keep walking."
    D)   "We don't need help from untrained persons. You're more dangerous than useful."

21.   Recruit officers in the Academy are told that they should never use their radios at the scene of a possible bomb. It would be most correct for the recruits to conclude that the primary concern behind this rule is that use of radios could:

    A)   Tip off the press, whose presence could cause additional problems.
    B)   Cause a panic among persons who have not yet been evacuated from the premises.
    C)   Trigger the premature detonation of the explosive device.
    D)   Block other important transmissions on the frequency.

NYPD - TEST PREPARATION KIT

<u>**NUMBER FACILITY**</u> - This ability involves adding, subtracting, multiplying and dividing quickly and correctly. Some samples of questions using this ability follow:

22.   In physical training class, Student Officer Chan completed the mile and a half run in 15 minutes. What is this speed in miles per hour?

    A)   3.75   B)   6   C)   16.666   D)   22.5

The recruit officers are told by their Social Sciences instructor that the quizzes they take in class are an important part of their evaluation. Since the quizzes are of different length, they vary in their importance. However, the recruit officers are told that they must have correctly answered 70% of their total classroom quiz questions in order to pass the course. The members of Recruit Officer Chan's study group have obtained the following scores:

Recruit Officer	Quiz 1 Score 20 questions total	Quiz 2 Score 45 questions total	Quiz 3 Score 15 questions total	Quiz 4 Score 20 questions total	Quiz 5 Score 50 questions total
Chan	15 correct	35 correct	13 correct	19 correct	44 correct
Fox	12 correct	34 correct	10 correct	15 correct	33 correct
Monzetti	18 correct	38 correct	14 correct	13 correct	38 correct
Vole	16 correct	40 correct	11 correct	17 correct	40 correct

23.   Which one of the following recruit officers is most likely to fail the Social Science course due to low scores on quizzes?

    A)   Chan   B)   Fox   C)   Monzetti   D)   Vole

NYPD - TEST PREPARATION KIT

MATHEMATICAL REASONING - This ability involves being able to reason abstractly using quantitative concepts and symbols. It includes reasoning through mathematical problems in order to determine appropriate operations that can be performed to solve them.

24. Police Officer Thomas O'Toole is assigned to verify that all the equipment assigned to the Coney Island detail is still on hand. Officer O'Toole counts the following property:

Quantity	Item
23	Barriers
15	Portable Radios
2	3 Wheel Scooters
3	2 Wheel Scooters
1	Portable Telephone

Officer O'Toole is required to make an entry in his memo book regarding the total number of items he has counted. Which one of the following formulas would Officer O'Toole be correct to use?

A) 23+15+2(3)+3(3)+1
B) 23+15+3+1
C) 23+15+2+3+1
D) 23+15+2+3+3+2+1

25. Police Officer Sam Jackson has arrested Bill Gorman for burglary. The following is a list of currency Mr. Gorman possessed at the time of his arrest.

Denomination	Number Possessed
$1	12
$5	4
$10	5
$20	12

Officer Jackson must count the money and inform the desk officer of the total amount of money taken from the suspect. Which one of the following formulas should Officer Jackson use to correctly calculate the total amount?

A) $1+12+$5+4+$10+5+$20+12
B) 12+4+5+12
C) $12+$5(4)+$10(5)+$20(12)
D) $1+$5+$10+$20

NYPD – TEST PREPARATION KIT

26. Officer Karen Campisi issued the following summonses during a four week period.

Week Number	Moving Summonses	Parking Summonses
1	12	24
2	11	36
3	8	40
4	13	28

Officer Campisi is required to list the total number of summonses in her Activity-Log at the end of the four week period. Which one of the following formulas will provide an accurate amount of summonses issued.

A) 1(12+24) + 2(11+36) + 3(8+40) + 4(13+28)
B) 12 + 11 + 8 + 13 + 24 + 36 + 40 + 28
C) 12 + 11 + 8 + 13
D) 24 + 36 + 40 + 28

NYPD – TEST PREPARATION KIT

ANSWERS

1.	C		14.	A
2.	D		15.	B
3.	B		16.	D
4.	A		17.	B
5.	B		18.	B
6.	C		19.	C
7.	A		20.	C
8.	C		21.	C
9.	B		22.	B
10.	A		23.	B
11.	C		24.	C
12.	B		25.	C
13.	B		26.	B

Exercise 2

TEST PREPARATION KIT

Social Security No.	_____
Room No.	_____
Seat No.	_____
Location	_____

MEMORY BOOKLET

POLICE OFFICER SERIES
PRACTICE EXAM No. 1

DO NOT OPEN THIS BOOKLET UNTIL THE SIGNAL IS GIVEN!

Write your Social Security Number, Room Number, Seat Number, and Location in the appropriate spaces at the top of this page. You MUST follow the instructions below.

ANYONE DISOBEYING ANY OF THE INSTRUCTIONS FOUND IN THE TEST INSTRUCTION BOOKLET MAY BE DISQUALIFIED AND RECEIVE A ZERO ON THE ENTIRE TEST.

This booklet contains several wanted posters. Study these wanted posters and try to remember as many details as you can. Pay equal attention to the descriptions and faces shown in the pictures and sketches. Do not write or make any notes while studying the wanted poster.

FIRST SIGNAL: **OPEN MEMORY BOOKLET.** You will be given 10 minutes to try to remember as many details about the posters as you can. You may not write or make any notes during this time. DO NOT TURN TO ANY OTHER PAGE DURING THIS TIME.

SECOND SIGNAL: **TURN TO NEXT PAGE.** Answer the four questions on the answer sheet. You will have 5 minutes to complete this section. DO NOT TURN TO ANY OTHER PAGE DURING THIS TIME. YOU MAY NOT LOOK BACK AT THE PICTURE, ANSWER STRICTLY FROM MEMORY.

THIRD SIGNAL: **CLOSE MEMORY BOOKLET.** It will be collected by the monitor. The Test Booklet will then be distributed. You may not write or make any notes during this time. DO NOT OPEN THE TEST BOOKLET.

DO NOT OPEN THIS BOOKLET UNTIL THE SIGNAL IS GIVEN!

TEST PREPARATION KIT

WANTED
RAPE

NAME........................Adam Antler
AGE...........................35
RACE.......................White
HEIGHT....................6'6"
WEIGHT...................230 lbs.
HAIR.........................Black
EYES.........................Brown
COMPLEXION..........Medium
SCARS/MARKS.........Scar on left forehead.

Wanted for multiple rapes in the 125 Pct.
Threatens victims with machete. Uses fire escape
to gain access to apartments through window.

WANTED
DRUG SALE

NAME........................Beverly Rhodes
AGE...........................35-40
RACE.......................Black
HEIGHT....................5'4"
WEIGHT...................120 lbs.
HAIR.........................Brown
EYES.........................Brown
COMPLEXION..........Medium
SCARS/MARKS.........Beauty mark
(mole) on left cheek. Usually wears thick
glasses.

Wanted for felony sale of Cocaine and
LSD Drives a white BMW. Often
accompanied by a young male Hispanic who
goes by the nickname of "Snow."

TEST PREPARATION KIT

WANTED
FORGERY

NAME.........................	Matthew Maples
AGE............................	25
RACE.........................	Black
HEIGHT....................	5'8"
WEIGHT....................	170 lbs.
HAIR.........................	Black
EYES.........................	Brown
COMPLEXION..........	Dark
SCARS/MARKS........	Heart-shaped

tattoo on left shoulder, walks with a limp.

Wanted for forging checks. Poses as a doctor. Follows postal workers and steals checks from mailboxes.

WANTED
AUTO THEFT

NAME.........................	Juana Lopez
AGE............................	21
RACE.........................	Hispanic
HEIGHT....................	5'11"
WEIGHT....................	190 lbs.
HAIR.........................	Brown
EYES.........................	Blue
COMPLEXION..........	Medium
SCARS/MARKS.......	Missing ring finger on

left hand.

Wanted for running a "Chop Shop" and multiple thefts of luxury autos - particularly late model Mercedes-Benz convertibles.

TEST PREPARATION KIT

WANTED
MATERIAL WITNESS

NAME.........................	Johnny Wong
AGE.............................	25
RACE...........................	Asian
HEIGHT.....................	6'
WEIGHT....................	180 lbs.
HAIR...........................	Brown
EYES...........................	Brown
COMPLEXION...........	Light
SCARS/MARKS.........	Withered left arm.

Birthmark on middle of forehead.
Blind in left eye.

Wanted as a material witness to a
multiple murder in New Jersey.

WANTED
ASSAULT

NAME..........................	John Colorodo
AGE.............................	23
RACE...........................	White
HEIGHT.....................	5'8"
WEIGHT....................	145 lbs.
HAIR...........................	Blonde
EYES...........................	Hazel
COMPLEXION.........	Ruddy
SCARS/MARKS.........	Wooden left leg.

Wanted for assaulting his girlfriend.
Almost always accompanied by his
sheepdog named "Martha."

TEST PREPARATION KIT

YOU MAY <u>NOT</u> LOOK BACK AT THE MEMORY BOOKLET.

Answer questions 1 through 4 on the basis of the sketches in the memory booklet.

1. With regard to the person who committed assault, which one of the following choices is correct?

    (A) The person poses as a doctor.
    (B) The person drives a Mercedes-Benz convertible.
    (C) The person is blind in his left eye.
    (D) The person has a wooden left leg.

2. With regard to the person wanted for auto theft, which one of the following choices is correct?

    (A) The person is missing a ring finger on their left hand.
    (B) The person drives a white BMW.
    (C) The person goes by the nickname of "Snow."
    (D) The person walks with a limp.

3. Which one of the persons below is wanted for forgery?

(A) (B) (C) (D)

4. Which one of the persons below is wanted for rape?

(A) (B) (C) (D)

ENTER YOUR ANSWERS ON THE ANSWER SHEET.
STOP WORK ON SIGNAL

TEST PREPARATION KIT

Social Security No. _____

Room No. _____

Seat No. _____

Location _____

TEST BOOKLET

POLICE OFFICER SERIES
PRACTICE EXAM No. 1
Written Test: Weight 100

Time Allowed: 50 minutes (Questions 5-44)

DO NOT OPEN THIS BOOKLET UNTIL THE SIGNAL IS GIVEN!

Record your answers on the official Answer Sheet before the last signal. If you wish, you may also record your answers in the Test Booklet, before the last signal is given.

This test booklet contains procedures which are to be used to answer certain questions. These procedures are not necessarily those of the New York City Police Department. However, you are to answer these questions solely on the basis of the material given.

After the signal is given, open this test booklet and begin work. You will have 50 minutes to complete this portion of the test.

You may make notes in this booklet and use the scrap paper on your desk. If you need additional scrap paper, ask the monitor.

Remember, only your official Answer Sheet will be rated, so be sure to mark <u>all</u> your answers on the official Answer Sheet before the signal. <u>No</u> additional time will be given for marking your answers after the test has ended.

ON SIGNAL: **OPEN TEST BOOKLET** and begin work. This part consists of 40 questions (5-44). Check to make sure that the Test Booklet goes up to and includes question No. 44, and is <u>not</u> defective. You will have 50 minutes from this signal to complete all the questions.

DO NOT OPEN THIS BOOKLET UNTIL THE SIGNAL IS GIVEN!

TEST PREPARATION KIT

Answer questions 5 through 8 solely on the basis of the following passage.

Police Officers Bret Clemens and Sam Harte are dispatched to 83-67 Richardson Boulevard, Apt. 23F, at 8:53 P.M., on November 18, 1992, in response to a burglary reported by a Mr. Kegler. They arrive at the apartment at 8:58 P.M., ring the doorbell and are greeted by Mr. and Mrs. Kegler. Mr. Kegler tells the officers that he left for his foreman's job at the telephone company at 7:00 A.M. and that his wife left for her secretary's job 10 minutes later. After work, Mr. Kegler picked up his wife and they returned to their apartment at 8:40 P.M., having eaten dinner out. When Mrs. Kegler entered the bedroom, she noticed her jewelry box on the floor. She told her husband, who then called the police. While the Keglers waited for the police to arrive, they discovered that all of Mrs. Kegler's jewelry and Mr. Kegler's coin collection, as well as approximately $175.00 in cash, were missing.

While Officer Harte begins to fill out a crime report, Officer Clemens goes to other apartments on the same floor to interview neighbors who might have additional information about the burglary.

Mrs. Johnston, age 35, a housewife, who lives in Apt. 23C located directly opposite the elevator, tells Officer Clemens that she heard voices in the hallway outside her apartment door at 4:30 P.M. She thought that the voices were those of a neighbor's children who sometimes play in the hallway. She opened her door to chase them away but, instead, saw two strange males standing by the elevator. They wore green work clothes. She noticed that the taller man was white, about 28 years old, 5'11", 165 lbs., with brown hair and was carrying a square leather case. The other man was Hispanic, about 21 years old, 5'7", 150 lbs., with black hair and a scar on the left side of his face.

Officer Clemens then contacts other residents at apartment 23D, 23E, and 23G. All of them tell the officer that they did not see or hear anything unusual. Officer Clemens then returns to the Keglers' apartment to tell his partner what he learned. In the meantime, Officer Harte had been told by Mr. Kegler that his coin collection was in a square brown leather carrying case.

Officer Harte was also told that Mr. Kegler is 42 years old. His telephone number at work is 827-6138 and his work address is 273 Eastern Avenue. Mrs. Kegler's telephone number at work is 746-3279 and her work address is 131 South Moore Street. The Kegler's home telephone number is 653-3946. Mrs. Johnston's telephone number at home is 653-2714.

Officers Harte and Clemens finish their investigation and complete the crime report.

5.   Which one of the following apartments is directly opposite the elevator?

A. 23B   B. 23C   C. 23F   D. 23G

TEST PREPARATION KIT

6. Which one of the following was <u>not</u> stolen during the burglary of the Kegler's apartment?

A. $175.00   C. Mr. Kegler's coin collection
B. Mrs. Kegler's jewelry   D. Credit cards

7. What is the approximate age of the taller of the two strangers seen standing near the elevator?

A. 21   B. 28   C. 42   D. 57

8. Which one of the following identifying marks is part of the description of the shorter male stranger seen standing near the elevator?

A. Scar   B. Tattoo   C. Birthmark   D. Mole

9. While on patrol, Officer James responds to a traffic accident. The following details were obtained at the scene:

Place of Accident:	Intersection of 3rd Ave. and 43rd St.
Time of Accident:	4:30 P.M.
Vehicle Involved:	1983 Volvo
Driver:	Joe Bedford
Damage:	Vehicle struck a lamppost causing a dented front bumper.

Officer James is completing a report of the incident. Which one of the following expresses the above information <u>most clearly, accurately and completely</u>?

A. A 1983 Volvo driven by Joe Bedford struck a lamppost at the intersection of 3rd Ave. and 43rd St. at 4:30 P.M., causing a dented front bumper.

B. A car was involved in an accident at the intersection of 3rd Ave. and 43rd St. at 4:30 P.M. It struck a lamppost causing a dented front bumper. Joe Bedford has a 1983 Volvo.

C. At 4:30 P.M. Joe Bedford was at the intersection of 3rd Ave. and 43rd St. A 1983 Volvo was involved in an accident when it struck a lamppost causing a dented front bumper.

D. A 1983 Volvo struck Joe Bedford causing a dented front bumper at the intersection of 3rd Ave. and 43rd St. at 4:30 P.M.

TEST PREPARATION KIT

10. While on patrol, Officer Jones responds to a grand larceny. The following details were obtained at the scene:

Place of Crime: In front of 1430 5th Avenue
Time of Crime: Between 8:30 A.M. and noon
Victim: Andrea Jason
Crime: Purse Snatching
Suspect: Unidentified

Officer Jones is completing a report of the incident. Which one of the following expresses the above information <u>most clearly, accurately and completely</u>?

A. Between 8:30 A.M. and noon, Andrea Jason was in front of 1430 5th Ave. A purse was snatched by an unidentified person.
B. A purse was snatched in front of Andrea Jason at 1430 5th Ave. between 8:30 A.M. and noon by an unidentified person.
C. An unidentified person in front of 1430 5th Ave. snatched a purse between 8:30 A.M. and noon. Andrea Jason has a purse.
D. An unidentified person snatched Andrea Jason's purse in front of 1430 5th Ave. between 8:30 A.M. and noon.

11. While on patrol, Officer Andre responds to a grand larceny. The following details were obtained at the scene:

Place of Crime: In front of 118-92 Shore Avenue
Time of Crime: Between midnight and 8:30 A.M.
Victim: Richard Alvin
Crime: Car Theft
Vehicle Stolen: 1992 Ford
Suspect: Unidentified

Officer Andre is completing a report of the incident. Which one of the following expresses the above information <u>most clearly, accurately and completely</u>?

A. A 1992 Ford was stolen in front of Richard Alvin at 118-92 Shore Avenue between midnight and 8:30 A.M. by an unidentified person.
B. Between midnight and 8:30 A.M. Richard Alvin was in front of 118-92 Shore Avenue. A 1992 Ford was stolen by an unidentified person.
C. An unidentified person in front of 118-92 Shore Avenue stole a car between midnight and 8:30 A.M. Richard Alvin has a 1992 Ford.
D. An unidentified person stole Richard Alvin's 1992 Ford in front of 118-92 Shore Avenue between midnight and 8:30 A.M.

TEST PREPARATION KIT

12.   While on patrol, Officer Wilson responds to a traffic accident. The following details
were obtained at the scene:

Place of Accident: Intersection of 13th Avenue and 83rd Street
Time of Accident: 6:30 P.M.
Vehicle Involved: 1993 Buick
Driver: Elizabeth Pollock
Damage: Vehicle struck a guard rail causing a dented front fender.

Officer Wilson is completing a report of the incident. Which one of the following
expresses the above information <u>most clearly, accurately and completely</u>?

A.   At 6:30 P.M. Elizabeth Pollock was at the intersection of 13th Ave. and 83rd
Street. A 1993 Buick was involved in an accident when it struck a guard rail
causing a dented front fender.
B.   A car was involved in an accident at the intersection of 13th Ave. and 83rd St.
at 6:30 P.M. It struck a guard rail causing a dented front fender. Elizabeth
Pollock has a 1993 Buick.
C.   A 1993 Buick driven by Elizabeth Pollock struck a guard rail at the intersection
of 13th Ave. and 83rd St. at 6:30 P.M., causing a dented front fender.
D.   A 1993 Buick struck Elizabeth Pollock causing a dented front fender at the
intersection of 13th Ave. and 83rd St. at 6:30 P.M.

Answer question 13 solely on the basis of the following information.

A police officer is prohibited from either accepting awards, gifts, loans or things of value to defray
or reimburse any fine or penalty, or accepting a reward for the performance of police service except:

1. Awards from the City of New York Employees' Suggestion Board.
2. Official awards of Departmental recognition.
3. Awards to a member of an officer's family for a brave or meritorious act, from a
   metropolitan newspaper.

TEST PREPARATION KIT

13.   Police Officer Gold captures a bank robber in the act of holding up a bank. To show appreciation, the bank manager gives the officer a check for $100.00. Officer Gold accepts the check. Officer Gold's action in accepting the $100.00 is:

   A.   Proper, because the money was given for performance of a brave act.
   B.   Improper, because the capture of the bank robber was not a meritorious act deserving of a reward.
   C.   Proper, because the money was given as a substitute for Departmental recognition.
   D.   Improper, because a police officer is not allowed to accept a reward from a bank for performance of his duties.

Answer questions 14 through 16 solely on the basis of the definitions given before each question.

   Rape - The crime of rape is committed when:

      1.   A male, being 21 yrs. of age or more, engages in sexual intercourse with a female under 17 yrs. of age;
            or
      2.   A male, being 18 yrs. of age or more, engages in sexual intercourse with a female under 14 yrs. of age;
            or
      3.   A male, being 16 yrs. of age or more, engages in sexual intercourse with a female under 11 yrs. of age.

14.   According to the definition given, which one of the following is the best example of rape?

   A.   Ricky, a 17 year old male, engages in sexual intercourse with a 12 year old female.
   B.   Gil, a 15 year old male, engages in sexual intercourse with a 10 year old female.
   C.   Tim, a 20 year old male, engages in sexual intercourse with a 15 year old female.
   D.   Tony, a 17 year old male, engages in sexual intercourse with a 10 year old female.

   Missing Person - The New York City Police Department classifies a missing person as any person missing from a New York City residence who is:

   1.   Under 18 years of age, or
   2.   Likely to commit suicide, or
   3.   Mentally or physically handicapped, or
   4.   Absent under suspicious circumstances, or
   5.   A possible victim of drowning.

TEST PREPARATION KIT

15. According to this definition, which one of the following should <u>not</u> be classified as a missing person?
    A. Glen Greber, an 18 year old male, is reported missing from his home in lower Manhattan. He had just returned home from vacation.
    B. Bobby Brody, a 22 year old man, is reported missing from his Queens home. He was last seen swimming at a Coney Island beach in very choppy waters.
    C. George Gilliam, a 17 year old male, is reported missing from his Brooklyn home by his parents. He had an argument with his mother and walked out of the house 4 days earlier.
    D. Sally Sanders, a 15 year old female who is mentally retarded, is reported missing after she wandered away from her Bronx home.

<u>**Reckless Endangerment**</u> - The crime of reckless endangerment is committed when a person performs an act, realizing that he is unjustifiably creating a great risk that one may be seriously injured or killed, and disregards the risk.

16. According to the definition given, which one of the following is the best example of reckless endangerment?

    A. Al Green, an exterminator, sprays Bob Boyd's house with a powerful chemical insecticide as Boyd requested. Nobody is supposed to be in the house since inhaling the chemical could cause death. Unknown to Green, one of Boyd's children is sleeping upstairs during the spraying.
    B. Joe Brown, a trapeze artist, performs for a circus. As part of his act, he dangles from a rope 250 feet in the air without a safety net beneath him. There are no spectators seated nearby.
    C. Bill White, a construction worker, is removing bricks from a foot bridge 30 feet above a highway. Since he has nothing in which to cart the bricks away, he decides to drop them down onto the highway, where he sees many autos passing below.
    D. Jimmy Ocher, a teenager, receives a set of darts as a present. Because he has no dart board, he throws his darts at the wall in his bedroom when no one else is home, realizing he could be causing serious damage to the property.

TEST PREPARATION KIT

Answer questions 17 and 18 solely on the basis of the following information.

While making an arrest, a police officer may find that the prisoner has a substance which the officer suspects to be narcotics. After the arrest has been made, the following procedures concerning the suspected narcotics should be used, in the order given:

1. The arresting police officer should notify a ranking officer that the suspected narcotics will be taken to the Police Laboratory for analysis.
2. The police officer must record such notification in his Activity Log.
3. A ranking officer must sign Activity Log under police officer's name.
4. At Police Laboratory, police officer will complete a Narcotics Analysis Request Form in duplicate.
    a. Original copy should be given to Police Laboratory personnel.
    b. Duplicate should be retained by arresting police officer and given to a ranking officer upon return to precinct.

17. Police Officer Ferris, while making an arrest, found a substance that he suspected to be narcotics. Ferris has already notified a ranking officer that he intends to take the substance to the Police Laboratory for analysis. Which one of the following actions should Police Officer Ferris take next?

A. Complete Narcotics Analysis Request Form in duplicate.
B. Record notification in his Activity Log.
C. Ask a ranking officer to sign Activity Log.
D. Have copy of Narcotics Analysis Request Form forwarded to a ranking officer.

18. Police Officer Johnson suspects that a substance he found in the pocket of a man he has arrested may be cocaine. Johnson has already completed all the appropriate actions through completion of Narcotics Analysis Request Form in duplicate at the Police Laboratory.

Which one of the following actions should Police Officer Johnson take next?

A. Give duplicate copy of Narcotics Analysis Request Form to a ranking officer.
B. Give original copy of Narcotics Analysis Request Form to Police Lab personnel.
C. Notify a ranking officer.
D. Record notification in Activity Log.

TEST PREPARATION KIT

Answer questions 19 and 20 solely on the basis of the following information.

Police officers may find it necessary to stop the driver of a vehicle in order to give the driver a summons, or to arrest or question the occupants. In such situations, police officers should follow the following procedures, in the order given:

1. Inform radio dispatcher of location, reason for stopping the vehicle, and description of vehicle and its occupants.
2. Position the police vehicle 6 to 10 feet behind the stopped vehicle.
3. Each police officer is to watch for any suspicious actions by the stopped vehicle's driver or passengers before approaching the vehicle.
4. Determine whether driver is to be summonsed or arrested.
5. If driver is to be given a summons, one police officer is to write the summons while the other observes the driver and passengers for any suspicious action.
6. If arrest is necessary, and additional police officers are required, the additional officers should be summoned by informing the radio dispatcher.

19. Police Officers Fenster and Dickens stop the driver of a 1982 Dodge in order to issue a summons for a traffic violation. There are two passengers in the car. If all appropriate steps have been taken prior to the issuing of the summons, while Police Officer Dickens is writing a summons for the driver, Fenster should be:

A. Checking to ensure that the police vehicle is 6 to 10 feet behind the stopped vehicle.
B. Summoning the radio dispatcher for additional police officers.
C. Watching the driver and passengers for any suspicious action.
D. Informing the radio dispatcher of their location, reason for stopping vehicle, description of vehicle, and description of occupants.

20. Police Officers Benson and Jenson stopped a vehicle in order to question the driver and three occupants. The officers have already completed all appropriate actions through determining that the driver and other occupants should be arrested and that additional police officers are needed. Which one of the following actions should the officers take next?

A. Inform the radio dispatcher that additional police officers are to be summoned.
B. Inform the radio dispatcher of location and reason for stopping the vehicle.
C. Write out summons and give it to the driver.
D. Position police vehicle 6 to 10 feet behind stopped vehicle.

TEST PREPARATION KIT

Answer questions 21 through 24 solely on the basis of the following map. The flow of traffic is indicated by the arrows. You must follow the flow of traffic.

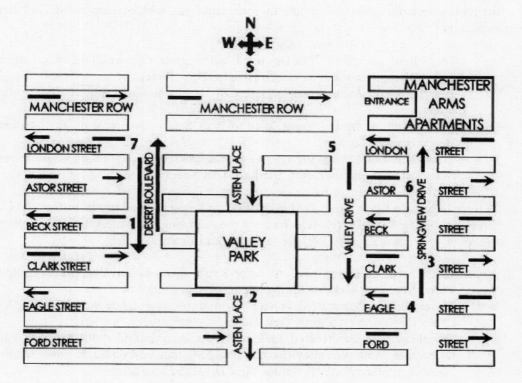

21. If you are located at Manchester Row and Desert Blvd. and travel east on Manchester Row to Valley Drive then turn south onto Valley Drive to Clark Street, and then turn east on Clark Street you will be closest to point:

A. 2   B. 3   C. 6   D. 5

22. If you are located at point 4 and travel north on Spring View Drive to London Street, then west on London Street to Desert Blvd., you will be closest to point:

A. 1   B. 7   C. 5   D. 2

TEST PREPARATION KIT

23.   You are located at Astor Street and Spring View Drive. You receive a call of a crime in progress at the intersection of Beck Street and Desert Blvd. Which one of the following is the most direct route for you to take in your patrol car, making sure to obey all traffic regulations?

   A.   Travel north on Spring View Drive to London Street, then west on London Street to desert Blvd., then south on Desert Blvd. to Beck Street.
   B.   Travel west on Astor Street to Desert Blvd. then south on Desert Blvd. to Beck Street.
   C.   Travel south on Spring View Drive to Beck Street, then west on Beck Street to Desert Blvd.
   D.   Travel south on Spring View Drive to Eagle Street, then west on Eagle Street to Desert Blvd., north on Desert Blvd. to Beck Street.

24.   You are located on Clark Street and Desert Blvd. and must respond to a disturbance at Clark Street and Spring View Drive. Which one of the following is the most direct route for you to take in your patrol car, making sure to obey all traffic regulations?

   A.   Travel north on Desert Blvd. to Astor Street, then east on Astor Street to Spring View Drive then south on Spring View Drive to Clark Street.
   B.   Travel south on Desert Blvd. to Beck Street, then east on Eagle Street to Spring View Drive, then north on Spring View Drive to Astor Street.
   C.   Travel north on Desert Blvd. to Astor Street, then east on Astor Street to Valley Drive, then south on Valley Drive to Eagle St., then east on Eagle Street to Spring View Drive, then north on Spring View Drive to Clark Street.
   D.   Travel north on Desert Blvd. to Astor Street, then east on Astor Street to Valley Drive, then south on Valley Drive to Clark Street, then east on Clark Street to Spring View Drive.

TEST PREPARATION KIT

Answer question 25 solely on the basis of the following information.

25.   On April 27, 1993, several drug-related homicides were committed at different locations. Based on the descriptions of eyewitnesses, it is believed that the same person committed all the homicides. Police officers are provided with the following description: The suspect is an Hispanic male, with long curly black hair, approximately 150 lbs., missing two fingers on his left hand, and is wearing a purple wind-breaker.

Officer Lopez has stopped four Hispanic males for questioning. Which one of the items of information provided by the witnesses should Officer Lopez consider the <u>most</u> helpful in identifying the suspect?

    A.   The suspect is missing two fingers.
    B.   The suspect is wearing a purple wind-breaker.
    C.   The suspect has long hair.
    D.   The suspect weighs approximately 150 lbs.

26.   While Officer Dean is on patrol, an alarm is transmitted over the police radio regarding a past robbery. The suspect is described as a male, white, blond hair, brown eyes, wearing a brown sweater. The suspect has a moustache and walks with a limp. Police Officer Dean stops four white males for questioning. Which one of the pieces of information provided by the victims should Officer Dean consider the <u>most</u> helpful in identifying the suspect?

    A.   The suspect has blond hair.
    B.   The suspect walks with a limp.
    C.   The suspect is wearing a brown sweater.
    D.   The suspect has a moustache.

TEST PREPARATION KIT

Answer questions 27 and 28 solely on the basis of the following information.

Officer Duggan is assigned to the Evans Housing Development on West 259th Street and April Avenue. Duggan familiarizes himself with the crime statistics of the four buildings in the development for September. All the robberies took place at 20 West 259th Street. All the assaults took place at 5 April Avenue. Mailboxes were broken into only at 7 April Avenue. All the rapes took place at 22 West 259th Street. All the assaults happened between 3 P.M. and 4 P.M. Robberies occurred between 11 A.M. and 1 P.M. The mailboxes were broken into shortly after the mail delivery between 1:30 P.M. and 2:30 P.M. Rapes occurred early in the morning when women left for work from 8 A.M. to 9 A.M.

When Duggan is working an 8 AM to 4 PM tour, he must divide his time among the four buildings to prevent these crimes.

27. To reduce the number of rapes he should patrol

A. 20 West 259th St. from 11 A.M. to 1 P.M.
B. 5 April Avenue from 1:30 A.M. to 2:30 P.M.
C. 12 West 259th St. from 8 A.M. to 9 A.M.
D. 22 West 259th St. from 8 A.M. to 9 A.M.

28. To reduce the number of assaults he should patrol

A. From 3 P.M. to 4 P.M. at 5 April Avenue.
B. From 8 A.M. to 9 AM at 7 April Avenue.
C. From 11 A.M. to 1 P.M. at 5 April Avenue.
D. From 3 P.M. to 4 P.M. at 7 April Avenue.

Answer questions 29 and 30 on the basis of the following:

A police officer may have to place barricades or signals on a roadway to warn motorists of hazardous spots on the road.

29. For which one of the following should an officer place a barricade on the roadway?

A. A one-lane country road.
B. A road with several sharp turns.
C. A road with two filled-in potholes.
D. A road with a broken water main.

TEST PREPARATION KIT

30.   For which of the following should an officer place a barricade on the roadway?

    A.   A 4-lane road with no emergency phone.
    B.   A narrow 2-lane road with an obstruction in the middle.
    C.   A road recently repaved.
    D.   A road covered with dry leaves.

31.   A police officer may have to evacuate people from a dangerous area. From which one of the following areas should a police officer evacuate people?

    A.   A crowded disco.
    B.   A crowded subway station.
    C.   A building where gas is leaking.
    D.   A parking lot where a minor traffic accident has occurred.

32.   A police officer may be called upon to help settle disputes. Which one of the following situations should the officer help settle?

    A.   Two men talking about sports outside a bar.
    B.   A shopkeeper arguing with a customer over an unpaid bill.
    C.   Four teenagers discussing fashion with a shopkeeper.
    D.   A man and a woman running for political office having a debate.

TEST PREPARATION KIT

Answer questions 33 through 36 on the basis of the following sketches. The first face, on the left, is a sketch of an alleged criminal based on witnesses' descriptions at the crime scene. One of the four sketches to the right is the way the suspect looked after changing appearance. <u>Assume that NO surgery has been done on the suspect.</u> Select the face which is most likely that of the suspect.

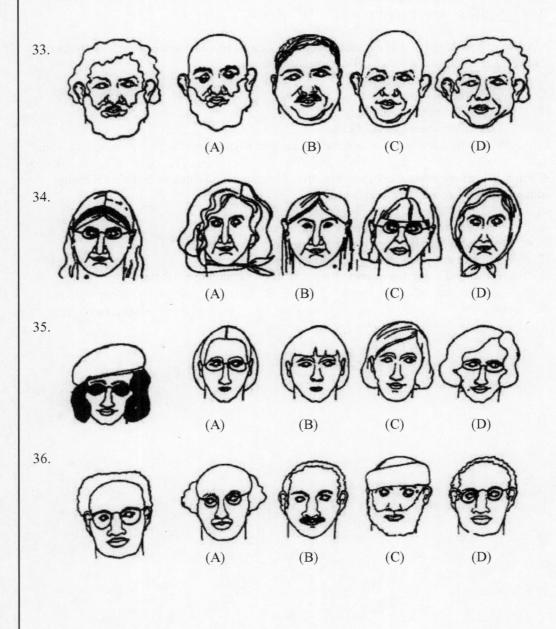

33.

             (A)   (B)   (C)   (D)

34.

             (A)   (B)   (C)   (D)

35.

             (A)   (B)   (C)   (D)

36.

             (A)   (B)   (C)   (D)

TEST PREPARATION KIT

Answer question 37 solely on the basis of the following information.

37. Police Officer Smith has arrested a burglary suspect. The following is a list of the property and dollar value of each item confiscated from the suspect.

Quantity	Items	Dollar Value
1	Radio	$ 95.
2	TVs	$320. each
3	Watches	$200. each
1	Bracelet	$325.
2	Pendants	$ 25. each

Officer Smith is required to voucher the property as evidence. Which one of the following formulas would Officer Smith be correct to use to calculate the total value of the vouchered property?

A. $95 + 5($320+$200)+325+$25
B. $95+$320+5($200+$325+$25)
C. 7($95+$320+$200+$325)+$25
D. $95+2($320)+3($200)+$325+2($25)

38. P.O. Wilson is completing her weekly P.O. Activity Report, in which she lists the police services she rendered during the previous week. The following is a listing of the number of parking summonses she issued during the first week of April:

Day	Parking Summonses
April 5	3
April 6	6
April 7	12
April 8	0
April 9	4

Which one of the following formulas should P.O. Wilson use to calculate the total number of summonses issued during the first week in April?

A. 5 + 3; 6 + 6; 7 + 12; 8 + 0; 9 + 4
B. 5 + 6 + 7 + 8 + 9 x 3 + 6 + 12 + 0 + 4
C. 3 + 6 + 12 + 0 + 4
D. 3 x 6 x 12 x 0 x 4

TEST PREPARATION KIT

Answer questions 39 solely on the basis of the following information.

39. Police Officer Jones has been sent by her sergeant to the property clerk to pick up the following equipment:

Quantity	Item
15	Portable Radios
10	Batteries
15	Radio Cases
1	Battery Charger (Type A)
4	Battery Chargers (Type B)

Officer Jones is required to make a notation in her memo book regarding the total number of items being picked up. Which one of the following formulas would Officer Jones be correct to use?

A. $15 + 10 + 16(2)$
B. $1 + 15(10) + 4(1)$
C. $15 + 10 + 15 + 1 + 4$
D. $15 + 10(15+1)(4)$

Answer question 40 solely on the basis of the following information.

40. P.O. Jones has arrested a suspect for assault. The following is a list of the currency possessed by the suspect at the time of the arrest:

Denomination	Number Possessed
$50	2
$20	8
$10	3
$ 5	1
$ 1	17

TEST PREPARATION KIT

Officer Jones is required to count the money found on the suspect before returning it to her and noting the amount in her memo book. Which of the following formulas would Officer Jones be correct to use to calculate the total amount?

A. 50 + 20 + 10 + 5 + 17
B. 50(2) + 20(8) + 10(3) + 5 + 17
C. 50 + 50 + 20(4) + 10 + 5 + 3 + 17
D. 50 + 2 + 20 + 8 + 10 + 3 + 5 + 1 + 1 + 17

41. P.O. Doe responded to 235 East 20th Street to investigate a report that a man who lived alone had died. Officer Doe arrived at the scene and searched the apartment of the deceased. He found the following items:

Property	# Items	Dollar Value (each)
Ring	1	$ 350.00
Cash	1	$ 100.00
Stamp Collection	1	$1,500.00
Cameras	3	$ 500.00

Officer Doe is preparing a voucher for the recovered property. Which one of the following choices is the total value of the property recovered?

A. $3,450.00
B. $1,750.00
C. $2,000.00
D. $4,450.00

42. P.O. Scott arrested a suspect for illegal sale of narcotics. The suspect possessed the following packages of narcotics:

Weight/Package	# Of Packages
2 lbs. Marijuana	6
6 oz. Cocaine	2
3 oz. Heroin	9

TEST PREPARATION KIT

P.O. Scott is preparing a report of the arrest. Which one of the following choices correctly states the total weight for each narcotic?

A.   8 lbs. Marijuana; 8 oz. Cocaine; 12 oz. Heroin
B.   26 lbs. Marijuana; 12 oz. Cocaine; 39 oz. Heroin
C.   12 lbs. Marijuana; 6 oz. Cocaine; 7 oz. Heroin
D.   12 lbs. Marijuana; 12 oz. Cocaine; 27 oz. Heroin

43.   P.O. Jones has been told by his sergeant to distribute 36 radios equally among the six different squads assigned to the precinct. Which one of the following choices correctly states the number of radios which are to be assigned to each squad?

A.   4
B.   5
C.   36
D.   6

44.   P.O. Jones has arrested John Dunn, a shoplifter at A.S. Department Store. Mr. Dunn had the following stolen items in his possession:

3   Sweaters each valued at $275.00
2   Pants each valued at $73.00
1   Tie valued at $19.00
2   Shirts each valued at $25.00

Which one of the following is the total value of the stolen property?

A. $1,040.00
B. $1,000.00
C. $ 392.00
D. $ 932.00

TEST PREPARATION KIT

ANSWERS

1.	D	12.	C	23.	A	34.	A
2.	A	13.	D	24.	D	35.	D
3.	C	14.	D	25.	A	36.	D
4.	B	15.	A	26.	B	37.	D
5.	B	16.	C	27.	D	38.	C
6.	D	17.	B	28.	A	39.	C
7.	B	18.	B	29.	D	40.	B
8.	A	19.	C	30.	B	41.	A
9.	A	20.	A	31.	C	42.	D
10.	D	21.	B	32.	B	43.	D
11.	D	22.	B	33.	C	44.	A

1 - 4   MEMORY

5 - 8   WRITTEN COMPREHENSION

9 - 12   WRITTEN EXPRESSION

13 - 16 DEDUCTIVE REASONING

17 - 20 INFORMATION ORDERING

21 - 24 SPATIAL ORIENTATION

25 - 28 INDUCTIVE REASONING

29 - 32 PROBLEM SENSITIVITY

33 - 36 VISUALIZATION

37 - 40 MATHEMATICAL REASONING

41 - 44 NUMBER FACILITY

ANSWER SHEET: PRACTICE EXAMINATION 2

1. (A)(B)(C)(D)
2. (A)(B)(C)(D)
3. (A)(B)(C)(D)
4. (A)(B)(C)(D)
5. (A)(B)(C)(D)
6. (A)(B)(C)(D)
7. (A)(B)(C)(D)
8. (A)(B)(C)(D)
9. (A)(B)(C)(D)
10. (A)(B)(C)(D)
11. (A)(B)(C)(D)
12. (A)(B)(C)(D)
13. (A)(B)(C)(D)
14. (A)(B)(C)(D)
15. (A)(B)(C)(D)
16. (A)(B)(C)(D)
17. (A)(B)(C)(D)
18. (A)(B)(C)(D)
19. (A)(B)(C)(D)
20. (A)(B)(C)(D)
21. (A)(B)(C)(D)
22. (A)(B)(C)(D)
23. (A)(B)(C)(D)
24. (A)(B)(C)(D)
25. (A)(B)(C)(D)

26. (A)(B)(C)(D)
27. (A)(B)(C)(D)
28. (A)(B)(C)(D)
29. (A)(B)(C)(D)
30. (A)(B)(C)(D)
31. (A)(B)(C)(D)
32. (A)(B)(C)(D)
33. (A)(B)(C)(D)
34. (A)(B)(C)(D)
35. (A)(B)(C)(D)
36. (A)(B)(C)(D)
37. (A)(B)(C)(D)
38. (A)(B)(C)(D)
39. (A)(B)(C)(D)
40. (A)(B)(C)(D)
41. (A)(B)(C)(D)
42. (A)(B)(C)(D)
43. (A)(B)(C)(D)
44. (A)(B)(C)(D)
45. (A)(B)(C)(D)
46. (A)(B)(C)(D)
47. (A)(B)(C)(D)
48. (A)(B)(C)(D)
49. (A)(B)(C)(D)
50. (A)(B)(C)(D)

51. (A)(B)(C)(D)
52. (A)(B)(C)(D)
53. (A)(B)(C)(D)
54. (A)(B)(C)(D)
55. (A)(B)(C)(D)
56. (A)(B)(C)(D)
57. (A)(B)(C)(D)
58. (A)(B)(C)(D)
59. (A)(B)(C)(D)
60. (A)(B)(C)(D)
61. (A)(B)(C)(D)
62. (A)(B)(C)(D)
63. (A)(B)(C)(D)
64. (A)(B)(C)(D)
65. (A)(B)(C)(D)
66. (A)(B)(C)(D)
67. (A)(B)(C)(D)
68. (A)(B)(C)(D)
69. (A)(B)(C)(D)
70. (A)(B)(C)(D)
71. (A)(B)(C)(D)
72. (A)(B)(C)(D)
73. (A)(B)(C)(D)
74. (A)(B)(C)(D)
75. (A)(B)(C)(D)

76. (A)(B)(C)(D)
77. (A)(B)(C)(D)
78. (A)(B)(C)(D)
79. (A)(B)(C)(D)
80. (A)(B)(C)(D)
81. (A)(B)(C)(D)
82. (A)(B)(C)(D)
83. (A)(B)(C)(D)
84. (A)(B)(C)(D)
85. (A)(B)(C)(D)
86. (A)(B)(C)(D)
87. (A)(B)(C)(D)
88. (A)(B)(C)(D)
89. (A)(B)(C)(D)
90. (A)(B)(C)(D)
91. (A)(B)(C)(D)
92. (A)(B)(C)(D)
93. (A)(B)(C)(D)
94. (A)(B)(C)(D)
95. (A)(B)(C)(D)
96. (A)(B)(C)(D)
97. (A)(B)(C)(D)
98. (A)(B)(C)(D)
99. (A)(B)(C)(D)
100. (A)(B)(C)(D)

ANSWER SHEET: PRACTICE EXAMINATION 2

CHAPTER 10: PRACTICE EXAMINATION 2

National Criminal Justice Officer Selection Inventory

INSTRUCTIONS

- Please answer ALL of the questions in this booklet.
- Select only ONE answer for each question.
- Calculators and electronic spelling aids are NOT allowed.
- Use the space in the margins of your test booklet for scratch paper.
- If you do not know an answer, narrow down your choices and select your "best guess."

SECTION I

Items 1 through 2 are based on the following passage.

When an officer is conducting an investigation of a crime, there are several factors that may influence the ease with which the officer concludes the investigation. The first factor, which is not under the control of the officer, is the type of crime that is being investigated. Typically, more serious crimes such as murder, rape, and armed robbery are more difficult to investigate due to their complicated nature. The amount of physical evidence that is available to the investigating officer may also influence the outcome of an investigation. The greater the amount of physical evidence, the more likely a successful investigation will result. In the same way, the number of available witnesses may affect the success of an investigation. Therefore, it is important for the investigating officer to interview the available witnesses according to the legal guidelines. Finally, the resources available to the officer may determine the success of an investigation. Limited resources will make any investigation more difficult and may even lead to an inconclusive outcome.

1. According to the above passage, how many factors might influence the ease of an officer's investigation?
   (A) One
   (B) Two
   (C) Three
   (D) Four

2. Crimes that are more difficult to investigate are typically
   (A) more serious crimes.
   (B) not complicated.
   (C) those with witnesses.
   (D) those with physical evidence.

Items 3 through 4 are based on the following passage.

Officer Nelson is the Crime Prevention Officer (CPO) in her department. As the CPO it is her responsibility to plan and coordinate crime prevention activities in the community that her department serves. One of her current projects is to educate the local SADD (Students Against Drunk Driving) chapter on the dangers of drunk driving. Her strategy is to educate the members of SADD so that they can in turn educate their peers on the dangers of drunk driving. The goal of this SADD chapter is to reduce the number of drunk driving accidents that occur next year to one-half the number of accidents that occurred this year.

3. What does CPO stand for?
   (A) Certified Public Officer
   (B) Students Against Drunk Driving
   (C) Crime Prevention Officer
   (D) Coordinating and Planning Officer

4. The goal of the local SADD chapter is to reduce the number of drunk driving accidents that occur next year by
   (A) 100 percent.
   (B) 50 percent.
   (C) 200 percent.
   (D) 75 percent.

Items 5 through 6 are based on the following chart.

CHARGES AGAINST JUVENILES

Age (in years)	Charges
7 years or less	No criminal charges can be filed in any court.
7 years or more, but less than 14 years.	Criminal charges can be filed ONLY in Juvenile Court.
14 years or more, but less than 17 years	Criminal charges are filed in Juvenile Court; request for transfer to adult Court is made or ordered by Court for certain crimes.
17 years or more	Criminal charges are filed in adult Court.

5. At what age is there most likely to be a dispute about whether criminal charges may be filed?
   (A) 7 years old
   (B) 11 years old
   (C) 14 years old
   (D) 17 years old

6. A request for transfer to Adult Court may be made for those who are
   (A) 7 years old or less
   (B) 7 years old or more
   (C) 14 years old or less
   (D) 14 years old or more

Items 7 through 10 are based on the following passage.

In recent years, an increasing amount of pressure has been placed on State Police Officers to prove their cases in criminal trials. As a result, State Police Officers have been encouraged to take greater care to ensure the proper collection of evidence. In order to ensure that evidence is used properly, it is important that all evidence be carefully collected, correctly identified, properly packaged, and secured. Once the evidence is secured, it should be accurately described in all State Police entries, journals, logs, forms, and reports.

When collecting evidence, it is also important to keep a careful record of who has come into contact with the evidence. A careful log of who has handled, examined, transported, or stored the evidence will establish a chain of custody that begins the moment the evidence is discovered. This will assure the court that the evidence was not altered in any way before presentation at trial.

When State Police Officers are collecting evidence for presentation at a criminal trial, it is also important for them to be conscious of the fact that the evidence they collect may either implicate or exonerate a person only if the evidence is reliable and valid. Thus, the way the evidence is collected and handled is equally important as the nature of the evidence that is discovered.

7. The chain of custody of the evidence begins
(A) when the evidence is identified.
(B) when the evidence is packaged.
(C) when the evidence is collected.
(D) when the evidence is discovered.

8. In the passage above, the meaning of the word "exonerate" is
(A) to declare someone as guilty.
(B) to declare someone as blameless.
(C) to declare something as greater than it is.
(D) to declare something as worth less than it is.

9. Which of the following is NOT necessary in order to ensure that evidence is used properly?
(A) Identification of the evidence
(B) Proper packaging of the evidence
(C) Cleaning of the evidence
(D) Careful collection of the evidence

10. Police Officer Wendell is the first officer to enter a crime scene. His first action is to collect the evidence that is relevant to the crime. He then carefully packages the evidence and places it in a secure storage bin back at the station. Police Officer Wendell has acted
(A) correctly.
(B) incorrectly; he did not handle the evidence.
(C) incorrectly; he did not clean the evidence.
(D) incorrectly; he did not identify the evidence.

Use the following terminology to answer questions 11 through 12.

Contraband: Any property other than narcotics or other controlled substances that comes into the possession of a police department as a result of confiscation or seizure, or property taken from an arrested person, including material that is not illegal to possess but may serve as evidence.

Controlled substances: All narcotics, and illegal drugs.

Found property: Property that is discovered by a civilian and is turned over to the police department or any Police Officer.

Property custodian: The commanding officer of each Station/Unit who is directly responsible for the control of evidence, contraband, controlled substances, and found, unclaimed, or abandoned property, and who has the responsibility to comply with all applicable procedures.

Unclaimed/abandoned property: Any property that is brought into the police department by any Police Officer.

11. Officer Rivera was patrolling an urban neighborhood when she discovered some children looking through a suitcase that they had apparently found on the side of the road. When she approached the children she discovered that the suitcase contained clothes and some jewelry. She explained to the children that she needed to return the suitcase to its owner and brought it into the police department. What is the best label for the suitcase?
    (A) Contraband
    (B) Controlled substance
    (C) Lost property
    (D) Unclaimed/abandoned property

12. Officer Chan has just arrested a man for threatening his wife and children with a baseball bat. After placing the man in the custody of his police department, Officer Chan gave the baseball bat to an officer at the station. The best label for the baseball bat is
    (A) contraband.
    (B) controlled substance.
    (C) found property.
    (D) property custodian.

Items 13 through 17 are based on the following passage.

Officer St. John was called to a hazardous materials spill at 5:35 p.m. The spill happened on County Road 42 while Officer St. John was on Commonwealth Avenue, which is a 5-minute drive away. The first thing that Officer St. John did when he arrived at the scene was to identify the material involved in the spill. By reading the placards on the tanker truck that had crashed, Officer St. John determined that the liquid that was leaking from the tanker was benzene. He then called the Station Desk Officer, who determined that benzene is a highly flammable liquid and could pose a serious threat to those in the area.

Officer St. John then determined if there was anyone in the area who was at risk of injury from the spill. He noticed that the driver of the truck was unconscious inside the cab of the tanker, but there did not appear to be any other individuals involved in the accident. After ascertaining that there would be no serious risk of injury, Officer St. John removed the driver from the truck and provided basic medical care until other rescue personnel arrived.

After an ambulance and a cleanup team from the Department of Environmental Protection (DEP) had arrived, Officer St. John established a perimeter around the accident. Activity within the perimeter was limited to authorized rescue and cleanup personnel. He then directed traffic around the perimeter to ensure that no other individuals would be at risk of injury.

13. Who determined that benzene is a highly flammable liquid?
(A) Officer St. John
(B) The DEP
(C) The cleanup team
(D) The Station Desk Officer

14. At what time did Officer St. John arrive at the scene of the spill?
(A) 5:35
(B) 5:40
(C) 5:45
(D) 5:50

15. Who is NOT allowed within the perimeter established by Officer St. John?
(A) Local citizens
(B) The cleanup team
(C) Rescue personnel
(D) The DEP

16. How did Officer St. John determine that the material leaking from the tanker was benzene?
(A) He recognized the smell.
(B) He asked the Station Desk Officer.
(C) He read the placards on the tanker.
(D) He asked the DEP.

17. Which of the following represents the order of Officer St. John's activities at the scene?

(A) Provided medical care to the driver, removed the driver from his truck, determined if anyone was in the area, noticed the driver was unconscious, noticed that no one else was involved in the accident, determined there was no risk of injury to himself

(B) Determined if anyone was in the area, noticed that no one else was involved in the accident, provided medical care to the driver, removed the driver from his truck, noticed the driver was unconscious, determined there was no risk of injury to himself

(C) Determined there was no risk of injury to himself, noticed that no one else was involved in the accident, provided medical care to the driver, determined if anyone was in the area, removed the driver from his truck, noticed the driver was unconscious

(D) Determined if anyone was in the area, noticed the driver was unconscious, noticed that no one else was involved in the accident, determined there was no risk of injury to himself, removed the driver from his truck, provided medical care to the driver

Items 18 through 19 are based on the following passage.

A recent report that was released by researchers hired by the department revealed that crimes tended to take place in certain patterns. Officer Costos obtained the following information on crimes in her patrol area: homicides tended to take place from 9 p.m. to 2 a.m., rapes occurred from 10 p.m. to 6 a.m., burglaries tended to occur between 10 a.m. and 2 p.m., and drug-related crimes tended to take place between 10 p.m. and 4 a.m. Rapes generally happened on Friday, Saturday, and Sunday; drug-related crimes usually occurred from Thursday through Saturday; burglaries tended to occur on Monday, Wednesday, and Thursday; and homicides usually occurred on Sunday through Tuesday. The drug-related crimes usually happened on Webster Ave., rapes tended to happen on California St., burglaries usually took place on McNalley Rd., and homicides usually occurred on Austin Rd.

18. In order to reduce the number of homicides, where should Officer Costos concentrate her patrol?

(A) McNalley Rd.

(B) Texas Ave.

(C) Webster Ave.

(D) Austin Rd.

19. Drug-related crimes have been one of the biggest problems on Officer Costos' patrol. How should she concentrate her patrol to reduce the number of drug-related crimes?
    (A) 9 p.m. to 2 a.m. on Friday through Sunday
    (B) 10 p.m. to 4 a.m. on Thursday through Saturday
    (C) 10 p.m. to 6 a.m. on Sunday through Tuesday
    (D) 9 p.m. to 2 a.m. on Thursday through Saturday

Item 20 is based on the following passage.

Officer Simmons was recently involved in a violent confrontation with a suspect that resulted in serious injuries to the suspect. The suspect sustained such intense injuries that he will no longer be able to walk. Officer Simmons feels confident that he acted in a professional manner and only used the force that was necessary to prevent injury to himself and to the suspect. However, Officer Simmons has recently felt very depressed and has had a hard time focusing his attention on his duties.

20. Considering recent events, what is most likely the reason for Officer Simmons' reaction?
    (A) Job stress
    (B) Boredom
    (C) Drugs
    (D) Alcohol

Items 21 through 23 are based on the following passage.

The manager of an electronics store called the police to report that $5,000 worth of merchandise had been stolen the previous evening. When Officer Mills arrived on the scene, he met with the manager in her office. During the interview, the manager expressed her suspicion that one of her employees must have committed the crime. She was unwilling to make any specific claims about who might have taken the merchandise and became very agitated whenever Officer Mills questioned her about her possible involvement in the theft. The manager's anxious behavior created some suspicion in the mind of Officer Mills, who then decided to investigate the manager's background. A check on the manager's arrest history revealed five prior arrests for suspicion of fraud and suspicion of theft. However, the manager had never been convicted of any crime.

21. How many times has the manager been convicted of fraud?
    (A) 5
    (B) 7
    (C) 10
    (D) She has never been convicted.

22. Where did Officer Mills question the manager?
(A) In Officer Mills's office
(B) In the interrogation room
(C) In the manager's office
(D) Outside of the store

23. What does Officer Mills suspect is the reason for the manager's agitation?
(A) She is angry about the theft.
(B) She is nervous because she took the merchandise.
(C) She is upset about the stolen merchandise.
(D) She is shy around people she does not know.

Item 24 is based on the following passage.

Prior to any search of a crime scene, it is important for the scene to be thoroughly documented through photographs or videotape. Officers, investigators, and police equipment should not be included in any of the photographs. Objects of interest should be photographed or videotaped from all relevant angles and then examined for prints before being moved. Close-ups of the objects of interest should document fingerprints, bloodstains, tool marks, bite marks, damaged areas, skid marks, tire tracks, etc. In addition to objects of interest, it is also important to photograph the approaches to the scene, the surrounding area, and the area underneath a body after its removal.

24. Which of the following is NOT mentioned as a part of the crime scene that should be photographed?
(A) Fingerprints
(B) Bite marks
(C) Bloodstains
(D) Police equipment used

Items 25 through 26 are based on the following passage. The people in the passage are identified by the following code:

M = the ambulance
N = the driver
O = the witness
P = the Police Officer
Q = the victim
R = the backup officer

While patrolling her beat, P noticed O flagging her down. When P approached O, she noticed Q laying on the ground unconscious. P immediately called for M and began providing medical assistance to Q. While doing so, P asked O what had happened. O explained that Q was crossing the street legally when N came speeding around the corner, hit Q, and then sped off. P then called R and instructed him to pursue N.

25. Who notified the ambulance that someone needed medical assistance?
(A) The witness
(B) The victim
(C) The Police Officer
(D) The driver

26. Who told the Police Officer what had happened?
(A) The ambulance
(B) The driver
(C) The witness
(D) The victim

Items 27 through 30 are based on the following information.

The first officer to arrive at a crime scene should take responsibility for conducting the preliminary investigation and should not yield this responsibility until directed to do so by a supervisor or until the arrival of the Bureau of Investigative Services (BIS) Investigator assigned to conduct the investigation. While conducting the preliminary investigation, the officer should do the following (in the order listed):

1. Request immediate medical services for victims or suspects who have sustained injuries.
2. Seek to arrest the perpetrator when it is determined that a crime has occurred.
3. If the perpetrator has left the scene, all relevant information should be broadcast using all means available.
4. Preserve the integrity of the crime scene to ensure that evidence is not lost, damaged, or altered in a way that reduces or eliminates its usefulness.
5. Unless absolutely necessary, evidence should not be touched or moved until the arrival of evidence technicians.
6. Reliable witnesses should be identified and located so that they may be interviewed.
7. Detailed field notes should be made of all relevant information concerning the crime scene and evidence.
8. A complete and accurate written report should be made of the incident and all relevant information gathered.

27. If the perpetrator has left the crime scene, the first officer to arrive at the scene should
(A) broadcast all relevant information.
(B) seek to arrest the witnesses.
(C) request backup immediately.
(D) call the appropriate supervisor.

28. If at all possible, the first officer to arrive on the scene should NOT
   (A) request medical services.
   (B) move any evidence.
   (C) identify any witnesses.
   (D) seek to arrest the perpetrator.

29. Who is responsible for conducting the preliminary investigation once the BIS Investigator that is assigned to conduct the investigation has arrived on the scene?
   (A) The first officer on the scene
   (B) The first officer's supervisor
   (C) The assigned BIS Investigator
   (D) The investigation captain

30. If the suspect has sustained injuries, the first officer on the scene should begin by
   (A) arresting the perpetrator.
   (B) requesting medical services.
   (C) broadcasting all relevant information.
   (D) interviewing witnesses.

Items 31 through 33 are based on the following information.

As soon as an officer detects a traffic violation, he or she must attempt to stop the violator as quickly as possible. However, in order to ensure the safety of the violator, the Police Officer, and nearby citizens, it is sometimes better to not pursue or abandon pursuit of the violator. An officer should not pursue or abandon pursuit when:

1. The dangers of exposing the officer and the public to unnecessary risks are clearly too high.
2. The environmental conditions indicate that further pursuit would be futile.
3. The violator's offense is not serious enough to warrant aggressive enforcement.
4. A pursuit that is initiated on a limited access highway proceeds into a densely populated area.
5. The vehicles, roadways, or operators involved degenerate to an unsafe state.
6. A superior orders termination of pursuit.

31. Officer Davis is involved in a high-speed pursuit of a suspect. The road that the suspect is on eventually turns into a gravel road that is clearly unsafe to drive on at high speeds. If Officer Davis continues the pursuit, she is in violation of what rule?
   (A) She is not violating any rule.
   (B) 2
   (C) 3
   (D) 5

32. Officer Drake pulls over a driver for expired license plate tags. He checks the license plates and finds that the car "checks out." As he walks up to the window of the car, the driver speeds off. If Officer Drake pursues this driver, he is in violation of what rule?
    (A) He is violating all six rules.
    (B) 1
    (C) 2
    (D) 3

33. Officer Ferreira is in pursuit of a traffic violator. The pursuit began in a rural part of the city, but it is now headed for a highly populated area of the city. If Officer Ferreira pursues this driver, he is in violation of what rule?
    (A) He is not violating any rule.
    (B) 2
    (C) 3
    (D) 4

For the following items, please identify the choice that best completes the sentence.

34. All police _____ should be thoroughly inspected prior to each use.
    (A) cruisers
    (B) croosers
    (C) cruizers
    (D) croozers

35. The district _____ is the prosecutor for the State or Federal government in a specified district.
    (A) atorney
    (B) atterney
    (C) attorney
    (D) aterney

For the following items, please identify the correctly spelled word that best completes the sentence.

36. Mr. Connor called the police when he noticed a _____ person in his back yard.
    (A) suspishous
    (B) suspicious
    (C) suspicous
    (D) suspishious

37. The detective asked for a full medical report from the victim's _____.
   (A) physision
   (B) physician
   (C) fysicion
   (D) phisician

38. Detective Green is investigating a _____ scheme involving U.S. currency.
   (A) counterfeiting
   (B) counterfiting
   (C) counterfitting
   (D) counterfieting

39. The general _____ of a patrol car is the responsibility of the officer that is assigned to that vehicle.
   (A) manetenance
   (B) maintainance
   (C) maintanence
   (D) maintenance

40. The suspect was held in a State holding facility until his _____.
   (A) arainment
   (B) arrainment
   (C) araignment
   (D) arraignment

41. Department vehicles that are _____ used for transporting prisoners will be modified to ensure the safety of both the officer and prisoner.
   (A) rootenely
   (B) routienely
   (C) routinely
   (D) rootinely

42. During a bomb threat, State Police Officers may be in charge of the _____ of the premises, aircraft, or vessel involved.
   (A) evaacuation
   (B) evaquation
   (C) evaquasion
   (D) evacuation

43. It is necessary to establish guidelines for response to any _____ emergency situation.
   (A) extrordinary
   (B) extraordinary
   (C) extriordinary
   (D) extraordinairy

44. It is necessary to receive departmental approval prior for the _____ of any new program.
   (A) implimentation
   (B) implamation
   (C) implementation
   (D) implemantation

45. All leads should be _____ investigated before closing a case.
   (A) thuroughly
   (B) thorolly
   (C) thorouly
   (D) thoroughly

For the following items, please identify the misspelled word or the incorrectly used word.

46. Officer Harris pursuaded the burglar to put down his weapon, but the perpetrator refused to comply.
   (A) pursuaded
   (B) burglar
   (C) weapon
   (D) perpetrator

47. Officer Stanley's annual performance review showed that her work ethic is acceptional.
   (A) annual
   (B) performance
   (C) review
   (D) acceptional

48. Police Officers have no authority in any places acquired by the United States Governement for military, postal, or customs purposes.
   (A) authority
   (B) acquired
   (C) Governement
   (D) military

49. It is the responsability of the Troop Duty Officer to dispatch the appropriate personnel according to need while maintaining adequate police services within their command.
   (A) responsability
   (B) appropriate
   (C) personnel
   (D) maintaining

50. The police department is committed to officer safety and is responsible for contributing to the sychological, physical, and economic well-being of all of its officers.
   (A) committed
   (B) contributing
   (C) sychological
   (D) physical

51. In order to be qualified for service with the Special Forces Team, an officer must have a minimum of five consequtive years of experience with the State Police.
   (A) qualified
   (B) service
   (C) minimum
   (D) consequtive

52. Any barricaded situation should be handeled by the Hostage Negotiation Team.
   (A) barricaded
   (B) situation
   (C) should
   (D) handeled

53. Mounted Police Units may be dispached to any situation involving outdoor public gatherings.
   (A) Mounted
   (B) dispached
   (C) situation
   (D) involving

For the following items, choose the sentence that contains the misspelled word or words.

54. **(A)** The Bycycle Patrol is the newest addition to the department.
   (B) The man was arrested for numerous traffic violations.
   (C) The Hazardous Materials Team is responsible for handling chemical spills.
   (D) It is important for every officer to deal with job stress in a healthy manner.

55. **(A)** The Underwater Search and Rescue Team is on call 24 hours a day.
   (B) At a fire scene, it is often the police officer's duty to direct trafic away from the scene.
   (C) The station has exercise facilities that may be utilized by all officers.
   (D) The boys' parents were contacted because they were out past curfew.

56. **(A)** The Aerial Support Team may be used for reconnaissance operations.
   (B) Canine units are often involved in locating narcotics.
   (C) The couple had been involved in domestic disputes several times before.
   (D) The officers aprehended two suspects after talking with the witnesses.

57. **(A)** An officer is compensated for time spent in court as a witness for the State.
    (B) The firing range is open to officers on Tuesdays and Thursdays.
    (C) The witness was reluctent to identify herself.
    (D) Her injuries kept her from patrol duty.

58. **(A)** Each officer must sign for additional equipment.
    (B) He is retiring after twenty years of service.
    (C) It is often difficult to find fingerprints in a stolen car.
    (D) Her attitude indicated that she was not being entirely truthfull.

59. **(A)** All officers in the area were deployed to the scene of the shooting.
    (B) Her RADAR indicated that the moterist was traveling 10 mph above the legal limit.
    (C) The morning briefing indicated a lull in criminal activity.
    (D) The Christmas party was fun and also left us with a feeling of camaraderie.

For the following items, choose the word or phrase that correctly completes the sentence.

60. I think that Officer Engstrom _____ promoted to Sergeant next year.
    (A) has been
    (B) was
    (C) is going
    (D) will be

61. The other possibility is that the suspect _____ down the alley.
    (A) ran
    (B) runned
    (C) running
    (D) ranned

62. Without the help of the witnesses, the suspect

    _____.

    (A) would not been found
    (B) did not get founded
    (C) is not found
    (D) would not have been found

63. David _____ the Police Chief until his retirement last year.
    (A) is
    (B) were
    (C) was
    (D) will be

Which punctuation marks are missing from the following sentences?

64. The Police Officers utilize all of their resources in an attempt make their jobs as safe as possible.
   (A) apostrophe
   (B) colon
   (C) semicolon
   (D) none

65. Officer Stevens said that the stations briefing room needed more tables.
   (A) quotations
   (B) apostrophe
   (C) comma
   (D) colon

For the following items, please choose the best answer.

66. An urban university recently reported that 12 percent of its students had been victims of assault the previous year. If a total of 4,225 students were enrolled in this university last year, how many were victims of assault?
   (A) 500
   (B) 507
   (C) 512
   (D) 515

67. If for every mile per hour in speed that a squad car is traveling it takes ¾ of a foot to come to a complete stop, how many feet will it take a squad car traveling 30 mph to come to a complete stop?
   (A) 22.5 feet
   (B) 23 feet
   (C) 25 feet
   (D) 25.5 feet

68. A burglar broke into a photographer's store and stole three cameras valued at $175 each, eight rolls of film valued at $6 each, two lenses valued at $125 each, and five camera bags valued at $25 each. What is the total value of the stolen items?
   (A) $845
   (B) S870
   (C) $924
   (D) $948

69. Officer McNeil received a domestic dispute call at 3:25 p.m. and arrived at the scene at 3:29 p.m. She then mediated the dispute and left the scene at 4:10 p.m. How much time had elapsed from the time of the call until Officer McNeil left the scene?
    (A) 40 minutes
    (B) 43 minutes
    (C) 45 minutes
    (D) 47 minutes

70. Officers in Department X work 10-hour days for four days a week. If 15 percent of an officer's work week is spent on traffic stops, what is this amount of time in hours?
    (A) 4 hours
    (B) 5 hours
    (C) 6 hours
    (D) 7 hours

71. The average paycheck for a nonsupervisory Police Officer is $1,300 (paid every two weeks). Since there are fifty-two weeks in a year, what is the average yearly salary of a nonsupervisory Police Officer?
    (A) $32,000
    (B) $32,600
    (C) $33,000
    (D) $33,800

72. Employees of a 50-person police department are given $400 annually to use for equipment and uniforms. If 75 percent of the employees use the money for uniforms only, how much money do these employees spend on uniforms each year?
    (A) $14,000
    (B) $15,000
    (C) $16,000
    (D) $17.000

73. A typical no-incident crime report takes 10 minutes to complete. This is _____ of an hour.
    (A) ½
    (B) ⅓
    (C) ⅕
    (D) ⅙

Use the following chart to answer questions 74 through 76.

STATION CALLS BY TYPE AND YEAR

	1999	2000	2001	2002
Domestic Dispute	87	97	68	73
Car Accident	154	167	174	186
Auto Theft	56	48	59	43

74. How many domestic dispute calls were received in 2000?
   (A) 83
   (B) 97
   (C) 73
   (D) 104

75. How many more car accident calls were received in 2002 than in 1999?
   (A) 32
   (B) 33
   (C) 34
   (D) 35

76. What was the average number of auto theft calls from 2000 to 2002?
   (A) 47
   (B) 48
   (C) 49
   (D) 50

77. When Officer Fisk is on bicycle duty in the summer, she puts an average of 90 miles on her bicycle during a typical five-day workweek. If she usually puts 22 miles on her bicycle on Mondays, what is the average number of miles that she puts on her bicycle on the other four days of the week?
   (A) 14.5 miles
   (B) 15 miles
   (C) 16 miles
   (D) 17 miles

78. If a police helicopter is traveling at a steady rate of 75 miles per hour, how long will it take the pilot to travel 243 miles?
   (A) 3.24 hours
   (B) 3.42 hours
   (C) 3.43 hours
   (D) 3.58 hours

79. If the gas tank of a squad car holds twelve gallons, and regular-grade gasoline costs $1.34 per gallon, how much will it cost to fill the tank if it is exactly half full?
    (A) $8.00
    (B) $8.03
    (C) $8.04
    (D) $8.06

80. If a squad car holds ten road flares that burn for 2 hours, six flares that burn for a half hour, and three flares that burn for 4 hours, what is the total burn time for all of the flares in a squad car?
    (A) 31 hours
    (B) 32 hours
    (C) 33 hours
    (D) 35 hours

81. Employees of a 75-person police department have the option of taking an additional $50 out of each paycheck and putting it toward their retirement. If 48 percent of the employees gave the additional money to their retirement this year, how much additional money did employees put toward retirement this year (there are 26 paychecks in one year)?
    (A) $46,000
    (B) $46,800
    (C) $47,500
    (D) $48,000

82. In a robbery of an office, eight items were stolen. The total estimated value of the stolen items is $8,304. The most expensive item stolen was a computer scanner valued at $1,300. What is the estimated average value of the remaining items?
    (A) $1,000.57
    (B) $1,034.28
    (C) $1,146.68
    (D) $1,235.46

83. In city Y, a change in street address of 600 is equal in distance to 1 mile. If an officer is at 800 Main St. and is called to 2300 Main St., how far must the officer travel?
    (A) 2 miles
    (B) 2.5 miles
    (C) 3 miles
    (D) 3.5 miles

84. A music store reports that three cases of compact discs were stolen from their storage room. Each case holds 200 compact discs, which sell for $12.95 each. Based on the price per compact disc, what is the value of the stolen merchandise?
    (A) $6,840.35
    (B) $6,999.95
    (C) $7,435.25
    (D) $7,770.00

Items 85 through 86 are based on the following situation.

Four men are arrested for a telemarketing scam that they used to acquire $35,000 each. Each man is held on a bond that is equal to three times the amount that he acquired in the scam.

85. What is the total amount of money that the four men acquired in the telemarketing scam?
    (A) $125,000
    (B) $130,000
    (C) $140,000
    (D) $145,000

86. What is the total bond for each man?
    (A) $35,000
    (B) $70,000
    (C) $90,000
    (D) $105,000

87. Sixty-five watches are stolen from a display case. The total value of the stolen watches is $5,200. What is the average value of each watch?
    (A) $60
    (B) $73
    (C) $80
    (D) $92

88. The following items are listed on a sales invoice:

    | Stereo receiver | $435.72 |
    | CD player | $520.95 |
    | Speakers | $875.23 |

    If the sales tax is 8 percent, what is the total amount due?
    (A) $1,875.56
    (B) $1,895.43
    (C) $1,934.56
    (D) $1,978.45

89. If an officer is traveling to a crime scene at 60 mph and the scene is 15 miles away, how long will it take the officer to travel to the crime scene (assuming no stops are made)?
    (A) 15 minutes
    (B) 16 minutes
    (C) 17 minutes
    (D) 18 minutes

90. The decimal .20 is equivalent to what fraction?
    (A) ¼
    (B) ⅕
    (C) ⅙
    (D) ⅐

91. In Hewson County, Missouri, last year there were 563 domestic abuse calls, 425 car accident calls, 142 burglary calls, 219 trespassing calls, and 451 miscellaneous calls. Police station A received 600 of these calls last year. What percentage of the total number of calls did station A receive?
    (A) 30 percent
    (B) 33 percent
    (C) 35 percent
    (D) 36 percent

92. A recent report showed that 85 percent of arsonists are repeat offenders. If 60 arsonists were arrested in city Z last year, how many of them are likely to commit the same crime again?
    (A) 9
    (B) 15
    (C) 45
    (D) 51

93. A convenience store reports that an average of $6,284 worth of merchandise is stolen every year. They also report that an average of 2,124 items are found missing from the store every year. What is the average cost of each item that is stolen?
    (A) $2.96
    (B) $2.97
    (C) $3.08
    (D) $3.09

94. $3,250 worth of merchandise is stolen from a store every year. The owner estimates that an improved security system would cost $13,000 to install. How many years would the new system have to be in place for the cost of the system to be equal to the total amount of merchandise that is stolen?
    (A) 2
    (B) 3
    (C) 3.5
    (D) 4

95. Officer Kim responded to two very long calls today. He received the first call at 9:25 a.m. and arrived at the scene at 9:53 a.m. He received the second call at 2:56 p.m. and arrived at the scene at 3:24 p.m. How much total time did Officer Kim spend en route to these two calls?
    (A) 28 minutes
    (B) 45 minutes
    (C) 56 minutes
    (D) 70 minutes

96. A man came home to find that his house had been burglarized. The police report listed the stolen items as a TV valued at $542, a stereo valued at $1,594, a VCR valued at $258, 50 CDs valued at $12 each, and 8 video cassettes valued at $24 each. What is the total value of the items stolen?
    (A) $3,004
    (B) $3,089
    (C) $3,186
    (D) $3,193

97. What is 12 squared?
    (A) 144
    (B) 169
    (C) 196
    (D) 225

98. An officer is asked to spend one half hour of every 8-hour workday in briefing. What percentage of the workday is this?
    (A) 6.25 percent
    (B) 6.5 percent
    (C) 6.75 percent
    (D) 7.25 percent

99. A police department's policy on crowd control states that a large nonthreatening crowd, such as people at a sporting event, should have one police officer for every 75 people. If an event has 12,489 people in attendance, how many officers should be present?
(A) 164
(B) 165
(C) 166
(D) 167

100. If the ratio of Police Sergeants to Police Officers is 1:10, how many Sergeants are in a department with 70 Police Officers?
(A) 6
(B) 7
(C) 8
(D) 9

Answer Key

1. **(D)**	21. **(D)**	41. **(C)**	61. **(A)**	81. **(B)**
2. **(A)**	22. **(C)**	42. **(D)**	62. **(D)**	82. **(A)**
3. **(C)**	23. **(B)**	43. **(B)**	63. **(C)**	83. **(B)**
4. **(B)**	24. **(D)**	44. **(C)**	64. **(D)**	84. **(D)**
5. **(A)**	25. **(C)**	45. **(D)**	65. **(B)**	85. **(C)**
6. **(D)**	26. **(C)**	46. **(A)**	66. **(B)**	86. **(D)**
7. **(D)**	27. **(A)**	47. **(D)**	67. **(A)**	87. **(C)**
8. **(B)**	28. **(B)**	48. **(C)**	68. **(D)**	88. **(D)**
9. **(C)**	29. **(C)**	49. **(A)**	69. **(C)**	89. **(A)**
10. **(D)**	30. **(B)**	50. **(C)**	70. **(C)**	90. **(B)**
11. **(D)**	31. **(D)**	51. **(D)**	71. **(D)**	91. **(B)**
12. **(A)**	32. **(D)**	52. **(D)**	72. **(B)**	92. **(D)**
13. **(D)**	33. **(D)**	53. **(B)**	73. **(D)**	93. **(A)**
14. **(B)**	34. **(A)**	54. **(A)**	74. **(B)**	94. **(D)**
15. **(A)**	35. **(C)**	55. **(B)**	75. **(A)**	95. **(C)**
16. **(C)**	36. **(B)**	56. **(D)**	76. **(D)**	96. **(C)**
17. **(D)**	37. **(B)**	57. **(C)**	77. **(D)**	97. **(A)**
18. **(D)**	38. **(A)**	58. **(D)**	78. **(A)**	98. **(A)**
19. **(B)**	39. **(D)**	59. **(B)**	79. **(C)**	99. **(D)**
20. **(A)**	40. **(D)**	60. **(D)**	80. **(D)**	100. **(B)**

Explanatory Answers

1. **The correct answer is (D).** The passage lists four factors that may influence the ease of an officer's investigation: the type of crime committed, the amount of physical evidence, the number of available witnesses, and the resources available.

2. **The correct answer is (A).** The passage states that serious crimes are more difficult to investigate.

3. **The correct answer is (C).** CPO stands for Crime Prevention Officer.

4. **The correct answer is (B).** The goal of the SADD chapter is to reduce the number of drunk driving accidents that occur next year to one-half the number of accidents that occurred this year. In other words, they want to reduce the number of drunk driving accidents by 50 percent.

5. **The correct answer is (A).** There is most likely to be a dispute about what criminal charges may be filed when the juvenile is 7 years of age. A juvenile who is 7 years of age may fit into the first or second age bracket, which may lead to disputes about which age bracket the juvenile belongs in.

6. **The correct answer is (D).** The table indicates that a request for transfer to Adult Court may be made for those who are 14 years of age or more.

7. **The correct answer is (D).** The second paragraph states that the chain of custody of the evidence begins when the evidence is discovered.

8. **The correct answer is (B).** The word "exonerate" means "to declare someone as blameless." This is the opposite of the word "implicate," which means "to declare someone as guilty."

9. **The correct answer is (C).** The first paragraph does NOT state that evidence should be cleaned in order to ensure that it is used properly.

10. **The correct answer is (D).** The first paragraph states that evidence should be carefully collected, correctly identified, properly packaged, and secured. Therefore, Officer Wendell acted incorrectly because he did not identify the evidence.

11. **The correct answer is (D).** The suitcase should be considered "unclaimed/ abandoned property" because it was property brought into the police station by a Police Officer and the property was not discovered during an arrest.

12. **The correct answer is (A).** The best label for the baseball bat is "contraband." Although the bat itself is not illegal, it was found during an arrest and may serve as evidence.

13. **The correct answer is (D).** The last sentence of the first paragraph states that the Station Desk Officer determined that benzene is a highly flammable liquid.

14. **The correct answer is (B).** The selection states that Officer St. John received the call at 5:35 and was a 5-minute drive from the scene. Therefore, he arrived at the scene at 5:40.

15. **The correct answer is (A).** The last paragraph states that activity within the perimeter was limited to authorized rescue and cleanup personnel. This does not include local citizens.

16. **The correct answer is (C).** The first paragraph states that Officer St. John determined that the material in the tanker was benzene by reading the placards on the tanker.

17. **The correct answer is (D).** Choice (D) correctly describes the order in which Officer St. John conducted his activities at the scene.

18. **The correct answer is (D).** The selection states that homicides typically occurred on Austin Rd. This is where Officer Costos should concentrate her patrol.

19. **The correct answer is (B).** The selection states that drug-related crimes usually occur between 10 p.m. and 4 a.m. on Thursdays through Saturdays.

20. **The correct answer is (A).** Considering the results of Officer Simmons' recent confrontation with a suspect, it is likely that his depression and lack of focus are due to job stress.

21. **The correct answer is (D).** The passage states that the manager had been arrested several times for fraud but was never convicted.

22. **The correct answer is (C).** The passage states that Officer Mills met with the manager in the manager's office.

23. **The correct answer is (B).** Officer Mills suspects that the manager is nervous because she is actually the one who took the merchandise. The officer attempts to confirm his suspicions by checking the manager's arrest history.

24. **The correct answer is (D).** The passage states that police equipment should not be included in any of the photographs.

25. **The correct answer is (C).** When the letters are replaced with the respective people involved, the selection states that the Police Officer immediately called for the ambulance before providing medical assistance.

26. **The correct answer is (C).** When the letters are replaced with the respective people involved, the selection states that the witness told the Police Officer what had happened.

27. **The correct answer is (A).** The third point of the selection states that if the perpetrator has left the scene, the first officer on the scene should broadcast all relevant information.

28. **The correct answer is (B).** The fifth point of the selection states that evidence should not be moved unless absolutely necessary.

29. **The correct answer is (C).** The first paragraph states that when the BIS Investigator arrives, he or she is then in charge of conducting the preliminary investigation.

30. **The correct answer is (B).** The first point of the selection states that the first officer on the scene should begin by requesting medical services for suspects who have sustained injuries.

31. **The correct answer is (D).** Point 5 states that an officer should abandon pursuit when the roadway degenerates to an unsafe state. In other words, when the roadway is not in an acceptable condition for high-speed driving, the officer should abandon the pursuit.

32. **The correct answer is (D).** Since the driver was pulled over for expired tags and had no prior violations, pursuit by the officer would be in violation of rule 3. It may not be worth the risk to the officer, the violator, and nearby citizens to pursue a driver for such a minor offense.

33. **The correct answer is (D).** By pursuing a driver into a highly populated area, Officer Ferreira would be in violation of rule 4.

34. **The correct answer is (A).** The correct spelling is "cruisers."

35. **The correct answer is (C).** The correct spelling is "attorney."

36. **The correct answer is (B).** The correct spelling is "suspicious."

37. **The correct answer is (B).** The correct spelling is "physician."

38. **The correct answer is (A).** The correct spelling is "counterfeiting."

39. **The correct answer is (D).** The correct spelling is "maintenance."

40. **The correct answer is (D).** The correct spelling is "arraignment."

41. **The correct answer is (C).** The correct spelling is "routinely."

42. **The correct answer is (D).** The correct spelling is "evacuation."

43. **The correct answer is (B).** The correct spelling is "extraordinary."

44. **The correct answer is (C).** The correct spelling is "implementation."

45. **The correct answer is (D).** The correct spelling is "thoroughly."

46. **The correct answer is (A).** The misspelled word is "pursuaded" and should be spelled "persuaded."

47. **The correct answer is (D).** The misspelled word is "acceptional" and should be spelled "exceptional."

48. **The correct answer is (C).** The misspelled word is "Governement" and should be spelled "Government."

49. **The correct answer is (A).** The misspelled word is "responsability" and should be spelled "responsibility."

50. **The correct answer is (C).** The misspelled word is "sychological" and should be spelled "psychological."

51. **The correct answer is (D).** The misspelled word is "consequtive" and should be spelled "consecutive."

52. **The correct answer is (D).** The misspelled word is "handeled" and should be spelled "handled."

53. **The correct answer is (B).** The misspelled word is "dispached" and should be spelled "dispatched."

54. **The correct answer is (A).** Choice (A) contains the word "Bycycle," which should be spelled "Bicycle."

55. **The correct answer is (B).** Choice (B) contains the word "trafic," which should be spelled "traffic."

56. **The correct answer is (D).** Choice (E) contains the word "aprehended," which should be spelled "apprehended."

57. **The correct answer is (C).** Choice (C) contains the word "reluctent," which should be spelled "reluctant."

58. **The correct answer is (D).** Choice (D) contains the word "truthfull," which should be spelled "truthful."

59. **The correct answer is (B).** Choice (B) contains the word "moterist," which should be spelled "motorist."

60. **The correct answer is (D).** The sentence is talking about one person (Officer Engstrom) and is discussing a future event. Therefore, the phrase "will be" correctly completes the sentence.

61. **The correct answer is (A).** This sentence indicates that the past tense should be used. Therefore, "ran" correctly completes the sentence.

62. **The correct answer is (D).** This sentence indicates the past tense. Therefore, the phrase "would not have been found" correctly completes the sentence.

63. **The correct answer is (C).** This sentence also indicates that the past tense should be used. Therefore, "was" correctly completes the sentence.

64. **The correct answer is (D).** There are no punctuation marks missing from this sentence.

65. **The correct answer is (B).** This sentence is missing an apostrophe. It should read, "Officer Stevens said that the station's briefing room needed more tables."

66. **The correct answer is (B).** It is necessary to find 12 percent of 4,225. To do so, take 4225 times .12. This results in the answer, which is 507.

67. **The correct answer is (A).** For every mile per hour that a car is traveling, it takes $\frac{3}{4}$ of a foot to come to a complete stop. Therefore, it is necessary to find out what $\frac{3}{4}$ of 30 mph is. Take 30 times 3, which is 90, and divide this by 4. This results in the answer, which is 22.5 feet.

68. **The correct answer is (D).** In order to find the answer, take the value of the item and multiply that dollar amount by the number of items. $175 \times 3 = \$525$, $\$6 \times 8 = \$48$, $\$125 \times 2 = \$250$, $\$25 \times 5 = \$125$. Then take the result of each of these equations and add them together. $\$525 + \$48 + \$250 + \$125 = \$948$.

69. **The correct answer is (C).** From 3:25 p.m. to 4:10 p.m. is a period of 45 minutes.

70. **The correct answer is (C).** If officers in Department X work four 10-hour days per week, they work a total of 40 hours per week. 15% of 40 is equal to $40 \times .15 = 6$ hours.

71. **The correct answer is (D).** There are 52 weeks in a year. Since paychecks come every two weeks, there are $\frac{52}{2}$ paychecks in one year. If the average paycheck is $\$1,300$, then the average yearly salary is $\$1,300 \times 26 = \$33,800$ per year.

72. **The correct answer is (B).** If 75 percent of a 50-person police department use the $\$400$ for uniforms only, then $50 \times .75 = 37.5$ people use the money for uniforms only. Thus, these employees spend $\$400 \times 37.5 = \$15,000$ per year on uniforms.

73. **The correct answer is (D).** There are 60 minutes in every hour. 10 minutes is equal to $\frac{10}{60} = \frac{1}{6}$ of an hour.

74. **The correct answer is (B).** Take the total number of calls in 2000 minus the number of car accident and auto theft calls in 2000. $(312 - 167 + 48) = 97$.

75. **The correct answer is (A).** Take the number of car accident calls in 1993 minus the number of car accident calls in 1999. $186 - 154 = 32$.

76. **The correct answer is (D).** In order to find the average, add up the numbers of interest and divide by the number of numbers that you just added. $\frac{150}{3} = 50$.

77. **The correct answer is (D).** Officer Fisk puts an average of 90 miles on her bike during a five-day workweek. If she usually puts 22 miles on her bike on Mondays, then the average for the rest of the week should be equal to $90 - 22 = \frac{68}{4} = 17$ miles per day.

78. **The correct answer is (A).** It should take the pilot $\frac{243}{75} = 3.24$ hours.

79. **The correct answer is (C).** If the tank is exactly half full, the tank will hold an additional 6 gallons. At $1.34 per gallon, it would cost $1.34 × 6 = $8.04 to fill the tank.

80. **The correct answer is (D).** 10 × 2 = 20, 6 × .5 = 3, 3 × 4 = 12. 20 + 3 + 12 = 35 hours.

81. **The correct answer is (B).** 48 percent of 75 employees is equal to 75 × .48 = 36. If 36 employees took an additional $50 out of 26 paychecks this year, then $50 × 26 = $1,300; $1,300 × 36 = $46,800.

82. **The correct answer is (A).** If one of the items stolen costs $1,300, then the remaining seven items cost an average of $8,304 – $1,300 = $\frac{\$7,004}{7}$ = $1,000.57.

83. **The correct answer is (B).** A difference in street numbers of 600 is the same distance as 1 mile. Since the officer is traveling from 800 to 2300, take 2300 – 800 = $\frac{1500}{600}$ = 2.5 miles.

84. **The correct answer is (D).** Three cases were stolen and each case holds 200 CDs, so 200 × 3 = 600 CDs were stolen. If each CD sells for $12.95, then 600 × 12.95 = $7,770.00.

85. **The correct answer is (C).** Four men each acquired $35,000, so $35,000 × 4 = $140,000.

86. **The correct answer is (D).** The total bond for each man is equal to three times the amount that each man acquired. $35,000 × 3 = $105,000.

87. **The correct answer is (C).** $\frac{\$5,200}{65}$ = $80.

88. **The correct answer is (D).** Not including the sales tax, the total amount is $435.72 + $520.95 + S875.23 = $1,831.90. Including the sales tax, the total amount due is $1,831.90 × .08 = $146.55 + $1,831.90 = $1,978.45.

89. **The correct answer is (A).** There are 60 minutes in every hour. When traveling at a steady rate of 60 miles per hour, it takes 1 minute to travel 1 mile. Thus, at this rate, it should take 15 minutes to travel 15 miles.

90. **The correct answer is (B).** 1 divided by 5 is equal to .20.

91. **The correct answer is (B).** The total number of calls last year is equal to 563 + 425 + 142 + 219 + 451 = 1,800 calls. Station A received $\frac{600}{1800}$ = 33% of these calls.

92. **The correct answer is (D).** 85% of 60 is equal to 60 × .85 = 51.

93. **The correct answer is (A).** $\frac{\$6,284}{2124}$ = $2.96.

94. **The correct answer is (D).** $^{\$13,000}/_{\$3,250} = 4$.

95. **The correct answer is (C).** The first call required 28 minutes of travel time. The second call also required 28 minutes of travel time. Thus, the two calls together required $28 + 28 = 56$ minutes of travel time.

96. **The correct answer is (C).** $\$542 + \$1,594 + \$258 + (50 \times \$12 = \$600) + (8 \times \$24 = \$192) = \$3,186$.

97. **The correct answer is (A).** 12 squared is equal to $12 \times 12 = 144$.

98. **The correct answer is (A).** $^{.5}/_{8} = 6.25\%$.

99. **The correct answer is (D).** $^{12,489}/_{75} = 166.52$. Since we cannot have .52 of a Police Officer, we must have 167 officers present.

100. **The correct answer is (B).** $^{70}/_{10} = 7$.

ANSWER SHEET: PRACTICE EXAMINATION 3

1. (A) (B) (C) (D)
2. (A) (B) (C) (D)
3. (A) (B) (C) (D)
4. (A) (B) (C) (D)
5. (A) (B) (C) (D)
6. (A) (B) (C) (D)
7. (A) (B) (C) (D)
8. (A) (B) (C) (D)
9. (A) (B) (C) (D)
10. (A) (B) (C) (D)
11. (A) (B) (C) (D)
12. (A) (B) (C) (D)
13. (A) (B) (C) (D)
14. (A) (B) (C) (D)
15. (A) (B) (C) (D)
16. (A) (B) (C) (D)
17. (A) (B) (C) (D)
18. (A) (B) (C) (D)
19. (A) (B) (C) (D)
20. (A) (B) (C) (D)
21. (A) (B) (C) (D)
22. (A) (B) (C) (D)
23. (A) (B) (C) (D)
24. (A) (B) (C) (D)
25. (A) (B) (C) (D)

26. (A) (B) (C) (D)
27. (A) (B) (C) (D)
28. (A) (B) (C) (D)
29. (A) (B) (C) (D)
30. (A) (B) (C) (D)
31. (A) (B) (C) (D)
32. (A) (B) (C) (D)
33. (A) (B) (C) (D)
34. (A) (B) (C) (D)
35. (A) (B) (C) (D)
36. (A) (B) (C) (D)
37. (A) (B) (C) (D)
38. (A) (B) (C) (D)
39. (A) (B) (C) (D)
40. (A) (B) (C) (D)
41. (A) (B) (C) (D)
42. (A) (B) (C) (D)
43. (A) (B) (C) (D)
44. (A) (B) (C) (D)
45. (A) (B) (C) (D)
46. (A) (B) (C) (D)
47. (A) (B) (C) (D)
48. (A) (B) (C) (D)
49. (A) (B) (C) (D)
50. (A) (B) (C) (D)

51. (A) (B) (C) (D)
52. (A) (B) (C) (D)
53. (A) (B) (C) (D)
54. (A) (B) (C) (D)
55. (A) (B) (C) (D)
56. (A) (B) (C) (D)
57. (A) (B) (C) (D)
58. (A) (B) (C) (D)
59. (A) (B) (C) (D)
60. (A) (B) (C) (D)
61. (A) (B) (C) (D)
62. (A) (B) (C) (D)
63. (A) (B) (C) (D)
64. (A) (B) (C) (D)
65. (A) (B) (C) (D)
66. (A) (B) (C) (D)
67. (A) (B) (C) (D)
68. (A) (B) (C) (D)
69. (A) (B) (C) (D)
70. (A) (B) (C) (D)
71. (A) (B) (C) (D)
72. (A) (B) (C) (D)
73. (A) (B) (C) (D)
74. (A) (B) (C) (D)
75. (A) (B) (C) (D)

76. (A) (B) (C) (D)
77. (A) (B) (C) (D)
78. (A) (B) (C) (D)
79. (A) (B) (C) (D)
80. (A) (B) (C) (D)
81. (A) (B) (C) (D)
82. (A) (B) (C) (D)
83. (A) (B) (C) (D)
84. (A) (B) (C) (D)
85. (A) (B) (C) (D)
86. (A) (B) (C) (D)
87. (A) (B) (C) (D)
88. (A) (B) (C) (D)
89. (A) (B) (C) (D)
90. (A) (B) (C) (D)
91. (A) (B) (C) (D)
92. (A) (B) (C) (D)
93. (A) (B) (C) (D)
94. (A) (B) (C) (D)
95. (A) (B) (C) (D)
96. (A) (B) (C) (D)
97. (A) (B) (C) (D)
98. (A) (B) (C) (D)
99. (A) (B) (C) (D)
100. (A) (B) (C) (D)

CHAPTER 11: PRACTICE EXAMINATION 3

Memory Booklet

Directions: You will be given 10 minutes to study the six "Wanted Posters" below and to try to remember as many details as you can. You may not take any notes during this time.

WANTED FOR ASSAULT

Name: John Markham

Age: 27

Height: 5'11"

Weight: 215 lbs.

Race: Black

Hair color: black

Eye color: brown

Complexion: dark

Identifying marks: eagle tattoo on back of right hand; very hard of hearing

Suspect is a former boxer.

He favors brass knuckles as his weapon.

WANTED FOR RAPE

Name: Arthur Lee

Age: 19

Height: 5'7"

Weight: 180 lbs.

Race: Asian

Hair color: black

Eye color: brown

Complexion: medium

Identifying marks: none

Suspect carries a pearl-handled knife with an eight-inch curved blade. He tends to attack victims in subway passageways.

WANTED FOR ARMED ROBBERY

Name: Antonio Gomez

Age: 31

Height: 5'6"

Weight: 160 lbs.

Race: Hispanic

Hair color: brown

Eye color: brown

Complexion: medium

Identifying marks: missing last finger of right hand; tattoo on back says "Mother"; tattoo on left biceps says "Linda"; tattoo on right biceps says "Carmen"

Suspect was seen leaving the scene in a stolen yellow 1987 Corvette. He carries a gun and must be considered dangerous.

WANTED FOR CAR THEFT

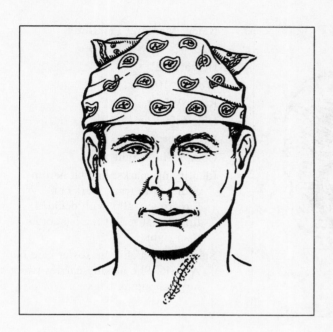

Name: Robert Miller

Age: 24

Height: 6'3"

Weight: 230 lbs.

Race: White

Hair color: brown

Eye color: blue

Complexion: light

Identifying marks: tracheotomy scar at base of neck; tattoo of dragon on right upper arm.

Suspect chain smokes unfiltered cigarettes. He always wears a red head scarf.

WANTED FOR MURDER

Name: Janet Walker

Age: 39

Height: 5'10"

Weight: 148 lbs.

Race: Black

Hair color: black

Eye color: black

Complexion: dark

Identifying marks: large hairy mole on upper left thigh; stutters badly

Suspect has frequently been arrested for prostitution. She often wears multiple ear and nose rings.

WANTED FOR ARSON

Name: Margaret Pickford

Age: 42

Height: 5'2"

Weight: 103 lbs.

Race: White

Hair color: red

Eye color: green

Complexion: light

Identifying marks: known heroin addict with track marks on forearms; walks with decided limp because left leg is shorter than right

Suspect has a child in foster care in Astoria. She usually carries two large shopping bags.

Test Question Booklet

Time: 3 Hours ▪ 90 Questions

> **Directions:** *Now that the Memory Booklets have been collected, you have 3 hours in which to answer the test questions. The first 10 questions are based on the information given on the "Wanted Posters." Answer these questions first. Then proceed directly to the remaining 80 questions. Choose the best answer to each question and mark its letter on your answer sheet.*

1. Which of the following suspects may have committed a crime in order to support a drug habit?

(A)

(C)

(B)

(D)

2. Which one of the following is missing a finger? The suspect wanted for
   (A) rape.
   (B) assault.
   (C) murder.
   (D) armed robbery.

3. Which of the suspects is most likely to be found in the subway?
   (A) John Markham
   (B) Margaret Pickford
   (C) Arthur Lee
   (D) Robert Miller

4. Which of these suspects has a dragon tattoo?

(A)

(C)
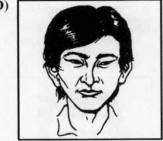

(B)

(D)

5. Which is an identifying mark of this suspect?

(A) Deafness
(B) A large mole
(C) A tattoo that reads "Mother"
(D) Needle tracks

6. Which one of the following is considered to be the most dangerous?

(A)

(C)

(B)

(D)

7. Which of these suspects is known to be a parent?
(A) The suspect who stutters
(B) The former boxer
(C) The smoker
(D) The suspect who limps

8. Which of these suspects escaped the scene of the crime in a stolen car?

(A)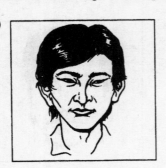

(C)

(B)

(D)

9. Which of these suspects would have the hardest time running from the police?
   (A) The heroin addict
   (B) The suspect who is nearly deaf
   (C) The suspect who wears lots of jewelry
   (D) The suspect with brass knuckles in his pocket

10. Which of these suspects is wanted for rape?

(A)

(C)
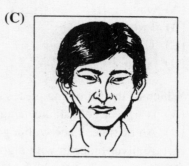

(B)
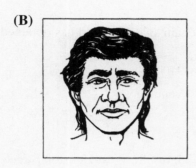

(D)
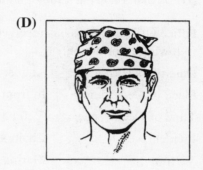

Please use the following information to answer questions 11–13.

Unsolved Homicide

On December 3, 1988, the body of a woman was found in a wooded area outside of Chicago, Illinois. The cause of death was homicide.

The victim is described as an African-American female between the ages of 18–24 with dark brown hair and brown eyes. She was approximately 5'3" tall and weighed 127 pounds. The victim was found wearing a gray sweatshirt, jeans, and white Adidas tennis shoes. She had a tattoo of a rose on her left ankle. She was found wearing six (6) pieces of jewelry: a pair (2) of silver stud earrings, an opal necklace with a gold chain, a plain gold band on her left ring finger, a diamond ring with a gold band on her right ring finger, and a gold bracelet with a silver heart charm.

Although the media devoted extensive coverage to this case, the woman has not yet been identified.

11. Approximately how old was the victim at the time of her death?
  (A) 15–18
  (B) 18–24
  (C) 24–28
  (D) 25–30

12. How many tattoos did the woman have on her body?
- **(A)** One
- **(B)** Two
- **(C)** Three
- **(D)** None

13. Which of the following pieces of jewelry was found on the victim?
- **(A)** A pair of gold stud earrings
- **(B)** An opal necklace with a gold chain
- **(C)** A silver bracelet with a gold charm
- **(D)** A diamond ring with a platinum band

14. Police Officer Barros has received a report of a chain snatching and has obtained the following information:

Date of Occurrence:	August 12, 1993
Place of Occurrence:	In front of 4312 Third Avenue
Time of Occurrence:	5:10 P.M.
Incident:	Chain snatching
Victim:	Marina Marzycki, age 35, of 887 West Houston Street
Witness:	Bonita Bonds, age 56, of 4309 Third Avenue
Suspect:	White male, about 18 years of age, 5'9", 165 lbs., dark brown hair, clean-shaven

Officer Barros is preparing a report on the incident. Which one of the following expresses the above information *most clearly* and *accurately*?
- **(A)** Marina Marzycki of 887 West Houston Street had her chain snatched in front of 4309 Third Avenue by a white male. Bonita Bonds saw it at 5:10 P.M.
- **(B)** A 5'9", 165 lbs. white male of 4312 Third Avenue snatched the chain of Marina Marzycki, age 35, at 5:10 P.M.
- **(C)** On August 12 at 5:10 P.M., Bonita Bonds of 4309 Third Avenue witnessed a chain snatching in front of 4312 Third Avenue. It was committed by an 18-year-old clean-shaven white male with brown hair.
- **(D)** Bonita Bonds says that Marina Marzycki's chain was snatched at 887 West Houston Street by a medium-sized teenager.

Items 15 through 16 are based on the following passage.

Officer Tonga was recently nominated for the State Police Medal of Honor. His willingness to expose himself to great personal risk and to work above and beyond the call of duty have earned him the greatest honor that a Police Officer can receive. Despite the praise that his peers gave him, Officer Tonga refused to take full responsibility for his actions. In his acceptance speech, he stated that he could not have saved the man's life without the help of his fellow officers.

15. Officer Tonga is best described as a(n) _____ man.
- **(A)** arrogant
- **(B)** lazy
- **(C)** proud
- **(D)** humble

16. The reason Officer Tonga was nominated for the Medal of Honor is
- **(A)** he is a good speaker.
- **(B)** he saved a man's life.
- **(C)** he is unwilling to take risks.
- **(D)** he is irresponsible.

17. Officer O'Callaghan has noticed that in her sector, most of the burglaries occur on Walnut Street, most of the robberies occur on Maple Street, and most of the auto thefts occur on Oak Street. Most of the robberies take place between 4:00 P.M. and 10:00 P.M. Most of the auto thefts occur between 9:00 P.M. and 3:00 A.M. Most of the burglaries occur between 11:00 P.M. and 6:00 A.M. Robberies occur most frequently on Wednesdays and Fridays. Most of the burglaries occur on Tuesdays and Saturdays. Most of the auto thefts occur on Wednesdays and Thursdays.

Officer O'Callaghan would be most likely to reduce the number of robberies by patrolling
- **(A)** Walnut Street on Wednesdays and Fridays between 4:00 P.M. and 10:00 P.M.
- **(B)** Maple Street on Wednesdays and Fridays between 4:00 P.M. and midnight.
- **(C)** Maple Street on Wednesdays and Thursdays between 4:00 P.M. and 10:00 P.M.
- **(D)** Walnut Street on Tuesdays and Fridays between 9:00 P.M. and 3:00 A.M.

Items 18 through 19 are based on the following information.

ALARS: <u>Automated License and Registrations System</u>, located at the Department of Motor Vehicles (DMV) headquarters in the state capitol. This system provides information on drivers' licenses and vehicle registrations issued by the State Registry of Motor Vehicles.

NCIC: <u>National Crime Information Center</u>, located in Washington, D.C., and run by the FBI. The NCIC is a computerized index of documented criminal justice information for use by law enforcement agencies throughout the country.

Subpoena Duces Tecum: This is a type of subpoena/summons that demands the production of documents or records and is directed toward the keeper of records of a business. The summons will provide a list of the documents desired.

Warrant Notification: This is a form used by the Police Department to officially notify an individual that the State Police are in possession of a warrant for their arrest.

18. A Police Officer is driving behind a vehicle with expired tags. In order to determine if the vehicle is registered, the officer should use
    (A) ALARS.
    (B) NCIC.
    (C) Subpoena Duces Tecum.
    (D) Warrant Notification.

19. An investigator suspects that a company is committing tax fraud. In order to obtain the company's financial records, the investigator should use
    (A) ALARS.
    (B) NCIC.
    (C) Subpoena Duces Tecum.
    (D) Warrant Notification.

Answer questions 20 through 25 on the basis of the following paragraph:

On Friday, February 2, at 8:30 A.M., Assistant Bridge Operator Henry Jones started to clean the walk of the Avenue X Bridge. It was snowing heavily, and the surface of the road was slippery. At 8:32 A.M., Jones saw a westbound station wagon skid and strike a westbound sedan about 50 feet from the barrier. Both cars were badly damaged. The station wagon overturned and came to rest 8 feet from the barrier. The driver of the station wagon, Harriet White, was thrown clear and landed in the middle of the road. The other car was smashed against the barrier. The driver of the sedan, Tom Green, was pinned behind the steering wheel and suffered cuts about the face. Jones called the Bridge Operator, Frank Smith, who telephoned for an ambulance. First aid was given to both drivers. They were taken to the Avenue W Hospital by an ambulance driven by James Doe that had arrived upon the scene at 9:07 A.M. Police Officer John Brown, Badge No. 71162, had arrived before the ambulance and recorded all the details of the accident, including the statements of Henry Jones and of Jack Black, another eyewitness.

20. The station wagon was driven by
    (A) Jane Brown.
    (B) Jane White.
    (C) Harriet White.
    (D) Harriet Brown.

21. The barrier was
    (A) struck by the sedan.
    (B) struck by the station wagon.
    (C) struck by both cars.
    (D) not struck by either car.

22. Tom Green was the
    (A) driver of the ambulance.
    (B) driver of the sedan.
    (C) other eyewitness.
    (D) Police Officer.

23. The woman driver
    (A) was pinned behind the wheel.
    (B) suffered face cuts.
    (C) was thrown clear.
    (D) was trapped in the car.

24. The name of the Bridge Operator was
    (A) Frank Smith.
    (B) John Smith.
    (C) Henry Jones.
    (D) Frank Jones.

25. When the accident occurred,
    (A) the station wagon was 20 feet from the barrier.
    (B) the cars were 50 feet from the barrier.
    (C) the sedan was 60 feet from the barrier.
    (D) the sedan was 8 feet from the barrier.

26. Foreign diplomats cannot be arrested or personally served with a summons. When a Police Officer arrives at the scene of an incident involving a diplomat, the officer must:

1. Take necessary action to protect life and property.

2. Obtain the name and title of the diplomat and his government.

    a. Ask to see the diplomat's identification.

    b. If the diplomat cannot produce identification, telephone the Operations Unit for verification.

3. If a vehicle bearing DPL license plates is unoccupied, illegally parked, and creating a safety hazard, place a summons on the windshield.

As Police Officer Schuman is patrolling her assigned area, she is approached by an agitated citizen carrying a black bag. The gentleman identifies himself as Dr. Forster. Dr. Forster has been called by the hospital to attend to a patient, but a double-parked car with DPL license plates is blocking his car. Officer Schuman notices that there is a person sitting in the back seat of the car with DPL plates. The passenger identifies himself as a diplomat and produces identification. He does not move the car. Officer Schuman suggests to Dr. Forster that he had better take a cab to the hospital. Schuman writes a parking summons and places it on the windshield of the vehicle. Police Officer Schuman's action in giving the car a parking summons is

(A) appropriate, because the car created a safety hazard in blocking a doctor's car.

(B) inappropriate; Schuman should have checked first with the Operations Unit.

(C) appropriate; a summons cannot be handed to a diplomat but may be placed on a diplomat's car.

(D) inappropriate; the car was not unoccupied.

27. Housing Police Officers, whether patrolling on foot or in a vehicle, are often the first to notice fires in apartment buildings. A Housing Police Officer who spots a fire must:

1. Send an alarm or make sure one has been sent.

2. Direct a responsible person to remain at the alarm box to direct fire engines if fire is not in view.

3. Park a patrol car so as to divert traffic to prevent interference with firefighting operations.

4. Warn and assist occupants in evacuation of building.

5. Take appropriate action to protect lives and property.

Housing Police Officer Patel is patrolling the interior streets of a large city housing project in his patrol car when he sees smoke pouring from a third-story window of a building that faces into another courtyard. Officer Patel uses his police radio to call in the fire alarm and to give the precise location of the fire. What should Officer Patel do next?

(A) Ask a woman who is walking her dog to wait at the corner to direct firefighters to the fire.

(B) Park the patrol car so that it blocks all access to the courtyard on which the fire building faces.

(C) Enter the building to alert residents.

(D) Grab a hall fire extinguisher and enter the burning apartment.

For the following sentences, please fill in the blank with the correctly spelled word.

28. Officer Pryce rushed to a reception hall where an elderly man had _____ to see if he could be of any assistance.
(A) callapsed
(B) calapsed
(C) collapsed
(D) colappsed

29. The _____ specialist located carpet fibers on the victim's body that are believed to have come from the trunk of the primary suspect's car.
(A) phorensics
(B) forensics
(C) fourensics
(D) forensicks

30. While on foot patrol on July 6, Police Officer Cartozian is stopped by a pedestrian and is told that a little boy in the neighborhood has been bitten by a dog. Officer Cartozian investigates and gathers the following information:

Date of Occurrence:	July 5
Occurrence:	dog bite, lower right leg
Victim:	Nicholas Christophe, age 8
Address of Victim:	612 Tenth Avenue, Apt. 3L
Witness:	Mary Murta of 721 Ninth Avenue
Location of Occurrence:	in front of 718 Ninth Avenue
Description of dog:	mixed-breed, black and white, spaniel-sized
Location of dog:	unknown

With the current rabies epidemic, Officer Cartozian takes this report very seriously and transmits the information right away to the precinct and to the canine control unit. Which of the following expresses the information *most clearly* and *accurately*?

(A) Nicholas Cristophe was bitten on the leg by a little black and white dog yesterday. He is 8 years old and lives at 721 Ninth Avenue, Mary Murta said.

(B) Eight-year-old Nicholas Cristophe of 612 Tenth Ave. was bitten by a small to midsize black and white mutt on July 5. Mary Murta of 721 Ninth Avenue observed this from her window.

(C) Mary Murta of 721 Ninth Avenue reports that a black and white dog bit Nicholas Christophe on his right leg yesterday.

(D) A black and white dog of 718 Ninth Avenue bit Nicholas Christophe on his leg at 612 Tenth Avenue. He is 8 years old, says Mary Murta, a witness.

31. CRIMINAL MISCHIEF is committed when

1. A person intentionally damages property belonging to another and the amount of the damage is $250 or more; or

2. A person intentionally damages property in any amount by means of an explosive.

According to the definition given, which one of the following is the best example of criminal mischief?

(A) On the last night of the school year, Jim and Ben put a lighted cherry bomb into the Marlin's $90 mailbox, blowing away the mailbox.

(B) A noisy party at the Browns' house is disturbing Mary's concentration on the book she is reading. Mary angrily goes into the street and scratches one guest's car with a letter opener. Repair of the paint job costs $180.

(C) Peter is admiring Paul's new B-B gun. The gun fires and the stray B-B shatters the O'Briens' $400 living room picture window.

(D) Katie's foot slips off the brake pedal and her mother's car, which she is driving without her mother's permission, smashes into a utility pole. Damage to the car is $2,500 and to the pole, $300.

For the following question, please choose the word or phrase that correctly completes the sentence.

32. The woman _____ that she saw prostitutes congregating on the corner of Washington and Main nearly every night.
    (A) have complained
    (B) complaining
    (C) was complained
    (D) complained

33. Housing Police Officer Tomassi has taken into custody a man caught running from the scene of an apartment burglary with a pillow case slung over his shoulder. At the station house, the booking sergeant takes inventory of the contents of the pillowcase. The contents consist of:

    2 silver candlesticks, each valued at $110.00

    1 diamond bracelet valued at $1,200.00

    3 18-kt. gold chains, each valued at $250.00

    Cash in the sum of $719.00

    What is the total value of the contents of the pillowcase?
    (A) $2,279
    (B) $2,639
    (C) $2,889
    (D) $2,989

Answer questions 34 through 36 on the basis of the following map. The flow of traffic is indicated by the arrows. You must follow the flow of traffic.

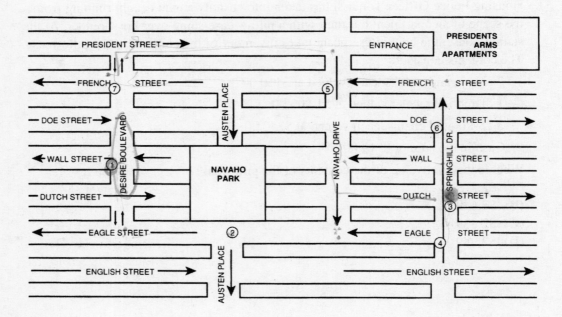

34. If you are located at point (1) and travel north three blocks, then turn east and travel one block, then turn south and travel five blocks, then turn west and travel one block, you will be closest to point
   (A) 2
   (B) 3
   (C) 5
   (D) 7

35. You are located at Desire Boulevard and Wall Street and receive a call to respond to the corner of Dutch Street and Springhill Drive. Which of the following is the most direct route for you to take in your patrol car, making sure to obey all traffic regulations?
    (A) Travel two blocks south on Desire Boulevard to Eagle Street, then three blocks east to Springhill Drive, then north one block to Dutch Street.
    (B) Travel three blocks north on Desire Boulevard to President Street, then one block east to Navaho Drive, then two blocks south to Austin Place, then one block east to Springhill Drive, then two blocks to Dutch Street.
    (C) Travel two blocks north on Desire Boulevard to French Street, then three blocks east to Springhill Drive, then three blocks south to Dutch Street.
    (D) Travel one block north on Desire Boulevard to Doe Street, then east two blocks to Navaho Drive, then south two blocks to Dutch Street, then east one block to Springhill Drive.

36. The call to Dutch Street and Springhill Drive turns out to be a false alarm, but your patrol car radio suddenly alerts you to a disturbance in the entryway of the President's Arms Apartments. You must get to the site of the disturbance in the quickest legal way. Which way should you go?
    (A) Travel north three blocks on Springhill Drive to French Street, then turn left onto French Street and go one block to Navaho Drive, then turn right and go one block on Navaho Drive to the entrance.
    (B) Travel north three blocks on Springhill Drive to French Street, then turn left onto French Street and follow it to Desire Boulevard, then go right onto Desire Boulevard one block to President Street, then go east on President Street to the apartment house entrance.
    (C) Travel south one block on Springhill Drive to Eagle Street, then go west on Eagle Street to Desire Boulevard, then turn right onto Desire Boulevard and follow it five blocks to President Street, then go east on President Street into the entrance.
    (D) Travel north one block on Springhill Drive to Wall Street, then west on Wall Street one block to Navaho Drive, then south on Navaho Drive two blocks to Eagle Street, then follow Eagle Street west to Desire Boulevard, then turn right onto Desire Boulevard and go to President Street, then turn right onto President Street and go to the entrance.

Items 37 through 39 are based on the following information.

In the event of a bomb threat, officers responding to the call should:

1. Turn off all radio communications devices within 500 feet of the threat
2. Open all windows and doors if the threat is in a building and it can be done safely
3. NOT touch or move any suspicious devices or objects
4. NOT turn any electrical devices on or off
5. NOT manipulate any appliance controls
6. NOT use a flashlight, unless equipped with a red lens (to prevent activation of a photoelectric cell)
7. NOT use a camera flash unless authorized by the Bomb Technician in charge of the scene
8. NOT allow any citizen or officer to enter the inner perimeter, unless authorized by the Bomb Technician

37. An officer is called to the scene of a bomb threat. The threat is in a building in a densely populated part of the city. The officer notices that much of the building's exterior is made of glass and therefore could cause extensive damage if the bomb exploded. The bomb technician instructs the officer to go inside the building and open all the windows and doors to keep them from shattering if the bomb does explode. The officer enters the building and turns on the lights in order to make his way to the windows. He opens all the windows and doors that the bomb technician indicated were safe to move.

    This officer is in violation of what rule?
    (A) 1
    (B) 2
    (C) 3
    (D) 4

38. Officer Philips is the first to arrive on the scene of a bomb threat. The threat is in a man's home, which is located in a residential neighborhood. The first thing Officer Philips does is establish an inner perimeter around the house. She then waits for the bomb technician to arrive. While she is waiting, another officer arrives who offers to search the home for any suspicious devices. She allows him to search the home while she stands guard outside the home.

    Officer Philips is in violation of what rule?
    (A) She is not in violation of any rule.
    (B) 4
    (C) 7
    (D) 8

39. A camera flash may be used at the scene of a bomb threat if
    (A) it is equipped with a red lens.
    (B) the Bomb Technician authorizes its use.
    (C) all radio communications are stopped.
    (D) there are no suspicious devices present.

40. A Police Officer who has determined that a child with whom he or she is in contact has run away from home should do the following in this order:

A) Bring the child to the Precinct.

B) Prepare Juvenile Report (PD-902).

C) Interview child to determine whereabouts of parent or guardian.

    b. Attempt to contact parent or guardian.

    c. If parent or guardian appears, release child to custody of parent or guardian.

    d. If parent or guardian cannot be reached or refuses to appear, contact Runaway Unit.

Transit Police Officer Schmidt has determined that the 9-year-old boy he has observed hanging about in the subway station all morning has run away from home. He takes the child to the Precinct, asks him his name, address, and telephone number, and goes to the telephone to call his parents. Officer Schmidt has acted

(A) properly; he had to call the parents so as to release the child to their custody.

(B) improperly; he should have first inquired where the parents could be found at that time.

(C) properly; children should not be permitted to hang around in subway stations.

(D) improperly; he should have first prepared a Juvenile Report.

41. A desk officer who receives a report that a suicide is being attempted must do the following in this order:

1. Ask the precise location where the attempt is occurring.

2. Ask for the sex and race of the attempter, approximate age, and name, if known.

3. Ask for the name of the person reporting the attempt.

4. Request the address from which the report is coming.

5. Ask if the caller knows the victim. If so,

    a. ask about motive.

    b. request names of others who might be of influence in dissuading victim.

Police Officer Swenson at the Precinct desk receives a telephoned report from a caller that a woman is about to jump off a bridge. Officer Swenson first asks, "Which bridge?" What should Swenson do next?

(A) Ask, "From what number are you calling?"

(B) Ask, "Can you tell me the race and age of the jumper?"

(C) Ask, "Is the person threatening suicide a man or a woman?"

(D) Notify the rescue squad at once.

Please use the information in the following passage to answer question 42.

Officer Denver is patrolling a neighborhood around 4:45 a.m. when she notices a car that must be traveling at least 20 miles over the speed limit. She pulls the car over for a traffic stop. As she steps out of the squad car, the driver of the car steps out of his vehicle and walks toward her with his license and registration. Before Officer Denver can say a word, the driver apologizes for speeding and explains that he had just received a call about an emergency at home. He shows Officer Denver his driver's license and says that he hopes that the situation can be taken care of quickly. The man seems alert and agitated; his speech is clear, and he does not seem to have problems walking. Officer Denver orders the man to go back inside his car. She adds that she will also need to see proof of insurance. The man offers to go back to the car and get the proof of insurance for her. Officer Denver again orders the man to return to his car. The man snaps, "Why can't we just take care of this here?" He immediately apologizes for losing his temper; however, Officer Denver must order him to return to his car for a third time before he complies.

42. Based on the above information, what, if anything, is most likely to be the man's problem?
   (A) The man is not familiar with what is expected of him during a traffic stop.
   (B) The man is just impatient to return home so that he can deal with a family emergency.
   (C) The man is under the influence of alcohol.
   (D) The man has something in his car that he does not want Officer Denver to see.

43. Police Officer Hua has noticed that most of the robberies in her sector occur on Greene Street, most of the auto thefts occur on Linda Lane, and most of the assaults occur on Battle Hill. The robberies occur most frequently between 6:00 P.M. and 10:00 P.M., the auto thefts most frequently occur between 9:00 P.M. and 2:00 A.M., and the assaults tend to occur between 6:00 A.M. and 9:00 A.M. and between 3:00 P.M. and 7:00 P.M. The departmental schedule is about to be altered, and Officer Hua's supervisor is asking for recommendations as to which shifts should be assigned more officers in order to reduce the general crime rate. Officer Hua should recommend that more officers should be assigned to patrol from
   (A) midnight to 8:00 A.M.
   (B) 8:00 A.M. to 4:00 P.M.
   (C) noon to 8:00 P.M.
   (D) 4:00 P.M. to midnight.

Please use the following information to answer questions 44–46.

Sick Leave Policies:

- If an employee of the police department knows that he or she will be late due to an illness or other emergency, that employee must contact his or her immediate supervisor before the shift begins to explain the situation and to provide an approximate time of arrival for duty.
- If an employee of the police department cannot work his or her shift due to illness or injury, then that employee must contact the highest-ranking supervisor available at the department at least 3 hours before the beginning of his or her shift. The supervisor will then notify on-duty members of the current shift that there is an opening in the upcoming shift. If no members of the current shift wish to work the upcoming shift, then members of the upcoming shift who have the day/night off will be contacted. Any members of the current or upcoming shift who fill the vacancy left by an ill or injured employee will be paid overtime.
- If an employee requires consecutive days off, the employee must contact the highest-ranking supervisor available at the department 3 hours before every shift that the employee will be unable to work. If an employee does not contact a supervisor the day/night after a sick day has been taken, then the supervisors will assume that the employee will work his/her assigned shift.
- If an employee fails to contact a supervisor if he/she is going to be late or absent, then that employee will be placed on leave without pay and will be subject to disciplinary action.

44. Officer Nelson has become violently ill with a virus. She goes to her local health clinic, and her doctor advises her to take tonight and the next two nights off so that she can rest. Which of the following must Officer Nelson do to notify her supervisor of her absence, according to the policies listed above?
    (A) She should call her supervisor 2 hours before her shift tonight and inform him/her that she will not be able to work tonight or the next two days.
    (B) She should call her supervisor1 hour before each shift that she must miss.
    (C) She should call her supervisor 3 hours before her shift tonight and inform him/her that she will not be able to work tonight or the next two days.
    (D) She should call her supervisor 3 hours before each shift that she must miss.

45. At a local police department, officers are currently working the 3 p.m. to 11 p.m. shift. An officer working on the midnight shift has just called in sick. Which of the following people will be offered the chance to work an extra shift FIRST?
    (A) Officer Hatori, who is an on-duty member of the current shift
    (B) Officer Sanchez, who is on-duty member of the midnight shift
    (C) Officer Giles, who is an off-duty member of the midnight shift
    (D) Officer McKellen, who is an off-duty member off the current shift

46. Officer Hewett is scheduled to report to duty at 3 p.m. this afternoon. He currently has severe bronchitis and feels that it would be best to call in sick. In order to conform to the policies above, he should contact his supervisor no later than
    (A) 9:00 a.m.
    (B) 11:00 a.m.
    (C) 12:00 p.m.
    (D) 2:30 p.m.

47. Police Officers are required to respond to areas where persons have become ill or been injured and to render necessary aid, take corrective action, and prepare prescribed forms. Upon arrival at a scene at which aid is required, a Police Officer should:

    1. Render reasonable aid to sick or injured person.

    2. Request an ambulance or doctor, if necessary.

    3. Wait in view to direct the ambulance or assign some responsible person to do so.

    4. If ambulance does not arrive in 20 minutes, make another call.

    5. Accompany unconscious or unidentified aided person to hospital in back of ambulance.

    Off-duty Police Officer McGonnigle is in the vicinity of a construction site where a heavy steel beam has fallen from the roof and struck a woman passing by on the sidewalk. Officer McGonnigle runs to the scene and finds that the woman is unconscious and is bleeding profusely from a wound to the groin. The first thing Officer McGonnigle should do is
    (A) identify himself as a Police Officer.
    (B) send for an ambulance.
    (C) attempt to stop the bleeding by applying pressure.
    (D) reassure the woman that he will go to the hospital with her.

Please use the following table to answer questions 48–50.

TOTAL PROPERTY CRIME IN YOUR STATE FROM 1989–2000

Year	Population	Burglary	Larceny	Motor Vehicle Theft	Total Property Crime	% Change	Property Crime Rate per 100,000	Rate Change
1989	12,797,318	289,254	583,702	102,086	975,042	—	7,619.1	—
1990	13,150,027	275,104	585,919	101,358	962,381	–1.30	7,318.5	–3.95
1991	13,195,952	264,749	603,922	102,852	971,523	0.95	7,362.3	0.60
1992	13,424,416	252,003	594,053	105,553	951,609	–2.05	7,088.6	–3.72
1993	13,608,627	245,353	594,793	114,632	954,778	0.33	7,016.0	–1.03
1994	13,878,905	233,006	617,195	122,839	973,040	1.91	7,010.9	–0.07
1995	14,149,317	213,050	605,751	109,610	928,411	–4.59	6,561.5	–6.41
1996	14,411,563	219,056	605,448	103,769	928,273	–0.01	6,441.2	–1.83
1997	14,712,922	214,894	599,190	108,872	922,956	–0.57	6,273.1	–2.61
1998	15,000,475	202,559	578,774	104,094	885,427	–4.07	5,902.7	–5.91
1999	15,322,040	180,785	532,462	92,243	805,490	–9.03	5,257.1	–10.94
2000	15,982,378	170,131	509,616	87,920	767,667	–4.70	4,803.2	–8.63

48. As the population increased from 1989–2000, what happened to the number of larcenies?

(A) They drastically increased from 1989–2000.

(B) They drastically decreased from 1989–2000.

(C) They mostly increased from 1989–1994 and decreased from 1995–2000.

(D) They mostly decreased from 1989–1994 and increased from 1995–2000.

49. During which year did the most motor vehicle thefts occur?

(A) 1989

(B) 1991

(C) 1994

(D) 1999

50. What was the average number of burglaries in your state from 1994–2000?

(A) 182,746

(B) 204,783

(C) 207,182

(D) 210,332

Items 51 through 52 are based on the following passage.

When there is concern about a lost or missing person, the public often contacts the State Police for advice, counsel, and aid. It is the duty of the State Police to put forth every effort to assist the public in locating such persons. When attempting to locate a missing person, it is important to remember that time is of the essence. An organized plan should be established as soon as possible after the police are notified. This will allow for a methodical search to begin as quickly as possible. While gathering information about possible areas to be searched, officers should remain calm and professional in an effort to calm and reassure the person reporting the incident. An officer's first priority is to locate the missing individual; however, it is also important for the officer to maintain the morale of those involved.

51. During a missing persons search, an officer not only provides technical information, but also
(A) supply funds.
(B) missing persons statistics.
(C) counsel and advice.
(D) the person's photograph.

52. Officers dealing with the missing persons' friends and family should remain calm and professional so that those who are concerned will feel
(A) anxious.
(B) reassured.
(C) apathetic.
(D) depressed.

Answer questions 53 through 55 based on the following map.

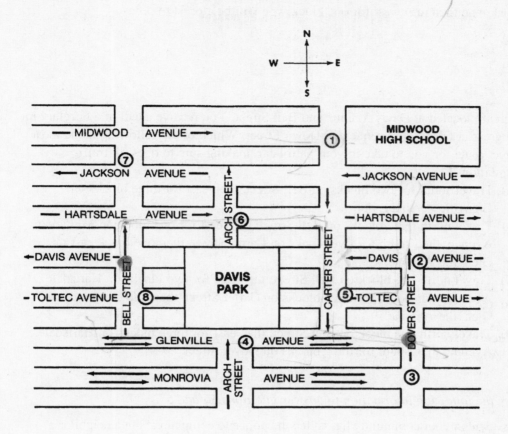

53. You are located at Carter Street and Davis Avenue. You receive a call to respond to a traffic accident at the intersection of Midwood Avenue and Carter Street. Which one of the following is the most direct route for you to take in your patrol car, making sure to obey all traffic regulations?

(A) Travel south on Carter Street for one block, then one block east on Toltec Avenue, then three blocks north on Dover Street, then one block west on Jackson Avenue, then one block north on Carter Street.

(B) Travel two blocks south on Carter Street, then west for two blocks on Glenville Avenue, then north for five blocks on Bell Street, then one block east on Midwood Avenue.

(C) Travel one block east on Davis Avenue, then two blocks north on Dover Street, then three blocks west on Jackson Avenue, then north for one block on Bell Street, then one block east on Midwood Avenue.

(D) Travel two blocks south on Carter Street, then east for one block on Glenville Avenue, then north for four blocks on Dover Street, then west for three blocks on Jackson Avenue, then north for one block on Bell Street, then east for one block on Midwood Avenue.

54. If you are located at point (4) and travel west for one block, turn north and travel three blocks, then turn east and travel one block, then turn north and travel one block, and then turn west for one block, you will be closest to point
    (A) 7
    (B) 6
    (C) 1
    (D) 8

55. You are located at Davis Avenue and Bell Street. You receive a call of a burglary in progress at Glenville Avenue and Dover Street. Which of the following is the most direct route for you to take in your patrol car, making sure to obey all traffic regulations?
    (A) Travel south for two blocks on Bell Street, then east for three blocks on Glenville Avenue.
    (B) Travel north three blocks on Bell Street, then east for one block on Midwood Avenue, then south for five blocks on Carter Street, then one block east on Glenville Avenue.
    (C) Travel north one block on Bell Street, then east for two blocks on Hartsdale Avenue, then south for three blocks on Carter Street, then one block east on Glenville Avenue.
    (D) Travel north one block on Bell Street, then east for three blocks on Hartsdale Avenue, then south for three blocks on Dover Street.

Please use the following information to answer questions 56 and 57.

A resident in your community has called the police to complain about a neighbor's teenage son, who is hosting a noisy party. You are sent to speak with the woman and record her complaint. Her statement consists of the following five sentences:
1. When I was getting ready for bed, I heard loud music and voices coming from the Konopasek home next door.
2. I informed her that if they didn't turn down the noise, I would call the police.
3. I went over to the Konopasek's home and knocked on the door.
4. A teenage girl, who I think is Nick's girlfriend, answered the door. I could see that the house was filled with about 20–30 teenagers.
5. I knew that Nick Konopasek's parents were away on vacation and that they had left Nick home alone for the long weekend.

56. Which of the following represents the most logical order of the above statements?
    (A) 1, 5, 3, 4, 2
    (B) 3, 5, 2, 4, 1
    (C) 2, 4, 5, 1, 3
    (D) 4, 5, 1, 3, 2

57. What happened immediately AFTER the teenage girl answered the door?

(A) The woman informed the girl that if they didn't turn down the noise, she would call the police.

(B) The woman knocked on the door of the Konopasek's home.

(C) The woman got ready for bed and heard loud music and voices coming from the Konopasek home next door.

(D) Nick Konopasek's parents left him alone for the weekend.

58. Police Officer Jaime Veldez, riding alone in his patrol car in the early morning of November 12, spots an active fire. Officer Veldez quickly notes the following information:

Location of Fire:	112 Lorelei Lane, just north of Industrial Highway.
Time of Report:	3:12 A.M.
Type of Structure:	plastics warehouse
Origin of Fire:	unknown
Extent of Involvement:	active and total; heavy, foul-smelling smoke

Officer Veldez must radio an alarm right away. Which of the following conveys all the information *most clearly* and *accurately*?

(A) A plastics warehouse caught fire all by itself at 3:12 A.M. today at 112 Lorelei Lane. It is north of Industrial Highway and smoking.

(B) There is a big fire at the plastics warehouse at Industrial Highway, North and 112 Lorelei Lane right now. It is November 12 and it is 3:12 A.M. so no one is at work, but it smells awful.

(C) A fire at 112 Lorelei Lane, a plastics warehouse, is burning out of control for unknown reasons north of Industrial Highway. Someone should put it out.

(D) It is 3:12 A.M. and I am approaching a major fire at the plastics warehouse at 112 Lorelei Lane just north of Industrial Highway. The smoke is heavy and may well be toxic.

59. **ROUTINE SICK AT HOME**—The New York City police department classifies as routine sick at home a call for service in which a sick person is aided at his or her residence and:

    a. Is conscious and properly identified;

    b. No other police service or notification is required;

    c. No dependent adults or uncared-for children are in the household; and

    d. No other investigation is needed.

According to the definition above, which of the following should be entered in a Police Officer's log as a routine sick at home call?

(A) Myrtle Cubbage, age 97, became dizzy in her apartment and fell to the living room floor. Her full-time live-in aide, Millie Mohan, was unable to lift her, so she called emergency services. Police Officer Ataturk responded to the call, helped Ms. Mohan in lifting Ms. Cubbage to her bed, and found Ms. Cubbage's vital signs to be normal. Ms. Mohan thanked Officer Ataturk for his assistance and assured him that she had the situation well under control.

(B) Police Officer Barbini responded to the call of Hattie Cool, who had cut herself very badly while splitting a three-day-old bagel. Officer Barbini noted that the baby appeared to be safely sleeping in his crib and called for an ambulance to transport Ms. Cool to the emergency room to have her hand sutured.

(C) Officer Kaliopolis was called to an apartment house airshaft where she found an unidentified man lying unconscious on the ground. Officer Kaliopolis summoned an ambulance and accompanied the victim to the hospital.

(D) Jimmy Jordan, age 9 and home alone, felt very nauseated and began vomiting. Police Officer Llewellyn, responding to Jimmy's call, found him feeling much better but frightened at having been sick all by himself.

60. Carol White, a woman with a record of convictions for prostitution, has been pointed out to police by a man who admits to having been her client and now accuses her of rifling through his pockets while he slept. Upon booking, Ms. White's valuables are removed from her possession and are inventoried. Among the items taken from Carol White:

1 woman's watch valued at		$80
2 woman's rings, each valued at		$120
1 pair earrings valued at		$40
1 woman's purse containing		$356
1 man's watch valued at		$625
2 gold chains, each valued at		$110
1 man's alligator wallet valued at		$250
containing:	6 bills @	$50
	10 bills @	$20
	5 bills @	$5
	7 bills @	$1

What was the total value of the inventoried items taken from Carol White?
(A) $2,113
(B) $2,338
(C) $2,343
(D) $2,443

For the following items, please identify the option that best completes the sentence.

61. It was necessary to establish guidelines for the _____ of firearms.
(A) utilization
(B) utilisation
(C) utilezation
(D) utilizacion

62. Special care should be taken when apprehending distraught mental _____.
(A) pashents
(B) patience
(C) pacients
(D) patients

63. Police Officer Phansonboom on foot patrol has surprised a suspect in the process of breaking into a car. He has taken the suspect into custody and has obtained the following information:

Suspect:	Nick Harrison, age 17
Address of Suspect:	8768 East 99th Street
Crime:	Attempted auto theft
Location of Crime:	in front of Kimberly Hotel
Date of Occurrence:	March 19
Time of Occurrence:	6:12 A.M.

Officer Phansonboom must write up his arrest for the booking officer. Which of the following expresses this information *most clearly* and *accurately*?

(A) Nick Harrison, age 17, who lives at the Kimberly Hotel, 8768 East 99th Street, tried to steal a car on March 19 at 6:12 A.M.

(B) 17-year-old Nick Harrison tried to steal a car in front of the Kimberly Hotel, 8768 East 99th Street, at 6:12 A.M. on March 19th.

(C) On March 19th at 6:12 A.M., Nick Harrison, 17, of 8768 East 99th Street, attempted to steal a car from the front of the Kimberly Hotel.

(D) The 17-year-old suspect, Nick Harrison of 8678 East 99th Street, attempted to steal a car parked in front of the Kimberly Hotel at 6:12 on the morning of March 19.

64. A Police Officer who stops a person under suspicion for driving under the influence of alcohol should follow this procedure:

1. Ask the driver to step out of the vehicle.

2. Pat down the driver for weapons.

3. Ask to see license and registration.

4. Ask driver to walk a straight line.

5. Smell breath.

6. Bring driver to police station for chemical testing.

Police Officer Gambino has been following a driver who has been weaving back and forth across the center line of the highway. Officer Gambino pulls the driver to the shoulder and asks to see her driver's license and registration. Officer Gambino has acted

(A) correctly, because the driver was weaving as if intoxicated.

(B) incorrectly, because the driver might have been armed.

(C) correctly, because there was alcohol on the driver's breath.

(D) incorrectly, because Officer Gambino should first have asked the driver to get out of the car.

65. Officer Miller is dispatched to a dispute between next-door neighbors. He is driving 25 mph, and the neighbors' homes are 2.5 miles away. Approximately how long will it take for Officer Miller to reach the neighbors' homes, assuming that he travels at a constant speed?
(A) 3 minutes
(B) 5 minutes
(C) 6 minutes
(D) 9 minutes

Please use the following table to answer questions 66 and 67.

Ann Palmer returned home late one evening from work and was shocked to find that her apartment had been burgled. Below is a list of a few of the items that were stolen along with their approximate value.

Stolen Item	Approximate Value
VCR	$150
Television	$600
Video Game System	$200
Stereo System	?
Computer	$1,500

66. If the total value of the stolen items listed above was $2,950, how much was the stereo system worth?
(A) $350
(B) $500
(C) $625
(D) $750

67. If Ms. Palmer replaces her television with a new set that costs approximately 25 percent more than the original, how much will her new television set cost?
(A) $690
(B) $710
(C) $750
(D) $830

For the following items, please identify the misspelled word or the incorrectly used word.

68. In situations that are unique and not specifically addressed by any procedure, an officer must rely upon his or her own descretion.
(A) situations
(B) unique
(C) addressed
(D) descretion

Questions 69–71 contain a set of letters, symbols, and numbers. Please choose ONLY ONE option that contains the exact pattern of letters, symbols, numbers, and spaces.

69. ∀√Kλ32.–8πθρΩς
    (A) ∀√Kλ32.–8πθρΩς
    (B) ∀√Kλ32.–8πθΡΩς
    (C) ∀√Kλ23.–8πθρΩς
    (D) ∀√Kλ32.–8πΟρΩς

70. [∴]≅?#BΔΦ♦♥3+!
    (A) [∴]≅?#BΔΦ♥♦3+!
    (B) [∴]=?#BΔΦ♦♥3+!
    (C) {∴}≅?#BΔΦ♦♥3+!
    (D) [∴]≅?#BΔΦ♦♥3+!

71. →ωBΓK÷•©©∝×≥∉γϑ
    (A) →ωBΓK+•©∝×≥∉γϑ
    (B) →ωBΓK÷•©∝×∠∉Yϑ
    (C) →ωBΓK÷•©∝×≥∉γϑ
    (D) →ωBLK÷•©∝×≥∉γϑ

For the following item, choose the sentence that contains the misspelled word or words.

72. (A) Officer Hill is now eligible for the Mounted Patrol Unit.
    (B) After running the plates, the officer found out that the car was stolen.
    (C) My guess is that a career crimanal committed this crime.
    (D) It is no secret that they have been arrested twice.

73. Police Officer Nygaard is making an inventory of the belongings of a deceased woman who lived alone and died in her apartment. The items include:

    1 gold wedding band valued at $110.00

    1 silver necklace valued at $70.00

    2 bracelets with semiprecious stones, each valued at $50.00

    1 marcasite brooch valued at $150.00

    contents of purse, total value $37.89

    What is the sum total value of the items inventoried?
    (A) $417.89
    (B) $428.89
    (C) $467.89
    (D) $468.89

74. Routine procedure upon arresting a suspect is to take fingerprints for purposes of positive identification. Fingerprinting is done in the following manner:

1. Ask the person to relax hands and fingers and let the officer do the rolling.

2. Prepare the fingerprint charts as follows:

   a. Two copies of Criminal Fingerprint Record

   b. One copy of FBI Fingerprint Chart

   c. One copy of State Fingerprint Chart

   d. If juvenile, one copy of State Juvenile Fingerprint Chart

3. Prepare two copies of palm prints.

4. Take photographs, full face and profile.

Police Officer Taormina responds to a call from Mitchell Rubin, owner of Motown Cleaners. Rubin complains of a woman who keeps darting behind the counter and tearing up plastic garment bags. The woman, who appears to be about 23 years of age, refuses to give her name or address. Officer Taormina takes her to the station house, asks her to relax her hands and fingers, and begins to roll fingerprints. Taormina prepares two sets for the woman's criminal record, one set for the FBI and one set for the State Fingerprint Chart. Next, Officer Taormina should

(A) prepare a set of fingerprints for the State Juvenile Chart.

(B) check the records to see if this woman is known to the police.

(C) take front face and profile photographs of the woman in duplicate.

(D) take palm prints.

75. The bank manager has summoned Police Officer Goola with an excited account of a break-in at the bank. Here is what he told to Officer Goola:

Occurrence:	Break-in, bank and vault
Date of Occurrence:	During the night January 5–6
Time of Occurrence:	Between 5:30 P.M. and 8:00 A.M.
Place of Occurrence:	First Fidelity Bank, Green Mall branch
Reporter:	Walter Briggs, bank manager
Crime Discovered by:	Marsha Szymborska, vault officer
Missing Objects:	Contents of safe deposit boxes 138 to 266 and one large canvas money sack, serial #9088098

Officer Goola must write up this event for the department's investigators and for a preliminary report to be sent to the Treasury Department. Which of the following expresses the information *most clearly* and *accurately*?

(A) During the night of January 5–6, thieves broke into the vault of the Green Mall branch of First Fidelity Bank and took contents of over 100 safe deposit boxes and money sack #9088098. The crime was discovered by the vault officer, Marsha Szymborska, after 8:00 A.M., January 6, and was reported by the bank manager, Walter Briggs.

(B) Marsha Szymborska discovered that the bank had been robbed when she came to work at 5:30 on January 6. She said that safe deposit boxes 138–266 had been emptied into a money sack. The bank manager, Walter Briggs, told me that the bank is in the Green Mall and the money sack was #9088098.

(C) Walter Briggs, the manager of First Fidelity Bank, told me that Marsha Szymborska broke into the vault of safe deposit boxes 138–266 and took a money sack #9088098. This happened between closing on January 5 and opening on January 6 at the Green Mall.

(D) A money sack #9088098 is missing from First Fidelity Bank in Green Mall full of safe deposit boxes 138–266 said Marsha Szymborska and Walter Briggs between 5:30 P.M. and 8:00 A.M. on January 5th or 6th.

For the following items, choose the word or phrase that correctly completes the sentence.

76. It is important that the first officers on an accident scene act _____.
   (A) quickest
   (B) quicker
   (C) quickly
   (D) quick

77. Police Officer McDaniel, _____ courage should be commended, saved the little boy's life.
   (A) whom
   (B) whose
   (C) that
   (D) who

78. **HARASSMENT** is committed when a person intends to harass, annoy, or alarm another person and does so by striking, shoving, kicking, or otherwise subjecting the other person to physical contact. According to the above definition, which of the following is the best example of harassment?
   (A) Peter's dog has overturned Darlene's garbage can once too often, and Darlene is tired of cleaning up the mess. Darlene sprinkles rat poison on chicken bones in the garbage can.
   (B) As he is trying to get off a very crowded subway car, Bruce tugs a folded newspaper from Philip's arm, thinking it is his own.
   (C) In hopes of extorting money, Michael writes letters to Jackson, threatening to expose an extramarital affair in which Jackson has been involved unless Jackson pays him handsomely.
   (D) Six-foot-two-inch Lawrence grabs five-foot-seven-inch Eric by the shoulders and shakes him hard while saying, "Stay away from my little brother. If I catch you smoking reefer with him, I'll shake you to death."

79. A Police Officer who responds to the scene of a serious crime should proceed as follows:

1. Look quickly over the scene and assess the nature and severity of the crime.

2. Interview the complainant and witnesses.

3. Gather evidence.

4. Prepare a Complaint Report.

5. Determine if complaint can be closed or where it should be referred for further investigation.

Police Officer Yves Montand on foot patrol discovers an unconscious middle-aged well-dressed man lying in the gutter. Officer Montand rolls the man over and notes that the man is lying in a small pool of blood and has a gunshot wound to the shoulder but that he is not bleeding profusely. Officer Montand radios for an ambulance. The next thing Montand should do is

(A) interview the man.

(B) look for a bullet.

(C) decide where to refer the case for further investigation.

(D) interview the witnesses.

Items 80 through 81 are based on the following passage.

Officer Petty has been using her RADAR gun to catch speeding motorists all week. Following is a chart of the number of tickets she has issued this month.

NUMBER OF TICKETS

Day of the Week	Week 1	Week 2	Week 3	Week 4
Monday	7	3	8	9
Tuesday	6	4	5	5
Wednesday	4	10	7	6
Thursday	6	12	9	9
Friday	10	11	9	9

80. What was the average number of tickets that Officer Petty issued on Thursdays?

(A) 8

(B) 9

(C) 10

(D) 11

81. What percentage of tickets during Week 4 were issued on Tuesday?

(A) 13 percent

(B) 14 percent

(C) 15 percent

(D) 16 percent

82. Officer Hendrickson received a burglary call at 8:29 P.M. He arrived on the scene of the burglary at 8:37 P.M., talked with the owner of the home until 9:12 P.M., and arrived back at the station at 9:18 P.M. How much time elapsed from the time of the call until Officer Hendrickson arrived back at the station?
    (A) 46 minutes
    (B) 47 minutes
    (C) 48 minutes
    (D) 49 minutes

83. A recent crime report stated that 475 drunk driving accidents occurred in State Z last year. The governor proposed a plan that would reduce the number of drunk driving accidents by 32 percent for the next year. If the governor's plan works, how many drunk-driving accidents will occur next year?
    (A) 323
    (B) 325
    (C) 330
    (D) 339

84. If Officer Panagua works 50 hours per week and spends about 10 hours per week doing paperwork, what percentage of her time is spent doing paperwork?
    (A) 18 percent
    (B) 20 percent
    (C) 23 percent
    (D) 24 percent

85. **ARSON** is committed when an individual intentionally starts a fire that causes damage to a building or that ignites an explosion. According to this definition, which of the following is the best example of arson?
    (A) Lou and Pete have had too much to drink and are looking for trouble. They pass a man they identify as being gay, wrestle him to the ground, pour lighter fluid on him, and set him afire.
    (B) Jenny is taking a short cut through a used car lot and is smoking a cigarette. She absently tosses away her cigarette, which lands in a puddle of gasoline that has leaked under a car. The gasoline bursts into flame, the flames lick the car, and the car explodes.
    (C) As Sheldon is driving along a heavily wooded section of highway, his old car shudders and smoke pours from under the hood. Sheldon jumps out and into the street just as the car explodes. Fire from the car ignites dry leaves and soon grows into a major forest fire.
    (D) Bob has been working for farmer White for six months without a raise and is very angry. He starts a fire in the chicken yard, and soon the chicken coop goes up in flames. Many chickens perish.

Answer questions 86 through 90 on the basis of the following sketches. The first face on top is a sketch of an alleged criminal based on witnesses' descriptions at the crime scene. One of the four sketches below that face is the way the suspect might look after changing his or her appearance. Assume that NO surgery has been done on the suspect's face.

86.

(A)

(C)

(B)

(D)

87.

(A)

(C)

(B)

(D)

88.

(A)

(C)

(B)

(D)

89.

(A)

(C)

(B)

(D)

90.

(A)

(C)

(B)

(D)

Answer Key

1. **(B)**	19. **(C)**	37. **(D)**	55. **(C)**	73. **(C)**
2. **(D)**	20. **(C)**	38. **(D)**	56. **(A)**	74. **(D)**
3. **(C)**	21. **(A)**	39. **(B)**	57. **(A)**	75. **(A)**
4. **(A)**	22. **(B)**	40. **(D)**	58. **(D)**	76. **(C)**
5. **(B)**	23. **(C)**	41. **(B)**	59. **(A)**	77. **(B)**
6. **(B)**	24. **(A)**	42. **(D)**	60. **(C)**	78. **(D)**
7. **(D)**	25. **(B)**	43. **(D)**	61. **(A)**	79. **(B)**
8. **(C)**	26. **(D)**	44. **(D)**	62. **(D)**	80. **(B)**
9. **(A)**	27. **(C)**	45. **(A)**	63. **(C)**	81. **(A)**
10. **(C)**	28. **(C)**	46. **(C)**	64. **(D)**	82. **(D)**
11. **(B)**	29. **(B)**	47. **(C)**	65. **(C)**	83. **(A)**
12. **(A)**	30. **(B)**	48. **(C)**	66. **(B)**	84. **(B)**
13. **(B)**	31. **(A)**	49. **(C)**	67. **(C)**	85. **(D)**
14. **(C)**	32. **(D)**	50. **(B)**	68. **(D)**	86. **(B)**
15. **(D)**	33. **(C)**	51. **(C)**	69. **(A)**	87. **(B)**
16. **(B)**	34. **(A)**	52. **(B)**	70. **(D)**	88. **(D)**
17. **(B)**	35. **(D)**	53. **(B)**	71. **(C)**	89. **(C)**
18. **(A)**	36. **(B)**	54. **(A)**	72. **(C)**	90. **(B)**

Explanatory Answers

1. **The correct answer is (B).** Margaret Pickford is a known heroin addict.

2. **The correct answer is (D).** Antonio Gomez is wanted for armed robbery. He is missing the last finger of his right hand.

3. **The correct answer is (C).** Arthur Lee often attacks his victims in subway passageways.

4. **The correct answer is (A).** Robert Miller has a tattoo of a dragon on his right upper arm.

5. **The correct answer is (B).** Janet Walker has a large hairy mole on her upper left thigh.

6. **The correct answer is (B).** Antonio Gomez carries a gun. Arthur Lee carries a wicked-looking knife, but Lee is not offered among the choices.

7. **The correct answer is (D).** Margaret Pickford, who walks with a limp because her left leg is shorter than her right, has a child in foster care, so she obviously is a parent.

8. **The correct answer is (C).** Antonio Gomez escaped from the scene of a recent armed robbery in a stolen yellow 1987 Corvette.

9. **The correct answer is (A).** Margaret Pickford, who is a drug addict, has a severe limp caused by one leg being shorter than the other, so she would have a hard time running from police.

10. **The correct answer is (C).** Arthur Lee is wanted for rape.

11. **The correct answer is (B).** The victim was described as between the ages of 18–24.

12. **The correct answer is (A).** The victim had one tattoo, depicting a rose, on her left ankle.

13. **The correct answer is (B).** The victim was found wearing an opal necklace with a gold chain. Each of the other choices is incorrect in some way. Be sure to read the passage carefully.

14. **The correct answer is (C).** All other choices confuse addresses, thereby giving misinformation.

15. **The correct answer is (D).** Officer Tonga is best described as a humble man because he would not take all of the credit for saving the man's life. Rather than keep all of the praise for himself, he pointed out that he could not have saved the man's life without the help of his fellow officers.

16. **The correct answer is (B).** The last sentence of the passage indicates that the reason Officer Tonga was nominated for the Medal of Honor is that he saved a man's life.

17. **The correct answer is (B).** Robberies occur most frequently on Maple Street on Wednesdays and Fridays between 4:00 P.M. and 10:00 P.M. Patrolling from 4:00 P.M. to midnight certainly covers the time span.

18. **The correct answer is (A).** The ALARS system provides information on drivers' licenses and vehicle registrations and would be a good resource to use when investigating if a car has been reported stolen.

19. **The correct answer is (C).** The Subpoena Duces Tecum is useful when an investigator needs to gain access to a business's documents.

20–25. If you made any mistakes, read again.

26. **The correct answer is (D).** The car was not unoccupied.

27. **The correct answer is (C).** Officer Patel used his radio, so firefighters already know the location of the fire. Surely, he should not block the entrance; firefighters must be able to reach the fire. Residents must be alerted and evacuated to safety. Firefighters are best equipped to put out the fire.

28. **The correct answer is (C).** The correct spelling of the word is "collapsed."

29. **The correct answer is (B).** The correct spelling of the word is "forensics."

30. **The correct answer is (B).** Only this choice gives all the needed information correctly.

31. **The correct answer is (A).** The damage, though not expensive, was caused by an explosion. In choice **(B)**, the cost of the damage without an explosion does not place it into the criminal mischief category. In choices **(C)** and **(D)**, there is no intent.

32. **The correct answer is (D).** This question requires the use of the simple past tense. Because the subject is singular, the only correct choice is **(D)**.

33. **The correct answer is (C).**　silver candlesticks

$$2 \times \$110 = \$\ 220.00$$

diamond bracelet　　$\$\ 120.00$

18-kt gold chains

$$3 \times \$250 = \$\ 750.00$$

cash　　　　　　　$\underline{+719.00}$

$\$2889.00$

34. **The correct answer is (A).**

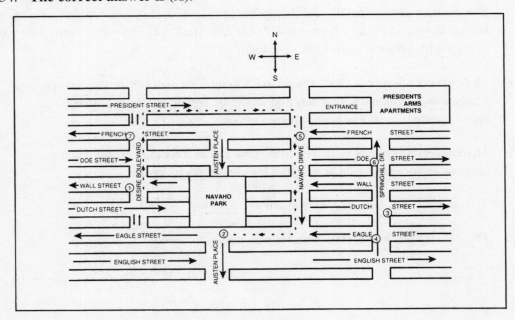

35. **The correct answer is (D).** Choice **(A)** is wrong because Eagle Street is one-way westbound; choice **(B)** is wrong because going south on Navaho Drive will never get you to Austin Place, which is parallel to Navaho; and choice **(C)** is wrong because French Street is one-way westbound.

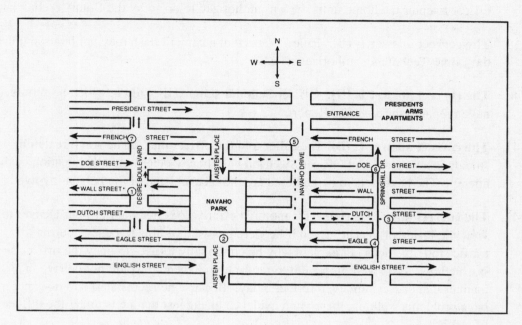

36. **The correct answer is (B).** Choice **(A)** is wrong because Navaho Drive is one-way southbound; choice **(C)** is wrong because Springhill Drive is one-way northbound; choice **(D)** is legal, but it most certainly is not the shortest route.

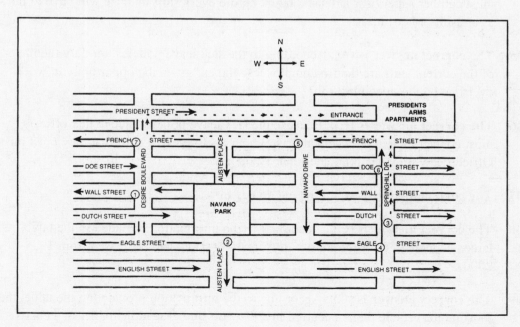

37. **The correct answer is (D).** The officer in this scenario turned on the lights in the building, which is in violation of rule 4.

38. **The correct answer is (D).** Officer Philips should not have allowed the other officer to enter the home until she was authorized to do so by the Bomb Technician.

39. **The correct answer is (B).** Rule 7 states that a camera flash may not be used unless the Bomb Technician authorizes its use.

40. **The correct answer is (D).** Officer Schmidt skipped the step in which he should have prepared the Juvenile Report.

41. **The correct answer is (B).** The caller told the officer that the person threatening suicide is a woman, and Officer Swenson has already determined the location of the attempt. The next facts to be gathered are the race and age of the person involved.

42. **The correct answer is (D).** This motorist clearly does not want Officer Denver to view the inside of his car. Even if he were unaware of how to behave during a traffic stop, this does not explain why he continually refuses to obey the officer's instructions. If he were impatient to return home, then he would not behave in a manner that causes him even further delay. Because he seems alert and does not have problems walking, there is no evidence to suggest that he is under the influence of alcohol.

43. **The correct answer is (D).** Most crimes occur in this time span.

44. **The correct answer is (D).** According to the sick leave policies, Officer Nelson must call her supervisor at least 3 hours before every shift that she will have to miss as a result of her illness.

45. **The correct answer is (A).** According to the sick leave policies, on-duty members of the current shift are the first employees who are given the opportunity to work overtime on the upcoming shift.

46. **The correct answer is (C).** Because the sick leave policies dictate that officers must contact their supervisors at least 3 hours before every shift that they must miss, Officer Hewitt may call no later than 12:00 p.m.

47. **The correct answer is (C).** First aid comes first.

48. **The correct answer is (C).** According to the information provided in the table, larcenies increased for the most part from 1989–1994 and decreased from 1995–2000.

49. **The correct answer is (C).** According to the information provided in the table, the most motor vehicle thefts occurred in 1994. Be sure to read the tables and charts carefully in these types of questions.

50. **The correct answer is (B).** To obtain the average number of burglaries, add together the number of burglaries that have taken place from 1994–2000. 233,006 + 213,050 + 219,056 + 214,894 + 202,559 + 180,785 + 170,131 = 1,433,481. You must then divide this total by the number of years measured. 2000–1994 = 7 years. 1,433, 481 divided by 7 = 204,783.

51. **The correct answer is (C).** During a missing persons search, an officer not only directs the technical aspects of the search, but also provides counsel and advice to those concerned.

52. **The correct answer is (B).** Officers involved in a missing persons search should remain calm and professional in an attempt to reassure those who are concerned.

53. **The correct answer is (B).** Choice **(A)** is wrong because Carter Street is one-way southbound; choice **(C)** is wrong because Davis Avenue is one-way westbound; and choice **(D)** is legal but unnecessarily long and roundabout.

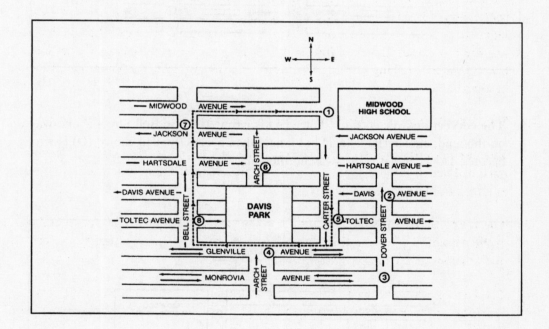

54. **The correct answer is (A).**

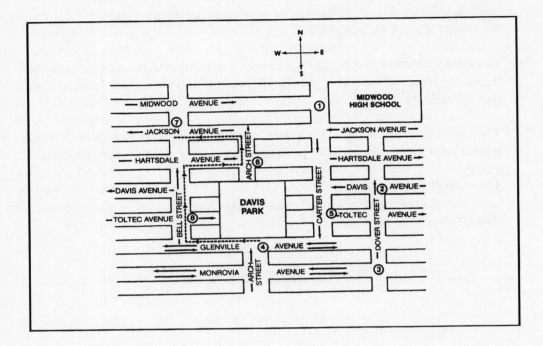

55. **The correct answer is (C).** Choice **(A)** is wrong because Bell Street is one-way northbound; choice **(B)** is legal but longer than necessary; and choice **(D)** is wrong because Dover Street is one-way northbound.

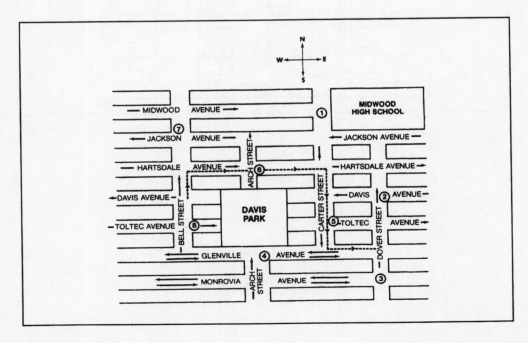

56. **The correct answer is (A).** Read the sentences carefully for words such as "before," "then," or "after." Choice **(A)** represents the most logical order of the statements.

57. **The correct answer is (A).** According to the most logical order of the sentences (as determined by question 56), after the teenage girl answered the door, the woman informed her that she would call the police if they didn't turn down the noise.

58. **The correct answer is (D).** All the choices place the fire correctly and give the most vital information, but choice **(D)** is clearest and most easily followed.

59. **The correct answer is (A).** In choice **(B)**, action was required and there was an infant in the household; in choice **(C)**, further action was taken; and in choice **(D)**, there was a child needing care.

60. **The correct answer is (C).**

woman's watch		$80
woman's rings	2 × $120 =	240
earrings		40
woman's purse		356
man's watch		625
gold chains	2 × $110	220
man's alligator wallet		250
$50 bills	6 × $50 =	300
$20 bills	10 × $20 =	200
$5 bills	5 × $5 =	25
$1 bills	7 × $1 =	+ 7
		$2343

61. **The correct answer is (A).** The correct spelling is "utilization."

62. **The correct answer is (D).** The correct spelling is "patients."

63. **The correct answer is (C).** Choices **(A)** and **(B)** confuse locations of crime and residence; choice **(D)** reverses digits in the suspect's address.

64. **The correct answer is (D).** These rules are for the officer's protection. The suspect should be removed from the vehicle and checked for weapons before license and registration are requested.

65. **The correct answer is (C).** To solve this problem, you must create a proportion. 25 miles/60 minutes = 2.5 miles/x minutes. To determine the value of x, multiply 2.5 by 60 (60 times 2.5 = 150). 150/25 = 6. It will take 6 minutes for Officer Miller to reach the homes if he travels at a constant speed of 25 miles per hour.

66. **The correct answer is (B).** To determine the value of the stereo system, you must first add together the approximate values given of the other items. 150 + 600 + 200 + 1,500 = 2,450. Then you must subtract 2,450 from the grand total of 2,950. You will then find that the approximate value of the stereo system is $500.

67. **The correct answer is (C).** To determine the cost of the new television set, you must first calculate what 25 percent of 600 is. 600 times .25 = 150. Then you add $150 to the cost of the original television set. 600 + 150 = 750. The new television costs $750.

68. **The correct answer is (D).** The misspelled word is "descretion" and should be spelled "discretion."

69–71. Look *very* carefully at the combinations presented in the question and in the answer options. The correct answers all represent the exact combinations of letters, symbols, and numbers. The incorrect answer choices are different in some way— the difference between the answer choices may be very subtle. Give yourself plenty of time to answer these types of questions to the best of your ability.

72. **The correct answer is (C).** Choice (C) contains the word "crimanal," which should be spelled "criminal."

73. **The correct answer is (C).**

gold wedding band		$110.00
silver necklace		$70.00
bracelets	2 × $50.00 =	$100.00
marcasite brooch		$150.00
contents of purse	+	$37.89
		$467.89

74. **The correct answer is (D).** The suspect is not a juvenile, so the next step is to take palm prints.

75. **The correct answer is (A).** Choice (B) does not identify the bank; choices (C) and (D) are garbled and incorrect.

76. **The correct answer is (C).** The word that correctly completes the sentence is "quickly."

77. **The correct answer is (B).** The word that correctly completes the sentence is "whose."

78. **The correct answer is (D).** Choice (C) presents an intimidating situation, but since there is no physical contact, it does not fit the definition of harassment.

79. **The correct answer is (B).** The man is unconscious so cannot be interviewed, and there is no mention of witnesses. (One can assume that witnesses might have drawn the officer's attention to the man in the gutter rather than leaving it to the officer to stumble upon him.) Officer Montand should now look for evidence, such as a bullet.

80. **The correct answer is (B).** To find the average number of arrests made on Thursdays, add all of the numbers and then divide by the number of numbers. $6 + 12 + 9 + 9 = 36/4 = 9$.

81. **The correct answer is (A).** Divide the number of arrests that took place on Tuesday during week 4 by the total number of arrests in week $4.5/38 = .13$, which is equal to 13 percent.

82. **The correct answer is (D).** From 8:29 to 9:18 is 49 minutes.

83. **The correct answer is (A).** 32 percent of 475 is equal to $475 \times .32 = 152$. Since the governor wants to reduce the number of accidents by 32 percent, the number of drunk driving accidents that occur next year should be equal to $475 - 152 = 323$.

84. **The correct answer is (B).** In order to find out the percentage, divide 10 by 50. $10/50 = .20$, which is equal to 20 percent.

85. **The correct answer is (D).** In choice **(A)**, there is no building; in choice **(B)**, there is no intent; and in choice **(C)**, there is neither intent nor a building.

86. **The correct answer is (B).** The suspect in choice **(A)** has larger eyes; the suspect in choice **(C)** has different ears; and the suspect in choice **(D)** has a fuller face.

87. **The correct answer is (B).** The suspect in choice **(A)** has a smaller nose; the suspect in choice **(C)** has a fuller face and fuller lips; and the suspect in choice **(D)** has lighter eyes and thinner lips.

88. **The correct answer is (D).** The suspect in choice **(A)** has a different nose; the suspect in choice **(B)** has different ears; and the suspect in choice **(C)** has an entirely different head and face shape.

89. **The correct answer is (C).** The suspect in choice **(A)** has a much finer nose; the suspect in choice **(B)** has a narrower jaw structure; and the suspect in choice **(D)** has different ears.

90. **The correct answer is (B).** The suspect in choice **(A)** has a smaller nose; the suspect in choice **(C)** has lighter eyes and a wider mouth; and the suspect in choice **(D)** has a fuller face and thinner lips.

ANSWER SHEET: PRACTICE EXAMINATION 4

1. A B C D	26. A B C D	51. A B C D	76. A B C D
2. A B C D	27. A B C D	52. A B C D	77. A B C D
3. A B C D	28. A B C D	53. A B C D	78. A B C D
4. A B C D	29. A B C D	54. A B C D	79. A B C D
5. A B C D	30. A B C D	55. A B C D	80. A B C D
6. A B C D	31. A B C D	56. A B C D	81. A B C D
7. A B C D	32. A B C D	57. A B C D	82. A B C D
8. A B C D	33. A B C D	58. A B C D	83. A B C D
9. A B C D	34. A B C D	59. A B C D	84. A B C D
10. A B C D	35. A B C D	60. A B C D	85. A B C D
11. A B C D	36. A B C D	61. A B C D	86. A B C D
12. A B C D	37. A B C D	62. A B C D	87. A B C D
13. A B C D	38. A B C D	63. A B C D	88. A B C D
14. A B C D	39. A B C D	64. A B C D	89. A B C D
15. A B C D	40. A B C D	65. A B C D	90. A B C D
16. A B C D	41. A B C D	66. A B C D	91. A B C D
17. A B C D	42. A B C D	67. A B C D	92. A B C D
18. A B C D	43. A B C D	68. A B C D	93. A B C D
19. A B C D	44. A B C D	69. A B C D	94. A B C D
20. A B C D	45. A B C D	70. A B C D	95. A B C D
21. A B C D	46. A B C D	71. A B C D	96. A B C D
22. A B C D	47. A B C D	72. A B C D	97. A B C D
23. A B C D	48. A B C D	73. A B C D	98. A B C D
24. A B C D	49. A B C D	74. A B C D	99. A B C D
25. A B C D	50. A B C D	75. A B C D	100. A B C D

CHAPTER 12: PRACTICE EXAMINATION 4

Memory Booklet

Directions: You will be given 10 minutes to study the scene below and to try to notice and remember as many details as you can. You may not take any notes during this time.

Test Question Booklet

Time: 2 Hours, 45 Minutes • Questions: 85

> **Directions:** Now that the Memory Booklets have been collected, you have 2 hours and 45 minutes in which to answer the test questions. The first 14 questions are based on the scene that you just studied. Answer these questions first. Then proceed directly to the remaining 71 questions. Choose the best answer to each question and mark its letter on your answer sheet.

Answer questions 1 through 14 on the basis of the scene in the memory booklet.

1. A person arriving at this reception area by elevator and wishing to go to room 2-J would have to walk past the
   (A) information desk.
   (B) exit.
   (C) wall clock.
   (D) director's office.

2. The person in the personnel manager's doorway is a
   (A) white woman wearing a business suit.
   (B) man with a gun.
   (C) well-dressed man wearing glasses.
   (D) well-dressed man not wearing glasses.

3. The time at which this hostage situation is occurring is
   (A) 10:25
   (B) 11:20
   (C) 4:40
   (D) 5:45

4. The person who is bald is
   (A) blind.
   (B) requesting information.
   (C) sitting beside an umbrella.
   (D) holding a newspaper.

5. The total number of people in this scene is
   (A) 6
   (B) 8
   (C) 9
   (D) 11

6. The weapon carried by the kneeling man is
   (A) no weapon.
   (B) a handgun.
   (C) a machete.
   (D) a submachine gun.

7. The receptionist is
   (A) talking on the telephone.
   (B) consulting the appointment book.
   (C) left-handed.
   (D) wearing her hair in corn rows.

8. The number of floors serviced by this elevator is
   (A) 4
   (B) 5
   (C) 6
   (D) 7

9. On the table in front of the person with both feet on the floor is
   (A) *Health* magazine.
   (B) a pile of newspapers.
   (C) *Elle* magazine.
   (D) an ashtray.

10. The youngest person in this scene
   (A) is wearing a ponytail.
   (B) is not wearing glasses.
   (C) came with a dog.
   (D) is sitting with feet crossed at the ankles.

11. The person holding the automatic rifle
   (A) has it pointed at the receptionist.
   (B) is wearing work clothes.
   (C) is being watched by a dog.
   (D) is equipped with lots of ammunition.

12. The person with right leg crossed over left is
   (A) a black woman.
   (B) seated in front of *New York* magazine.
   (C) a terrorist.
   (D) wearing high-heeled sandals.

13. At the end of the bench next to the man reading a newspaper is
   (A) a potted plant.
   (B) an umbrella stand.
   (C) an umbrella.
   (D) a floor lamp.

14. On the floor between the elevator and the stairs is
    (A) a water cooler.
    (B) a waste container.
    (C) a coat rack.
    (D) nothing at all.

Please use the following passage to answer questions 15–17.

Officer Charise Jackson is called to the scene of a domestic dispute. She speaks with the victim, a 27-year-old woman named Laurie Farnsworth, and the victim's neighbor, a 53-year-old man named Jorge Sanchez. Mr. Sanchez claims that he heard a loud argument between Mrs. Farnsworth and her husband, Jeff Farnsworth. Because he thought that he heard Mr. Farnsworth beating his wife, Mr. Sanchez called the police. Mrs. Farnsworth claims that her husband came home drunk after spending the evening with his friends at the apartment belonging to Lee Vracek. Her husband became very angry over the price of their latest grocery bill and began to beat and kick her. Mrs. Farnsworth's right eye is swollen shut, and she feels that her right arm might be sprained. Mrs. Farnsworth says that after her husband beat her, he took their car and drove away. The paramedics arrive shortly after Officer Jackson speaks to Mrs. Farnsworth and her neighbor. Mrs. Farnsworth is transported to Mercy Hospital to be treated for her injuries.

Officer Jackson and a team of fellow officers are now looking for Mr. Farnsworth. Mr. Farnsworth is a 29-year-old white male with medium-length blonde hair and brown eyes and is 6'1" tall. He has a tattoo of an eagle on his right shoulder and a scar across his left cheek. He is most likely to be driving a black Volkswagen Jetta with the license plate number S652 Z19. Because he is said to be very drunk, the officers are anxious to find Mr. Farnsworth before he causes a traffic collision or further injuries to himself or others.

15. Which of the following is the most accurate description of Jeff Farnsworth?
    (A) A 53-year-old white male with medium-length blonde hair and brown eyes
    (B) A 29-year-old white male, 6'2" tall, with short blonde hair and brown eyes
    (C) A 32-year-old white male, 6'1" tall, with a tattoo of an eagle on his left shoulder and a scar across his left cheek
    (D) A 29-year-old white male with medium-length blonde hair and a tattoo of an eagle on his right shoulder

16. Which of the following individuals was the first to contact police about this matter?
    (A) Laurie Farnsworth
    (B) Lee Vracek
    (C) Jorge Sanchez
    (D) Jeff Farnsworth

17. Jeff Farnsworth is most likely to be driving a black Volkswagen Jetta with the license plate number _____.
    (A) S652 Z19
    (B) Z19 S652
    (C) S19 Z652
    (D) Z652 S19

18. Police Officer Ruiz on patrol in a residential area arrives at the scene of a fire and, after speaking with a bystander on the street, makes the following notes:

Place of Occurrence:	1520 Clarendon Road, Brooklyn
Time of Occurrence:	6:32 a.m.
Type of Building:	two-family frame dwelling
Event:	fire; suspected arson
Suspect:	male, white, approx. 6-foot, wearing jeans
Witness:	Mary Smith of 1523 Clarendon Road, Brooklyn

    Officer Ruiz must now write up a report of the incident. Which of the following expresses the information *most clearly*, *accurately*, and *completely*?
    (A) At 6:32 a.m., Mary Smith of 1523 Clarendon Road, Brooklyn, saw a white male wearing approximately 6-foot blue jeans running from the building across the street.
    (B) A white male wearing blue jeans ran from the house at 1520 Clarendon Road at 6:32 a.m. Mary Smith saw him.
    (C) At 6:32 a.m., a 6-foot white male wearing blue jeans ran from a burning two-family frame structure at 1520 Clarendon Road, Brooklyn. He was observed by a neighbor, Mary Smith.
    (D) A two-family frame house is on fire at 1520 Clarendon Road in Brooklyn. A white male in blue jeans probably did it. Mary Smith saw him run.

Items 19 through 21 are based on the following passage.

Officer Ellingson was called to investigate a car that had been left in front of a man's house and was suspected to be abandoned. When she arrived on the scene, the man who made the call approached her and explained that the car had been left there over a week ago with the doors unlocked and the windows down. Before investigating the vehicle, Officer Ellingson entered the license plates into her computer. After a few minutes, the computer informed her that the plates on the car were fictitious. She then suspected that the car had been stolen. In order to confirm this, she found the Vehicle Identification Number (VIN) of the car and entered it into her computer. This time, the computer indicated that the car belonged to a local woman and was reported stolen about two weeks ago. Officer Ellingson then conducted a thorough search of the vehicle, including a search for fingerprints, but did not find much that could be clearly linked to the car thief. The only piece of evidence that she found was a fingerprint on the rearview mirror. The print most likely belongs to the owner of the vehicle, but Officer Ellingson felt that it was significant enough to send to the crime lab.

19. When did Officer Ellingson confirm that the vehicle had been stolen?
    (A) When the caller told her it was stolen
    (B) When she discovered the fictitious plates
    (C) When she entered the VIN number
    (D) When she found the fingerprint

20. The fingerprint that Officer Ellingson found on the rearview mirror most likely belongs to
    (A) Officer Ellingson.
    (B) the caller.
    (C) the thief.
    (D) the car's owner.

21. Which of the following represents the order of Officer Ellingson's actions at the scene?
    (A) Talked to the caller, entered the license plates, entered the VIN number, and conducted a search of the car
    (B) Entered the license plates, entered the VIN number, talked to the caller, and conducted a search of the car
    (C) Conducted a search of the car, entered the license plates, entered the VIN number, and talked to the caller
    (D) Talked to the caller, entered the VIN number, entered the license plates, and conducted a search of the car

Questions 22 and 23 are based on the following situation:

On a hot summer afternoon, three prisoners are missing from the state penitentiary located on the wooded outskirts of a small upstate city. Their means of escape has not yet been established, so search parties are dispatched near and far.

22. Police car 43 leaves the city traveling west on highway 9. After 3 miles, the car makes a right turn onto route 21. Two miles up route 21, a dirt road forks off in a diagonal right. Car 43 turns onto the dirt road and continues until it reaches a farmhouse on the right-hand side of the road. The car turns into the driveway, and both officers get out. When the driver gets out, in which direction is she facing?
    (A) Northeast
    (B) Southwest
    (C) East
    (D) South

23. Correction Officers English and Miller leave the prison by the south gate, turn right, and run into the woods. They run halfway around a large boulder that lies directly in their path and continue looking to the right and to the left. They stop and peer into a dense clump of bushes on their left. In what direction are they looking?
(A) East
(B) North
(C) South
(D) West

Items 24 through 26 are based on the following passage.

The nature of a line officer's job requires him or her to perform various roles, often under extreme conditions, and to provide police services to anyone requesting or requiring them. The demanding nature of the job can often lead officers to become "run down" and unmotivated. In order to avoid these negative outcomes, it is important for officers to be provided with opportunities to set and achieve goals. The Officer Training Program is a program designed to address these issues by providing officers with the information and competency skills necessary to advance their knowledge of law enforcement.

The main focus of the Officer Training Program is to assist line officers in developing the skills and knowledge necessary to advance to supervisory, mid-management, and executive management positions within the agency. However, the Department recognizes that not all officers desire these positions and that many wish to remain within their current operational areas. Regardless of the end goal, the Officer Training Program will provide officers with information, knowledge, and skills that will help them to perform their jobs more effectively. This will provide officers with a concrete goal to strive toward, whether it is advancement within the department or advancement of personal knowledge.

24. The demanding nature of a line officer's job can lead officers to become
(A) angry.
(B) efficient.
(C) unmotivated.
(D) supervisors.

25. The idea behind the Officer Training Program is to provide officers with
(A) better salaries.
(B) goals.
(C) various roles.
(D) more work.

26. Many officers are not interested in supervisory or management positions. These officers would prefer to
(A) retire early.
(B) remain in their current position.
(C) not have any concrete goals.
(D) avoid the Officer Training Program.

Answer questions 27 and 28 solely on the basis of the following procedure:

Police Officers responding to complaints of loud or violent disagreements between members of a family are directed to follow the procedure below:

1. When knocking on the door of the premises in which the dispute is taking place, do not stand directly in front of it.
2. Separate the parties taking part in the dispute by taking them into different rooms.
3. Attempt to calm the people involved while interviewing them.
4. Stay out of the dispute; do not take sides.
5. If an insult is directed at you, ignore it.
6. Advise the parties in the argument where they may go for counseling.
7. Do not say anything that will direct the people's anger at you.
8. Make no arrests unless one of the participants is hurt.

27. Officers Claymore and Peron, arriving at the scene of a family dispute, separate a screaming couple into different rooms. The wife shouts that her husband is having an affair with his secretary and that she is going to file for divorce. The wife picks up the ringing telephone, listens briefly, and then slams it down. She shouts to her husband, "Your secretary just called, but she didn't leave a message." At this point, it would be proper for one of the Police Officers to advise that the
(A) husband end this affair at once.
(B) wife go ahead with her divorce plans.
(C) wife trust her husband.
(D) couple seek the help of local marriage counselors.

28. Two officers respond to a complaint of gunshots and loud arguing taking place in an apartment. They approach the apartment and hear a television set playing. They stand in front of the door, knock on it, and are told to enter. A man and a woman are sitting on a couch watching a murder mystery on television. The couple states that they have been watching the program for almost 2 hours. The officers evaluate the situation and decide that a mistake has been made. They apologize and leave. One of the actions taken by the officers does not conform to the procedure for dealing with this type of situation. This occurred when they
(A) determined that a mistake had been made and then apologized and left the premises.
(B) interviewed both people in the same room.
(C) investigated the complaint even though they could hear no argument.
(D) stood in front of the door while knocking on it.

For questions 29–31, determine which word in the sentence is spelled incorrectly. There will be only one misspelled word in each sentence.

29. Becuase of his outstanding performance, Officer Dolan received a promotion.
    (A) Becuase
    (B) outstanding
    (C) performance
    (D) promotion

30. All oficers are expected to comply with the new uniform regulations.
    (A) oficers
    (B) comply
    (C) uniform
    (D) regulations

31. At the sentencing heering, the judge sternly reminded the defendant that his reckless driving caused an innocent father of three to lose his life.
    (A) sentencing
    (B) heering
    (C) defendant
    (D) innocent

Items 32 through 34 are based on the following passage. The people in the passage are identified by the following code:

> **F** = the car's owner
> **G** = witness (pedestrian)
> **H** = the car thief
> **J** = the Police Officer
> **K** = the backup office

At 11:26 p.m., J was called to the scene of an auto theft. When she arrived on the scene, F was clearly agitated and was speaking about the incident with G. J spoke with F, who stated that he came home from work to find his car missing. He said that he did not get a look at H, but that G noticed someone sneaking around F's house at about 11:15 p.m. J then interviewed G to get a description of H. J then called K and advised him to look for someone who fit her description of H.

32. Who appeared to be agitated?
    (A) The car thief
    (B) The witness
    (C) The car's owner
    (D) The Police Officer

33. Who spoke with the backup officer about what the thief looked like?
- **(A)** The Police Officer
- **(B)** The car's owner
- **(C)** The witness
- **(D)** The car thief

34. What are the genders of the Police Officer and the witness, respectively?
- **(A)** Male, male
- **(B)** Female, female
- **(C)** Female, male
- **(D)** Male, female

Please use the following passage to answer question 35.

Many teenagers in the area had been looking forward to the rock concert for months; the show had sold out within minutes as soon as the tickets went on sale. The night of the concert, the backstage area was particularly hectic. The band's drummer had been missing for most of the evening. The opening bands played, and their shows went smoothly. However, the crowd was certainly eager to see the main act. They were forced to wait more than 2 hours after the last opening band while the main act waited for their drummer to arrive; the crowd started to boo. Finally, minutes before the other members of the band were ready to cancel the concert, the drummer finally showed up at the arena, clearly intoxicated. Band members were not sure whether or not they would be able to perform. Police working at the concert were told to remain alert for any signs of trouble.

35. Which of the following is the MOST likely reason that police had to remain alert in this situation?
- **(A)** The drummer could possibly hurt himself in his intoxicated state.
- **(B)** A fight could break out between the band members and the drummer.
- **(C)** The crowd could riot if their favorite band cancelled the concert at the last minute.
- **(D)** The drummer could have illegal substances in his possession.

Please use the following information to answer questions 36–38.

The following are policies regarding warrantless searches.
- Officers may search a person or a person's property when that person provides the officer with voluntary oral permission to do so. A person may withdraw his or her consent to a search of his or her person or property at any time, and the search will cease. Any evidence that is found before the person withdraws his or her consent will be retained by the officers.
- Officers may stop a person if the officers have a reasonable suspicion that he or she has committed, is committing, or will commit a crime in order to gain information about the crime from that person. If at any time during this

temporary detention an officer believes that the person is carrying a deadly weapon, the officer will search that person (and/or the person's property and car) for the weapon.

- If officers have probable cause to believe that contraband items or pieces of evidence have been hidden in a vehicle, the officers may search the vehicle where such items or evidence could be found.
- Officers may search property or vehicles if they know that a crime has been committed in that location and if the location has been classified as a crime scene. They are allowed to search the scene during a time period that is deemed reasonable to conduct an investigation of the crime and to gather evidence.

36. Officer Chopak pulls over a vehicle belonging to Bill Coddington Sr. Officer Chopak has probable cause to believe that Mr. Coddington is hiding a murder weapon and other evidence of homicide in his car. When Officer Chopak searches Mr. Coddington's car, Mr. Coddington exclaims, "Hey, you can't do that! You don't have a warrant!" Officer Chopak then locates a knife with traces of blood on the blade and handle in the glove compartment. Has Officer Chopak followed the above policies?
    (A) Yes, because Officer Chopak found the knife before Mr. Coddington withdrew his consent to the search.
    (B) Yes, because officers may search a vehicle if they have probable cause to believe that contraband items or pieces of evidence are hidden there.
    (C) No, because Officer Chopak did not have Mr. Coddington's permission to search his property.
    (D) No, because officers may never search a vehicle without a warrant.

37. Officers are called to the scene of an alleged sexual assault. A teenage girl claims that her boyfriend sexually assaulted her in her bedroom. Officers plan to search the bedroom for any additional evidence. How long do they have to conduct an investigation and gather evidence?
    (A) Personnel may take as long as they need to gather all necessary evidence of the crime at the crime scene.
    (B) Personnel have 24 hours to gather all necessary evidence of the crime at the crime scene.
    (C) Personnel have 48 hours to gather all necessary evidence of the crime at the crime scene.
    (D) Personnel are allowed to search the scene during a time period that is deemed reasonable to conduct an investigation and gather evidence.

38. Officers Gary and Hammond go to the apartment of Debra Griffith, a former girlfriend of a man who was reported missing several weeks earlier. Although they have not been issued a search warrant, they ask her if they can search her apartment, and Ms. Griffith agrees. During the search, Ms. Griffith becomes anxious and angry when Officers Gary and Hammond go through some personal items. She asks them to stop the search and leave her apartment. After she says this, Officer Hammond finishes looking through a box she was searching and finds what could very well be a key piece of evidence. Officers Gary and Hammond then end their search and leave Ms. Griffith's residence. Will the officers be able to use the evidence?

(A) No, because Officer Hammond did not ask Ms. Griffith's permission as to whether she could take the piece of evidence with her.

(B) No, because Officer Hammond found the piece of evidence after Ms. Griffith asked them to stop, and they do not have a warrant.

(C) Yes, because Ms. Griffith had given the officers permission to search her apartment.

(D) Yes, because they immediately ended their search after Ms. Griffith asked them to stop.

39. Beverly Bowers, who has been convicted of aggravated assault and who has exhausted all appeals, surrenders herself at the Women's Correctional Facility to serve her sentence. Ms. Bowers hands over her purse, and the contents of her wallet are inventoried thus:

5 $20 bills

7 $10 bills

13 $5 bills

2 $1 bills

9 quarters

21 dimes

17 nickels

8 pennies

How much money was in Ms. Bowers' purse?

(A) $237.88

(B) $242.28

(C) $243.06

(D) $244.68

Answer questions 40 and 41 on the basis of the following procedure:

1. When a prisoner requests medical attention or is in apparent need of it, the Police Officer should arrange for the prisoner to be promptly examined by a doctor.

2. In the event that a prisoner is in need of medical treatment, the Police Officer should notify a supervisor immediately so that an ambulance can be sum-

moned. Prisoners who are drug addicts and who are in need of treatment for their addiction should be taken to a hospital by a radio car.

3. Under no circumstances should a Police Officer prescribe any medication for a prisoner.

4. A Police Officer should not attempt to diagnose a prisoner's illness or injury and should not attempt to treat the prisoner except in a situation where first aid is required. First aid should be administered promptly.

5. A doctor is the only one authorized to administer medicine to a prisoner. When a doctor is not available, the Police Officer in charge of the prisoner should then give him or her the medicine and watch him or her take it.

40. Alan Fox, a prisoner well known to police because of his long record, is in custody when he claims that he has a severe headache as a result of being badly beaten. There are no apparent signs of a physical injury, but the prisoner is demanding medical attention. The Police Officer in charge of Alan Fox should

(A) consider the prisoner's long record before deciding to call a doctor.

(B) give the prisoner two aspirins.

(C) ignore the prisoner's request for medical attention since there are no apparent physical injuries.

(D) see that Alan Fox is promptly examined by a doctor.

41. It is a hot summer day, and Officer Stone has in his custody a prisoner who is a drug addict. The prisoner opens his shirt to reveal a large unhealed wound that is obviously infected. Officer Stone suggests to the prisoner that he call a doctor in to examine him, but the prisoner refuses, saying the wound is of no consequence. In this instance, Officer Stone should

(A) request that his supervisor call an ambulance.

(B) closely examine the wound in order to evaluate its severity.

(C) adhere to the prisoner's wishes and do nothing about the matter.

(D) take the prisoner at once to a hospital in a radio car.

For the following items, please identify the option that best completes the sentence.

42. The _____ investigation indicated that the woman was not involved.

(A) perliminary

(B) praliminary

(C) preliminary

(D) pirliminary

43. Investigators are required to have _____ skills developed through experience in law enforcement.

(A) speshalized

(B) spiecialized

(C) specialised

(D) specialized

Please use the following table to answer questions 44–46.

TOTAL SEXUAL OFFENSES COMMITTED IN YOUR STATE FROM 1990–2000.

Year	Number of Offenses	Year	Number of Offenses
1990	257	1996	434
1991	372	1997	428
1992	418	1998	392
1993	562	1999	377
1994	475	2000	345
1995	446		

44. During which of the following years did the most sexual offenses occur?
  (A) 2000
  (B) 1998
  (C) 1993
  (D) 1990

45. A program was instituted in 1993 to educate the public (especially young women in high school and college) about sexual offenses and crime prevention. According to the information above, this program was
  (A) ineffective, because sexual offenses increased from 1993–2000.
  (B) ineffective, because the number of sexual offenses did not change from 1993–2000.
  (C) effective, because the number of sexual offenses decreased by 50 percent in 1994.
  (D) effective, because the number of sexual offenses steadily decreased from 1993–2000.

46. In 2001, 10 percent fewer sexual offenses were committed than in the year 2000. The number of sexual offenses committed in 2001 is _____.
  (A) 379.5
  (B) 332.3
  (C) 310.5
  (D) 292.8

47. In a police academy exercise, a recruit is handed the following information collected by a Police Officer arriving at the scene of a robbery immediately after it had occurred:

Time:	5:28 p.m.
Place:	Aneke's Bridal Fashions, 280 Second Avenue
Reporter:	Aneke Blau, owner
Event:	knife-point robbery; $200 taken
Suspect:	white woman, red hair, blue jeans, white T-shirt

The Police Officer is calling in a report so that cars in the vicinity can search for the suspect. Which of the following expresses this information *most clearly*, *accurately*, and *completely*?

(A) Aneke Blau reported at 5:28 p.m. her store Aneke's Bridal Fashions was robbed at knifepoint at 280 Second Avenue. A white woman with red hair took $200 from her wearing blue jeans and white T-shirt.

(B) At 5:28 p.m., a red-haired woman took $200 from 280 Second Avenue at Aneke's Bridal Fashions owned by Aneke Blau who was robbed by a white woman. She was wearing blue jeans and a white T-shirt and used a knife.

(C) In a robbery that occurred at knifepoint, a red-haired white woman robbed the owner of Aneke's Bridal Fashions. Aneke Blau, the owner of the 280 Second Avenue store was robbed of $200. She said she was wearing blue jeans and white T-shirt at 5:28 p.m.

(D) Just before 5:28 p.m., Aneke Blau, owner of Aneke's Bridal Fashions located at 280 Second Avenue, was robbed of $200 at knifepoint. The suspect is a white female with red hair, wearing blue jeans and white T-shirt.

For the following items, please identify the misspelled word or the incorrectly used word.

48. There may be some cases in which a uniformed officer becomes actively involved in the investigation of a crime.
(A) uniformed
(B) activelly
(C) involved
(D) investigation

49. A confidential informent is a person who provides confidential information and investigative leads to the police and wishes to remain anonymous.
(A) informent
(B) information
(C) investigative
(D) anonymous

Answer questions 50 and 51 on the basis of the following definitions:

Burglary is committed when an individual, without authorization, enters or remains in a building with the intent of committing a crime.

Criminal mischief is committed when a person intentionally damages the property of another person, having neither the right to do so nor any reasonable ground to believe that he has the right to do so.

Larceny is committed when a person intentionally deprives another of property or wrongfully takes, obtains, or withholds property from the owner of that property without the use of force, violence, or threat of injury. Larceny is committed, for example, when property is obtained under false pretenses, when lost property is found and not returned, or when a bad check is intentionally issued.

Robbery is committed when a person, against another person's will, takes property from that person.

50. Jane Wills finds a diamond ring on the sidewalk of a busy street. She keeps it. According to the definitions, Wills committed
   (A) the crime of larceny.
   (B) the crime of burglary.
   (C) the crime of robbery.
   (D) none of the listed crimes.

51. Elwood Tompkins is waiting at a bus station to hand over a package of expensive jewelry to a representative of the XYZ Transfer Company. Phil Shore learns of the shipment and decides to steal the package. He goes to the bus station, presents himself to Tompkins, and says he is from XYZ. Tompkins gives Shore the package, believing he is from XYZ. Shore is not armed. The definitions indicate that Shore committed the crime of
   (A) robbery.
   (B) burglary.
   (C) criminal mischief.
   (D) larceny.

Answer questions 52 through 54 on the basis of the following procedure:

A Police Officer responding to a situation that involves a person or persons who seem to be dead should take the following steps:
1. The officer should assume that the person is alive unless the officer is absolutely sure that he or she is dead.
2. If the officer is absolutely sure that the person is dead, and if the body is in public view, the body should be covered with a waterproof covering.
3. The officer should summon a sergeant to the scene.
4. The officer should immediately call the homicide detectives if the death is suspicious.

5. The body should be searched for identification if the death took place in a public area. In the event that the death took place in the home of a person who lived alone, both the body and the home are to be searched. All searches must be witnessed by a sergeant.

6. Property of a dead person may be released only to a relative who lived with the deceased.

7. Do not notify relatives or family of a death over the telephone. However, if you receive a call from a relative concerning the person's condition, you may inform the relative of the death.

52. A Police Officer is summoned to the scene of an accident. The victim, a young woman, is lying on the street, apparently dead. She is surrounded by bystanders. In this situation, the officer should first
(A) cover the body with a waterproof covering.
(B) notify the homicide detectives.
(C) search the body to determine its identity.
(D) check to see if the woman is alive.

53. A Police Officer is sent to the apartment of an elderly man who obviously has been dead for a few days. The officer closes the door to the apartment and is now alone with the body. His first act should be to
(A) summon a sergeant.
(B) search the apartment.
(C) search the body.
(D) cover the body.

54. A Police Officer, while searching the home of a dead man who had lived alone, is approached by the man's sister, who requests permission to remove a few family albums from the apartment. The officer, in this instance, should
(A) give her the albums since she is the dead man's sister.
(B) not give her the albums since she did not live with the dead man.
(C) give her the albums since they contain only family pictures.
(D) not give her the albums until she proves that she is the deceased's sister.

Please use the following information to answer questions 55 and 56.

Officer Stiles is sent to Maple Avenue to help settle a dispute between two neighbors, John Garson and Harry Weber. Officer Stiles speaks with each neighbor separately. The following five statements are part of Harry Weber's account of the incident:

1. John threatened my wife and children and punched me in the face.
2. I noticed that there were bike tracks on my lawn, and my wife's flowers had been crushed. I suspected John's kids were involved because I had seen them playing in our yard before.
3. I got home from work around 5:30 p.m.

4. I told John that his kids needed to stay off my lawn.

5. John answered the door when I went to his house to confront him. I could smell the alcohol on his breath.

55. Which of the following would be the MOST logical order of the above statements?
   (A) 5, 3, 1, 2, 4
   (B) 3, 2, 5, 4, 1
   (C) 1, 4, 3, 2, 5
   (D) 2, 5, 3, 1, 4

56. According to Harry Weber's account of the incident, which of the following occurred immediately BEFORE Mr. Weber noticed that there were bike tracks on his lawn?
   (A) John Garson threatened his wife and children.
   (B) John Garson opened the door; he had obviously been drinking.
   (C) Harry Weber told Mr. Garson that his kids needed to stay off the Webers' lawn.
   (D) Harry Weber arrived home from work.

For the following item, choose the sentence that contains the misspelled word or words.

57. **(A)** Officer Merchant has an exceptional service record.
   (B) The thief fell as he ran from the store owner.
   (C) His patrol area spans 2 square miles.
   (D) Domestic despute is one of the most common calls.

58. Officer Parks is dispatched to the scene of an apparent suicide. She is driving 42 mph to a home that is 4.5 miles away. Approximately how long will it take her to arrive at the scene?
   (A) 8 minutes
   (B) 7.5 minutes
   (C) 6.4 minutes
   (D) 5.2 minutes

Answer questions 59 and 60 on the basis of the following Employee Leave Regulations:

As a full-time permanent city employee under the Career and Salary Plan, Officer Peter Smith earns an "annual leave allowance." This consists of a certain number of days off a year with pay and may be used for vacation, for personal business, or for observing religious holidays. During his first eight years of city service, he will earn an "annual leave allowance" of twenty days off a year (an average of one and two thirds days off a month). After he has finished eight full years of working for the city, he will begin earning an additional five days off a year. His "annual leave allowance" will then be twenty-five days a year and will remain at this amount for seven full years. He will begin earning an additional two days off a year after he has completed a total of fifteen years of city employment.

A "sick leave allowance" of one day a month is also given to Officer Smith, but it can be used only in case of actual illness. When Smith returns to work after using "sick leave allowance," he *must* have a doctor's note if the absence is for a total of more than three days, but he may also be required to show a doctor's note for absences of one, two, or three days.

59. According to the preceding passage, Mr. Smith's "annual leave allowance" consists of a certain number of days off a year that he
    (A) does not get paid for.
    (B) gets paid for at time and a half.
    (C) may use for personal business.
    (D) may not use for observing religious holidays.

60. According to the preceding passage, when he uses "sick leave allowance," Mr. Smith may be required to show a doctor's note
    (A) even if his absence is for only one day.
    (B) only if his absence is for more than two days.
    (C) only if his absence is for more than three days.
    (D) only if his absence is for three days or more.

Answer questions 61 and 62 on the basis of the drawing below. This drawing shows some vital interior parts of a police revolver and the order in which they fit together.

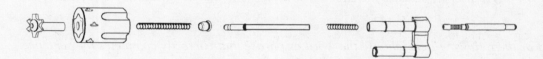

61. The part that goes between  and is

    (A)
    (B)
    (C)
    (D)

62. The part that does NOT belong to this portion of the revolver is

   (A)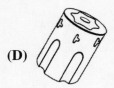

   (B)

   (C)

   (D)

63. Police Officers are often assigned to the scene of a fire to control traffic and, at times, to close off a street to all traffic except emergency vehicles. Two officers assigned to this duty arrive in a radio car, which they park across one end of a street, blocking traffic. After locking their radio car, they then proceed to the other end of the street on foot to block off traffic at that end. The action taken by these Police Officers should be considered

   (A) improper, because they should have remained in their car in order to be able to move quickly if they were needed.

   (B) proper, since a person who may have started the fire would be effectively trapped.

   (C) improper, because their car was left unattended and therefore could not be moved to permit emergency vehicles to enter.

   (D) proper, because the street is now closed to all but emergency vehicles.

For the following item, choose the word or phrase that correctly completes the sentence.

64. The juvenile denied that he _____ at the store last night during the theft.

   (A) is

   (B) will be

   (C) was

   (D) shall be

65. It is mid-January, and many members of the precinct house staff are out with the flu. Officer Seguaro is covering the dispatcher's desk on an emergency basis. Officer Seguaro receives a call reporting alleged child abuse and consults the following rules for the procedure to be followed in prescribed order:

1. Ask for the name, address, and telephone number of the caller.

2. Ask for the name and address of the person being abused.

3. Ask the nature of the abuse.

4. Ask for the name of the abuser.

5. Dispatch police to the scene of the alleged abuse.

6. If the reporter is at a location not proximate to the scene of the abuse and abused, dispatch police to interview caller.

7. Ask caller his or her relationship to abused and abuser.

8. Assure caller that all information will be kept confidential.

Officer Seguaro asks the caller his name, address, and telephone number, then asks for the name and address of the person being abused. She learns that the caller lives in the apartment directly across the hall from the little girl, who is being beaten by a shouting male, unidentified since the beating is taking place behind closed doors. Officer Seguaro immediately dispatches a patrol car to the scene. The next thing for Officer Seguaro to do is

(A) dispatch another patrol car to interview the caller.

(B) ask the caller his relationship to the abused.

(C) ask the names of likely suspects.

(D) assure the caller that all information will be kept confidential.

66. Cory Schumann is pulled over for speeding in a construction zone. He was driving 85 mph in a construction zone. His fines are as follows: a $75 fine for speeding, a $150 fine for speeding in a construction zone, and a $50 fine for not wearing his seatbelt while operating his vehicle. Mr. Schumann goes to court to contest the ticket. The judge determines that the speeding and construction zone fines will stand, but the seat belt citation will be dismissed, and Mr. Schumann will not have to pay for the seat belt citation. How much will Mr. Schumann have to pay in all?

(A) $300

(B) $275

(C) $225

(D) $200

67. Officer O'Brien is hired at his department with a starting annual salary of $31,000. One year later, he is given a 6 percent raise, in accordance with his union contract. How much is Officer O'Brien's salary during his second year at the department?

(A) $32,860

(B) $33,290

(C) $33,540

(D) $34,160

68. A fire truck with lights flashing and siren wailing pulled out of the firehouse and headed north toward the site of a fire. After one block, the fire truck turned right. At the next corner, it turned right again, proceeding for two blocks before turning left. At successive corners, the fire truck then turned right and right again. At the next intersection, an impatient motorist crossed the path of the fire truck, and the fire truck hit the car on its right side. In which direction was the car traveling?

(A) North

(B) South

(C) East

(D) West

Questions 69–71 contain a set of letters, symbols, and numbers. Please choose ONLY ONE option that contains the exact pattern of letters, symbols, numbers, and spaces.

69. ʻ†??ï????e12¦

    (A) ʻ†??ï????e21¦

    (B) ʻ†??ï?!??!e12¦

    (C) ʻ†??ï????e12¦

    (D) ʻ†??ï????e12¦

70. ?????9.828IU;n

    (A) ?????98.28IU;n

    (B) ?????9.828IU;n

    (C) ?????9828I.U;n

    (D) ?????9.8281U;n

71. ¤??46*99¦?~?l‹

    (A) ¤??46*99¦?~?l‹

    (B) ¤??46*99¦?~?I‹

    (C) ¤??469*9¦?~?l‹

    (D) ¤??46*99¦?=?l‹

72. Twelve percent of an officer's calls are related to domestic violence. If an officer receives an average of 30 calls in a week, how many of them are likely to be related to domestic violence?

    (A) 3.2

    (B) 3.6

    (C) 3.7

    (D) 3.9

73. Officer Maxwell must travel on city streets for 3 miles, on the highway for 5 miles, and on city streets again for 2 miles in order to make it to the scene of a robbery. On the city streets she travels at an average speed of a half mile per minute. On the highway she travels at an average speed of 1 mile per minute. How long does it take her to get to the scene?
(A) 14 minutes
(B) 15 minutes
(C) 16 minutes
(D) 17 minutes

Answer question 74 on the basis of the following definitions:

Felony murder is committed when a person, acting alone or with others, commits or attempts to commit the crimes of robbery, burglary, kidnapping, arson, or rape, and in the course and furtherance of such crime, or immediate flight therefrom, he, or another participant, if there be any, causes the death of a person other than one of the participants.

Murder is committed when a person, following a period of lengthy planning, intentionally causes the death of another person.

74. The difference between murder and felony murder is that
(A) in murder, someone is killed; in felony murder, the crime may be attempted.
(B) in the case of felony murder, some other crime must be committed along with the murder.
(C) murder is planned; felony murder may be incidental to another crime.
(D) felony murder is part of a calculated crime; murder may be impulsive, based upon extreme provocation or emotional stress.

Answer question 75 on the basis of the following paragraph:

Proper firearms training is one phase of law enforcement that cannot be ignored. No part of the training of a law officer is more important or more valuable. The officer's life, and often the lives of his or her fellow officers, depend directly upon skill with the weapon he or she is carrying. Proficiency with the revolver is not attained exclusively by the volume of ammunition used and the number of hours spent on the firing line. Supervised practice and the use of training aids and techniques help make the shooter. It is essential to have a good firing range where new officers are trained and older personnel practice in scheduled firearms sessions. The fundamental points to be stressed are grip, stance, breathing, sight alignment, and trigger squeeze. Coordination of thought, vision, and motion must be achieved before the officer gains confidence in shooting ability. Attaining this ability will make the student a better officer and enhance his or her value to the force.

75. The paragraph best supports the statement that
    (A) skill with weapons is a phase of law enforcement training that is too often ignored.
    (B) the most useful and essential single factor in the training of a law officer is proper firearms training.
    (C) the value of an officer to the force is enhanced by the officer's self-confidence and coordination.
    (D) the lives of law enforcement officers always depend directly upon the skill with weapons displayed by fellow officers.

76. An off-duty Police Officer visiting a friend in another city stops to fill his tank with gasoline and discovers a holdup in progress at the gas station. When he identifies himself as a law officer, the robber takes off at high speed and the officer gives chase. They proceed west on the highway for 3 miles. Then they make a right turn off the highway onto a secondary road for another 1½ miles, and then a left turn onto a dirt road. Driving at high speed on the dirt road, the holdup man's car develops a flat tire. The man jumps out of the driver's seat and runs directly into the woods. The Police Officer follows on foot but loses sight of his suspect. The Police Officer then turns around to walk back to his car. In what direction is he walking?
    (A) North
    (B) South
    (C) East
    (D) West

77. At the scene of an apparent homicide, the following procedure must be rigidly followed:

    1. Pull on gloves.

    2. Check for signs of life in all victims.

    3. If any victim is alive, summon ambulance without delay.

    4. Make a quick sketch of the scene so as to show relative locations and positions of bodies, weapons, possible points of entry and exit, and both large and small objects.

    5. Seal off premises and permit access only to police and medical personnel.

    6. Remain at premises until a superior officer arrives.

    Police Officer Blitz arrives at an apartment in which a small massacre has taken place. Two men and a woman are lying face down in the living room with bullet holes in the backs of their heads. A teenage girl is lying face up on a bed with her neck slashed.

A baby is lying in its crib with a stomach wound. Officer Blitz pulls on her gloves, takes out a pocket mirror, and holds the mirror to each person's mouth. The mirror fogs slightly when she holds it to the baby's mouth, so Officer Blitz immediately calls for an ambulance. She then opens her memo book to an empty page and makes a rough sketch of this scene of carnage. The doorbell rings and Officer Blitz learns that the person at the door lives in this apartment. Officer Blitz should now

(A) check this occupant of the apartment for injuries and possible need for medical care.

(B) refuse admittance to this person.

(C) leave because the owner of the apartment has returned.

(D) cover the bodies.

Answer questions 78 and 79 on the basis of the map below. The flow of traffic is indicated by the arrows. If there is only one arrow shown, then traffic flows only in the direction indicated by the arrow. If there are two arrows shown, then traffic flows in both directions. You must follow the flow of traffic.

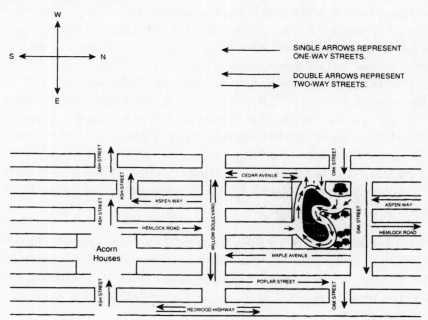

78. Police Officers Patel and Mohan are in their patrol car on Ash Street at the corner of Hemlock Road when they receive word of a car being vandalized on Aspen Way at the corner of Oak Street. Which is the fastest legal route for the officers to take to apprehend the vandals?
    (A) Take Hemlock Road straight into the park. Follow the park drive around and exit at Aspen Way on Oak Street.
    (B) Take Hemlock Road to Willow Boulevard. Go west on Willow Boulevard to Aspen Way. Go south on Aspen Way one block to Ash Street. Turn right onto Ash Street and right again onto Cedar Avenue. Follow Cedar Avenue past the park and go east on Oak Street to Aspen Way.
    (C) Follow Ash Street to Cedar Avenue. Make a right turn onto Cedar Avenue to Oak Street. Go right on Oak Street to Aspen Way.
    (D) Drive through the grounds of Acorn Houses, exiting at Maple Avenue. Turn left onto Willow Boulevard to Cedar Avenue. Make a right onto Cedar Avenue and follow it to Oak Street. Turn south on Oak Street to Aspen Way.

79. When Officers Mohan and Patel arrive at the corner of Aspen Way and Oak Street, they discover that the problem is not vandalism but rather keys locked inside the car. They assist in opening the car, then are alerted to a burglary in progress on Poplar Street just south of Oak Street. What route should they take to get to the scene?
    (A) Proceed east on Oak Street and turn left onto Poplar Street.
    (B) Proceed east on Oak Street and turn right onto Poplar Street.
    (C) Enter the park at Aspen Valley Way and follow the park drive around to the exit at Cedar Avenue. Turn left onto Cedar Avenue to Willow Boulevard. Turn left onto Willow Boulevard and continue to Poplar Street. Turn north onto Poplar Street to the scene of the crime.
    (D) Take Oak Street to Maple Avenue. Turn right onto Maple Avenue and proceed to Willow Boulevard. Make a left onto Willow Boulevard for one block, then another left onto Poplar Street.

80. When Officer Shavez is 10 feet from his target at the firing range, he shoots with 100 percent accuracy. After this distance, his accuracy decreases by 3 percent for every additional 10 feet in distance from his target. What is his shooting accuracy if he is 50 feet from the target?
    (A) 88 percent
    (B) 87 percent
    (C) 86 percent
    (D) 85 percent

81. A woman called the police department to report that her car had been burglarized. She listed the items that were taken as a stereo valued at $486, 26 CDs valued at $14 each, a cellular phone valued at $294, and a leather jacket valued at $319. What was the total value of the items taken from her car?
   (A) $1,113
   (B) $1,182
   (C) $1,297
   (D) $1,463

82. Department Y will provide safety vests for any of its 592 officers that request them. Each of these vests costs the department $895. If 528 officers request the vests, how much will this cost the department?
   (A) $558,043
   (B) $529,840
   (C) $541,527
   (D) $472,560

83. In city Z last year, 582 assaults were reported. Of these reports, 92 were given by individuals who were reporting a second incident. If the population of city Z is 24,500, what percentage of the population was assaulted only one time last year?
   (A) 2 percent
   (B) 3 percent
   (C) 4 percent
   (D) 5 percent

84. A Police Officer who observes a merchant selling liquor to a person who appears to the officer to be underage should take the following steps in this order:

   1. Ask the purchaser for information.
   2. If the purchaser is a minor, as defined by the liquor laws, ask to see what identification was shown to the salesclerk.
   3. Ask the salesperson what identification the purchaser presented.
   4. If the salesperson did not request adequate proof, serve a summons on the person and on the establishment.
   5. If the minor presented fraudulent proof, take the minor into custody.

   Police Officer Murphy, on foot patrol, passes a liquor store and observes a youth leaving with a brown paper bag in his hand. Officer Murphy suspects that the youth is underage, stops him, and asks to see his identification. The young man produces a driver's license that indicates that he is 21 years of age and a picture ID from his place of employment.

   Officer Murphy should now
   (A) ask the salesperson what identification the young man presented.
   (B) release the young man and serve a summons on the salesclerk.
   (C) release the young man and continue patrolling her post.
   (D) take the young man into custody.

85. Police Officer Davis, patrolling the park by motorcycle on a bitterly cold day, hears cries from the direction of the partially frozen lake. He runs to the sound and sees that a large dog has fallen through the ice in a shallow area near the edge of the lake. A teenage girl is calling to the dog and shouting that someone should save it. Officer Davis radios for immediate assistance from a car with blankets, then wades in and rescues the dog. In the warm police car that arrives promptly, Officer Davis dries the dog and takes these notes:

Location:	south shore of Muddy Lake, Clover Park
Date:	February 4
Time:	4:10 p.m.
Incident:	rescued dog that fell through ice in shallow water
Dog's Owner:	Peggy Wilson, 15, of 1979 Sunrise Drive, Apt. 12B
Assisted By:	Officer Kalish in police car #66

When Officer Davis is warm and dry, he writes up a report of this incident. Which of the following expresses the information *most clearly, accurately, and completely?*

(A) Peggy Wilson's dog fell through the ice into Muddy Lake in Clover Park at 4:10 p.m. I rescued it and police car #66 with Officer Kalish helped me.

(B) At 4:10 p.m. on February 4, a dog owned by Peggy Wilson who is 15 years old and lives at 1979 Sunset Drive, Apt. 12 B was rescued from the icy water in the lake by Officer Kalish of police car #66.

(C) Peggy Wilson who is 15 years old was in Muddy Lake in Clover Park with her dog at 4:10 p.m. through the ice. Officer Kalish in police car #66 answered my radio call and we rescued her at 1979 Sunrise Drive, Apt. 12B on February 4.

(D) On February 4 at 4:10 p.m. at the shallow end of Muddy Lake in Clover Park, I rescued the dog of 15-year-old Peggy Wilson of Apt. 12B, 1979 Sunrise Drive. Officer Kalish of car #66 assisted with warming and transportation.

Answer Key

1. (B)	18. (C)	35. (C)	52. (D)	69. (D)
2. (D)	19. (C)	36. (B)	53. (A)	70. (B)
3. (A)	20. (D)	37. (D)	54. (B)	71. (A)
4. (D)	21. (A)	38. (B)	55. (B)	72. (B)
5. (C)	22. (A)	39. (B)	56. (D)	73. (B)
6. (B)	23. (C)	40. (D)	57. (D)	74. (C)
7. (C)	24. (C)	41. (A)	58. (C)	75. (B)
8. (C)	25. (B)	42. (C)	59. (C)	76. (A)
9. (A)	26. (B)	43. (D)	60. (A)	77. (B)
10. (B)	27. (D)	44. (C)	61. (D)	78. (C)
11. (C)	28. (D)	45. (D)	62. (B)	79. (D)
12. (D)	29. (A)	46. (C)	63. (C)	80. (A)
13. (D)	30. (A)	47. (D)	64. (C)	81. (D)
14. (B)	31. (B)	48. (B)	65. (B)	82. (D)
15. (D)	32. (C)	49. (A)	66. (C)	83. (A)
16. (C)	33. (A)	50. (A)	67. (A)	84. (C)
17. (A)	34. (B)	51. (D)	68. (A)	85. (D)

Explanatory Answers

1. **The correct answer is (B).** A sign on the wall indicates that rooms 2I-S are to the right. The stairs are to the right of the elevator.

2. **The correct answer is (D).** The man peeking from the personnel manager's office is not wearing glasses.

3. **The correct answer is (A).** The time indicated on the clock is 10:25. If there is a clock, expect a time question.

4. **The correct answer is (D).** The bald black man has a newspaper on his lap.

5. **The correct answer is (C).** There are nine people in the scene. Always count people in a memory picture.

6. **The correct answer is (B).** The kneeling terrorist has a handgun.

7. **The correct answer is (C).** The receptionist has close-cropped hair and is looking straight ahead. She is holding a pencil in her left hand, so it is reasonable to assume that she is left-handed.

8. **The correct answer is (C).** The indicator above the elevator goes from L to 5. This makes six floors in all.

9. **The correct answer is (A).** The woman terrorist has both boots on the floor. *Health* magazine is on the table in front of her.

10. **The correct answer is (B).** The young boy is sitting on one leg and is not wearing glasses. The seeing-eye dog undoubtedly came with the blind woman.

11. **The correct answer is (C).** The seated woman terrorist is wearing an army camouflage jumpsuit and has her gun pointed at the opposite bench. The dog is watching her. It is the man terrorist who is obviously carrying extra ammunition.

12. **The correct answer is (D).** The Hispanic woman sitting in front of the pile of newspapers is wearing high-heeled sandals and has her right leg crossed over her left.

13. **The correct answer is (D).** The floor lamp is next to the black man. The potted plant is next to the receptionist's desk; the umbrella is leaning on the opposite bench; there is no umbrella stand.

14. **The correct answer is (B).** There is a waste container between elevator and stairs. Neither water cooler nor coat rack is shown in this scene.

15. **The correct answer is (D).** According to the passage, Jeff Farnsworth is 29 years old with medium-length blonde hair and a tattoo of an eagle on his right shoulder.

16. **The correct answer is (C).** According to the passage, Jorge Sanchez called the police when he thought that he heard Mr. Farnsworth beating his wife.

17. **The correct answer is (A).** According to the passage, the Farnsworths' license plate is S652 Z19.

18. **The correct answer is (C).** Choices (A) and (B) neglect to mention the fire. Choice (D) leaves out the time and expresses an opinion. A report should be factual, not conjectural.

19. **The correct answer is (C).** The selection states that Officer Ellingson suspected that the car was stolen after she discovered the fictitious plates. However, she did not confirm this until she entered the VIN number; therefore, choice (C) is correct.

20. **The correct answer is (D).** The selection states that the fingerprint most likely belongs to the owner of the vehicle.

21. **The correct answer is (A).** Officer Ellingson talked to the caller, entered the license plates, entered the VIN number, and conducted a search of the car. Therefore, choice (A) is correct.

22. **The correct answer is (A).**

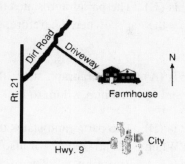

23. **The correct answer is (C).**

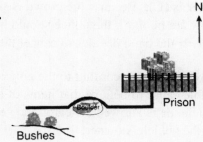

24. **The correct answer is (C).** The beginning of the selection states that the demanding nature of a line officer's job can lead officers to become unmotivated.

25. **The correct answer is (B).** The main idea of this selection is that regardless of whether or not an officer wishes to advance or simply improve his knowledge, the Officer Training Program provides officers with goals.

26. **The correct answer is (B).** The second paragraph indicates that some officers that may take advantage of the Officer Training Program may want to remain in their current positions.

27. **The correct answer is (D).** Rule 4 explains why the other choices are wrong. Choice **(D)** conforms with rule 6.

28. **The correct answer is (D).** The officers violated rule 1. The officers had no way of knowing that there was no gun and no argument. If there were, a knock at the door might easily provoke a shot at the door.

29. **The correct answer is (A).** The correct spelling of the word is "Because."

30. **The correct answer is (A).** The correct spelling of the word is "officers."

31. **The correct answer is (B).** The correct spelling of the word is "hearing."

32. **The correct answer is (C).** The paragraph states that F was clearly agitated. The code indicates that F = the car's owner. Therefore, the car's owner appeared to be agitated.

33. **The correct answer is (A).** The paragraph states that J (the police officer) called K (the backup officer) and advised him whom to look for.

34. **The correct answer is (B).** The paragraph states that J (the police officer) was called to the scene: "When SHE arrived. . ." It also states that J told K to "look for someone who fit her (G's) description. . ." Therefore, both the Police Officer and the witness are female.

35. **The correct answer is (C).** Because the crowd is starting to become agitated after the long delay (they are booing), the police should be concerned about a riot in this situation, especially if the band decides to cancel the concert at the last minute.

36. **The correct answer is (B).** According to the policies provided, because Officer Chopak has probable cause to believe that items of evidence are hidden in Mr. Coddington's vehicle, he is allowed to search the vehicle, even if he does not have the permission of the vehicle's owner.

37. **The correct answer is (D).** According to the policies provided, personnel may search a crime scene during a time period that is deemed reasonable to conduct an investigation and gather evidence.

38. **The correct answer is (B).** According to the policies provided, if the officers do not have a warrant, they may still search the premises if they receive the person's voluntary oral permission to do so. However, if a person withdraws his or her consent at any time during the search, the search must cease. The evidence found by Officer Hammond would be inadmissible because it was discovered after the search should have ended.

39. **The correct answer is (B).**

40. **The correct answer is (D).** Rule 1 governs. An officer should never assume the responsibility of deciding whether or not a prisoner requires the services of a doctor.

41. **The correct answer is (A).** Rule 2 governs. It is apparent that the prisoner requires medical attention even though there is no emergency. Medical attention is required for the prisoner's wound, not for his drug addition; therefore, an ambulance should be called.

42. **The correct answer is (C).** The correct spelling is "preliminary."

43. **The correct answer is (D).** The correct spelling is "specialized."

44. **The correct answer is (C).** According to the table, the greatest number of sexual offenses committed in a year was 562. These assaults took place in 1993.

45. **The correct answer is (D).** According to the table, the number of sexual offenses steadily decreased from 1993–2000. Therefore, the program could be considered a success.

46. **The correct answer is (C).** To determine how many sexual offenses took place in 2001, one must first determine what exactly is 10 percent of 345, the number of sexual offenses that took place in 2000. 345 times .10 = 34.5. You must then subtract this number from 345. 345 − 34.5 = 310.5.

47. **The correct answer is (D).** Who was robbed and by whom? Who was wearing what? When and where did it happen? Choice **(D)** tells it best.

48. **The correct answer is (B).** The incorrectly spelled word is "activelly" and should be spelled "actively."

49. **The correct answer is (A).** The incorrectly spelled word is "informent" and should be spelled "informant."

50. **The correct answer is (A).** According to the definition of *larceny,* one may be considered guilty of this crime if found property is not returned to its owner. Since the question makes no reference to a search for the rightful owner, one must assume intent to keep the ring.

51. **The correct answer is (D).** *Larceny* also involves obtaining property under false pretenses, the situation here.

52. **The correct answer is (D).** In compliance with Rule 1, the first thing the officer must do is ascertain that the woman is indeed dead.

53. **The correct answer is (A).** The officer is certain that the man is dead, and the body is in the apartment, not in public view. Rule 3 requires that the officer now summon a sergeant to the scene.

54. **The correct answer is (B).** The sister did not live with the dead man, so according to Rule 6, the albums may not be released to her.

55. **The correct answer is (B).** Be sure to read each sentence of the account carefully. Be sure to look for words such as "before," "after," and "then" to determine the most logical order of the sentences.

56. **The correct answer is (D).** According to the most logical order of the sentences contained in Mr. Weber's account of the incident, Mr. Weber arrived home from work just before he noticed the bike tracks on his lawn.

57. **The correct answer is (D).** Choice **(D)** contains the word "despute," which should be spelled "dispute."

58. **The correct answer is (C).** To determine how long it took for the officer to reach her destination, you must create a proportion. 42 miles/60 minutes = 4.5 miles/x minutes. 60 times 4.5 = 270. 270/42 = 6.4 minutes.

59. **The correct answer is (C).** The second sentence lists the permissible uses of annual leave allowance.

60. **The correct answer is (A).** According to the last sentence of the paragraph, he *may* be required to show a doctor's note for absences of one, two, or three days.

61. The **correct answer is (D).**

62. The **correct answer is (B).**

63. **The correct answer is (C).** The officers were assigned to close off the street to all traffic except emergency vehicles. They have used poor judgment. Their unattended parked police car cannot be easily moved to permit arriving emergency vehicles to enter the street.

64. **The correct answer is (C).** The word "was" correctly completes this sentence because it is phrased in the past tense.

65. **The correct answer is (B).** Officer Seguaro has followed the procedure properly through step 5. Since the caller is just across the hall from the location of the child abuse, there is no reason to send a second car. The caller has already said that he does not know the identity of the abuser, so there is no point to asking his relationship to the abuser. However, the caller might be related to the child being beaten. Officer Seguaro must ask.

66. **The correct answer is (C).** To determine the total fine, you must add $75 + $150 = $225. Remember that the seat belt citation was dismissed; you do not have to add this fine to the total.

67. **The correct answer is (A).** To determine Officer O'Brien's second-year salary, you must first calculate what exactly is 6 percent of 31,000. 31,000 times .06 = 1,860. Then you must add the 6 percent to the first-year salary. 31,000 + 1,860 = 32,860.

68. **The correct answer is (A).**

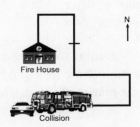

69–71. Read the combination presented in the question and in the answer choices *very* carefully. Only one answer choice has the exact combination of letters, numbers, and symbols as in the question. The differences may be very subtle, so give yourself plenty of time to answer this type of question.

72. **The correct answer is (B).** In order to find the percentage of a number, multiply the decimal form of the percentage by the number. $30 \times .12 = 3.6$.

73. **The correct answer is (B).** Officer Maxwell must travel on city streets for a total of 5 miles. The passage states that she travels at a rate of ½ mile per minute on the city streets. Thus, it should take her 10 minutes to travel 5 miles on city streets. She must also travel on the highway for 5 miles at a rate of 1 mile per minute. Thus, it should take her 5 minutes to travel 5 miles on the highway. The total travel time to the scene is $5 + 10 = 15$ minutes.

74. **The correct answer is (C).** The definitions make it quite clear that murder is planned and intentional, while felony murder refers to accidental death that occurs during commission or *attempted commission*—which is why choice **(B)** is wrong—of another crime.

75. **The correct answer is (B).** If no part of the training of a law officer is more important or more valuable (sentence 2), then clearly the most useful and essential single factor in the training of a law officer is proper firearms training. Choice **(A)** is incorrect because the first sentence says only that firearms training *cannot* be ignored, not that it *is* ignored. Choice **(D)** is an overstatement; lives often depend directly upon weapons skills but not always.

76. **The correct answer is (A).**

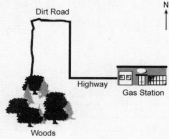

77. **The correct answer is (B).** Rule 5 is very clear. Access is permitted only to police and medical personnel.

78. **The correct answer is (C).** Choice **(A)** is incorrect because one cannot exit the park at Aspen Way; choice **(B)** is legal but is surely not the quickest, most direct route; and choice **(D)** is incorrect because Ash Street is westbound, so the officers cannot enter the grounds of Acorn Houses from Ash and Hemlock. Choice **(D)** is further impossible because Oak Street runs east, not south.

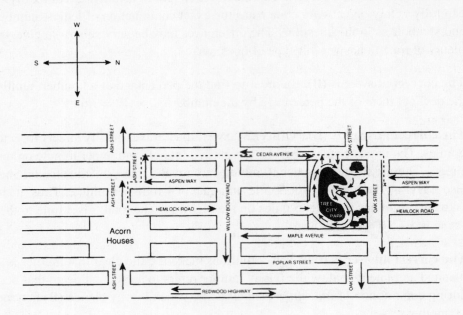

79. **The correct answer is (D).** Choice **(A)** is incorrect because a left turn onto Poplar will take them away from the scene of the burglary; choice **(B)** is incorrect because Poplar is one-way northbound and a right off Oak would send them south; and choice **(C)** is an unnecessarily long and circuitous route.

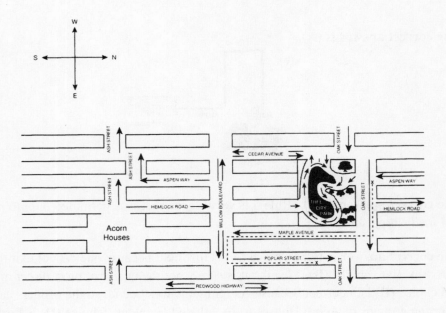

80. **The correct answer is (A).** Officer Shavez is 50 feet from his target. At a distance of 10 feet, he shoots with 100 percent accuracy. Now his accuracy will decrease by 3 percent for every additional 10-foot distance from his target. After the first 10 feet, there are four 10-foot intervals (40 feet) left. 4 × 3 percent = 12 percent. Thus, at a distance of 50 feet, Officer Shavez should shoot with 100 percent − 12 percent = 88 percent accuracy.

81. **The correct answer is (D).** The total value of the items stolen is $486 + $14(26) + $294 + $319 = $1,463.

82. **The correct answer is (D).** If 528 officers request the vests, the total cost to the department will be 528 × $895 = $472,560.

83. **The correct answer is (A).** If 92 of the reports were given by individuals who were reporting a second incident, then 582 − 92 = 490 individuals were assaulted only one time last year. This is equal to 2 percent of the population.

84. **The correct answer is (C).** The facts as presented indicate that Officer Murphy's suspicion was unfounded. The young man is of legal age, and there is no reason to question the salesperson.

85. **The correct answer is (D).** Choice (A) inadequately describes Peggy Wilson; choice (B) credits Officer Kalish with the rescue; and choice (C) places Peggy Wilson in the lake with her dog.

ANSWER SHEET: PRACTICE EXAMINATION 5

1. Ⓐ Ⓑ Ⓒ Ⓓ	26. Ⓐ Ⓑ Ⓒ Ⓓ	51. Ⓐ Ⓑ Ⓒ Ⓓ	76. Ⓐ Ⓑ Ⓒ Ⓓ
2. Ⓐ Ⓑ Ⓒ Ⓓ	27. Ⓐ Ⓑ Ⓒ Ⓓ	52. Ⓐ Ⓑ Ⓒ Ⓓ	77. Ⓐ Ⓑ Ⓒ Ⓓ
3. Ⓐ Ⓑ Ⓒ Ⓓ	28. Ⓐ Ⓑ Ⓒ Ⓓ	53. Ⓐ Ⓑ Ⓒ Ⓓ	78. Ⓐ Ⓑ Ⓒ Ⓓ
4. Ⓐ Ⓑ Ⓒ Ⓓ	29. Ⓐ Ⓑ Ⓒ Ⓓ	54. Ⓐ Ⓑ Ⓒ Ⓓ	79. Ⓐ Ⓑ Ⓒ Ⓓ
5. Ⓐ Ⓑ Ⓒ Ⓓ	30. Ⓐ Ⓑ Ⓒ Ⓓ	55. Ⓐ Ⓑ Ⓒ Ⓓ	80. Ⓐ Ⓑ Ⓒ Ⓓ
6. Ⓐ Ⓑ Ⓒ Ⓓ	31. Ⓐ Ⓑ Ⓒ Ⓓ	56. Ⓐ Ⓑ Ⓒ Ⓓ	81. Ⓐ Ⓑ Ⓒ Ⓓ
7. Ⓐ Ⓑ Ⓒ Ⓓ	32. Ⓐ Ⓑ Ⓒ Ⓓ	57. Ⓐ Ⓑ Ⓒ Ⓓ	82. Ⓐ Ⓑ Ⓒ Ⓓ
8. Ⓐ Ⓑ Ⓒ Ⓓ	33. Ⓐ Ⓑ Ⓒ Ⓓ	58. Ⓐ Ⓑ Ⓒ Ⓓ	83. Ⓐ Ⓑ Ⓒ Ⓓ
9. Ⓐ Ⓑ Ⓒ Ⓓ	34. Ⓐ Ⓑ Ⓒ Ⓓ	59. Ⓐ Ⓑ Ⓒ Ⓓ	84. Ⓐ Ⓑ Ⓒ Ⓓ
10. Ⓐ Ⓑ Ⓒ Ⓓ	35. Ⓐ Ⓑ Ⓒ Ⓓ	60. Ⓐ Ⓑ Ⓒ Ⓓ	85. Ⓐ Ⓑ Ⓒ Ⓓ
11. Ⓐ Ⓑ Ⓒ Ⓓ	36. Ⓐ Ⓑ Ⓒ Ⓓ	61. Ⓐ Ⓑ Ⓒ Ⓓ	86. Ⓐ Ⓑ Ⓒ Ⓓ
12. Ⓐ Ⓑ Ⓒ Ⓓ	37. Ⓐ Ⓑ Ⓒ Ⓓ	62. Ⓐ Ⓑ Ⓒ Ⓓ	87. Ⓐ Ⓑ Ⓒ Ⓓ
13. Ⓐ Ⓑ Ⓒ Ⓓ	38. Ⓐ Ⓑ Ⓒ Ⓓ	63. Ⓐ Ⓑ Ⓒ Ⓓ	88. Ⓐ Ⓑ Ⓒ Ⓓ
14. Ⓐ Ⓑ Ⓒ Ⓓ	39. Ⓐ Ⓑ Ⓒ Ⓓ	64. Ⓐ Ⓑ Ⓒ Ⓓ	89. Ⓐ Ⓑ Ⓒ Ⓓ
15. Ⓐ Ⓑ Ⓒ Ⓓ	40. Ⓐ Ⓑ Ⓒ Ⓓ	65. Ⓐ Ⓑ Ⓒ Ⓓ	90. Ⓐ Ⓑ Ⓒ Ⓓ
16. Ⓐ Ⓑ Ⓒ Ⓓ	41. Ⓐ Ⓑ Ⓒ Ⓓ	66. Ⓐ Ⓑ Ⓒ Ⓓ	91. Ⓐ Ⓑ Ⓒ Ⓓ
17. Ⓐ Ⓑ Ⓒ Ⓓ	42. Ⓐ Ⓑ Ⓒ Ⓓ	67. Ⓐ Ⓑ Ⓒ Ⓓ	92. Ⓐ Ⓑ Ⓒ Ⓓ
18. Ⓐ Ⓑ Ⓒ Ⓓ	43. Ⓐ Ⓑ Ⓒ Ⓓ	68. Ⓐ Ⓑ Ⓒ Ⓓ	93. Ⓐ Ⓑ Ⓒ Ⓓ
19. Ⓐ Ⓑ Ⓒ Ⓓ	44. Ⓐ Ⓑ Ⓒ Ⓓ	69. Ⓐ Ⓑ Ⓒ Ⓓ	94. Ⓐ Ⓑ Ⓒ Ⓓ
20. Ⓐ Ⓑ Ⓒ Ⓓ	45. Ⓐ Ⓑ Ⓒ Ⓓ	70. Ⓐ Ⓑ Ⓒ Ⓓ	95. Ⓐ Ⓑ Ⓒ Ⓓ
21. Ⓐ Ⓑ Ⓒ Ⓓ	46. Ⓐ Ⓑ Ⓒ Ⓓ	71. Ⓐ Ⓑ Ⓒ Ⓓ	96. Ⓐ Ⓑ Ⓒ Ⓓ
22. Ⓐ Ⓑ Ⓒ Ⓓ	47. Ⓐ Ⓑ Ⓒ Ⓓ	72. Ⓐ Ⓑ Ⓒ Ⓓ	97. Ⓐ Ⓑ Ⓒ Ⓓ
23. Ⓐ Ⓑ Ⓒ Ⓓ	48. Ⓐ Ⓑ Ⓒ Ⓓ	73. Ⓐ Ⓑ Ⓒ Ⓓ	98. Ⓐ Ⓑ Ⓒ Ⓓ
24. Ⓐ Ⓑ Ⓒ Ⓓ	49. Ⓐ Ⓑ Ⓒ Ⓓ	74. Ⓐ Ⓑ Ⓒ Ⓓ	99. Ⓐ Ⓑ Ⓒ Ⓓ
25. Ⓐ Ⓑ Ⓒ Ⓓ	50. Ⓐ Ⓑ Ⓒ Ⓓ	75. Ⓐ Ⓑ Ⓒ Ⓓ	100. Ⓐ Ⓑ Ⓒ Ⓓ

CHAPTER 13: PRACTICE EXAMINATION 5

The time allowed for the entire examination is 3 hours.

> **Directions:** Each question has four suggested answers, lettered (A), (B), (C), and (D). Decide which one is the best answer, and on the sample answer sheet, locate the question number and darken the area corresponding to your answer choice with a soft pencil.

Questions 1 through 15 are to be answered on the basis of the description of the police action that follows. You will have 10 minutes to read and study the description. Then you will have to answer the 15 questions about the incident without referring to the description of the incident.

Police Officers Smith and Jones were working a midnight-to-8 A.M. tour of duty. It was a Saturday morning in the month of July, and the weather was clear. At about 4:30 A.M., Officers Smith and Jones received a radio call reporting a burglary in progress at 777 Seventeenth Street, the address of an appliance store.

Upon their arrival at the scene, the officers could not find evidence of a break-in. However, as the officers continued their investigation, they heard noises coming from the rear of the building. As the officers raced to the rear of the building, they saw four people alighting from the roof, by way of a ladder, and climbing over a fence that leads to the rear of a warehouse. As the officers climbed over the fence, they observed two of the people running into an alleyway on the west side of the warehouse and the other two people running into a parking lot on the east side of the warehouse.

Officer Smith, using a walkie-talkie, called for assistance and proceeded to give chase after the two persons who entered the alley. The description of the two individuals was as follows: One was a male white, wearing light pants, a blue shirt, and white sneakers, with long blond hair, and carrying what appeared to be a portable TV set. The other was also a male white, wearing dungarees, a white T-shirt, and cowboy boots, with short dark hair, and carrying what appeared to be a portable cassette-stereo-radio.

Officer Jones continued to give chase to the two individuals who had entered the parking lot. The description of these two individuals was as follows: One was a male Hispanic, wearing dark pants, a yellow shirt, and dark shoes, with long dark hair, and carrying what appeared to be a video recorder. The other was a male black, wearing dungarees, a white T-shirt, and white sneakers, with a bald head, and carrying what appeared to be a baseball bat and portable TV set.

As Officer Smith emerged from the alley onto the sidewalk, he again observed the two individuals he had been chasing. They were entering a dark blue Chevrolet with New York license plates, beginning with the letters AKG. The vehicle drove west on Seventh Street. The male with the long blond hair appeared to be driving.

As Officer Jones reached the parking lot, he observed the two individuals he was pursuing speed off in a white station wagon, heading west on Seventh Street. The license plates could not be discerned. Officer Jones found a broken portable TV set in the parking lot.

Officer Smith broadcast this additional information, and both officers then quickly returned to their radio car to conduct a search of the area.

Do not refer to the description while answering questions 1 through 15.

1. Officers Smith and Jones responded to a "burglary in progress" call at approximately
   (A) midnight.
   (B) 8:00 A.M.
   (C) 4:30 P.M.
   (D) 4:30 A.M.

2. The suspects in the burglary gained entrance to the store by
   (A) breaking a front window.
   (B) breaking a rear window.
   (C) breaking in from an adjoining warehouse.
   (D) using a ladder to get to the roof.

3. The suspects, when fleeing from the burglary,
   (A) all ran into an alleyway.
   (B) all ran into a parking lot.
   (C) all ran into a warehouse.
   (D) went in different directions.

4. The male white with the long blond hair was carrying what appeared to be a
   (A) portable TV set.
   (B) portable cassette-stereo-radio.
   (C) video recorder.
   (D) portable cassette player.

5. The male Hispanic was carrying what appeared to be a
   (A) video recorder.
   (B) portable cassette-stereo-radio.
   (C) portable TV set.
   (D) portable cassette player.

6. The male white with the short hair was carrying what appeared to be a
   (A) portable TV set.
   (B) portable cassette-stereo-radio.
   (C) video recorder.
   (D) portable cassette player.

7. The suspect wearing cowboy boots was the
   (A) male white with long blond hair.
   (B) male black.
   (C) male Hispanic.
   (D) male white with short hair.

8. The suspect wearing light pants and blue shirt was the
   (A) male black.
   (B) male white with long blond hair.
   (C) male Hispanic.
   (D) male white with short hair.

9. The suspect wearing dark pants and a yellow shirt was the
   (A) male white with long blond hair.
   (B) male black.
   (C) male white with short hair.
   (D) male Hispanic.

10. When the suspects were fleeing, the two male whites entered a
    (A) blue station wagon with unknown license plates.
    (B) white station wagon with New York license plates, beginning with the letters AKG.
    (C) blue Chevrolet with New York license plates, beginning with the letters AKG.
    (D) white Chevrolet with unknown license plates.

11. From reading the description of the incident, one could assume
    (A) that Seventh Street is one-way westbound.
    (B) that Seventh Street is a two-way street.
    (C) that Seventh Street is one-way eastbound.
    (D) None of the above

12. Upon entering the parking lot, Officer Jones found a broken portable TV set that had apparently been dropped by the
    (A) male white with blond hair.
    (B) male white with dark hair.
    (C) male black.
    (D) male Hispanic.

13. The male black was
   (A) bald, wearing dark pants, a yellow shirt, and dark shoes.
   (B) bald, wearing dungarees, a white T-shirt, and white sneakers.
   (C) wearing dungarees, a white T-shirt, and cowboy boots and had dark hair.
   (D) bald, wearing light pants and a blue shirt.

14. The suspect who was carrying the baseball bat was also carrying what appeared to be a
   (A) portable TV set.
   (B) video recorder.
   (C) portable cassette-stereo-radio.
   (D) portable cassette player.

15. A description of the suspects was broadcast to other police units so that they could assist in searching the area. This was done by
   (A) both Officers Jones and Smith, as they both had walkie-talkies.
   (B) Officer Jones, as he had a walkie-talkie.
   (C) Officer Smith, as he had a walkie-talkie.
   (D) both officers upon returning to their radio car.

Items 16 through 17 are based on the following passage.

At any time during an investigation, the officer who is working on the case may recommend to the Unit Commander the suspension of any further investigative activity on the case. Recommendations for case suspension must be fully approved by the Unit Commander. If the recommendation is approved, the case must be entered into the casebook review log as a suspended case. When a case has been formerly suspended, it is not excluded from being reopened for any reason. Cases of a serious nature (e.g., rape, murder, and armed robbery) are not eligible for suspended status.

16. When a case has been formerly suspended from further investigative activity, it is NOT
   (A) allowed to be reopened.
   (B) in the casebook review log.
   (C) to be discussed by anyone.
   (D) excluded from being reopened.

17. An example of a case that may be suspended from further investigative activity is
   (A) murder.
   (B) shoplifting.
   (C) rape.
   (D) armed robbery.

Items 18 through 19 are based on the following passage.

Police Officers Wilson and Fitch were dispatched to 44 Larson Rd. at 11:32 P.M. The officers arrived on the scene at 11:35 P.M. and were greeted at the door of the residence by a distraught man in his mid-thirties. The man explained to the officers that his wife was in labor and that he was afraid that taking her to the hospital on his own would be unsafe.

The man led the officers into the bedroom, where his wife was lying on the bed. She appeared to be in good condition but was very anxious. Wilson asked the woman if she was in severe pain and checked her vital signs. The woman told her that she was in pain, but it was bearable and that her contractions were about 12 minutes apart. Wilson instructed the woman to do her best to relax because an ambulance would arrive shortly to take her to the hospital.

At 11:39 P.M., the ambulance arrived on the scene. The EMT personnel brought a stretcher into the bedroom and the two of them, along with the two Police Officers, lifted the woman onto the stretcher. As she was brought out to the ambulance, Fitch assured the woman's husband that everything seemed to be going well and that he had made the right choice by calling 911. Fitch then helped the man into the ambulance so that he could ride to the hospital with his wife. The officers left the scene at 11:47 P.M.

18. Who checked the woman's vital signs?
    (A) Officer Fitch
    (B) The EMT personnel
    (C) The woman's husband
    (D) Officer Wilson

19. How long was the call?
    (A) 5 minutes
    (B) 7 minutes
    (C) 10 minutes
    (D) 15 minutes

20. An escaped prisoner has been wounded and is lying flat on his stomach with his head turned to one side. In order to make it most difficult for the prisoner to fire quickly and accurately at the Police Officer, from which direction should the Police Officer approach?
    (A) Directly behind the prisoner's head
    (B) Facing the top of the prisoner's head
    (C) Facing the prisoner's face
    (D) Facing the prisoner's heels

21. A gas main explosion has caused some property damage. Examination by an emergency repair crew clearly indicates that no further explosions will occur. Nevertheless, rumors are circulating that more explosions and greater damage are going to occur. This situation has resulted in a high degree of fear among local residents. The best of the following actions for a Police Officer on duty at the scene to take *first* would be to
    (A) ignore the rumors since they are false and no real danger exists.
    (B) inform the people of the true circumstances of the emergency.
    (C) question several people at the scene in an attempt to determine the source of the rumors.
    (D) order everyone to leave the area quickly and in an orderly fashion.

Item 22 is based on the following passage.

At the beginning of every shift, Officer Hibbard records how many total miles are on her squad car and runs through the standard automotive checklist before going anywhere in her car. At the end of her shift, she again records how many miles are on her squad car. On one Monday morning, she was running through her standard checklist and recorded 53,283 miles as her starting mileage. This troubled her because when she looked at the mileage that she entered at the end of the day on Friday, it read 53,264 miles. Officer Hibbard did not work over the weekend, and this was the first time she had been in her squad car since Friday evening.

22. The mileage reading on Monday morning suggests
    (A) the car was not used this weekend.
    (B) the mileage counter does not work.
    (C) someone used the car this weekend.
    (D) Officer Hibbard worked this weekend.

23. While a Police Officer in plainclothes is following and watching a suspect in a homicide case, the officer becomes convinced that the suspect realizes he is being watched. The police know the suspect's identity, but the suspect is known to have changed his place of residence frequently during the past few months. The officer does not have sufficient evidence to arrest the suspect at this time. Of the following, the best action for the officer to take is to
    (A) approach the suspect, inform him that he is being followed, and demand an explanation of his suspicious past conduct.
    (B) continue to follow the suspect until an opportunity is presented for the officer to telephone for a replacement.
    (C) continue to follow the suspect since he will probably commit an illegal act eventually.
    (D) discontinue following the suspect and attempt to gain evidence by other means.

24. While issuing a summons to the manager of a movie theater for allowing a child under 16 to remain in the theater without a parent or guardian at an R-rated movie, a Police Officer requests identification from the manager. The manager hands his wallet to the officer and says that his operator's license is in the wallet. The officer should NOT accept the wallet mainly

(A) because the sorting of papers and cards contained in the wallet would be too time-consuming for the officer.

(B) to discourage the manager from any possible bribery offer.

(C) to lessen the possibility that the manager will later claim that money or papers were taken from the wallet.

(D) to minimize the temptation for the officer to look at papers or cards of a personal nature.

25. Probationary Police Officers A and B are given a special assignment by the sergeant. Officer B does not fully understand some of the instructions given by the sergeant concerning the carrying out of the assignment. Of the following, it would be best for Officer B to

(A) proceed with those parts of the assignment he understands and ask for an explanation from the sergeant when he can go no further.

(B) observe Officer A's work carefully in order to determine how the assignment is to be carried out.

(C) ask the sergeant to explain the portion of the instructions that he does not fully understand before starting the assignment.

(D) suggest to Officer A that he supervise the operation since he probably understands the sergeant's instructions better.

Items 26 through 28 are based on the following passage.

In order to keep track of who has come into contact with the evidence of a case, it may be necessary to mark the evidence. This will help to establish a chain of custody, or a record of who has handled the evidence. The investigating officer typically marks the evidence that he or she discovers by placing his or her initials or State Police identification number on each piece of evidence. An exception to this rule is when the evidence is jewelry or precious metals that have a high monetary value. These items, along with other pieces of evidence that may not be marked, are to be placed in containers and sealed. The containers can then be marked appropriately.

It is important to mark evidence immediately as the items are discovered. This will prevent any confusion about who first came into contact with the evidence. Markings should be made with a diamond- or Carborundum-point pencil and should be placed where they will least affect the item's appearance or evidentiary value. Soft pieces of evidence, such as clothing or paper, may be marked with a piece of tape that has the officer's initials or State Police identification number on it.

26. The "chain of custody" is
    (A) a record of who has handled the evidence.
    (B) a standard set of handcuffs used by officers.
    (C) a plastic "cuff" used for large-scale arrests.
    (D) a record of who owns the collected evidence.

27. If a piece of clothing is used as evidence, it should be marked with
    (A) a diamond-point pencil.
    (B) a Carborundum-point pencil.
    (C) a high monetary value.
    (D) a piece of tape.

28. Evidence should be placed in an appropriately marked container when
    (A) the item itself may not be marked.
    (B) the item is soft, such as a piece of clothing.
    (C) the item does not have a high monetary value.
    (D) the item has already been marked with tape.

29. While on patrol, you are informed by the manager of a supermarket that an object, which appears to be a homemade bomb, has been discovered in his market. Your first reaction should be to
    (A) go to the market and make sure that everyone leaves it immediately.
    (B) go to the market, examine the bomb, and then decide what action should be taken.
    (C) question the manager in detail in an effort to determine whether this really is a bomb.
    (D) telephone the bomb squad for instructions as to how the bomb should be rendered harmless.

30. A Police Officer on post would be most likely to make a regular hourly signal-box call to the precinct, rather than an immediate call, when he or she
    (A) discovers that a traffic signal light is not functioning properly.
    (B) discovers what appears to be an abandoned car on the post.
    (C) notices a street-name sign that has been damaged.
    (D) overhears a conversation between two groups of teenagers relating to a possible disturbance.

31. The most reasonable advice that a Police Officer can give to a merchant who asks what he should do if he receives a telephone call from a person he doesn't recognize regarding an alleged emergency at his store after ordinary business hours is that the merchant should go to the store and, if Police Officers are not at the scene, he should
    (A) continue past the store and call the police for assistance.
    (B) continue past the store and return and enter it if there doesn't appear to be an emergency.
    (C) enter the store and ascertain whether the alleged emergency exists.
    (D) enter the store only if there is no one apparently loitering in the vicinity.

32. A citizen asks a Police Officer for directions to a candy store that the officer knows is under observation for suspected bookmaking activity. In such a situation, the Police Officer should
(A) give the proper directions to the citizen.
(B) give the proper directions to the citizen but explain that the store is under observation.
(C) pretend not to know the location of the store.
(D) tell the citizen that he may be arrested if the store is raided.

33. Whenever a crime has been committed, the criminal has disturbed the surroundings in one way or another by his or her presence. The *least* valid deduction for the police to make from this statement is that
(A) clues are thus present at all crime scenes.
(B) even the slightest search at crime scenes will turn up conclusive evidence.
(C) the greater the number of criminals involved in a crime, the greater the number of clues likely to be available.
(D) a completely clueless crime is rarely encountered in police work.

For the following items, please identify the option that best completes the sentence.

34. The caller was very nervous because the person in her back yard had _____ from sight.
(A) disappeared
(B) dissappeared
(C) disapeared
(D) dissapeared

35. There are several effective _____ for using physical force to apprehend a resisting suspect.
(A) teckniques
(B) techniqes
(C) techniques
(D) techneques

Answer questions 36 through 45 on the basis of the following legal definitions.

Burglary is committed when a person enters a building to commit a crime therein.

Larceny is committed when a person wrongfully takes, obtains, or withholds the property of another.

Robbery is the forcible stealing of property. If a person, while committing a larceny, uses or threatens the *immediate* use of force, the crime changes from larceny to robbery.

Sexual Abuse is committed when a person subjects another person to sexual contact without the second person's consent or when a person has sexual contact with another person less than 17 years of age. (A person less than 17 years of age cannot legally consent to any sexual conduct.) "Sexual contact" may be defined as touching the sexual or other intimate parts of a person to achieve sexual gratification.

Sexual Misconduct is committed when a male has sexual intercourse with a consenting female who is at least 13 years of age but less than 17 years of age.

Harassment is committed when a person intends to harass, annoy, or alarm another person and does so by striking, shoving, kicking, or otherwise subjecting the other person to physical contact.

Assault is committed when a person unlawfully causes a physical injury to another person.

36. James Kelly enters the home of Mary Smith with the intention of taking Mary's portable TV set. While Kelly is in the apartment, Mary wakes up and attempts to retrieve her TV set from Kelly. Kelly punches Mary in the face and flees with the TV set. Kelly can be charged with
    (A) burglary and larceny.
    (B) burglary only.
    (C) robbery and larceny.
    (D) burglary and robbery.

37. John Page enters a department store with the intention of doing some shopping. Page has a .38 caliber revolver in his coat pocket and also has a criminal conviction for armed robbery. As he passes the jewelry counter, he notices an expensive watch lying on the showcase. He checks to see if anyone is watching him, and, when he feels that he is not being observed, he slips the watch into his pocket and leaves the store. Page could be charged with
    (A) larceny.
    (B) burglary and larceny.
    (C) burglary and robbery.
    (D) robbery.

38. Tom Murphy enters a crowded subway car. He positions himself behind a woman and starts to touch her buttocks with his hand. The woman becomes very annoyed and starts to move away. As she does so, Murphy reaches into her pocketbook and removes $10. He then exits the train at the next station. Murphy could be charged with
    (A) robbery, larceny, and sexual misconduct.
    (B) burglary, robbery, and sexual abuse.
    (C) burglary, larceny, and sexual misconduct.
    (D) larceny and sexual abuse.

39. Ed Saunders entered the apartment of Jane Robers with the intent to sexually abuse her. However, Robers was not at home, and Saunders left the apartment. Saunders could be charged with
(A) sexual abuse.
(B) sexual misconduct.
(C) burglary.
(D) none of the above, as a crime did not take place because Robers was not at home.

40. Frank Taylor entered the apartment of his 16-year-old girlfriend, Doris, to have sexual intercourse with her. Doris consented to this sexual conduct, and they engaged in intercourse. Taylor could be charged with
(A) burglary.
(B) sexual misconduct.
(C) both burglary and sexual misconduct.
(D) no crime, as Doris consented to the activity.

41. Brian Jones asks his 17-year-old girlfriend, Mary, if she would like to go to a motel and have sexual intercourse. She agrees, and they go to the motel. Jones could be charged with
(A) burglary.
(B) sexual misconduct.
(C) both burglary and sexual misconduct.
(D) no crime, as she consented to the activity.

42. Bill is at a party at Joan's house. An argument ensues among several of the guests. Bill overhears Helen make a derogatory comment about him. He walks up to Helen and demands she "apologize or else." Helen refuses to apologize; Bill slaps her in the face and then rushes from the apartment. Bill could be charged with
(A) assault.
(B) burglary and assault.
(C) harassment.
(D) burglary and harassment.

43. Joe is on his way to work. He is in a very bad mood. As he enters the warehouse where he works, he slips and falls to the floor. This only escalates his foul mood. As he is getting up, he sees a fellow worker who had made some unkind remarks to him two days before. Joe picks up a piece of board that is lying on the floor, walks up to the other worker, and hits him across the arm. This causes the other worker to suffer a broken arm. Joe could be charged with
(A) assault.
(B) burglary and assault.
(C) harassment.
(D) none of the above, as Joe was emotionally upset.

44. Jim enters a school through a rear window at 2:00 A.M. He wants to take a movie projector that he knows is kept in a specific room. He enters the room, takes the projector, and starts to leave when he is confronted by a security guard. The guard attempts to grab Jim; however, Jim slips away. As the guard again attempts to apprehend him, Jim swings the projector, striking the guard in the face. The guard falls to the floor unconscious and suffers a broken nose. Jim could be charged with
(A) burglary, larceny, and robbery.
(B) robbery, larceny, and assault.
(C) burglary, larceny, and assault.
(D) burglary, robbery, and assault.

45. Sue invites Tom to her apartment for dinner. After dinner, Tom decides that he would like to have a sexual encounter with Sue. She attempts to discourage his advances. Tom then proceeds to hold her down on the couch and to fondle her breasts and touch her private parts. When Sue starts to scream, Tom rushes from the apartment. Tom could be charged with
(A) burglary and sexual abuse.
(B) burglary and sexual misconduct.
(C) sexual abuse.
(D) no crime, as Sue invited him to her apartment.

For the following items, please identify the misspelled word or the incorrectly used word.

46. This manual will describe the gidelines for scheduled escort services.
(A) manual
(B) describe
(C) gidelines
(D) scheduled

47. The Public Relations Unit focuses mainly on the delivery of crime prevention programs thrughout the community.
(A) Relations
(B) prevention
(C) thrughout
(D) community

For the following two items, choose the sentence that contains the misspelled word or words.

48. **(A)** She was checking for speeding violations on the hiway.
(B) Mr. Little's business was robbed last Thursday.
(C) The center of the city seems to experience the most burglaries.
(D) She decided to pursue the suspect on foot.

49. **(A)** All injuries should be immediately reported to the proper supervisor.
     (B) She was concerned that her boyfriend would return to the apartment.
     (C) His insureance will most likely cover the damage from the accident.
     (D) She will begin by interviewing all of the witnesses in the area.

50. "Undoubtedly, the police have an important contribution to make to the welfare of youth." Of the following, the principal reason for this is that
     (A) effectiveness is a result of experience, and the police have had the longest experience in youth work.
     (B) no other agency can make use of the criminal aspects of the law as effectively as the police.
     (C) the police are in a strategic position to observe children actually or potentially delinquent and the conditions contributing thereto.
     (D) welfare agencies lack an understanding of the problems of youth.

51. An apparently senile man informs a Police Officer that he is returning from a visit to his daughter and that he is unable to find his way back home because he has forgotten his address. Of the following courses of action, the *first* one that should be taken by the officer is to
     (A) question the man in an effort to establish his identity.
     (B) request the police missing persons section to describe to you any person recently reported as missing.
     (C) suggest that the man return to his daughter for travel directions to his home.
     (D) telephone a description of the man to the precinct station house.

52. Of the following facts about a criminal, the one that would be of most value in apprehending and identifying the criminal would be that he
     (A) drives a black 1980 Chevrolet sedan with chrome license-plate holders.
     (B) invariably uses a .38 caliber Colt blue steel revolver with walnut stock and regulation front sight.
     (C) talks with a French accent and has a severe stutter.
     (D) usually wears three-button single-breasted "Ivy League" suits with white oxford cloth button-down-collar shirts.

For the following item, choose the word or phrase that correctly completes the sentence.

53. _____ they had left the scene of the argument, the two men began to fight again.
     (A) After
     (B) While
     (C) Until
     (D) Whether

54. If there should be one K-9 unit for every 60 police officers and there are 22,980 police officers in State Y, how many K-9 units should be in State Y?
    (A) 298
    (B) 327
    (C) 367
    (D) 383

55. Eight items that totaled $2,854 were stolen from a store. What was the average price of each item?
    (A) $356.75
    (B) $364.50
    (C) $380.65
    (D) $387.50

56. If the gas tank of a squad car holds 11.5 gallons of gasoline, and regular-grade gasoline costs $1.22 per gallon, how much will it cost to fill the tank if it is completely empty?
    (A) $13.29
    (B) $13.98
    (C) $14.03
    (D) $14.73

Use the following chart to answer questions 57 through 59.

NUMBER OF DWI ARRESTS				
COUNTY	1982	1987	1994	2002
Dakota	461	470	325	348
Aldridge	529	506	467	420
Lexington	241	284	115	164
Garrison	441	457	461	408

57. What was the average number of DWI arrests in Dakota County during these four years?
    (A) 386
    (B) 395
    (C) 401
    (D) 409

58. What was the average number of DWI arrests in these four counties during 2002?
    (A) 300
    (B) 325
    (C) 335
    (D) 350

59. The average number of DWI arrests in all four counties decreased from 1982 to 2002 by

(A) 80

(B) 83

(C) 88

(D) 91

60. Officers assigned to regular posts for an extended period of time should try to establish friendly relations with the people in the area. For officers to follow this procedure is generally

(A) advisable, mainly because the officers will be more likely to get the cooperation of the residents when needed.

(B) inadvisable, mainly because it will take the officers' attention away from their regular duties.

(C) advisable, mainly because it will help officers to impress their superior officers.

(D) inadvisable, mainly because the people may be encouraged to take advantage of this friendliness to commit minor violations.

Use the following samples as a guide for questions 61 through 66.

Assume that a Police Officer at a certain location is equipped with a two-way radio to keep him in constant touch with his security headquarters. Radio messages and replies are given in code form, as follows:

Radio Code for Situation	J P M F B
Radio Code for Action to be Taken	o r a z q
Radio Response for Action Taken	1 2 3 4 5

Assume that each of the above capital letters is the radio code for a particular type of situation, that the small letter below each capital letter is the radio code for the action a Police Officer is directed to take, and that the number directly below each small letter is the radio response the Police Officer should make to indicate what action was actually taken.

In questions 61 through 66 below, the code letter for the action directed (Column 2) and the code number for the action taken (Column 3) should correspond to the capital letters in Column 1.

- If only Column 2 is different from Column 1, mark choice **(A)**.
- If only Column 3 is different from Column 1, mark choice **(B)**.
- If both Column 2 and Column 3 are different from Column 1, mark choice **(C)**.
- If both Columns 2 and 3 are the same as Column 1, mark choice **(D)**.

SAMPLE QUESTION

Column 1	Column 2	Column 3
JPFMB	orzaq	12453

The code letters in Column 2 are correct, but the numbers "53" in Column 3 should be "35." Therefore, the correct answer is **(B)**.

	Column 1	Column 2	Column 3
61.	**PBFJM**	rqzoa	25413
62.	**MPFBJ**	zrqoa	32541
63.	**JBFPM**	oqzra	15432
64.	**BJPMF**	qaroz	51234
65.	**PJFMB**	rozaq	21435
66.	**FJBMP**	zoqra	41532

Answer questions 67 through 76 solely on the basis of the following narrative and Assistance Report. The report contains twenty numbered boxes. First read the narrative and the information given concerning the form, and then study the form thoroughly before answering the questions.

It was 9:30 A.M., Sunday, June 14, 1989. Officers Whelan and Murphy of the 2nd Precinct, riding in patrol car 1294, received a radio call of an injury at the northwest corner of Seventh Avenue and 83rd Street. The location of the injury was within the confines of the 3rd Precinct; however, the 3rd Precinct did not have any cars available to respond.

Upon arriving at the scene, Officers Whelan and Murphy found a male white, approximately 28 years of age, lying on the sidewalk. The man was bleeding moderately from a cut on the forehead. When questioned by the officers, the man identified himself as John Mandello, and he stated that someone ran up behind him and pushed him to the ground, causing him to strike his head on the sidewalk. The person who pushed him to the ground also took a wallet containing $100 from his rear left pocket. Officer Whelan informed Mr. Mandello that an ambulance was on the way. Mr. Mandello stated that he would take care of the injury himself and did not want any medical assistance.

Officer Whelan cancelled the ambulance and proceeded to take the information to be included in the report. As he was doing so, Officer Whelan noticed that the corner street light was not working.

Just as Officer Whelan was finishing getting the information, he and Officer Murphy heard what sounded like brakes screeching and cars colliding. The two officers ran around the corner and saw a car on the southeast corner sidewalk of 82nd Street and Seventh Avenue. They also observed a van, lying on its side, in the intersection of 82nd Street and Seventh Avenue. Officer Murphy ran back to his patrol car and put in a call for an additional 2nd Precinct patrol car to handle traffic conditions. The accident had occurred within the confines of the 2nd Precinct.

Officer Whelan checked the car that was on the sidewalk. The car, after colliding with the van, apparently drove onto the sidewalk and went through the front window of a men's clothing store, setting off the burglar alarm. The driver was lying on the front seat with moderate bleeding from a cut on his head and had what appeared to be a broken arm. The driver of the car was identified as Joe Serrano, a male white, 29 years of age, residing at 384 Lincoln Place, Apt. 4E, Brooklyn, NY.

Officer Murphy went to the van and, with the help of several passersby, pulled the driver out. The driver was unconscious. A search of the unconscious van driver's wallet identified him as Juan Rodriguez, a male Hispanic, 24 years of age, residing at 98 Fourth Avenue, Apt. 1, Newark, NJ.

An ambulance from Washington Hospital arrived at the scene. The ambulance attendant, John Francis, administered first aid to both drivers, who were then transported to Washington Hospital.

Further investigation produced two witnesses to the accident. The first witness was Mary Randolph of 876 First Avenue, Apt. 2S, NYC; the second was Helen Sweeney of 684 Broadway, Apt. A, NYC. The witnesses stated to Police Officer Whelan that the traffic light at the intersection of 82nd Street and Seventh Avenue was not working.

Mr. Thomas Serrano of 384 Lincoln Place, Apt. 4E, phone 287-8777, was notified that his brother, Joe, was admitted to Washington Hospital. The admission number for Joe Serrano was 18764.

No friends or relatives of Juan Rodriguez could be notified that he was admitted to Washington Hospital. His admission number was 18763.

ASSISTANCE REPORT

1. Date	2. Last name First name M.I.	3. Age	4. Sex	5. Color

6. Time

7. Residence (including county, apt. # & Zip Code)

8. Location of occurrence (including county, apt. # & Zip code)

9. Illness or injury	10. Precinct and report number

11. Check:
- ☐ sick
- ☐ injured
- ☐ mentally ill
- ☐ dead

12. Taken to: Name of
- ☐ hospital   (   )
- ☐ morgue   (   )

13. Admission number	14. Name of Doctor or ambulance attendant

15. Person notified	Relationship

16. Witnesses

17. Remarks

18. Additional required reports (Check appropriate boxes, if any)
- ☐ Crime report
- ☐ Vehicle accident report
- ☐ Morgue report
- ☐ Street injury report

19. Other agency notifications

20. Reporting Officer

Rank	Name	Number	Precinct

A Police Officer is required to prepare an Assistance Report whenever an occurrence that requires that a person receive medical aid or assistance comes to the officer's attention. However, if a person is sick at his or her own residence, an Assistance Report is not required. The officer then need only make a log book entry.

Box #1 is to indicate the date that the report is being prepared. If the occurrence happened on a date that is different from the date of the report, the date of occurrence will be listed under Remarks, box #17. The reason for the delay in reporting the incident is to be noted under Remarks, box #17.

Box #8 is for the specific location of the occurrence (e.g., 374 First Street, Apt. ID; Front of 374 First Street on sidewalk; northwest corner of 86th Street and First Avenue).

Box #9 is to indicate, to the best of your knowledge, the illness or injury sustained (e.g., cut on forehead, dizziness). The official doctor's or hospital's diagnosis, if available, is to be listed under Remarks, box #17.

Box #10 is to list the precinct of the site of the incident and the precinct report number. Check the appropriate circumstance in box #11.

Check the appropriate disposition in box #12. If a person is treated at his or her home and is not removed to another location, no report is required. If a person is removed to a hospital or morgue, check the appropriate box and list the name of the hospital or morgue. If a person refuses medical assistance, write "refused assistance" in box #12. If a person is treated at another location other than his or her home and is not removed to a hospital or morgue, state such facts under Remarks, box #17.

The hospital admission number is to be listed in box #13 only if a relative or a friend cannot be notified that the person is being admitted to the hospital.

Box #14 is to indicate the name of the doctor or ambulance attendant who treated the individual.

Box #15 is to list the name and address of the friend or relative who was notified of the person's admission to the hospital. The relationship of the person notified to the person admitted will also be listed (e.g., friend, wife, brother).

Box #16 is to indicate the names and addresses of any witnesses.

Box #17 is to contain a short description of the incident.

In box #18, check the appropriate box for any additional forms that may be needed. Check *crime report* if medical assistance was made necessary as the result of a criminal act. Check *vehicle accident report* if the incident involved a motor vehicle accident. Check *morgue report* if the individual involved dies. Check *street injury report* if the person was injured as a result of a defect in a street or sidewalk.

Box #19 is to list the names of any other city agencies that may have to be notified (e.g., damaged or broken traffic or street lights—Traffic Department; potholes in the street or broken sidewalks—Department of Highways; broken or damaged fire hydrants or water mains—Department of Water Supply).

Box #20 is for the rank, name, and command of the Police Officer making the report.

All other boxes not specifically mentioned are self-explanatory.

Questions 67 through 70 are to be answered solely on the basis of the information relating to the case of John Mandello.

67. An assistance report
   (A) would not be required because Mr. Mandello refused medical assistance.
   (B) would not be required; only a Police Officer's log entry would be necessary.
   (C) would be required, and the precinct that would be listed in box #10 would be the 2nd Precinct.
   (D) would be required, and the precinct number that would be listed in box #20 would be the 2nd Precinct.

68. In box #9, the officer would
   (A) enter the official hospital diagnosis when it became available.
   (B) enter the description of the illness or injury in his own words.
   (C) make a reference to see box #17, Remarks, for the official diagnosis.
   (D) enter "refused medical assistance."

69. In box #18, the officer would check the box(es) for
   (A) street injury report, because Mr. Mandello was injured when his head struck the sidewalk.
   (B) street injury report, because the injury was incurred when Mr. Mandello's head struck the sidewalk, and crime report, because he was apparently the victim of a robbery.
   (C) crime report only.
   (D) No additional report would be required because Mr. Mandello refused medical assistance.

70. In box #19, the officer would
   (A) enter Traffic Department.
   (B) enter Department of Highways.
   (C) enter both Traffic Department and Department of Highways.
   (D) make no entry, as no additional agency would have to be notified.

Answer questions 71 through 76 based on the information given regarding Joe Serrano and Juan Rodriguez.

71. Box #13 would be
   (A) filled in only in the case of Mr. Serrano.
   (B) filled in only in the case of Mr. Rodriguez.
   (C) filled in for the cases of both Mr. Serrano and Mr. Rodriguez.
   (D) left blank in both cases.

72. The official hospital diagnoses of Mr. Serrano's injuries were a laceration of the forehead and a fracture of the right arm. This information would
    (A) be listed in box #17, Remarks.
    (B) be listed in box #9, Illness or injury.
    (C) be listed in box #14 next to the doctor's name.
    (D) not be listed in the report.

73. In regard to the proper preparation of the Assistance Report, select the correct answer from the choices given below.
    (A) In box #10, the number of the precinct that would be entered would be the 2nd Precinct.
    (B) In box #20, the number of the precinct that would be entered would be the 3rd Precinct.
    (C) In box #10, the number of the precinct that would be entered would be the 3rd Precinct.
    (D) The admission number for Mr. Serrano, 18763, would be entered in box #13.

74. In box #18, the additional report(s) that would be required is (are)
    (A) a crime report.
    (B) a street injury report.
    (C) a vehicle accident report.
    (D) a vehicle accident report and a crime report.

75. Based on the information given by the witnesses, box #19 would contain the name(s) of which other agency or agencies?
    (A) Traffic Department
    (B) Traffic Department and Highway Department
    (C) Highway Department
    (D) Building Department

76. In preparing the Assistance Report,
    (A) the caption "sick" would be checked in box #11.
    (B) the relationship of the person notified in the case of Mr. Serrano would be "father" and would be entered in box #15.
    (C) the location of the occurrence would be the intersection of 83rd Street and Seventh Avenue and would be entered in box #8.
    (D) the name John Francis would be entered in box #14.

Answer questions 77 through 80 on the basis of the information given in the following passage.

The public often believes that the main job of a uniformed officer is to enforce laws simply by arresting people. In reality, however, many of the situations that an officer deals with do not call for the use of the power of arrest. In the first place, an officer spends much of his or her time *preventing* crimes from happening, by spotting potential violations or suspicious behavior and taking action to prevent illegal acts. In the second place, many of the situations in which officers are called on for assistance involve elements like personal arguments, husband-wife quarrels, noisy juveniles, or emotionally disturbed persons. The majority of these problems do not result in arrests and convictions, and often they do not even involve illegal behavior. In the third place, even in situations where there seems to be good reason to make an arrest, an officer may have to exercise very good judgment. There are times when making an arrest too soon could touch off a riot, result in the detention of a minor offender while major offenders escaped, or cut short the gathering of necessary on-the-scene evidence.

77. The passage implies that most citizens
   (A) will start to riot if they see an arrest being made.
   (B) appreciate the work that law enforcement officers do.
   (C) do not realize that making arrests is only a small part of law enforcement.
   (D) never call for assistance unless they are involved in a personal argument or a husband-wife quarrel.

78. According to the passage, one way in which law enforcement officers can prevent crimes from happening is by
   (A) arresting suspicious characters.
   (B) letting minor offenders go free.
   (C) taking action on potential violations.
   (D) refusing to get involved in husband-wife quarrels.

79. According to the passage, which of the following statements is NOT true of situations involving emotionally disturbed persons?
   (A) It is a waste of time to call on law enforcement officers for assistance in such situations.
   (B) Such situations may not involve illegal behavior.
   (C) Such situations often do not result in arrests.
   (D) Citizens often turn to law enforcement officers for help in such situations.

80. The last sentence in the passage mentions "detention of a minor offender." Of the following, which best explains the meaning of the word "detention" as used here?
   (A) Sentencing someone
   (B) Indicting someone
   (C) Calling someone before a grand jury
   (D) Arresting someone

Answer questions 81 through 84 on the basis of the information given in the following passage.

Automobile tire tracks found at the scene of a crime constitute an important link in the chain of physical evidence. In many cases, these are the only clues available. In some areas, unpaved ground adjoins the highway or paved streets. A suspect will often park his or her car off the paved portion of the street when committing a crime, sometimes leaving excellent tire tracks. Comparison of the tire track impressions with the tires is possible only when the vehicle has been found. However, the initial problem facing the police is the task of determining what kind of car probably made the impressions found at the scene of the crime. If the make, model, and year of the car that made the impressions can be determined, it is obvious that the task of elimination is greatly lessened.

81. The one of the following that is the most appropriate title for this passage is
    (A) "The Use of Automobiles in the Commission of Crimes."
    (B) "The Use of Tire Tracks in Police Work."
    (C) "The Capture of Criminals by Scientific Police Work."
    (D) "The Positive Identification of Criminals through Their Cars."

82. When searching for clear signs left by the car used in the commission of a crime, the most likely place for the police to look would be on the
    (A) highway adjoining unpaved streets.
    (B) highway adjacent to paved streets.
    (C) paved streets adjacent to a highway.
    (D) unpaved ground adjacent to a highway.

83. Automobile tire tracks found at the scene of a crime are of value as evidence in that they are
    (A) generally sufficient to trap and convict a suspect.
    (B) the most important link in the chain of physical evidence.
    (C) often the only evidence at hand.
    (D) circumstantial rather than direct.

84. The primary reason that the police try to determine the make, model, and year of the car involved in the commission of a crime is to
    (A) compare the tire tracks left at the scene of the crime with the type of tires used on cars of that make.
    (B) determine if the mud on the tires of the suspected car matches the mud in the unpaved road near the scene of the crime.
    (C) reduce, to a large extent, the amount of work involved in determining the particular car used in the commission of a crime.
    (D) alert the police forces to question the occupants of all automobiles of this type.

Answer Key

1. **(D)**	22. **(C)**	43. **(A)**	64. **(A)**
2. **(D)**	23. **(B)**	44. **(D)**	65. **(D)**
3. **(D)**	24. **(C)**	45. **(C)**	66. **(A)**
4. **(A)**	25. **(C)**	46. **(C)**	67. **(D)**
5. **(A)**	26. **(A)**	47. **(C)**	68. **(B)**
6. **(B)**	27. **(D)**	48. **(A)**	69. **(C)**
7. **(D)**	28. **(A)**	49. **(C)**	70. **(A)**
8. **(B)**	29. **(A)**	50. **(C)**	71. **(B)**
9. **(D)**	30. **(C)**	51. **(A)**	72. **(A)**
10. **(C)**	31. **(A)**	52. **(C)**	73. **(A)**
11. **(D)**	32. **(A)**	53. **(A)**	74. **(C)**
12. **(C)**	33. **(B)**	54. **(D)**	75. **(A)**
13. **(B)**	34. **(A)**	55. **(A)**	76. **(D)**
14. **(A)**	35. **(C)**	56. **(C)**	77. **(C)**
15. **(C)**	36. **(D)**	57. **(C)**	78. **(C)**
16. **(D)**	37. **(A)**	58. **(C)**	79. **(A)**
17. **(B)**	38. **(D)**	59. **(B)**	80. **(D)**
18. **(D)**	39. **(C)**	60. **(A)**	81. **(B)**
19. **(D)**	40. **(C)**	61. **(D)**	82. **(D)**
20. **(A)**	41. **(D)**	62. **(C)**	83. **(C)**
21. **(B)**	42. **(C)**	63. **(B)**	84. **(C)**

Explanatory Answers

1. **The correct answer is (D).** Refer to the third sentence of the description.

2. **The correct answer is (D).** The officers observed the suspects alighting from the roof by way of a ladder.

3. **The correct answer is (D).** The two male whites ran into an alleyway, and the male black and male Hispanic ran into a parking lot.

4. **The correct answer is (A).** This information is included in the description of the male white with long blond hair.

5. **The correct answer is (A).** This information is included in the description of the male Hispanic.

6. **The correct answer is (B).** This information is included in the description of the male white with short hair.

7. **The correct answer is (D).** This information is included in the description of the male white with short hair.

8. **The correct answer is (B).** This information is included in the description of the male white with long blond hair.

9. **The correct answer is (D).** This information is included in the description of the male Hispanic.

10. **The correct answer is (C).** This is the description of the vehicle in which the two male whites fled.

11. **The correct answer is (D).** The description states only that the escape vehicles fled west on Seventh Street. There is no information as to what type of street Seventh Street is.

12. **The correct answer is (C).** Both the male black and male Hispanic entered the parking lot. However, it was the male black who was carrying what appeared to be a portable TV set.

13. **The correct answer is (B).** This information is included in the description of the male black.

14. **The correct answer is (A).** This information is included in the description of the male black.

15. **The correct answer is (C).** The description refers only to Officer Smith using a walkie-talkie and broadcasting information.

16. **The correct answer is (D).** The passage states that when a case has been formerly suspended, it is not excluded from being reopened for any reason.

17. **The correct answer is (B).** The passage states that serious cases, such as those involving murder, rape, or armed robbery, may not be suspended. Only cases that are less serious in nature, such as one involving shoplifting, may be suspended.

18. **The correct answer is (D).** The selection states that Officer Wilson checked the woman's vital signs.

19. **The correct answer is (D).** The call was received at 11:32 P.M. and ended at 11:47 P.M. Therefore, the call lasted 15 minutes.

20. **The correct answer is (A).** The prisoner would have to either roll over or turn his head completely around to see the officer in order to shoot accurately. The time required for this type of movement would allow the officer to take cover or to fire the first shot.

21. **The correct answer is (B).** Ignoring the rumors or not supplying the true circumstances of the emergency as soon as they are available only increases the fear people may have and may result in a possible panic situation.

22. **The correct answer is (C).** The mileage that Officer Hibbard recorded on Monday morning was greater than the mileage she recorded on Friday evening. Since Officer Hibbard did not work this weekend, someone must have used the car this weekend.

23. **The correct answer is (B).** If the plainclothes officer were to stop following the suspect now, the latter would be difficult to locate again since he is known to have changed residences frequently.

24. **The correct answer is (C).** The Police Officer should always request that only the needed identification papers be produced. If the Police Officer accepts the wallet and goes through it for identification papers, there is a possibility that a complaint could be made that money and other personal items were missing when the wallet was returned.

25. **The correct answer is (C).** If a Police Officer doesn't fully understand the instructions given by a supervisor, the officer should immediately ask for clarification from the person giving the instructions so that he or she can carry out the assignment properly.

26. **The correct answer is (A).** The first paragraph states that the "chain of custody" is a record of who has handled the evidence.

27. **The correct answer is (D).** The last sentence of the selection states that soft pieces of evidence, such as clothing, should be marked with a piece of tape.

28. **The correct answer is (A).** The first paragraph states that items should be placed in a marked container when the item itself may not be marked.

29. **The correct answer is (A).** If there is the slightest chance that the object could be a bomb, all persons should be removed from the location for safety reasons.

30. **The correct answer is (C).** All of the other choices require immediate police action; a damaged street-name sign does not.

31. **The correct answer is (A).** The call could be a setup for robbing both the owner and his store. If there were a real emergency, the police would most likely be on the scene.

32. **The correct answer is (A).** The citizen may have a legitimate reason for going to the store. Information regarding a criminal investigation should not be divulged to the public.

33. **The correct answer is (B).** In most cases, it takes a thorough search of the crime scene to uncover the clues left by the criminal. Most clues in and of themselves are not conclusive. However, when used collectively, they form the foundation for proving the guilt or innocence of the suspect.

34. **The correct answer is (A).** The correct spelling is "disappeared."

35. **The correct answer is (C).** The correct spelling is "techniques."

36. **The correct answer is (D).** The situation fits both the definition of burglary (to enter a building to commit a crime) and of robbery (stealing by force—in this case, the punch in the face).

37. **The correct answer is (A).** John Page can be charged with larceny only since there was no intent to commit a crime when he entered the store and there was no force used.

38. **The correct answer is (D).** The charges are sexual abuse (touching of the buttocks) and larceny (taking $10 from the pocketbook). No force was used to remove the money, thus eliminating the charge of robbery.

39. **The correct answer is (C).** To charge a person with burglary, it must only be shown that the building was entered with the intention of committing a crime therein. (In this case, the crime was sexual abuse.) Despite the fact that Saunders was not successful in committing the crime he intended, the intention was there.

40. **The correct answer is (C).** Taylor's intention for entering the apartment was to have sexual intercourse with his 16-year-old girlfriend, a crime because she is less than 17 years of age. He could be charged with burglary (intent to commit a crime) and sexual misconduct (sexual intercourse with a female less than 17 years of age).

41. **The correct answer is (D).** Mary is 17 years old and gave her consent.

42. **The correct answer is (C).** There was neither any intention to commit a crime when Bill entered the building nor was there any injury incurred. For the charge to be assault, there must be some kind of injury.

43. **The correct answer is (A).** Joe had no intent to commit a crime before he entered the warehouse. He caused an injury to a fellow worker, a broken arm, by his actions; therefore, the charge of assault could be made. Emotional disturbance is not a valid excuse for such actions.

44. **The correct answer is (D).** The charges are burglary (entering the school with the intention of taking a movie projector), robbery (using force on the security guard to take the projector), and assault (causing an injury, the broken nose, to the security guard).

45. **The correct answer is (C).** Because Tom used force to touch Sue's private parts, he could be charged with sexual abuse. Since there was no intention to commit the crime prior to his entering her apartment, the possibility of a burglary charge is eliminated.

46. **The correct answer is (C).** The misspelled word is "gidelines" and should be spelled "guidelines."

47. **The correct answer is (C).** The incorrectly spelled word is "thrughout" and should be spelled "throughout."

48. **The correct answer is (A).** Choice (A) contains the word "hiway," which should be spelled "highway."

49. **The correct answer is (C).** Choice (C) contains the word "insureance," which should be spelled "insurance."

50. **The correct answer is (C).** When the police observe potential delinquent-producing conditions, they can take immediate action to correct them.

51. **The correct answer is (A).** By questioning the man first, the officer may be able to ascertain who he is and where he lives and thereby return him to his home without any further delay.

52. **The correct answer is (C).** The suspect's accent and stuttering are more or less permanent conditions. The other habits mentioned could be readily changed as needed.

53. **The correct answer is (A).** The word "After" correctly completes this sentence because the two men began to fight at some time after they had left the scene of the argument.

54. **The correct answer is (D).** If there must be one K-9 unit for every 60 police officers, find 22,980/60 = 383.

55. **The correct answer is (A).** In order to find the average price of each item, divide the total value of the items by the number of items: $2,854/8 = $356.75.

56. **The correct answer is (C).** Each gallon of gasoline costs $1.22. Since the car holds 11.5 gallons, 11.5 × $1.22 = $14.03.

57. **The correct answer is (C).** The average number of DWI arrests in Dakota County during these four years is equal to 461 + 470 + 325 + 348 = 1604. 1604/4 = 401.

58. **The correct answer is (C).** The average number of DWI arrests in these four counties during 1998 is equal to 348 + 420 + 164 + 408 = 1340. 1340/4 = 335.

59. **The correct answer is (B).** The average number of DWI arrests in all four counties decreased from 1978 to 1998 by 418 − 335 = 83.

60. **The correct answer is (A).** Once the people in the neighborhood get to know the Police Officer who is regularly assigned, they are more likely to cooperate. People don't generally cooperate with strangers, even if the stranger is a Police Officer.

61. **The correct answer is (D).** All the letters in Column 2 and all the numbers in Column 3 are in sequence with the capital letters in Column 1.

62. **The correct answer is (C).** When compared to Column 1, the letters (Column 2) *z, q, o,* and *a* and the numbers (Column 3) 5 and 4 are out of sequence.

63. **The correct answer is (B).** When compared to Column 1, all the letters in Column 2 are in their proper sequence; however, the numbers 2 and 3 in Column 3 are out of sequence.

64. **The correct answer is (A).** When compared to Column 1, all the numbers in Column 3 are in their proper sequence; however, the letters *a* and *o* in Column 2 are out of sequence.

65. **The correct answer is (D).** When compared to Column 1, all the letters in Column 2 and all the numbers in Column 3 are in proper sequence.

66. **The correct answer is (A).** When compared to Column 1, all the numbers in Column 3 are in proper sequence, however, the letters *r* and *a* in Column 2 are out of sequence.

Assistance Report on John Mandello Completed with Information Supplied

<table>
<tr><td colspan="6" align="center">**ASSISTANCE REPORT**</td></tr>
<tr>
<td>**1. Date**

6/14/89</td>
<td colspan="2">**2. Last name   First name   M.I.**

Mandello, John</td>
<td>**3. Age**
Approx.
28</td>
<td>**4. Sex**

M</td>
<td>**5. Color**

W</td>
</tr>
<tr>
<td>**6. Time**

9:30 A.M.</td>
<td colspan="5">**7. Residence (including county, apt. # & Zip Code)**</td>
</tr>
<tr>
<td colspan="6">**8. Location of occurrence (including county, apt. # & Zip code)**

N.W. Corner, Seventh Avenue and 83rd Street, New York</td>
</tr>
<tr>
<td colspan="4">**9. Illness or injury**

Cut on forehead</td>
<td colspan="2">**10. Precinct and report number**

3</td>
</tr>
<tr>
<td colspan="2">**11. Check:**
☐ sick   ☐ mentally ill
☒ injured ☐ dead</td>
<td colspan="2">**12. Taken to:**
Refused ☐ hospital (
assitance ☐ morgue (</td>
<td colspan="2">**Name of**

)
)</td>
</tr>
<tr>
<td colspan="2">**13. Admission number**</td>
<td colspan="4">**14. Name of Doctor or ambulance attendant**</td>
</tr>
<tr>
<td colspan="4">**15. Person notified**</td>
<td colspan="2">**Relationship**</td>
</tr>
<tr>
<td colspan="6">**16. Witnesses**</td>
</tr>
<tr>
<td colspan="6">**17. Remarks**

Victim was pushed from behind; fell to sidewalk and struck forehead; wallet containing $100.00 was removed from pocket.</td>
</tr>
<tr>
<td colspan="6">**18. Additional required reports (Check appropriate boxes, if any)**
☒ Crime report   ☐ Morgue report
☐ Vehicle accident report   ☐ Street injury report</td>
</tr>
<tr>
<td colspan="6">**19. Other agency notifications**
Traffic Department</td>
</tr>
<tr>
<td colspan="6">**20. Reporting Officer**

Rank   Name Whelan   Number   Precinct 2</td>
</tr>
</table>

Assistance Report on Juan Rodriguez Completed with Information Supplied

---

ASSISTANCE REPORT

1. Date 6/14/89	2. Last name First name M.I. Rodriguez, Juan	3. Age 24	4. Sex M	5. Color Hispanic

6. Time
Shortly after 9:30 A.M.

7. Residence (including county, apt. # & Zip Code)
98 Fourth Ave., Apt. 1, Newark, N.J.

8. Location of occurrence (including county, apt. # & Zip code)
82 Street and Seventh Ave., New York, N.Y.

9. Illness or injury
Unconscious

10. Precinct and report number
2nd

11. Check:
☐ sick   ☐ mentally ill
☒ injured   ☐ dead

12. Taken to:
☒ hospital   (Washington)
☐ morgue   ( )
Name of

13. Admission number
18763

14. Name of Doctor or ambulance attendant
John Francis, ambulance attendant

15. Person notified

Relationship

16. Witnesses
Mary Randolph, 876 First Ave., Apt. 2S, N.Y.C.
Helen Sweeney, 684 Broadway, Apt. A, N.Y.C.

17. Remarks
Collision of car and van at intersection of inoperative signal. Car mounted sidewalk and entered window of men's clothing store, setting off burglar alarm. Both drivers injured. No other injuries.

18. Additional required reports (Check appropriate boxes, if any)
☐ Crime report   ☐ Morgue report
☒ Vehicle accident report   ☐ Street injury report

19. Other agency notifications
Traffic

20. Reporting Officer

Rank   Name   Number   Precinct 2

Assistance Report on Joe Serrano Completed with Information Supplied

ASSISTANCE REPORT

1. Date 6/14/89

2. Last name First name M.I. Serrano, Joe

3. Age 29

4. Sex M

5. Color W

6. Time Shortly after 9:30 A.M.

7. Residence (including county, apt. # & Zip Code) 384 Lincoln Place, Apt. 4E, Brooklyn, N.Y. (Kings)

8. Location of occurrence (including county, apt. # & Zip code) 82nd St. and Seventh Ave., N.Y.C.

9. Illness or injury bleeding from cut on head; possible broken arm

10. Precinct and report number 2nd

11. Check: ☐ sick ☐ mentally ill ☒ injured ☐ dead

12. Taken to: ☒ hospital (Washington) ☐ morgue ( )

13. Admission number

14. Name of Doctor or ambulance attendant John Francis, ambulance attendant

15. Person notified Thomas Serrano 384 Linclon Place, Apt. 4E Brooklyn, N.Y. 287-8777

Relationship brother

16. Witnesses Mary Randolph, 876 First Ave, Apt. 25, N.Y.C. Helen Sweeney, 684 Broadway, Apt. A, N.Y.C.

17. Remarks Collision of car and van at intersection of inoperative signal. Car mounted sidewalk and entered window of men's clothing store setting off burglar alarm. Hospital diagonsis of forehead laceration and right arm fracture. Other driver injured.

18. Additional required reports (Check appropriate boxes, if any) ☐ Crime report ☒ Vehicle accident report ☐ Morgue report ☐ Street injury report

19. Other agency notifications Traffic

20. Reporting Officer Rank Name Number Precinct 2

67. **The correct answer is (D).** The person is treated at a location other than his home. If he were treated at home, a report would not be required. The reporting officer is from the 2nd Precinct. The incident occurred in the 3rd Precinct.

68. **The correct answer is (B).** The directions for box #9 state that the officer will enter the nature of the illness or injury to the best of his or her knowledge.

69. **The correct answer is (C).** Mr. Mandello was the victim of a robbery; therefore, a crime report is required. A street injury report is not required because he was not injured as a result of a defect in the sidewalk.

70. **The correct answer is (A).** As he was taking the information for the Assistance Report, Officer Whelan noticed that the corner streetlight was not working.

71. **The correct answer is (B).** An admission number is required only when a relative or friend can't be notified that a person was admitted to a hospital. This is true only in the case of Mr. Rodriguez.

72. **The correct answer is (A).** The directions for preparing the report state that the official diagnosis will be listed in box #17, Remarks.

73. **The correct answer is (A).** The incident involving Mr. Serrano and Mr. Rodriguez occurred in the 2nd Precinct. Mr. Serrano's admission number is not recorded because his brother was notified that he was taken to the hospital. In addition, the number listed for Mr. Serrano in choice (D) is incorrect.

74. **The correct answer is (C).** Only a vehicle accident report is required. There was no crime involved, and the accident was not caused by a defect in the roadway, thus eliminating a street injury report.

75. **The correct answer is (A).** The witnesses state that the traffic light was not working; therefore, the Traffic Department should be notified.

76. **The correct answer is (D).** John Francis was the ambulance attendant who responded. The victims were not sick; they were injured. Mr. Serrano's brother, not his father, was notified as to his injury in an accident that occurred on Seventh Avenue and 82nd Street.

77. **The correct answer is (C).** Refer to the first sentence of the passage.

78. **The correct answer is (C).** Refer to the third sentence of the passage.

79. **The correct answer is (A).** It is stated in the fourth sentence that many of the situations in which police assistance is required involve emotionally disturbed persons.

80. **The correct answer is (D).** A Police Officer arrests; the courts sentence, indict, or call people before a grand jury. Detention is to hold in custody.

81. **The correct answer is (B).** The passage talks exclusively about tire tracks. No mention is made of autos being used in the commission of crimes, of scientific police work, or of positive identification through cars.

82. **The correct answer is (D).** Refer to sentences 3 and 4 of the passage.

83. **The correct answer is (C).** Refer to the second sentence of the passage.

84. **The correct answer is (C).** Refer to the last sentence of the passage.

FOUR

TRAINING

CHAPTER 14: THE POLICE ACADEMY

The First Step in Your Career by Steve Albrecht

Steve Albrecht is nationally known for his written work on Police Officer safety and tactics. He has been with the San Diego Police Department since 1984, first as a regular officer and now as a reserve. He is a member of the American Society of Law Enforcement Trainers and contributes articles to police publications across the country. He is the author of *STREETWORK: The Way To Police Officer Safety & Survival* (Paladin) and is co-author, with John Morrison, of *CONTACT & COVER: Two-Officer Suspect Control* (Charles C. Thomas).

The Need for Training

Police work is a profession that puts a tremendous emphasis upon training. You start your law enforcement career in a training mode and, as long as you wear the badge of a Police Officer, you spend a large part of your time learning on the job. You need to have an extraordinarily broad range of knowledge on many different subjects. During an average patrol shift, you are called upon to solve a variety of problems, mediate disputes, investigate criminal cases, and respond to any number of different service requests ranging from the life-threatening to the mundane.

New Police Officers like to think of themselves as true "crime fighters." Equipped with a badge, gun, and uniform, many envision themselves chasing "bad guys," making dozens of felony arrests, and solving major crimes on a constant basis. However, law enforcement studies indicate that you will spend only 20 percent of your patrol time actually in an enforcement position. As a Police Officer, you answer citizen complaints, questions, and requests; write reports; participate in administrative or training tasks; or just randomly patrol your area waiting for calls. The 20 percent figure that relates to enforcement—issuing citations, making arrests, and protecting life and property—is certainly an important part of your job as a Police Officer, but it's really only one of your many job functions.

Every town, city, and suburb is filled with people who have different cultural backgrounds, ethical values, and moral standards. The residents interact with the police in a variety of matters, not just during enforcement situations. You need to have good "people" skills to assist them with the many different situations that may occur. The citizens of this country look to the police for protection and service, and by its nature, police work is a reactive, service "business."

If you are hired as a Police Officer, you have already met a number of high standards. You passed a series of rigorous mental, physical, medical, and psychological tests. You convinced key city and police department personnel that you have the high morals, positive ethical values, and stable personality traits needed to do the job in a humane and intelligent manner. But surviving the hiring process is only the start of your exposure to the world of police service. The next phase of your development as an officer—your introduction to law enforcement—begins in the police academy.

Once hired, the next four to six months of your life are spent at the police academy, learning what it means to be a Police Officer. This chapter gives you an overview of a typical police academy facility, including the information you need to have before you begin your training. Note that the information provided covers the overall police training experience. Check with your police academy for specific area requirements since different agencies require different things from their trainees. For example, some police departments, such as the LAPD, stress extensive physical training sessions and spend a significant amount of time teaching recruits to speak Spanish. This emphasis on second-language skills reflects the cultural necessities of their area.

Other agencies, like the San Diego Police Department, established a "phase training" program where Police Officer trainees rotate back and forth between academy classes and actual participation in street patrol with senior Field Training Officers. This hands-on experience prepares new officers for the stress of police work by introducing them to it in carefully controlled stages.

Some police academies require recruits to live at the facility—much like the military. Federal and state law enforcement agencies usually require their trainees to live on-site, while city and county academies allow their cadets to commute from home. Other police training centers operate in conjunction with state universities or with local community college facilities.

No matter how or where the academy for your agency functions, the values you learn are the same. On the west or east coast, from a small midwestern training center or from a large southern regional facility that covers an entire state, you will come away from your academy experience with the following traits and abilities:

- **Discipline.** You will know how to take orders and give them, especially during moments of extreme stress.
- **Teamwork.** You will recognize the need to work together as a unit, with a partner or even with several dozen other officers.
- **Camaraderie.** You will establish personal friendships that last for your entire career and beyond.
- **Esprit-de-corps.** You will forge an intense commitment to your "brothers and sisters in arms" that permeates your working relationships and even your entire way of life.
- **Courtesy, tact, and control.** You will use these traits to handle any situation, politely, safely, humanely, and above all, professionally.
- **Tactical survival skills.** You will receive the best officer safety material available and learn the latest patrol theories designed to save your life.
- **Professionalism.** You will become a total law enforcement professional, taught to protect and serve with skill and a strong sense of commitment that the career you have chosen is both right and necessary in our society today.

Pre-Academy Preparations

Your entrance into the police academy really begins long before you get there. An old police maxim fits here: *Forewarned is forearmed.* The more you can prepare yourself for the rigors of academy training, both mentally and physically, the better you will do. This may sound simplistic and obvious, but the reasoning is clear. A little preparation before you start can save you from an enormous amount of hardship later.

Police academy training instructors know of many Police Officer candidates who had all the "on-paper" qualifications to make it to the academy and seemed to have it all. They scored well on written tests, showed impressive skills during the many interviews, and even had the strength and health to pass the physical and medical tests. However, once they arrived at the academy—with its built-in stressors and physical requirements—they folded under the pressure. Some candidates who reach the academy stage find themselves quite disillusioned by the pressure, the workload, and the physical side of police work. This often leads to their dismissal because of low test scores and poor physical performance or they quit on their own.

To get through a typical police academy, you need more than just high test scores and physical strength; you need mental toughness as well. The biggest, "baddest," or smartest people don't always make it because the police academy calls for so many other characteristics from its students. Humility, internal courage, and enthusiasm count for just as much as physical virtues.

Another common mistake is underestimating the amount of classroom study required. Most academy programs are designed around a college curriculum, offering from 12 to 18 units to officer-graduates. To learn and retain this much material, academy students must spend much of their off-time studying their notes and reading their textbooks. With today's academy programs, it's just not possible to get by without extensive studying since the classroom work is demanding and calls for mental discipline. Scanning your criminal law book and reading a few cryptic notes will not suffice. If you don't devote a substantial portion of your off-hours to studying this large amount of material, you won't make it to graduation day.

The skills you bring to the academic portion of the academy are largely in place when you get there. Here are some tips to make the most of those skills:

- Read up on how to study efficiently.
- Take good notes.
- Manage your time effectively.
- Maximize your in-class time.
- Work at home at a specific pace.
- Follow a planned study schedule.

Except for reviewing some helpful techniques, there is very little you can do to improve upon the common sense you already carry. Reading legal textbooks and police training manuals may give you an idea of what to expect, but for the most part, your instructors will teach you everything you'll need to know to function in the field. Since you can't really prepare for the academic rigors, focus your attention on one key area you can improve: your level of physical fitness. Most academy physical fitness programs stress the same three elements:

1. Upper body strength
2. Cardiovascular endurance
3. Joint and muscle flexibility

The key to your success in these demanding areas starts with your pre-academy fitness level. It's just not possible to "work" yourself into shape once you get there. You've probably seen or heard stories about professional athletes who come to training camp for their sport grossly overweight or out of shape. They quickly fall behind their teammates and spend most of their time in a catch-up position.

If you train correctly and work hard before your academy classes begin, the exercise programs at the academy will seem much easier. You don't want to start off with the handicap of being out of shape. Come to the academy in great shape and try to improve upon that once the physical training sessions begin.

In some academy programs, you are given a list of equipment to purchase before you arrive. Usually, you are required to buy your uniforms, dress jacket, cold and rainy weather clothes, footwear, and leather gear. Most departments give you a duty weapon, a baton, a helmet, a whistle, Mace, and other similar department-issue items. These items belong to the agency, even though you will use them for your entire career. If you decide to leave the department, you must return any equipment issued to you. In most programs, you are also given the textbooks, paperwork, report forms, and other written materials needed to complete the academic portions of the academy.

If your agency requires you to buy uniforms, it is wise to buy the best you can afford. With uniforms, your appearance is critical to your professionalism both inside the academy and out in the field. Buy quality uniforms and have them tailored to fit your body.

Nowhere is this sense of quality more important than with your leather gear and police equipment. The quality and durability of your holster, handcuff case, and baton ring could affect your safety. Respected, name-brand equipment may save you from injuries or death; poor-quality "knockoffs" could threaten your survival if they fail. Buy the best leather gear and equipment you can afford and then take care of it as if your life depended on it, because it just might.

Some police agencies issue a badge and a photo identification card to trainees just before the academy formally begins. If your agency does this, you will get instructions on how and when to wear your badge, including some careful admonishments about off-duty considerations and the potential for misuse and abuse of your new authority. Most agencies, though, issue it only after you complete the academy, usually at the graduation ceremony.

With an understanding of the nature of police work, the goals of police academy training, and the mental and physical preparations you need, you're ready to look at academy life—one of the most exciting and demanding parts of your law enforcement career.

Dealing with the "Boot Camp" Environment

It's no secret that the police academy is much like military basic training. You are required to respond to orders quickly, march in a structured fashion to and from various locations, salute when necessary, answer your training officers with a stout "Yes Sir!" or "Yes Ma'am!" when called upon, and generally assume a role of the classic "cadet," "recruit," or "trainee." It may seem as if the academy training officers are always yelling—and mostly at you. There are good reasons for this: Discipline, obedience, and unity are the orders of the day.

On the first day at the academy, the training officers in charge of your class will carefully point out the rules and regulations of the facility. They will also teach you how to walk, how to talk, how to act, and how to move on command. Any attempt at horseplay, showing-off, or other childish moves that jeopardize the safety and success of your classmates are met with swift and decisive punishment. As one veteran instructor puts it, "Unless you want to spend all of your time doing push-ups or writing 500-word essays on the importance of discipline, you had better 'toe the mark' and do what we tell you."

There are many reasons police training academies follow a military model. The reasons are based upon safety concerns (especially when dealing with firearms, defensive tactics, pursuit-driving, and other potentially dangerous training programs); the need to unite, train, and control a large group of people in a minimal amount of time; and linked to the histories and traditions of that particular agency.

Police work is similar to the military in more than just its use of titles—Officer, Sergeant, Lieutenant, Captain, Commander, Chief, etc. Both organizations deal with life-and-death situations in many hostile environments. Each requires its people to respond to specific orders during periods of great personal danger and stress. In many foreign countries, the police and the military work in conjunction with each other, even to the point of near interchangeability.

Some new recruits are quite comfortable with this emphasis on the paramilitary, while other trainees find it terrifying and have a hard time concentrating on the tasks at hand. Those who adjust the best have prior military experience; they still remember how to march and how to speak to superiors, giving them a significant edge over their classmates. Academy training officers usually recognize these recruits and assign them "squad leader" roles to help guide and instruct their peer recruits.

Most officers who have gone through the academy experience say that after a short period, it is easier to respond in this military fashion. What seems difficult at first will get easier, especially if you concentrate and work hard to conform. Still, you will do much better if you develop a thick skin before you begin the academy program. The trick is to follow the orders, complete the tasks you're given, and show effort and enthusiasm at all times. An important tip is to keep in mind that verbal abuse from your training officers or instructors is not a personal attack.

Rest assured that training officers have your best interests in mind. They want you to make it to graduation day, and they will never hit you, curse you, or allow you to do anything unsafe or dangerous. Keep in mind that they aren't picking on you. They are merely exercising their lungs and reinforcing the level of discipline that must pervade the academy setting. It's all for your own good, although it's often difficult to keep this in mind as you complete your fiftieth push-up on a hot summer day.

One key element of police work is the strong sense of camaraderie and unity. Large academy classes are often broken into two separate squads, each competing against the other for the top class honors. Some academy classes, like those of the LAPD, use full-size military flags with their class colors, emblem, and slogan printed on them. Many academy classes have a "fight" slogan that they yell out at the beginning and end of each day, before each break, and during rigorous physical training sessions. These class slogans serve to reinforce the concepts of teamwork, unity of command, tradition, pride, and aggressive-ness—all good qualities for today's Police Officers.

The concept of the "Thin Blue Line"—that the police are the first and only defense against the criminals in our society—continually permeates the academy training process. Training officers want you to think and act as individuals but never at the expense of the group. They teach you how to help each other survive not only the academy process but life on the streets as well.

This concept runs throughout the academy. Few people go out of their way to help a Police Officer in dire need, either because they dislike the police or, more likely, because they don't want to get involved. Fellow Police Officers come to each other's aid under any circumstance. Law enforcement is a team effort, and this is emphasized every day at the academy.

The rewards and punishments doled out by your training officers have a "one size fits all" flavor. You are usually rewarded as a group and punished as one, too. Class unity is a constant goal, so if one trainee violates the rules, his or her associates may share the blame. This isn't to say that individual punishments don't exist, but rather that the instructors use their knowledge of group dynamics to teach discipline and order by involving everyone.

The best way to deal with the discipline and paramilitary structure of academy training is to accept it as a part of your law enforcement training process. Don't take anything too personally—it won't last forever. Monitor your stress level the best you can, and realize that your training officers want you to succeed.

Classroom Conduct

The time you spend in the academy classroom environment represents about 60 percent of your total training time. Another 20 percent is spent with physical training and defensive tactics activities, and the last 20 percent is spent outside the classroom, with driving and firearms training, role plays, and trips to off-site agencies. Since the majority of your training time is in classes, it helps to know what to expect, what to ask, and how to respond to questions, orders, and requests.

The positions of Academy Training Officer and Academy Course Instructor are highly coveted jobs, so the competition among officers is fierce. This competition almost guaran-tees that you will get some of the finest teachers available. They know their subjects and can spice the classroom lectures with some carefully chosen "war stories" that illustrate the need to do things correctly in the field.

The course material itself is specifically written and created to stress the most important parts of each subject. Course organizers know they have a limited amount of time to teach you and your classmates a wide variety of necessary information; they do not spend time covering subjects that do not apply to a Police Officer career. Nearly everything your instructors discuss relates to material that you must know to pass an exam. Instructors are also responsible for explaining core material mandated by your state since each state has its own learning requirements for its Police Officers.

Academy classroom etiquette is similar to that of most college classrooms, with a few important exceptions. In a college class, the room level is fairly informal, and the discussions usually bounce back and forth between students and the teacher. In the academy, discipline in the classroom is much more important. To ask a question, you need to raise your hand, wait to be called on, and stand to address the instructor formally, "Sir, Trainee Jones. I wanted to ask about . . ."

Your course instructors will tell you how to address them once their class begins. This formal style serves a few purposes. It shows respect to the instructors, builds a foundation of discipline in the classroom, and allows each student to speak without interruption.

Most academy subjects are taught in blocks of instruction, ranging from 2-hour overviews to 80-hour, in-depth looks. Lectures for these blocks, however, usually last for 50 minutes at a time to allow for frequent breaks. At many academies, the break procedure is the same: dismissal by the instructor, "fall in" to ranks outside the classroom, wait to be marched to the break area by a training officer or chosen student, and then dismissal for a break.

Lectures and Exams

It's hard to overstress the importance of good study habits. Academy courses are dense and force you to cover a lot of material in a short period. Your success in the classroom lies in your ability to take good notes, ask appropriate questions when you need further clarification, study efficiently, and score well on the exams.

TAKING NOTES DURING LECTURES

Effective studying starts with good note taking. One of the easiest ways to take notes efficiently is to use a technique called "mind-mapping." Start with a clean sheet of paper and write the title or the subject of the lecture right in the center of the page. From there, draw lines that radiate from the center, attaching a word, phrase, or key piece of information to each line. Each time you hear a new piece of information, start a new line or add it to an existing line. Some people call these "spider diagrams" because they look like webs. They are also called "mind-maps" because the ideas look like cities and the lines look like roads.

When you take notes during a lecture, be sure to listen carefully to the instructor. He or she will usually tell you what material you'll "see again," meaning that it relates to test questions. Make extra notes about these items and study them in particular later.

STUDYING FOR AND TAKING EXAMS

Since most academy courses are taught in core modules, that's how you will take the exams as well—in sections. Instead of one huge 500-question test that covers all your knowledge, you will usually take a series of 10- to 50-question multiple-choice tests on each subject. Most academies use multiple-choice exams because they're easier to create and grade, and they aren't completely subjective in the grading, as are essay tests.

In most instances, the test follows the conclusion of the last block of instruction for that subject. That means you'll have a test about every two weeks. Your master schedule should list when each subject concludes and when the exam blocks will arrive. This gives you ample time to plan your study sessions accordingly.

Many academies use electronic scoring machines to grade exams. Since tests can be reused with future classes, you mark your answers on a special tally sheet rather than on the test itself. The machine can score several hundred exams in a short period so you can get the results back immediately. This can do wonders for your morale, because you won't have to worry about your scores overnight or, worse, over a weekend.

A passing exam grade is 70 percent and above; anything below that means you have to retake the test. If you fail an exam, you are usually given one opportunity to retake it. If you fail the exam the second time, you could fail out of the academy program. While this sounds harsh, it illustrates the need for good study habits and hard work.

Some academy programs allow you to retake a failed exam the next day. Others let you take it at the end of the same day, allowing you ample study time to prepare again. It's important that you pass the first time since a failed exam can put you behind your fellow classmates. The academy program is stressful enough without having to retake exams. Further, you run the risk of expulsion if you don't pass the make-up exams.

After you receive your test papers back, your training officers go over each test question and answer with the entire class. This is an opportunity for you to learn from your mistakes and reinforce the material you've learned. This question-and-answer exam review serves an important purpose: It gives you the right to have certain test questions thrown out if a majority of your fellow classmates got the wrong answer as well. For example, if you took an extensive exam on first aid procedures and your instructor gave you one answer and the test asks for something completely different, you can ask to have that question deleted. This protects your grade and tells the training officers and instructors what parts of the lectures they might need to improve.

Study Groups

If you are apprehensive about the amount of study involved in the academy, consider getting help from your fellow classmates. One of the best ways to study is in groups. Informal study sessions are usually held at a student's home or some other convenient meeting place. Besides the obvious benefits of review and reinforcement, these study sessions also offer a good way to get to know your fellow officers.

However you study—alone or in groups—make sure you stay on track and current with the material. As with most college-type classes, academy courses require some cumulative knowledge, so things you learned in the first week will apply to courses that come later.

Academy Subjects

Here's an overview of the criminal law classes, patrol theory, first aid, and evidence courses required to graduate. The subjects may differ in scope and content, since different academies stress different subjects. For the most part, this list represents the core of a typical police academy program.

Alcoholic beverage control laws. This subject deals with the rules and regulations surrounding alcoholic beverage sales and distribution. It includes types of liquor store, bar, and restaurant licenses; underage minors violations; and the enforcement of similar vice laws. Patrol officers and detectives spend a good deal of their time dealing with alcohol-related problems in bars, taverns, and liquor stores. This class gives information crucial to the law enforcement aspects of these problems.

Chemical weapons training. Although most of the chemical weapons training calls for outdoor activities (and exposures), there is a significant amount of class time involved. You will learn the dynamics of chemical weapon assaults, chemical weapon types and ingredients, effective usage as a defensive weapon, first aid, and proper suspect handling techniques after exposure.

Citations. This training involves how and when to write citations for traffic, misdemeanor, drug, and alcohol violations. Sample citation forms are used to illustrate the written formats. Since "cite" writing makes up a large part of the police patrol function, the lectures include specific officer safety techniques. You will be given several "street scenarios" and will be asked to write a variety of sample citations for each.

Community relations. This section explains the customs of many races and how to build better cultural relations; meet community needs; follow noncultural, unbiased standards for law enforcement; conduct community meetings; form citizen awareness groups; make citizen contacts; and suggest referrals and recommend social service agencies. It also includes creating crime and drug prevention programs for neighborhoods, businesses, and schools.

Constitutional law. Here you will learn more about the Constitution, the Bill of Rights, and the amendments that relate specifically to the judicial system and to police work. This information is especially useful when coupled with patrol practices involving search and seizure, laws of arrest, interrogation, report writing, and court testimony.

Corrections. This module follows the booking procedures for arrested suspects, including bail, in-custody care, probation and parole, city and county jail procedures, the roles and functions of the Sheriff's Department, and an overview of the state prison system.

The court system. This overview covers the entire judicial process, including trials, hearings, and arraignments; pleas and plea bargains; complaints; indictments; appeals; felony and misdemeanor cases; district and city attorneys; subpoenas; traffic court; family court; and juvenile court. You will learn more about the arrest cycle from the initial arraignment and the preliminary hearing to the jury selection, the court case, the verdict, and the sentencing hearing.

Courtroom testimony. Focusing on courtroom etiquette and preparedness, this section explains court procedures, testimony techniques, and the use of reports as a prosecution and defense tool. You will probably see a mock trial, with careful explanations of your role in the court proceedings.

Criminal laws. This section is one of the most comprehensive parts of academy training. It covers all phases of the law as it pertains to police work. This includes the laws of arrest; search and seizure rules; stop and frisk requirements; detentions; the definitions of "reasonable suspicion" and "probable cause"; "Miranda" warnings; laws relating to property crimes, personal crimes, the Penal Code, Health and Safety codes, juvenile crimes, Welfare and Institution codes, and the Vehicle Code; citizens' arrests; and powers of arrest and release. This section is often taught by ranking district attorneys, city attorneys, or, in some cases, former Police Officers who have themselves become prosecuting attorneys.

Deadly force issues. Another of the important core elements in any academy training program, this section utilizes highly focused and detailed discussions, role playing, and video training simulations. The issues themselves include use of firearms, warning shots, "fleeing felon" decisions, the use of shotguns, the use-of-force continuum, deadly force decision-making techniques, stress control, and the potential for civil or criminal liability actions against officers who misuse deadly force.

Death cases. This topic includes death case procedures, crime scene and evidence protection, report writing, and an overview of the Coroner's Office.

Defensive tactics. The defensive tactics module emphasizes the defensive rather than offensive side of effective suspect control. It includes classroom lectures, gymnasium training, armed and unarmed handcuffing procedures, armed and unarmed self-defense, baton training, the carotid neck restraint, search procedures, the use of chemical weapons, high-risk arrest tactics, crowd and riot control, and the potential for civil liability of officers who misuse defensive tactics, arrest and control procedures, or police weaponry.

Disturbance calls. Since many officers are killed or injured while handling disturbance calls, this section explains the dynamics of disturbance calls, one- and two-officer safety issues, conflict management, cultural issues, family fights, child custody cases, emotionally disturbed persons, domestic violence, social services and referrals, report procedures, and arrest criteria.

Driver's licenses. Taught by State Motor Vehicle investigators, this class explains the issuance and use of driver's licenses, ID cards, vehicle license plates, and VIN numbers. Examples of fraudulent documents are shown to help you recognize them in the field.

DUI arrests. Because drunk driving arrests are growing in response to public awareness, this section shows how to identify, stop, arrest, and book the suspected driver. It includes discussions and examples of the Field Coordination Test; officer safety factors; accident scenes involving the drinking driver; public safety issues; awareness campaigns; arrest, impound, and booking procedures; reports; State Motor Vehicle requirements; and potential civil liability problems.

Evidence. Patrol officers are often called on to collect and recover evidence from crime scenes. This course explains collection techniques, impounding procedures, chain of custody, how to take photos and make crime scene diagrams, fruits of the crime, instrumentalities of the crime, and practical exercises to help recover trace amounts of evidence, such as fingerprints, hairs, fibers, and soil.

Firearms training. This is another significant core module, involving classroom lectures; gun safety rules; range practice; two-hand, one-hand, barricade, prone, and stress shooting; reloading; cleaning the weapon; shotgun training; and weapons identification.

First aid training. While this course probably won't make you a paramedic, it does provide enough information to allow you to stabilize most injury cases, from minor problems to life-threatening wounds. The subjects include first aid application and theory, CPR certification, field problems and role-play, and first aid testing and certification.

Interviews and interrogations. Since most crimes come to police attention "after the fact," a police investigation is only as good as the officer asking the questions. This course teaches techniques for interviewing victims and witnesses, techniques for interrogating suspects, and the dynamics of human communication, including "active listening," body language, and lie detection.

Officer safety and survival. This class is probably one of the most demanding and powerful sections of the academy. It goes over mental and physical awareness; patrol theory; radio call response; low- and high-risk arrest tactics; assaults involving knives, guns, and other weapons; disarmings; gun retention; role plays; the use of force; uses of gun, baton, and defensive tactics; stress control; and the survival mindset.

Patrol theory. This section teaches trainees how to patrol the streets, either on a foot beat or from the seat of a police car. It explains the proper response to radio calls, self-initiated activity, citations, field interviews, and referrals. It covers crimes in progress, building searches, using the police radio, car stops, pedestrian stops, observation techniques, officer safety, officer survival, and modern patrol practices.

Penal code. Coupled with detailed explanations in the law section, the discussion of the Penal Code shows officers how to use this law book and explains the crime elements, violations, and enforcement sections.

Physical training lectures. More than a few Police Officers in this country die of heart attacks, many of which are brought on by poor dietary habits, lack of exercise, and far too much stress. Other officers are forced into early retirement because of chronic back and knee ailments. The Physical Training classroom module discusses health issues that relate to Police Officers, including diet and exercise plans, injury prevention, and stress control.

Police history and ethical principles. This module is an overview of the history and principles of law enforcement in the United States, ethics and conduct, on- and off-duty habits, individual department policies and procedures, the police chain of command, and the administration of justice in the community.

Report writing. Most of your career as a Police Officer will be spent writing reports of some type. Report writing explains the nature and scope of police reports; terminology, procedures, and forms; narratives; interviews and interrogations; crime cases; arrest reports; impounds; narcotics arrests; drunk driver arrest reports; auto theft reports and recoveries; crime descriptions; courtroom procedures; and civil liability precautions.

Traffic accident investigation. This section explains the proper procedures to be used to respond to vehicle accidents, including safe response; flare patterns; injuries; evidence; vehicle impounds; collision reports; victim, driver, and witness statements; traffic direction; scene protection; measurements; and collision investigation techniques.

Vehicle code. This course offers detailed explanations of state traffic laws. The discussion of the Vehicle Code shows officers how to use this law book in the field, including the administrative and enforcement sections, and indicates specific traffic violations to remember.

Vehicle operations. A typical police patrol officer spends more time behind the wheel of a police car than nearly any other on-duty activity. This important section includes classroom study, emergency vehicle traffic laws, emergency vehicle operations, pursuit driving techniques, pursuit policies, accident prevention, and civil liability issues.

Physical Training

While the classroom portion of your academy training takes up the bulk of your time, you will spend a significant part of your days and weeks doing some kind of physical training (PT). How well you do during these PT sessions depends upon two things:

1. Your level of fitness before the academy begins
2. Your ability to work hard and ignore the pain and discomfort that comes with difficult physical exercise

The good news is that you can control each of these factors. The bad news is that if you don't, you can fail the academy program.

If you have any preconceived notions about Police Officers being the largest or heaviest people around, get rid of them. The old days of the burly, door-filling cops on the beat are over. Today's officers are leaner, more health-conscious, and more fit than ever before. More officers are exercising, eating correctly, quitting smoking, and actually working to reduce their on- and off-duty stresses.

Police work is a physically and mentally demanding occupation. It takes place in all kinds of weather, in some of the worst neighborhoods imaginable, and under the most difficult stressors a human being can face. Police work can be painful, involving severe bodily injury and even death to the officer. It requires upper- and lower-body strength, flexibility, cardiovascular stamina, and lastly, plain old-fashioned guts. If you lack some of these physical requirements, academy PT sessions will teach you to overcome physical pain and carry on. Like classroom work, police academy physical training can be extremely difficult.

The best way to succeed in PT is to be in shape before it begins. Some hard work on your part before the academy starts will save you much grief later. It's just not possible to get in shape when you get there since you don't have the luxury of time (or a stress-free training environment) to help you ease your way into it.

Your personal PT program should begin at least four months before the actual academy starts. This gives you plenty of time to get physically and mentally ready for the classroom courses and PT sessions. Consider these four steps as a part of your pre-academy training plan.

1. Quit Smoking

If you smoke, it's time to quit. The police academy theory of PT is based on one idea: constant movement. If you aren't running somewhere at double-time speed, you are marching or walking quickly. If you are a medium-to-heavy smoker, you will pay the price during these training and marching sessions. Quit now—you will certainly see a definite improvement in your fitness level.

Many progressive police academies actively discourage smoking. They know how harmful it is to the health and safety of their new officers, so they create barriers that make it hard for you to continue smoking. This includes no "smoke breaks," restricted smoking areas, and added peer pressure from training officers and fellow classmates to give up the habit.

2. Lose Weight

If you can lose any excess weight before the academy, it will be very easy to keep it off once the PT sessions start. In fact, you may even find you have to eat more food, more frequently, just to maintain your current weight. If you go through your academy program during hot summer or cold winter months, you will probably need to increase your intake of calories and fluids to keep up. The PT sessions can take a lot out of you.

Proper weight control also makes it easier for you to run long distances. Since it's no longer necessary to be built like a pro football player to work as a police officer, focus your pre-academy training efforts toward slimming down to a leaner body weight. Many new recruits who spend hours in the health spa "pumping iron" find that the extra muscle bulk actually hindered their performance. Carrying extra weight, even if it's mostly muscle, can slow you down.

The trick is to be strong and muscular, without any unnecessary muscle mass or fat. Unless you are an experienced athlete with years of work behind you, don't try to bring any extra muscle weight to the academy. If you are too heavy, you are probably too slow as well. Lean and mean is the idea here. You can certainly lift weights before and during the academy, but keep the weights light and the number of repetitions high to tone up rather than bulk up.

Start a sensible diet program when you begin your pre-academy conditioning program. Lose the extra weight slowly and safely by drinking plenty of water, taking vitamins, and eating a balanced and reduced-calorie diet as you train. Remember that you have to carry any extra pounds with you on those long academy training runs.

3. Walk/Run/Sprint

If you are more than a weekend athlete, you are probably used to running or jogging at least three or four times per week. If so, continue your present training pace and add some long runs, some sprints and speed work, and plenty of pre- and post-run stretching to your workouts. If you don't run regularly, do yourself a favor and start your training by walking first. Many overeager police cadets set themselves back with serious injuries by overtraining. Go to the bookstore and get a good book on walking. Follow the advice concerning the choice of shoes, walking courses, and training times. Start slowly, work hard during every session, and focus on strengthening your leg and back muscles as you walk. Some carefully planned walking workouts will prepare your body safely and efficiently for the runs to follow.

Once you've worked up to a brisk walking pace, you can start your pre-academy running program. Start by running at a "talking pace"—a speed where you can hold a conversation without gasping—for the first few weeks. Make sure you have a good pair of running shoes—not tennis or basketball sneakers—that support your ankles and protect your legs from the inevitable pounding from hard running surfaces.

While some experts say you can run on a near-daily basis as long as you alternate one "hard" day with one "easy" day, other sports trainers aren't so sure. A good rule of thumb is to run every other day so you can rest your legs, lungs, and heart on off days. Many people like to run on Mondays, Wednesdays, and Fridays, with a longer distance run on Sunday. Then they rest Monday and start up again Tuesday with the every-other-day pace. Pick a schedule that works for you and stick with it. If you want to increase your mileage, go up about 10 percent every other week. For example, if you can run 10 total miles per week with little difficulty, go up to 11, and so on.

Too much running can cause you a host of problems, from blisters to shin splints, stress fractures, and broken bones. Be sensible, run on well-cushioned surfaces, and concentrate on quality training sessions rather than quantity. Run in a way that causes you to roll along heel to toe, rather than on the balls of your feet. Run straight upright, so that your body doesn't bounce. If the horizon in front of you shakes about, you're probably moving your upper body too much.

To give you some variety during your running workouts, try some wind sprints. Go to a local high school football field and pace off 40 yards. Try running a few warm-up sprints at half-speed. Then run 6 to 10 full-speed sprints to get your heart rate up and increase your leg-muscle flexibility. Sprint workouts offer a good change of pace and can prepare you for a variety of academy running assignments. Remember to stretch before and after every running workout.

4. Use Your Body Weight

If you were to get a dime for every push-up you do in the police academy, you could retire at an early age. The standard gym-class push-up is a mainstay of most academy PT sessions. You will do them as punishment in a group and as punishment for an individual mistake, and you'll do them by the carload in your formal PT sessions.

As you're doing these push-ups with your classmates, you will collectively wonder when your training officers will get tired and ask you to stop. Unfortunately, they have several secret weapons at their disposal. First, if they get tired, they simply stand up and continue counting. So while they've stopped doing their push-ups at 37, you have to go on until 50. Secondly, if they get tired at 50, they just ask another instructor to take over until you reach 100. Lastly, if you don't yell loudly during the count portion, instructors may pretend they lost track, and you'll have to start again from push-up number one!

Since push-ups are so much a part of academy PT, you will want to do hundreds of them as part of your pre-academy training program. If you haven't done this type of exercise in some time, start slowly. Give yourself small goals and try to meet them each day. Start with 10 push-ups per session, go to 25, and then go to 50. Increase the number of times you practice push-ups from once or twice per day on up to 10 times per day. Use good form, breathe correctly (inhale going down, exhale coming up), and stick with them. The more you do now, the easier they are to do later, when you are at the academy.

Like push-ups, sit-ups are another standard-issue academy exercise. While push-ups build your arms, shoulders, and chest, sit-ups also strengthen your abdominal muscles and, to a lesser extent, your lower back and hip joint area. Many Police Officers retire early with long-term medical disabilities because of weak backs. Some problems stem from the constant wear and tear on your stomach muscles. Police gun belts, bulletproof vests, heavy shoes, and other equipment can add up to 30 pounds to an officer's body weight, causing stomach muscles to sag and become more prone to injuries like hernias, ruptures, and lateral low-back ailments. To prevent these problems, start a sit-up program with your push-up regimen. Choose a target number and meet it every day. Use good form, don't pull on the back of your neck with your hands, and protect your seat with a towel or pad.

Lastly, many training academies ask their officers to do pull-ups as a part of PT. The typical pull-up movement requires an above-average amount of upper-body strength, and it offers a good way to show improvements in overall fitness levels. As with your pre-academy conditioning exercises, start slowly and build yourself up to multiple pull-up sets. If you can't do one pull-up, make that your goal and work hard to achieve it. Use your determination and concentrate on good form. Try to do 1, 5, or 10 more of everything you did the previous day.

PT DISCIPLINE

The paramilitary model that covers the classroom discipline in the academy also reaches the PT sessions. Trainees with prior military experience will be fairly comfortable with the group exercise process. If you don't have a military background, you will have to make a few adjustments.

Most academy PT classes run for 1 hour to 1 hour and 15 minutes. Some sessions take place early in the morning, before classes begin; others start just before lunch, and still others cover the last hour of the work day. Nearly every session includes a running program followed by a vigorous session of mat work, which includes the usual push-ups, sit-ups, leg lifts, abdominal crunches, pull-ups, and even bar dips.

You begin with a set of warm-ups and calisthenics, which you do as a group, counting loudly enough to impress your training officers. From there, you form two single-file lines and begin the run of the day. Running in formation like this takes a careful step. Too close and you stomp on the person in front of you; too far away and you risk falling behind. Since most training runs are held on roads around the academy facility, pay strict attention to the terrain and the potential hazards in the street, such as curbs, fire hydrants, and mail boxes.

A few academy classes like to run in the traditional Army style, with everyone staying together and running at a comfortable pace so the slowest runner can keep up. Most PT instructors, however, prefer to start the class together and then let the faster runners set the pace. This tends to spread the group out in a long line but allows everyone to work at a rate that is personally best. To keep the "gazelles" under control, a training officer often sets a fast pace and keeps everyone else behind. Another training officer anchors the end of the line to encourage the stragglers with a few well-chosen words and to push them along.

If you are out of shape, this spread-out method can be unbearable. Just when you catch up to the leaders of the pack—who jog in place until you arrive—they start up again, giving you no break whatsoever. This should tell you how important pre-academy fitness is to your mental and physical health. Unless you want your eardrums to ring with the howls of your training officers, get in shape and be ready to run at a brisk pace when necessary.

The only thing that makes this kind of running enjoyable—besides knowing that it can't last forever—is the cadence calling. Just like the military, many academies use marching songs and rhymes to encourage the recruits and take their minds off their labored breathing. These songs, limericks, and marching poems are always inspirational, usually motivational, and occasionally humorous. They also encourage group unity, promote discipline, and help to pass the time a bit.

After a stimulating run, it's off to the gym room or exercise area for some more calisthenics. You usually line up in rows and begin a whole series of push-ups and sit-ups. These exercises aren't particularly difficult, but coupled with the running program, they can really tire you out.

As with all PT exercises, the more you do before the academy begins, the easier it is for you to complete each exercise session. During all sessions, try to stay up with the training officers and match them exercise for exercise. You will improve your conditioning, and this makes for a better impression among your peers and trainers.

If your PT program takes place before class begins, you should have just enough time to shower and dress for the start of the day. If the session ends at lunch or at the close of the day, take some extra time to eat properly and drink plenty of fluids, especially water. If you eat sensibly, minimizing the junk food, sodas, and fast-food items, you help your physical performance and feel better as well.

Besides the obvious cardiovascular and upper-body strength benefits, most academy PT sessions are designed to build the muscles of the abdomen, lower back, and back and knee joints. Since so many officers suffer career-threatening health problems in these vital areas, injury prevention is a critical part of your overall fitness plan while you attend the academy. Tell your instructors anytime you feel any unusual pains or anything other than normal muscle soreness.

Work hard to keep your knee joints strong and flexible. Concentrate on your stomach muscles to prevent back and stomach injuries. Run carefully and efficiently to avoid any foot or leg problems. Think of your academy PT sessions as the gateway to a career of lifelong fitness and injury prevention

Arrest and Control Classes

Many academies have what is known as a "mat room" specially designed for police defensive training. This area is covered with thick wrestling-style mats, and there are usually heavy boxing-type body punching bags in various locations around the room. The mats help protect you during defensive tactics training, and the bags are for baton strikes and punching practice. Except for the classroom courses, you'll go through most of your arrest and control classes and defensive tactics in the mat room.

Notice the key word *defensive*. By nature, police work is filled with opportunities for officers to prevent physical confrontations. Defensive tactics are used rather than offensive movements for a variety of reasons. The defensive mode promotes better officer safety tactics. It is also more effective as a suspect control technique and it prevents undue civil liability suits against officers and their departments.

Some trainers like to teach judo "safe-falling" techniques, tumbling movements, ground and foot fighting movements, boxing and wrestling techniques, and other "street" fighting maneuvers. For these defensive tactics drills, you partner up with a fellow classmate. Most of these activities call for one officer to be "the cop" and one to be "the crook." You then switch back and forth as you practice the hands-on techniques over the 1- to 2-hour class sessions.

Whether you are learning to use the police baton, a handcuffing technique, or an empty-hand control technique, the key to your success in defensive tactics training lies in correct practice and repetition. You must exercise the proper control to protect yourself and your partner from injuries. Some officers are badly injured during these sessions because of an overzealous partner or because they failed to practice safely and carefully. The only way you will learn to perform these techniques correctly (and safely) is to practice them over and over again.

The human body, in terms of police training, thrives on repetition. Constant, unrelenting practice involving several hundred or even several thousand repetitions builds a sense of muscle memory into your brain and muscles. With sufficient practice, each of these moves can become almost instinctive, requiring no thought, just action. Your defensive tactics training instructors know this, so you will spend most of your time learning new techniques and drilling them over and over again. The more you practice in the gym, the better you will follow the techniques in the field, where it really counts.

Many hands-on techniques for police work are based on the martial art aikido, which focuses on wrist, elbow, and shoulder-joint pressures and throwing techniques. You do not need any previous martial arts experience to learn these movements, but you may want to review some aikido or other martial arts books at the bookstore or library. Sometimes it helps to see these grappling techniques as they are broken down in step-by-step photographs.

Police baton training in the academy depends upon the equipment used by your local agency. Some police departments use the straight baton, and others use an expandable straight baton. Some agencies train officers to use the PR-24 side-handle baton, and others prefer the Orcutt Police Nunchakus. Whatever equipment you use, keep these rules in mind:

Train safely. These are potentially deadly weapons

Train consistently. Use many drills and repetitions to hone your skills.

Dress Codes

Most academies require their trainees to maintain three different types of uniform, each serving its own purpose:

1. **Dress uniform.** This is usually the uniform of the agency that hired you. Some academies have trainees wear the actual uniform of the police agency, while others use a training uniform of blue or khaki brown. In the latter example, you would begin wearing the traditional uniform of your agency at your graduation. In any case, the dress uniform is usually worn during the classroom sessions.

2. **Arrest and control uniform.** Most cadets wear "nametag" T-shirts with their last names printed on the front and back for ease in identification (and yelling at). Some academies have trainees wear T-shirts, standard blue jeans, and running shoes for defensive tactics classes, while other classes use T-shirts, sweatpants, and running shoes. In either case, the purpose of the uniform is comfort, durability, freedom of

movement, easy identification, and safety. Few academies want their people to wrestle and fight in dress uniforms, since it's expensive to fix torn clothes.

3. **PT uniform.** This uniform consists of the "nametag" T-shirt, running shorts, white socks, and running shoes. It is used strictly for PT sessions because it's cool and comfortable and allows free movement.

Since the word *uniform* is defined as "official clothing; one that does not vary," you can imagine that police academy clothing is all the same. You dress exactly the same as your classmates, even down to the color of your socks. You also have the same haircut, the same color dress shoes, and, one hopes, the same enthusiastic attitude. Only your training officers and instructors dress differently from you, and they do not particularly encourage your individuality.

For nearly every defensive tactics session, you wear the arrest and control uniform. You also wear your gun belt, baton, and unloaded handgun. Since safety is a constant issue, every arrest and control session starts with a handgun inspection to make certain no live ammunition is anywhere near your gun. Then, after a quick warm-up session involving some stretching and push-ups, you begin the course of instruction for the day.

Role Plays

A weary patrol officer once said that all of police work is just "street theater." This refers to an officer's ability to portray certain characters while out in the field. In some cases, you need to be the concerned and empathetic helper when talking to an emotionally disturbed or suicidal person. In others, you need to play the "heavy," the strict authoritarian figure, especially in the face of certain violence. And in others, you may need to act as if you aren't the slightest bit afraid, even though, inside, you may be shaking like a leaf. Police patrol work requires a great deal from its officers, and playing different roles is just part of the job. You learn to play these parts in the police academy.

As academy training begins to wind down, your training officers and instructors will begin to give you more autonomy, more leeway in your decision-making activities. You still have the discipline that is a part of academy life, but you are placed in certain situations and are asked to respond like a professional law enforcement officer. These situations are called *role plays*, and they resemble small theater skits in that they call for you to act out a part and respond to other people doing the same.

In a typical role-play scenario, you and your partner are asked to answer a radio call regarding some in-progress or after-the-fact crime. You go to the scene, meet the participants, and take the appropriate police action. During this role-play scenario, your training officers and instructors supervise your actions and grade your performance. Here, under the controlled conditions of the academy, you can make mistakes and learn from them. You don't always have that luxury in the field, where your mistakes could cost your life.

These role plays could involve something simple, like a burglary report, or something life-threatening, like a liquor store robbery or a high-risk vehicle stop. In each example, you are expected to respond just as you would if it were a real-life field problem. Now is the time to put your skills and training to use. Your success in role plays at the academy can mean continued success on the streets later.

Weapons Training

Besides the role-playing work, you spend a significant portion of your academy time at the police range, practicing with your duty firearm. Coupled with your classroom training on deadly force issues, the firearms module is critical to your development as a professional Police Officer.

Any time you are not at a police range or in some other training capacity, you are responsible for every bullet that leaves your gun. These days, it just doesn't matter that an officer says he or she "meant to do the right thing." Civil liability and deadly force go hand in hand. You must know when to draw your weapon and how to operate it safely. The instructors at the police range teach you how to do both.

As with the movements you make in the defensive tactics and arrest and control classes, safety and repetition are the keys to your success on the firing line. You must always realize that you are holding a loaded handgun, capable of delivering deadly force in a split-second. Discipline and attention to the details of safety are the rules of the police range. Rest assured that your instructors will make sure you pay attention and follow their explicit directions.

Some police agencies favor the standard .38-caliber police handgun while others favor the 9mm semi-automatic pistol. Barring damage or malfunction, you will carry the gun assigned to you for the rest of your police career. Your instructors will show you how to shoot your weapon from a variety of hand and body positions. They also teach you how to clean it, disassemble and reassemble it, and carry and draw it in a stressful situation. You will probably shoot more than 1,000 rounds before your academy training ends. Your practice includes shooting at night and in bright sunlight, shooting left-handed and right-handed, shooting from your knees and from your stomach, and shooting from behind barricades of all shapes and sizes. You also practice shooting at close range and over long distances, under timed conditions, with a partner, and on your own.

Since most law enforcement agencies use the standard police shotgun, you learn just as much about that weapon as you do about your handgun. By the end of your training, you will know how to break the shotgun down into pieces and rebuild it. Your practice includes shooting it in a variety of positions, settings, and lighting conditions, using different ammunition loads. Other agencies use police dries, involving similar training and repetition as with the police shotgun.

You will be under the watchful eyes of your training officers and firearms instructors at the shooting range. Like the role-play exercises, the police range is the place to make mistakes and learn from them. Mistakes involving a firearm that you make in the street could end in a tragedy.

Emergency Vehicle Driving

Other outdoor academy work takes place on the driving course. Since the majority of random patrol time is spent behind the wheel of a car, you need extensive training in emergency vehicle driving. Some large city law enforcement agencies average more than one police equipment accident per day. Not only is it expensive to repair these cars, but an accident often results in injuries to officers and civilians as well as the possibility of a court case against the officer and the department.

Since instructors assume you already have average or better-than-average behind-the-wheel skills, the driving portion of your academy training usually focuses on emergency techniques to help you during high-risk pursuit-type operations. This includes the following:

- "Speed" braking
- Driving in reverse
- "Slalom" turn driving
- High-speed turning
- Skid control

Because you spend so much time behind the wheel—and because a moving car can be just as much of a deadly weapon as a gun—it's essential that you appreciate your degree of responsibility every time you operate a police vehicle in a normal or emergency situation.

Field Trips

Some academies send their trainees out to various criminal justice facilities for familiarization training. Usually, the instructor for a particular subject leads a tour or arranges to have a representative take recruits around the facility. Since officers interact with other public service agencies, it helps to know where these places are located and how they operate. Your academy may schedule tours and short trips to the facilities listed below.

City and county jail. Since many city law enforcement agencies contract their custodial inmate services with the county sheriff, deputies rather than Police Officers work in these facilities. A jail tour helps new officers understand the booking and detention procedures as well as the duties and responsibilities of the sheriff's department for inmate housing, transportation, and care inside the jail.

Juvenile holding centers. Juvenile inmates are held in locations separate from those for adults. The laws and restrictions surrounding the housing of juvenile inmates are quite strict, so trainees must learn how arrest and booking procedures differ from those of adult suspects.

Family and child protective services. Many cities have social service facilities to care for abandoned, abused, or injured children. They also care for foster children, wards of the court, and other children involved in noncriminal matters.

Courthouse tour. This tour covers city or county courthouses and explains to new officers how and where the trials take place. Coupled with the classroom lectures that cover courtroom procedures, this trip takes recruits through the criminal justice cycle that begins after an arrest is made.

Coroner's office. The Coroner's Office tour supplements the classroom lectures for death cases and crime scene investigations. In some cities, police recruits watch an actual autopsy. Members of the Coroner's Office explain when an autopsy is necessary in a death case and how the evidence is collected, analyzed, and processed.

Field trips give recruits a different perspective on the criminal justice process and the social service organizations in their area by helping put some reality into academy training. They also expose recruits to available sources of help and information once they get into the field.

Graduation

The only event more important than starting the academy is finishing it. And the only day more exciting than the first one is graduation day. Here you'll see the payoff, the culmination of your hard work, the sweat, the exams, and the extra effort.

Graduation Day is an exciting time for all new officers. You receive your police badge and get to meet your Police Chief. You also get to meet the command staff. Once you have celebrated your achievement with family and friends, it is time to look ahead to the next step in your police officer career: field officer training.

Field Officer Training

There's an old saying in law enforcement: "The academy teaches you to be a Police Officer, and the streets teach you to be a cop." The distinction is an important one. The material you learned in the academy is a valuable and necessary part of your development as a Police Officer, but the only way you can earn the title of "street cop" is to hit the streets and prevent crime. Rest assured that you do not do this by yourself. For the first few months of your patrol career, you are under the wing of an experienced Field Training Officer (FTO).

Some new officers say the Field Training phase is even more stressful and difficult than the academy. This may be due to the fact that the academy is a relatively safe environment. No one can assault or injure you there, and, except for all the yelling and screaming done by the training officers, it's a fairly calm place. The streets, on the other hand, are rarely calm and hardly offer much safety, especially in some of the more vehemently anti-police neighborhoods.

Street patrol, with its hours of boredom interspersed with minutes of high excitement, offers a much more difficult learning environment than the academy. It is indeed possible to magnify the consequences of your mistakes, especially when it comes to your safety, the safety of your partner, and the safety of the people you are to protect. The ever-present news media hardly help the situation; your mistakes can now be captured for eternity on videotape. You're now in the "fishbowl," under constant public scrutiny, with many eyes upon you.

To minimize mistakes and make sure you learn to be a safe street cop, most police agencies have developed an entire program based on the training needs of new officers. Your initial meeting with your partner, the Field Training Officer, includes your introduction to the guide to street policing, the Critical Task book. Other agencies may refer to it differently, perhaps as the Patrol Guide, but whatever it's called, the book is basically a checklist of your duties and responsibilities as a patrol officer.

As its title suggests, the Critical Task book is a book filled with various critical and essential police tasks that you must identify and complete with the approval of your FTO. Your FTO will explain each of the tasks. The tasks range from checking the equipment in your police car before the beginning of a shift, to proper radio procedures, to handling domestic disturbance calls, to high-risk arrests, to issuing parking citations, to working with the computer records back at the station, and to writing complete and effective reports. If you do something as a Police Officer, you'll find it in this Critical Task book.

You may even be asked to complete "homework" assignments, ranging from map book location problems to sample arrest and crime case reports. These assignments are to be completed on your own and need to be turned in on time.

Besides teaching you how to do this demanding job safely and effectively, your FTO will document your daily activities on paper. The FTO's report includes an evaluation of your work habits, strengths, weaknesses, mistakes, and good points. Depending upon the length of time you spend with your FTO, he or she will write biweekly evaluation reports to show that you are on schedule and progressing in a timely manner.

These biweekly reports are reviewed by the training division personnel who also monitor your progress and by a number of other supervisors up the line. Rest assured that your agency wants you to make it through street patrol training and to become a full-fledged member of the department. Officers who can work alone or without constant supervision offer the best service to their department.

The length of the field training phase varies from agency to agency. Some departments put new academy graduates through a four-month program, rotating their partners, shift hours, and duty areas each month. Others cycle new officers back and forth each month between the academy classroom and the field until they graduate. Many departments send a new officer to his or her permanent duty assignment immediately upon graduation, with no area or shift rotation at all. Still other agencies assign new graduates to one station for their entire one-year (or eighteen-month) probationary period. After they clear probation, they can request a transfer to another station.

During this critical probationary period, officers must work hard and meet all of the required job performance objectives. Probationary officers have very few civil service rights and can be quickly terminated for crucial mistakes, judgment errors, or hazardous off-duty incidents. Where the veteran officer may have some protection from discharge by the civil service board, the probationary officer does not. The probationary period forces new officers to demonstrate their skills and knowledge to the police agency that hired them.

Getting through the field training phase is quite similar to succeeding in the academy: Listen, do as you're told, ask questions when necessary, and practice doing the right things over and over again. Your FTO will suggest ways to do the job more effectively. Take what you learn from each training officer you encounter in the field. Just like the academy training officers and course instructors, the Field Training Officers in your department are chosen for their police skills and their ability and desire to train new officers to function in the field. They're usually the finest officers in the department.

Listen to their suggestions, take their criticisms in stride, and learn from your mistakes. Don't rationalize your behavior with statements like, "What I really meant to do was . . ." or, "I meant to do that but didn't because . . . " Your FTO partners will try to give you the benefit of their experience. Watch how they work, observe their safety habits, and make these part of your own operating plan. Learn from them and continually tell yourself you can do this job safely and successfully.

Recruiting studies show that for every one person a police agency hires and puts through an academy, it turns away nearly ninety applicants, for one reason or another. Police work truly is a profession for an elite and qualified few. Consider yourself part of a proud and honorable calling.

Many people in this country admire law enforcement and have the utmost respect and admiration for Police Officers. Plenty of people will tell you, "You know, I always thought I could be a cop." The difference between them and you is that you put forth the effort and did what was asked. You became a law enforcement officer.

APPENDIX

Physical Fitness Course

In the law enforcement universe, much of the hiring decision is based upon a candidate's physical status. Considering the demands made upon the Police Officer's body, there is a great emphasis on physical fitness. From your own standpoint as a serious candidate, you need to devote as much attention preparing your body for the physical test as you do preparing your mind for the written exam.

To consider yourself a candidate for becoming a Police Officer, you must first determine if you are physically fit. It is wise to consult with your doctor before proceeding with the application process. Tell your doctor about the type of work you have in mind, describe the physical demands, and ask for an assessment of your potential to withstand these rigors. If your doctor foresees any potential problems, either in passing the exams or in facing the demands of the job, discuss corrective measures and remedial programs right now. Follow the medical advice you receive concerning diet and general lifestyle.

If the jurisdiction to which you are applying provides you with a description of the physical performance test you must take, describe it to your doctor. You may be able to pick up special tips from your doctor to prepare yourself to do well on your exam, such as a physical conditioning program to recommend. If not, design your own program. The following suggestions prepared by the President's Council on Physical Fitness can be used as a guide for a fitness program, or you can adapt it to a fitness program that you create based on your own needs and time requirements.

Defining Fitness

Physical fitness is to the human body what fine-tuning is to an engine. It enables us to perform up to our potential. Fitness can be described as a condition that helps us look, feel, and do our best. More specifically, it is:

> *"The ability to perform daily tasks vigorously and alertly, with energy left over for enjoying leisure-time activities and meeting emergency demands. It is the ability to endure, to bear up, to withstand stress, and to carry on in circumstances where an unfit person could not continue and is a major basis for good health and well-being."*

Physical fitness involves the performance of the heart, the lungs, and the muscles of the body. And, since what we do with our bodies also affects what we can do with our minds, fitness influences qualities such as mental alertness and emotional stability.

As you undertake your fitness program, it's important to remember that fitness is an individual quality that varies from person to person. It is influenced by age, sex, heredity, personal habits, exercise, and eating practices. You can't do anything about the first three factors. However, it is within your power to change and improve the others where needed.

KNOWING THE BASICS

Physical fitness is most easily understood by examining its components, or parts. There is widespread agreement that these five components are basic:

1. **CARDIORESPIRATORY ENDURANCE**—the ability to deliver oxygen and nutrients to tissues, and to remove wastes, over sustained periods of time. Long runs and swims are among the methods employed in measuring this component.
2. **MUSCULAR STRENGTH**—the ability of a muscle to exert force for a brief period of time. Upper-body strength, for example, can be measured by various weight-lifting exercises.
3. **MUSCULAR ENDURANCE**—the ability of a muscle, or a group of muscles, to sustain repeated contractions or to continue applying force against a fixed object. Push-ups are often used to test endurance of arm and shoulder muscles.
4. **FLEXIBILITY**—the ability to move joints and use muscles through their full range of motion. The sit-and-reach test is a good measure of flexibility of the lower back and hamstrings.
5. **BODY COMPOSITION**—the makeup of the body in terms of lean mass (muscle, bone, vital tissue, and organs) and fat mass. An optimal ratio of fat to lean mass is an indication of fitness, and the right types of exercises will help you decrease body fat and increase or maintain muscle mass.

A WORKOUT SCHEDULE

How often, how long, and how hard you exercise and what kinds of exercises you do should be determined by what you are trying to accomplish. Your goals, your present fitness level, age, health, skills, interest, and convenience are among the factors you should consider. For example, an athlete training for high-level competition would follow a different program than a person whose goals are good health and the ability to meet work and recreational needs.

Your exercise program should include something from each of the four basic fitness components described previously. Each workout should begin with a warm-up and end with a cool-down. As a general rule, space your workouts throughout the week and avoid consecutive days of hard exercise.

Here are the amounts of activity necessary for the average, healthy person to maintain a minimum level of overall fitness. Included are some of the popular exercises for each category.

- **WARM-UP**—5–10 minutes of exercises such as walking, slow jogging, knee lifts, arm circles, or trunk rotations. Low-intensity movements that simulate movements to be used in the activity can also be included in the warm-up.

- **MUSCULAR STRENGTH**—a minimum of two 20-minute sessions per week that include exercises for all the major muscle groups. Lifting weights is the most effective way to increase strength.
- **MUSCULAR ENDURANCE**—at least three 30-minute sessions each week that include exercises such as calisthenics, push-ups, sit-ups, pull-ups, and weight training for all the major muscle groups.
- **CARDIORESPIRATORY ENDURANCE**—at least three 20-minute bouts of continuous aerobic (activity requiring oxygen) rhythmic exercise each week. Popular aerobic conditioning activities include brisk walking, jogging, swimming, bicycling, rope-jumping, rowing, cross-country skiing, and some continuous action games like racquetball and handball.
- **FLEXIBILITY**—10–12 minutes of daily stretching exercises performed slowly, without a bouncing motion. This can be included after a warm-up or during a cool-down.
- **COOL-DOWN**—a minimum of 5–10 minutes of slow walking, low-level exercise, combined with stretching.

A MATTER OF PRINCIPLE

The key to selecting the right kinds of exercises for developing and maintaining each of the basic components of fitness are found in these principles:

- **SPECIFICITY**—Pick the right kind of activities to affect each component. Strength training results in specific strength changes. Also, train for the specific activity in which you're interested. For example, optimal swimming performance is best achieved when the muscles involved in swimming are trained for the movements required. It does not necessarily follow that a good runner is a good swimmer.
- **OVERLOAD**—Work hard enough, at levels that are vigorous and long enough to overload your body above its resting level, to bring about improvement.
- **REGULARITY**—You can't hoard physical fitness. At least three balanced workouts a week are necessary to maintain a desirable level of fitness.
- **PROGRESSION**—Increase the intensity, frequency, and/or duration of activity over periods of time in order to improve.

Some activities can be used to fulfill more than one of your basic exercise requirements. For example, in addition to increasing cardiorespiratory endurance, running builds muscular endurance in the legs, and swimming develops the arm, shoulder, and chest muscles. If you select the proper activities, it is possible to fit parts of your muscular endurance workout into your cardiorespiratory workout and save time.

MEASURING YOUR HEART RATE

Heart rate is widely accepted as a good method for measuring intensity during running, swimming, cycling, and other aerobic activities. Exercise that doesn't raise your heart rate to a certain level and keep it there for 20 minutes won't contribute significantly to cardiovascular fitness.

The heart rate you should maintain is called your **target heart rate**. There are several ways of arriving at this figure. One of the simplest is **maximum heart rate** (220 – age) × 70 percent. Thus, the target heart rate for a 40-year-old person would be 126.

Some methods for figuring the target rate take individual differences into consideration. Here is one method:

1. Subtract age from 220 to find **maximum heart rate.**
2. Subtract resting heart rate (see below) from maximum heart rate to determine **heart rate reserve.**
3. Take 70 percent of heart rate reserve to determine **heart rate raise.**
4. Add heart rate raise to resting heart rate to find **target rate**.

Resting heart rate should be determined by taking your pulse after sitting quietly for 5 minutes. When checking heart rate during a workout, take your pulse within 5 seconds after interrupting exercise because it starts to go down once you stop moving. Count pulse for 10 seconds and multiply by 6 to get the per-minute rate.

The Program for Women

ABOUT THE PROGRAM

The program below assumes that you have not been putting all of your muscles to any consistent use and that you are starting from close to "couch potato" status. If you are already in pretty good shape, you might be able to start more quickly. But do not overdo it. A gradual build-up makes sense.

The program starts with an orientation or "get-set" series of exercises that will allow you to bring all major muscles into use easily and painlessly.

There are then five graded levels. As you move from one to the next, you will be building toward a practical and satisfying level of fitness.

By building gradually, progressively, you will be building soundly.

WHAT THE EXERCISES ARE FOR

There are three general types of exercises:

1. **Warm-up exercises:** Stretch and limber up the muscles and speed up the action of the heart and lungs, thus preparing the body for greater exertion and reducing the possibility of unnecessary strain.
2. **Conditioning exercises:** Systematically planned to tone up abdominal, back, leg, arm, and other major muscles.
3. **Circulatory activities:** Produce contractions of large muscle groups for relatively longer periods than the conditioning exercises—to stimulate and strengthen the circulatory and respiratory systems.

The plan calls for doing ten mild exercises during the orientation period and, thereafter, the warm-up exercises and the seven conditioning exercises listed for each level. The first six exercises of the orientation program are used as warm-up exercises throughout the graded levels.

When it comes to the circulatory activities, you choose one per workout, alternately running and walking, skipping rope, and running in place. All are effective. You can choose running and walking on a pleasant day and one of the other exercises for use indoors when the weather is inclement. You can switch around for variety.

HOW YOU PROGRESS

A sound physical conditioning program should take into account your individual tolerance—your ability to execute a series of activities without undue discomfort or fatigue. It should provide for developing your tolerance by increasing the workload so you gradually become able to achieve more and more with less and less fatigue and with increasingly rapid recovery.

As you move from level to level, some exercises will be modified so they call for increased effort. Others will remain the same, but you will build more strength and stamina by increasing the number of repetitions. You will be increasing your fitness another way, as well.

At level 1, your objective is to gradually reduce, from workout to workout, the "breathing spells" between exercises until you can do the seven conditioning exercises without resting. You proceed in the same fashion with the more difficult exercises and increase repetitions at succeeding levels. The program is designed—and the progression carefully planned—to make this feasible. You are able to proceed at your own pace, competing with yourself rather than with anyone else, which is of great importance for sound conditioning.

Note: Gradually speeding up, from workout to workout, the rate at which you do each exercise will provide greater stimulation for the circulatory and respiratory systems and also help to keep your workouts short. However, the seven conditioning exercises should not be a race against time. Perform each exercise correctly to insure maximum benefit.

HOW LONG AT EACH LEVEL

Your objective at each level is to reach the point where you can do all the exercises called for, for the number of times indicated, without resting between exercises.

However, start slowly. It cannot be emphasized enough that by moving forward gradually, you will be moving forward solidly, avoiding sudden strains and excesses that could make you ache and hold you back for several days.

If you find yourself at first unable to complete any exercises—to continuously do all the repetitions called for—stop when you encounter difficulty. Rest briefly and then take up where you left off and complete the count. If you have difficulty at first, there will be less and less with succeeding workouts.

Stay at each level for at least three weeks. If you have not passed the prove-out test at the end of that time, continue at the same level until you do. The prove-out test calls for performing—in three consecutive workouts—the seven conditioning exercises without resting and satisfactorily fulfilling the requirement for one circulatory activity.

A MEASURE OF YOUR PROGRESS

You are, of course, able to observe the increase in your strength and stamina from week to week in many ways—including the increasing facility with which you do the exercises at a given level. In addition, there is a 2-minute step test you can use to measure and keep a running record of the improvement in your circulatory efficiency, one of the most important of all aspects of fitness.

The immediate response of the cardiovascular system to exercise differs markedly between well-conditioned individuals and others. The step test measures the response in terms of pulse rate taken shortly after a series of steps up and down onto a bench or chair.

Although it does not take long, the test is necessarily vigorous. Stop if you become overly fatigued while taking it. You should not try it until you have completed the orientation period.

THE STEP TEST

Use any sturdy bench or chair 15 to 17 inches in height.

Count 1—Place right foot on bench.
Count 2—Bring left foot alongside right and stand erect.
Count 3—Lower right foot to floor.
Count 4—Lower left foot to floor.

REPEAT the four-count movement 30 times a minute for 2 minutes.

THEN sit down on bench or chair for 2 minutes.

FOLLOWING the 2-minute rest, take your pulse for 30 seconds. Double the count to get the per-minute rate. (You can find the pulse by applying the middle and index finger of one hand firmly to the inside of the wrist of the other hand, on the thumb side.)

Record your score for future comparisons. In succeeding tests—about once every two weeks—you probably will find your pulse rate becoming lower as your physical condition improves.

Three important points:

1. For best results, do not engage in physical activity for at least 10 minutes before taking the test. Take it at about the same time of day and always use the same bench or chair.

2. Remember that pulse rates vary among individuals. This is an individual test. What is important is not a comparison of your pulse rate with that of anybody else, but rather a record of how your own rate is reduced as your fitness increases.

3. As you progress, the rate at which your pulse is lowered should gradually level off. This is an indication that you are approaching peak fitness.

YOUR PROGRESS RECORDS

Charts are provided for the orientation program and for each of the five levels. They list the exercises to be done and the goal for each exercise in terms of number of repetitions, distance, etc. They also provide space in which to record your progress in the following:

1. Completing the recommended 15 workouts at each level
2. Accomplishing the three prove-out workouts before moving on to a succeeding level
3. The results as you take the step test from time to time

A sample chart and progress record for one of the five levels is shown below. You do the warm-up exercises and the conditioning exercises along with one circulatory activity for each workout. Check off each workout as you complete it. The last three numbers are for the prove-out workouts, in which the seven conditioning exercises should be done without resting. Check them off as you accomplish them.

You are now ready to proceed to the next level. As you take the step test—at about two-week intervals—enter your pulse rate. When you move on to the next level, transfer the last pulse rate from the preceding level. Enter it in the margin to the left of the new progress record and circle it so it will be convenient for continuing reference.

Sample	Goal
Warm-up Exercises	Exercises 1–6 of Orientation Program
Conditioning Exercises	Uninterrupted Repetitions
1. Bend and stretch	10
2. Sprinter	6
3. Sitting stretch	15
4. Knee push-up	12
5. Sit-up (fingers laced)	10
6. Leg raiser	10 per leg
7. Flutter kick	30
Circulatory activity (choose one per workout)	
Jog-walk (jog 50, walk 50)	½ mile
Rope (skip 30 secs., rest 60 secs.)	3 series
Run in place (run 100, hop 25—2 cycles)	3 minutes
Water activities (see pages 493–494)	
Your progress record 1 2 3 4 5 6 7 8 9 10 11 12 13 14 15	
Step test (pulse)	Prove-out workouts

GETTING SET: ORIENTATION WORKOUTS

With the series of mild exercises listed in the chart that follows and described on the next two pages, you can get yourself ready—without severe aches or pains—for the progressive conditioning program.

Plan to spend a minimum of one week on preliminary conditioning. Don't hesitate to spend two or three weeks if necessary for you to limber up enough to accomplish all the exercises easily and without undue fatigue.

Note: The Police Officer physical performance test is identical for both men and women because all Police Officers must be able to perform all tasks. The demands of police work do not cater to weakness of any form. The women who can meet the physical standards take their places as full-fledged Police Officers, sharing equally in duties, responsibilities, risks, and hard work.

There are, of course, real physiological differences between men and women. Some conditioning exercises are modified in recognition of these differences. Women with the potential to pass the Police Officer physical performance test should find that the women's program described here, if followed faithfully, should prepare them well.

Orientation Program: Women	Goal
Conditioning Exercises	Repetitions
*1. Bend and stretch	10
*2. Knee lift	10 left, 10 right
*3. Wing stretcher	20
*4. Half knee bend	10
*5. Arm circles	15 each way
*6. Body bender	10 left, 10 right
7. Prone arch	10
8. Knee push-up	6
9. Head and shoulder curl	5
10. Ankle stretch	15
Circulatory Activity (choose one per workout)	
Walking	½ mile
Rope (skip 15 secs., rest 60 secs.)	3 series

* The first six exercises of the orientation program will be used as warm-up exercises throughout the graded levels.

Step Test Record: After completing the orientation program, take the 2-minute step test. Record your pulse rate here: _____. This will be the base rate with which you can make comparisons in the future.

1. Bend and Stretch

Starting position: Stand erect, feet shoulder-width apart.
Action: Count 1. Bend trunk forward and down, flexing knees. Stretch gently in attempt to touch fingers to toes or floor. Count 2. Return to starting position.
Note: Do slowly; stretch and relax at intervals rather than in rhythm.

2. Knee Lift

Starting position: Stand erect, feet together, arms at sides.
Action: Count 1. Raise left knee as high as possible, grasping leg with hands and pulling knee against body while keeping back straight. Count 2. Lower to starting position. Counts 3 and 4. Repeat with right knee.

3. Wing Stretcher

Starting position: Stand erect, elbows at shoulder height, fists clenched in front of chest.
Action: Count 1. Thrust elbows backward vigorously without arching back. Keep head erect, elbows at shoulder height. Count 2. Return to starting position.

4. Half Knee Bend

Starting position: Stand erect, hands on hips.
Action: Count 1. Bend knees halfway while extending arms forward, palms down. Count 2. Return to starting position.

5. Arm Circles

Starting position: Stand erect, arms extended sideward at shoulder height, palms up.
Action: Make small circles backward with arms. Keep head erect. Do 15 backward circles. Reverse, turn palms down, and do 15 small circles forward.

6. Body Bender

Starting position: Stand, feet shoulder-width apart, hands behind neck, fingers interlaced.
Action: Count 1. Bend trunk sideward to left as far as possible, keeping hands behind neck. Count 2. Return to starting position. Counts 3 and 4. Repeat to the right.

7. Prone Arch

Starting position: Lie face down, hands tucked under thighs.
Action: Count 1. Raise head, shoulders, and legs from floor. Count 2. Return to starting position.

8. Knee Push-up

Starting position: Lie on floor, face down, legs together, knees bent with feet raised off floor, hands on floor under shoulders, palms down.
Action: Count 1. Push upper body off floor until arms are fully extended and body is in straight line from head to knees. Count 2. Return to starting position.

9. Head and Shoulder Curl

Starting position: Lie on back, hands tucked under small of back, palms down.
Action: Count 1. Tighten abdominal muscles, lift head, and pull shoulders and elbows off floor. Hold for four seconds. Count 2. Return to starting position.

10. Ankle Stretch

Starting position: Stand on a stair, large book, or block of wood, with weight on balls of feet and heels raised.
Action: Count 1. Lower heels. Count 2. Raise heels.

CIRCULATORY ACTIVITIES

WALKING—Step off at a lively pace, swing arms, and breathe deeply.

ROPE—Any form of skipping or jumping is acceptable. Gradually increase the tempo as your skill and condition improve.

Women: Level One	Goal
Warm-up Exercises	Exercises 1–6 of Orientation Program
Conditioning Exercises	Uninterrupted Repetitions
1. Toe touch	5
2. Sprinter	8
3. Sitting stretch	10
4. Knee push-up	8
5. Sit-up (arms extended)	5
6. Leg raiser	5 each leg
7. Flutter kick	20
Circulatory Activity (choose one per workout)	
Walking (120 steps a minute)	½ mile
Rope (skip 30 sec., rest 60 sec.)	2 series
Run in place (run 50, straddle hop 10— 2 cycles)	2 minutes
Water activities (see pages 493–494)	
Your progress record 1 2 3 4 5 6 7 8 9 10 11 12 13 14 15	
Step test (pulse)	Prove-out workouts

1. Toe Touch

Starting position: Stand at attention.

Action: Count 1. Bend trunk forward and down, keeping knees straight, touching fingers to ankles. Count 2. Grasp ankles and pull down gently. Count 3. Grasp ankles and pull down gently. Count 4. Return to starting position.

2. Sprinter

Starting position: Squat, hands on floor, fingers pointed forward, left leg fully extended to rear.

Action: Count 1. Reverse position of feet in bouncing movement, bringing left foot to hands, extending right leg backward—all in one motion. Count 2. Reverse feet again, returning to starting position.

3. Sitting Stretch

Starting position: Sit, legs spread apart, hands on knees.

Action: Count 1. Bend forward at waist, extending arms as far forward as possible. Count 2. Return to starting position.

4. Knee Push-up

Starting position: Lie on floor, face down, legs together, knees bent with feet raised off floor, hands on floor under shoulders, palms down.

Action: Count 1. Push upper body off floor until arms are fully extended and body is in straight line from head to knees. Count 2. Return to starting position.

5. Sit-up (Arms Extended)

Starting position: Lie on back, legs straight and together, arms extended beyond head.

Action: Count 1. Bring arms forward over head, roll up to sitting position, sliding hands along legs, grasping ankles. Count 2. Roll back to starting position.

6. Leg Raiser

Starting position: Right side of body on floor, head resting on right arm.

Action: Lift left leg about 24 inches off floor, then lower it. Do required number of repetitions. Repeat on other side.

7. Flutter Kick

Starting position: Lie face down, hands tucked under thighs.

Action: Arch the back, bringing chest and head up, then flutter kick continuously, moving the legs 8 to 10 inches apart. Kick from hips and with knees slightly bent. Count each kick as one.

CIRCULATORY ACTIVITIES

WALKING—Maintain a pace of 120 steps per minute for a distance of ½ mile. Swing arms and breathe deeply.

ROPE—Skip or jump rope continuously using any form for 30 seconds, then rest 60 seconds. Repeat twice.

RUN IN PLACE—Raise each foot at least 4 inches off the floor and jog in place. Count one repetition each time left foot touches floor. Complete number of running steps called for in chart, then do specified number of straddle hops. Complete two cycles of alternate running and hopping for time specified on chart.

STRADDLE HOP—*Starting position:* At attention.

Action: Count 1. Swing arms sideward and upward, touching hands above head (arms straight) while simultaneously moving feet sideward and apart in a single jumping motion. Count 2. Spring back to starting position. Two counts in one hop.

Women: Level Two	Goal
Warm-up Exercises	Exercises 1–6 of Orientation Program
Conditioning Exercises	Uninterrupted Repetitions
1. Toe touch	15
2. Sprinter	12
3. Sitting stretch	15
4. Knee push-up	12
5. Sit-up (fingers laced)	10
6. Leg raiser	10 each leg
7. Flutter kick	30
Circulatory activity (choose one per workout)	
Jog-walk (jog 50, walk 50)	½ mile
Rope (skip 30 sec., rest 60 sec.)	3 series
Run in place (run 80, hop 15—2 cycles)	3 minutes
Water activities (see pages 493–494)	
Your progress record 1 2 3 4 5 6 7 8 9 10 11 12 13 14 15	
Step test (pulse)	Prove-out workouts

1. Toe Touch

Starting position: Stand at attention.
Action: Count 1. Bend trunk forward and down, keeping knees straight, touching fingers to ankles. Count 2. Grasp ankles and pull down gently. Count 3. Grasp ankles and pull down gently. Count 4. Return to starting position.

2. Sprinter

Starting position: Squat, hands on floor, fingers pointed forward, left leg fully extended to rear.
Action: Count 1. Reverse position of feet in bouncing movement, bringing left foot to hands, extending right leg backward—all in one motion. Count 2. Reverse feet again, returning to starting position.

3. Sitting Stretch

Starting position: Sit, legs spread apart, hands on knees.
Action: Count 1. Bend forward at waist, extending arms as far forward as possible. Count 2. Return to starting position.

4. Knee Push-up

Starting position: Lie on floor, face down, legs together, knees bent with feet raised off floor, hands on floor under shoulders, palms down.
Action: Count 1. Push upper body off floor until arms are fully extended and body is in straight line from head to knees. Count 2. Return to starting position.

5. Sit-up (Fingers Laced)

Starting position: Lie on back, legs straight and feet spread approximately one foot apart, fingers laced behind neck.

Action: Count 1. Curl up to sitting position and turn trunk to left. Touch right elbow to left knee. Count 2. Return to starting position. Count 3. Curl up to sitting position and turn trunk to right. Touch left elbow to right knee. Count 4. Return to starting position. Score one sit-up each time you return to starting position. Knees may be bent as necessary.

6. Leg Raiser

Starting position: Right side of body on floor, head resting on right arm.

Action: Lift left leg about 24 inches off floor, then lower it. Do required number of repetitions. Repeat on other side.

7. Flutter Kick

Starting position: Lie face down, hands tucked under thighs.

Action: Arch the back, bringing chest and head up, then flutter kick continuously, moving the legs 8 to 10 inches apart. Kick from hips with knees slightly bent. Count each kick as one.

CIRCULATORY ACTIVITIES

JOG-WALK—Jog and walk alternately for number of paces indicated on chart for distance specified.

ROPE—Skip or jump rope continuously using any form for 30 seconds and then rest 60 seconds. Repeat three times.

RUN IN PLACE—Raise each foot at least 4 inches off floor and jog in place. Count one repetition each time left foot touches floor. Complete number of running steps called for in chart, then do specified number of straddle hops. Complete two cycles of alternate running and hopping for time specified on chart.

STRADDLE HOP—*Starting position:* At attention.

Action: Count 1. Swing arms sideward and upward, touching hands above head (arms straight) while simultaneously moving feet sideward and apart in a single jumping motion. Count 2. Spring back to starting position. Two counts in one hop.

Women: Level Three	Goal
Warm-up Exercises	Exercises 1–6 of Orientation Program
Conditioning Exercises	Uninterrupted Repetitions
1. Toe touch	20
2. Sprinter	16
3. Sitting stretch (fingers laced)	15
4. Knee push-up	20
5. Sit-up (arms extended, knees up)	15
6. Leg raiser	16 each leg
7. Flutter kick	40
Circulatory Activity (choose one per workout)	
Jog-walk (jog 50, walk 50)	¾ mile
Rope (skip 45 sec., rest 30 sec.)	3 series
Run in place (run 110, hop 20—2 cycles)	4 minutes
Water activities (see pages 493–494)	
Your progress record 1 2 3 4 5 6 7 8 9 10 11 12 13 14 15	
Step test (pulse)	Prove-out workouts

1. Toe Touch

Starting position: Stand at attention.
Action: 1. Bend trunk forward and down, keeping knees straight, touching fingers to ankles. Count 2. Grasp ankles and pull down gently. Count 3. Grasp ankles and pull down gently. Count 4. Return to starting position.

2. Sprinter

Starting position: Squat, hands on floor, fingers pointed forward, left leg fully extended to rear.
Action: Count 1. Reverse position of feet in bouncing movement, bringing left foot to hands, extending right leg backward all in one motion. Count 2. Reverse feet again, returning to starting position.

3. Sitting Stretch (Fingers Laced)

Starting position: Sit, legs spread apart, fingers laced behind neck.
Action: Count 1. Bend forward at waist, reaching elbows as close to floor as possible. Count 2. Return to starting position.

4. Knee Push-up

Starting position: Lie on floor, face down, legs together, knees bent with feet raised off floor, hands on floor under shoulders, palms down.
Action: Count 1. Push upper body off floor until arms are fully flexed and body is in straight line from head to knees. Count 2. Return to starting position.

5. Sit-up (Arms Extended, Knees Up)

Starting position: Lie on back, legs straight, arms extended overhead.
Action: Count 1. Sit up, reaching forward with arms encircling knees while pulling them tightly to chest. Count 2. Return to starting position. Do this exercise rhythmically, without breaks in the movement.

6. Leg Raiser

Starting position: Right side of body on floor, head resting on right arm.
Action: Lift left leg about 24 inches off floor, then lower it. Do required number of repetitions. Repeat on other side.

7. Flutter Kick

Starting position: Lie face down, hands tucked under thighs.
Action: Arch the back, bringing chest and head up. Then flutter kick continuously, moving the legs 8 to 10 inches apart. Kick from hips with knees slightly bent. Count each kick as one.

CIRCULATORY ACTIVITIES

JOG-WALK—Jog and walk alternately for number of paces indicated on chart for distance specified.
ROPE—Skip or jump rope continuously using any form for 45 seconds and then rest 30 seconds. Repeat three times.
RUN IN PLACE—Raise each foot at least 4 inches off floor and jog in place. Count one repetition each time left foot touches floor. Complete number of running steps called for in chart, then do specified number of straddle hops. Complete two cycles of alternate running and hopping for time specified on chart.
STRADDLE HOP—*Starting position:* At attention.
Action: Count 1. Swing arms sideward and upward, touching hands above head (arms straight) while simultaneously moving feet sideward and apart in a single jumping motion. Count 2. Spring back to starting position. Two counts in one hop.

Women: Level Four	Goal
Warm-up Exercises	Exercises 1–6 of Orientation Program
Conditioning Exercises	Uninterrupted Repetitions
1. Toe touch (twist and bend)	15 each side
2. Sprinter	20
3. Sitting stretch (alternate)	20
4. Push-up	8
5. Sit-up (arms crossed, knees bent)	20
6. Leg raiser (whip)	10 each leg
7. Prone arch (arms extended)	15
Circulatory Activity (choose one per workout)	
Jog-walk (jog 100, walk 50)	1 mile
Rope (skip 60 sec., rest 30 sec.)	3 series
Run in place (run 145, hop 25—2 cycles)	5 minutes
Water activities (see pages 493–494)	
Your progress record 1 2 3 4 5 6 7 8	9 10 11 12 13 14 15
Step test (pulse)	Prove-out workouts

1. Toe Touch (Twist and Bend)

Starting position: Stand, feet shoulder-width apart, arms extended over head, thumbs interlocked.

Action: Count 1. Twist trunk to right and touch floor inside right foot with fingers of both hands. Count 2. Touch floor outside toes of right foot. Count 3. Touch floor outside heel of right foot. Count 4. Return to starting position, sweeping trunk and arms upward in a wide arc. On the next four counts, repeat action to left side.

2. Sprinter

Starting position: Squat, hands on floor, fingers pointed forward, left leg fully extended to rear.

Action: Count 1. Reverse position of feet in bouncing movement, bringing left foot to hands, extending right leg backward—all in one motion. Count 2. Reverse feet again, returning to starting position.

3. Sitting Stretch (Alternate)

Starting position: Sit, legs spread apart, fingers laced behind neck, elbows back.

Action: Count 1. Bend forward to left, touching forehead to left knee. Count 2. Return to starting position. Counts 3 and 4. Repeat to right. Score one repetition each time you return to starting position. Knees may be bent if necessary.

4. Push-up

Starting position: Lie on floor, face down, legs together, hands on floor under shoulders with fingers pointing straight ahead.

Action: Count 1. Push body off floor by extending arms so that weight rests on hands and toes. Count 2. Lower the body until chest touches floor.

Note: Body should be kept straight; buttocks should not be raised; abdomen should not sag.

5. Sit-up (Arms Crossed, Knees Bent)

Starting position: Lie on back, arms crossed on chest, hands grasping opposite shoulders, knees bent to right angle, feet flat on floor.

Action: Count 1. Curl up to sitting position. Count 2. Return to starting position.

6. Leg Raiser (Whip)

Starting position: Right side of body on floor, right arm supporting head.

Action: Whip left leg up and down rapidly lifting as high as possible off the floor. Count each whip as one. Reverse position and whip right leg up and down.

7. Prone Arch (Arms Extended)

Starting position: Lie face down, legs straight and together, arms extended to sides at shoulder level.

Action: Count 1. Arch the back, bringing arms, chest, and head up, and raising legs as high as possible. Count 2. Return to starting position.

CIRCULATORY ACTIVITIES

JOG-WALK—Jog and walk alternately for number of paces indicated on chart for distance specified.

ROPE—Skip or jump rope continuously using any form for 60 seconds and then rest 30 seconds. Repeat three times.

RUN IN PLACE—Raise each foot at least 4 inches off floor and jog in place. Count one repetition each time left foot touches floor. Complete number of running steps called for in chart, then do specified number of straddle hops. Complete two cycles of alternate running and hopping for time specified on chart.

STRADDLE HOP—*Starting position:* At attention.

Action: Count 1. Swing arms sideward and upward, touching hands above head (arms straight) while simultaneously moving feet sideward and apart in a single jumping motion. Count 2. Spring back to starting position. Two counts in one hop.

Women: Level Five	Goal
Warm-up Exercises	Exercises 1–6 of Orientation Program
Conditioning Exercises	Uninterrupted Repetitions
1. Toe touch (twist and bend)	25 each side
2. Sprinter	24
3. Sitting stretch (alternate)	26
4. Push-up	15
5. Sit-up (fingers laced, knees bent)	25
6. Leg raiser (on extended arm)	10 each side
7. Prone arch (fingers laced)	25
Circulatory Activity (choose one per workout)	
Jog-run	1 mile
Rope (skip 2 min., rest 45 sec.)	2 series
Run in place (run 180, hop 30—2 cycles)	6 minutes
Water Activities (see pages 493–494)	
Your progress record 1 2 3 4 5 6 7 8	9 10 11 12 13 14 15
Step test (pulse)	Prove-out workouts

1. Toe Touch (Twist and Bend)

Starting position: Stand, feet shoulder-width apart, arms extended over head, thumbs inter-locked.

Action: Count 1. Twist trunk to right and touch floor inside right foot with fingers of both hands. Count 2. Touch floor outside toes of right foot. Count 3. Touch floor outside heel of right foot. Count 4. Return to starting position, sweeping trunk and arms upward in a wide arc. On the next four counts, repeat action to left side.

2. Sprinter

Starting position: Squat, hands on floor, fingers pointed forward, left leg fully extended to rear.

Action: Count 1. Reverse position of feet in bouncing movement, bringing left foot to hands, extending right leg backward—all in one motion. Count 2. Reverse feet again, returning to starting position.

3. Sitting Stretch (Alternate)

Starting position: Sit, legs spread apart, fingers behind neck, elbows back.

Action: Count 1. Bend forward to left, touching forehead to left knee. Count 2. Return to starting position. Counts 3 and 4. Repeat to right. Score one repetition each time you return to starting position. Knees may be bent if necessary.

4. Push-up

Starting position: Lie on floor, face down, legs together, hands on floor under shoulders with fingers pointing straight ahead.
Action: Count 1. Push body off floor by extending arms so that weight rests on hands and toes. Count 2. Lower the body until chest touches floor.
Note: Body should be kept straight; buttocks should not be raised; abdomen should not sag.

5. Sit-up (Fingers Laced, Knees Bent)

Starting position: Lie on back, fingers laced behind neck, knees bent, feet flat on floor.
Action: Count 1. Sit up, turn trunk to right, touch left elbow to right knee. Count 2. Return to starting position. Count 3. Sit up, turn trunk to left, touch right elbow to left knee. Count 4. Return to starting position. Score one repetition each time you return to starting position.

6. Leg Raiser (On Extended Arm)

Starting position: Body rigidly supported by extended right arm and foot. Left arm is held behind head.
Action: Count 1. Raise left leg high. Count 2. Return to starting position slowly. Repeat on other side. Do required number of repetitions.

7. Prone Arch (Fingers Laced)

Starting position: Lie face down, fingers laced behind neck.
Action: Count 1. Arch the back, legs, and chest off floor. Count 2. Extend arms fully forward. Count 3. Return hands to behind neck. Count 4. Flatten body to floor.

CIRCULATORY ACTIVITIES

JOG-RUN—Jog and run alternately for distance specified on chart.
ROPE—Skip or jump rope continuously using any form for 2 minutes and then rest 45 seconds. Repeat twice.
RUN IN PLACE—Raise each foot at least 4 inches off floor and jog in place. Count one repetition each time left foot touches floor. Complete number of running steps called for in chart, then do specified number of straddle hops. Complete two cycles of alternate running and hopping in time specified on the chart.
STRADDLE HOP—*Starting position:* At attention.
Action: Count 1. Swing arms sideward and upward, touching hands above head (arms straight) while simultaneously moving feet sideward and apart in a single jumping motion. Count 2. Spring back to starting position. Two counts in one hop.

The Program for Men

ABOUT THE PROGRAM

The program assumes you have not—recently and consistently—been exposed to vigorous, all-around physical activity. This could be true even if you play golf once or twice a week or engage in some other sport; no one sport provides for balanced development of all parts of the body.

The plan starts with an orientation or "get-set" series of mild exercises to limber up all major muscle groups and help assure a painless transition.

There are then five graded levels. As you move up from one level to the next, you build toward a practical and satisfactory level of fitness. By building gradually—progressively—you will be building soundly.

WHAT THE EXERCISES ARE FOR

There are three general types of exercises:

1. **Warm-up exercises:** Stretch and limber up the muscles and speed up the action of the heart and lungs, thus preparing the body for greater exertion and reducing the possibility of unnecessary strain.
2. **Conditioning exercises:** Systematically planned to tone up abdominal, back, leg, arm, and other major muscles.
3. **Circulatory activities:** Produce contractions of large muscle groups for relatively longer periods than the conditioning exercises—to stimulate and strengthen the circulatory and respiratory systems.

The plan calls for doing ten mild exercises during the orientation period and, thereafter, the warm-up exercises and the seven conditioning exercises listed for each level. The first six exercises of the orientation program are used as warm-up exercises throughout the graded levels.

When it comes to the circulatory activities, you choose one per workout, alternately running and walking, skipping rope, and running in place. All are effective. You can switch around for variety.

HOW YOU PROGRESS

Right now, you have limited tolerance for exercise; you can do just so much without discomfort and fatigue. A sound conditioning program should gradually stretch your tolerance. It should give unused or little-used muscles moderate tasks at first, then make the tasks increasingly more demanding so you become able to achieve more and more with less and less fatigue and with increasingly rapid recovery.

As you move from level to level, some exercises will be modified so they call for more effort. Others will remain the same, but you build strength and stamina by increasing the number of repetitions.

At level 1, your objective is to gradually reduce, from workout to workout, the "breathing spells" between exercises until you can do the seven conditioning exercises without resting. You proceed in the same fashion with the more difficult exercises and increase repetitions at succeeding levels.

The program is designed—the progression carefully planned—to make this feasible. You are able to proceed at your own pace, competing with yourself rather than with anyone else, which is of great importance for sound conditioning.

Note: Gradually speeding up, from workout to workout, the rate at which you do each exercise will provide greater stimulation for the circulatory and respiratory systems and also help to keep your workouts short. However, the seven conditioning exercises should not be a race against time. Perform each exercise completely to insure maximum benefit.

WHEN AND HOW OFTEN TO WORK OUT

To be most beneficial, exercise should become part of your regular daily routine—as much as bathing, shaving, and dressing. Five workouts a week are called for throughout the program.

You can choose any time that is convenient. Preferably, it should be the same time every day—but it does not matter whether it's first thing in the morning, before dinner in the evening, just before retiring, or any other time.

The hour just before the evening meal is a popular time for exercise. The later afternoon workout provides a welcome change of pace at the end of the work day and helps dissolve the day's worries and tensions. Another popular time to work out is early morning, before the work day begins. Advocates of the early start say it makes them more alert and energetic on the job.

Among the factors you should consider in developing your workout schedule are personal preference, job and family responsibilities, availability of exercise facilities, and weather. It's important to schedule your workouts for a time when there is little chance that you will have to cancel or interrupt them because of other demands on your time.

You should not exercise strenuously during extremely hot, humid weather or within 2 hours after eating. Heat and/or digestion both make heavy demands on the circulatory system and in combination with exercise can be an overtaxing double load.

YOUR PROGRESS RECORDS

Charts are provided for the orientation program and for each of the five levels. They list the exercises to be done and the goal for each exercise in terms of number of repetitions, distance, etc.

They also provide space in which to record your progress in the following:

1. Completing the recommended 15 workouts at each level
2. Accomplishing the three prove-out workouts before moving on to a succeeding level
3. The results as you take the step test from time to time

A sample chart and progress record for one of the five levels is shown below. You do the warm-up exercises and the conditioning exercises along with one circulatory activity for each workout.

Check off each workout as you complete it. The last three numbers are for the prove-out workouts, in which the seven conditioning exercises should be done without resting. Check them off as you accomplish them. You are now ready to proceed to the next level.

As you take the step test—at about two-week intervals—enter your pulse rate. When you move on to the next level, transfer the last pulse rate from the preceding level. Enter it in the margin to the left of the new progress record and circle it so it will be convenient for continuing reference.

Sample	Goal
Warm-up Exercises	Exercises 1–6 of Orientation Program
Conditioning Exercises	Uninterrupted Repetitions
1. Toe touch	20
2. Sprinter	16
3. Sitting stretch	18
4. Push-up	10
5. Sit-up (fingers laced)	15
6. Leg raiser	16 each leg
7. Flutter kick	40
Circulatory Activity (choose one per workout)	
Jog-walk (jog 100, walk 100)	1 mile
Rope (skip 60 sec., rest 60 sec.)	3 series
Run in place (run 95, hop 15—2 cycles)	3 minutes
Water activities (see pages 493–494)	
Your progress record 1 2 3 4 5 6 7 8 9 10 11 12 13 14 15	
Step test (pulse)	Prove-out workouts

GETTING SET: ORIENTATION WORKOUTS

With the series of preliminary exercises listed in the chart that follows and described on the next two pages, you can get yourself ready—without severe aches or pains—for the progressive conditioning program.

Even if these preliminary exercises should seem easy—and they are deliberately meant to be mild—plan to spend a minimum of one week with them. Do not hesitate to spend two weeks or even three if necessary for you to limber up enough to accomplish all the exercises easily and without undue fatigue.

Orientation Program: Men	Goal
Conditioning Exercises	Repetitions
*1. Bend and stretch	10
*2. Knee lift	10 left, 10 right
*3. Wing stretcher	20
*4. Half knee bend	10
*5. Arm circles	15 each way
*6. Body bender	10 left, 10 right
7. Prone arch	10
8. Knee push-up	6
9. Head and shoulder curl	5
10. Ankle stretch	15
Circulatory activity (choose one per workout)	
Walking	½ mile
Rope (skip 15 sec., rest 60 sec.)	3 series

* The first six exercises of the orientation program will be used as warm-up exercises throughout the graded levels.

Step Test Record: After completing the orientation program, take the 2-minute step test. Record your pulse rate here:_____. This will be the base rate with which you can make comparisons in the future.

1. Bend and Stretch

Starting position: Stand erect, feet shoulder-width apart.
Action: Count 1. Bend trunk forward and down, flexing knees. Stretch gently in attempt to touch fingers to toes or floor. Count 2. Return to starting position.
Note: Do slowly; stretch and relax at intervals rather than in rhythm.

2. Knee Lift

Starting position: Stand erect, feet together, arms at sides.
Action: Count 1. Raise left knee as high as possible, grasping leg with hands and pulling knee against body while keeping back straight. Count 2. Lower to starting position. Counts 3 and 4. Repeat with right knee.

3. Wing Stretcher

Starting position: Stand erect, elbows at shoulder height, fists clenched in front of chest.
Action: Count 1. Thrust elbows backward vigorously without arching back. Keep head erect, elbows at shoulder height. Count 2. Return to starting position.

4. Half Knee Bend

Starting position: Stand erect, hands on hips.
Action: Count 1. Bend knees halfway while extending arms forward, palms down. Count 2. Return to starting position.

5. Arm Circles

Starting position: Stand erect, arms extended sideward at shoulder height, palms up.
Action: Make small circles backward with arms. Keep head erect. Do 15 backward circles. Reverse: turn palms down and do 15 small circles forward.

6. Body Bender

Starting position: Stand, feet shoulder-width apart, hands behind neck, fingers interlaced.
Action: Count 1. Bend trunk sideward to left as far as possible, keeping hands behind neck. Count 2. Return to starting position. Counts 3 and 4. Repeat to the right.

7. Prone Arch

Starting position: Lie face down, hands tucked under thighs.
Action: Count 1. Raise head, shoulders, and legs from floor. Count 2. Return to starting position.

8. Knee Push-up

Starting position: Lie on floor, face down, legs together, knees bent with feet raised off floor, hands on floor under shoulders, palms down.
Action: Count 1. Push upper body off floor until arms are fully extended and body is in straight line from head to knees. Count 2. Return to starting position.

9. Head and Shoulder Curl

Starting position: Lie on back, hands tucked under small of back, palms down.
Action: Count 1. Tighten abdominal muscles, lift head, and pull shoulders and elbows up off floor. Hold for four seconds. Count 2. Return to starting position.

10. Ankle Stretch

Starting position: Stand on a stair, large book, or block of wood, with weight on balls of feet and heels raised.
Action: Count 1. Lower heels. Count 2. Raise heels.

CIRCULATORY ACTIVITIES

WALKING—Step off at a lively pace, swing arms, and breathe deeply.

ROPE—Any form of skipping or jumping is acceptable. Gradually increase the tempo as your skill and condition improve.

Men: Level One	Goal
Warm-up Exercises	Exercises 1–6 of Orientation Program
Conditioning Exercises	Uninterrupted Repetitions
1. Toe touch	10
2. Sprinter	12
3. Sitting stretch	12
4. Push-up	4
5. Sit-up (arms extended)	5
6. Leg raiser	12 each leg
7. Flutter kick	30
Circulatory Activity (choose one per workout)	
Walking (120 steps a minute)	1 mile
Rope (skip 30 sec., rest 30 sec.)	2 series
Run in place (run 60, hop 10—2 cycles)	2 minutes
Water activities (see pages 493–494)	
Your progress record 1 2 3 4 5 6 7 8 9 10 11 12 13 14 15	
Step test (pulse)	Prove-out workouts

1. Toe Touch

Starting position: Stand at attention.

Action: Count 1. Bend trunk forward and down keeping knees straight, touching fingers to ankles. Count 2. Grasp ankles and pull down gently. Count 3. Grasp ankles and pull down gently. Count 4. Return to starting position.

2. Sprinter

Starting position: Squat, hands on floor, fingers pointed forward, left leg fully extended to rear.

Action: Count 1. Reverse position of feet in bouncing movement, bringing left foot to hands and extending right leg backward—all in one motion. Count 2. Reverse feet again, returning to starting position.

3. Sitting Stretch

Starting position: Sit, legs spread apart, hands on knees.

Action: Count 1. Bend forward at waist, extending arms as far forward as possible. Count 2. Return to starting position.

4. Push-up

Starting position: Lie on floor, face down, legs together, hands on floor under shoulders with fingers pointing straight ahead.

Action: Count 1. Push body off floor by extending arms, so that weight rests on hands and toes. Count 2. Lower the body until chest touches floor.

Note: Body should be kept straight; buttocks should not be raised; abdomen should not sag.

5. Sit-up (Arms Extended)

Starting position: Lie on back, legs straight and together, arms extended beyond head.

Action: Count 1. Bring arms forward over head and roll up to sitting position, sliding hands along legs, grasping ankles. Count 2. Roll back to starting position.

6. Leg Raiser

Starting position: Right side of body on floor, head resting on right arm.

Action: Lift left leg about 24 inches off floor, then lower it. Do required number of repetitions. Repeat on other side.

7. Flutter Kick

Starting position: Lie face down, hands tucked under thighs.

Action: Arch the back, bringing chest and head up, then flutter kick continuously, moving the legs 8 to 10 inches apart. Kick from hips with knees slightly bent. Count each kick as one.

CIRCULATORY ACTIVITIES

WALKING—Maintain a pace of 120 steps per minute for a distance of 1 mile. Swing arms and breathe deeply.

ROPE—Skip or jump rope continuously using any form for 30 seconds and then rest 30 seconds. Repeat twice.

RUN IN PLACE—Raise each foot at least 4 inches off floor and jog in place. Count one repetition each time left foot touches floor. Complete the number of running steps called for in chart, then do specified number of straddle hops. Complete two cycles of alternate running and hopping for time specified on chart.

STRADDLE HOP—*Starting position:* At attention.

Action: Count 1. Swing arms sideward and upward, touching hands above head (arms straight) while simultaneously moving feet sideward and apart in a single jumping motion. Count 2. Spring back to starting position. Two counts in one hop.

Men: Level Two	Goal
Warm-up Exercises	Exercises 1–6 of Orientation Program
Conditioning Exercises	Uninterrupted Repetitions
1. Toe touch	20
2. Sprinter	16
3. Sitting stretch	18
4. Push-up	10
5. Sit-up (fingers laced)	20
6. Leg raiser	16 each leg
7. Flutter kick	40
Circulatory Activity (choose one per workout)	
Jog-walk (jog 100, walk 100)	1 mile
Rope (skip 1 min., rest 1 min.)	3 series
Run in place (run 95, hop 15—2 cycles)	3 minutes
Water activities (see pages 493–494)	
Your progress record 1 2 3 4 5 6 7 8 9 10 11 12 13 14 15	
Step test (pulse)	Prove-out workouts

1. Toe Touch

Starting position: Stand at attention.
Action: Count 1. Bend trunk forward and down keeping knees straight, touching fingers to ankles. Count 2. Grasp ankles and pull down gently. Count 3. Grasp ankles and pull down gently. Count 4. Return to starting position.

2. Sprinter

Starting position: Squat, hands on floor, fingers pointed forward, left leg fully extended to rear. *Action:* Count 1. Reverse position of feet in bouncing movement, bringing left foot to hands, extending right leg backward—all in one motion. Count 2. Reverse feet again, returning to starting position.

3. Sitting Stretch

Starting position: Sit, legs apart, hands on knees.
Action: Count 1. Bend forward at waist, extending arms as far forward as possible. Count 2. Return to starting position.

4. Push-up

Starting position: Lie on floor, face down, legs together, hands on floor under shoulders with fingers pointing straight ahead.
Action: Count 1. Push body off floor by extending arms, so that weight rests on hands and toes. Count 2. Lower the body until chest touches floor.
Note: Body should be kept straight; buttocks should not be raised; abdomen should not sag.

5. Sit-up (Fingers Laced)

Starting position: Lie on back, legs straight and feet spread approximately 1 foot apart, fingers laced behind neck.

Action: Count 1. Curl up to sitting position and turn trunk to left. Touch right elbow to left knee. Count 2. Return to starting position. Count 3. Curl up to sitting position and turn trunk to right. Touch left elbow to right knee. Count 4. Return to starting position. Score one sit-up each time you return to starting position. Knees may be bent as necessary.

6. Leg Raiser

Starting position: Right side of body on floor, head resting on right arm.

Action: Lift left leg about 24 inches off floor, then lower it. Do required number of repetitions. Repeat on other side.

7. Flutter Kick

Starting position: Lie face down, hands tucked under thighs.

Action: Arch the back, bringing chest and head up, then flutter kick continuously, moving the legs 8 to 10 inches apart. Kick from hips with knees slightly bent. Count each kick as one repetition.

CIRCULATORY ACTIVITIES

JOG-WALK—Jog and walk alternately for number of paces indicated on chart for distance specified.

ROPE—Skip or jump rope continuously using any form for 60 seconds, then rest 60 seconds. Repeat five times.

RUN IN PLACE—Raise each foot at least 4 inches off floor and jog in place. Count one repetition each time left foot touches floor. Complete number of running steps called for in chart, then do specified number of straddle hops. Complete two cycles of alternate running and hopping for time specified on chart.

STRADDLE HOP—*Starting position:* At attention.

Action: Count 1. Swing arms sideward and upward, touching hands above head (arms straight) while simultaneously moving feet sideward and apart in a single jumping motion. Count 2. Spring back to starting position. Two counts in one hop.

Men: Level Three	Goal
Warm-up Exercises	Exercises 1–6 of Orientation Program
Conditioning Exercises	Uninterrupted Repetitions
1. Toe touch	30
2. Sprinter	20
3. Sitting stretch (fingers laced)	18
4. Push-up	20
5. Sit-up (arms extended, knees up)	30
6. Leg raiser	20 each leg
7. Flutter kick	50
Circulatory Activity (choose one per workout)	
Jog-walk (jog 200, walk 100)	1½ miles
Rope (skip 1 min., rest 1 min.)	5 series
Run in place (run 135, hop 20—2 cycles)	4 minutes
Water activity (see pages 493–494)	
Your progress record 1 2 3 4 5 6 7 8 9 10 11 12 13 14 15	
Step test (pulse)	Prove-out workouts

1. Toe Touch

Starting position: Stand at attention.

Action: Count 1. Bend trunk forward and down keeping knees straight, touching fingers to ankles. Count 2. Grasp ankles and pull down gently. Count 3. Grasp ankles and pull down gently. Count 4. Return to starting position.

2. Sprinter

Starting position: Squat, hands on floor, fingers pointed forward, left leg fully extended to rear.

Action: Count 1. Reverse position of feet in bouncing movement, bringing left foot to hands, extending right leg backward—all in one motion. Count 2. Reverse feet again, returning to starting position.

3. Sitting Stretch (Fingers Laced)

Starting position: Sit, legs spread apart, fingers laced behind neck, elbows back.

Action: Count 1. Bend forward at waist, reaching elbows as close to floor as possible. Count 2. Return to starting position.

4. Push-up

Starting position: Lie on floor, face down, legs together, hands on floor under shoulders with fingers pointing straight ahead.

Action: Count 1. Push body off floor by extending arms, so that weight rests on hands and toes. Count 2. Lower the body until chest touches floor.

Note: Body should be kept straight; buttocks should not be raised; abdomen should not sag.

5. Sit-up (Arms Extended, Knees Up)

Starting position: Lie on back, legs straight, arms extended overhead.
Action: Count 1. Sit up, reaching forward with arms encircling knees while pulling them tightly to chest. Count 2. Return to starting position. Do this exercise rhythmically, without breaks in the movement.

6. Leg Raiser

Starting position: Right side of body on floor, head resting on right arm.
Action: Lift left leg about 24 inches off floor, then lower it. Do required number of repetitions. Repeat on other side.

7. Flutter Kick

Starting position: Lie face down, hands tucked under thighs.
Action: Arch the back, bringing chest and head up, then flutter kick continuously, moving the legs 8 to 10 inches apart. Kick from hips with knees slightly bent. Count each kick as one repetition.

CIRCULATORY ACTIVITIES

JOG-WALK—Jog and walk alternately for number of paces indicated on chart for distance specified.
ROPE—Skip or jump rope continuously using any form for 60 seconds and then rest 60 seconds. Repeat five times.
RUN IN PLACE—Raise each foot at least 4 inches off floor and jog in place. Count one repetition each time left foot touches floor. Complete number of running steps called for in chart, then do specified number of straddle hops. Complete two cycles of alternate running and hopping for time specified on chart.
STRADDLE HOP—*Starting position:* At attention.
Action: Count 1. Swing arms sideward and upward, touching hands above head (arms straight) while simultaneously moving feet sideward and apart in a single jumping motion. Count 2. Spring back to starting position. Two counts in one hop.

Men: Level Four	Goal
Warm-up Exercises	Exercises 1–6 of Orientation Program
Conditioning Exercises	Uninterrupted Repetitions
1. Toe touch (twist and bend)	20 each side
2. Sprinter	28
3. Sitting stretch (alternate)	24
4. Push-up	30
5. Sit-up (arms crossed, knees bent)	30
6. Leg raiser (whip)	20 each leg
7. Prone arch (arms extended)	20
Circulatory Activity (choose one per workout)	
Jog	1 mile
Rope (skip 90 sec., rest 30 sec.)	3 series
Run in place (run 180, hop 25—2 cycles)	5 minutes
Water activity (see pages 493–494)	
Your progress record 1 2 3 4 5 6 7 8 9 10 11 12 13 14 15	
Step test (pulse)	Prove-out workouts

1. Toe Touch (Twist and Bend)

Starting position: Stand, feet shoulder-width apart, arms extended overhead, thumbs interlocked.

Action: Count 1. Twist trunk to right and touch floor inside right foot with fingers of both hands. Count 2. Touch floor outside toes of right foot. Count 3. Touch floor outside heel of right foot. Count 4. Return to starting position, sweeping trunk and arms upward in a wide arc. On the next four counts, repeat action to left side.

2. Sprinter

Starting position: Squat, hands on floor, fingers pointed forward, left leg fully extended to rear.

Action: Count 1. Reverse position of feet in bouncing movement, bringing left foot to hands, extending right leg backward—all in one motion. Count 2. Reverse feet again, returning to starting position.

3. Sitting Stretch (Alternate)

Starting position: Sit, legs spread apart, fingers laced behind neck, elbows back.

Action: Count 1. Bend forward to left, touching forehead to left knee. Count 2. Return to starting position. Counts 3 and 4. Repeat to right. Score one repetition each time you return to starting position. Knees may be bent if necessary.

4. Push-up

Starting position: Lie on floor, face clown, legs together, hands on floor under shoulders with fingers pointing straight ahead.

Action: Count 1. Push body off floor by extending arms, so that weight rests on hands and toes. Count 2. Lower the body until chest touches floor.

Note: Body should be kept straight, buttocks should not be raised, abdomen should not sag.

5. Sit-up (Arms Crossed, Knees Bent)

Starting position: Lie on back, arms crossed on chest, hands grasping opposite shoulders, knees bent to right angle, feet flat on floor.

Action: Count 1. Curl up to sitting position. Count 2. Return to starting position.

6. Leg Raiser (Whip)

Starting position: Right side of body on floor, right arm supporting head.

Action: Whip left leg up and down rapidly, lifting as high as possible off the floor. Count each whip as one. Reverse position and whip right leg up and down.

7. Prone Arch (Arms Extended)

Starting position: Lie face down, legs straight and together, arms extended to sides at shoulder level.

Action: Count 1. Arch the back, bringing arms, chest, and head up, and raising legs as high as possible. Count 2. Return to starting position.

CIRCULATORY ACTIVITIES

JOG—Jog continuously for 1 mile.

ROPE—Skip or jump rope continuously using any form for 90 seconds and then rest for 30 seconds. Repeat three times.

RUN IN PLACE—Raise each foot at least 4 inches off the floor and jog in place. Count one repetition each time left foot touches floor. Complete number of running steps called for in chart, then do specified number of straddle hops. Complete two cycles of alternate running and hopping in time specified on chart.

STRADDLE HOP—*Starting position:* At attention.

Action: Count 1. Swing arms sideward and upward, touching hands above head (arms straight) while simultaneously moving feet sideward and apart in a single jumping motion. Count 2. Spring back to starting position. Two counts in one hop.

Men: Level Five	Goal
Warm-up Exercises	Exercises 1–6 of Orientation Program
Conditioning Exercises	Uninterrupted Repetitions
1. Toe touch (twist and bend)	30 each side
2. Sprinter	36
3. Sitting stretch (alternate)	30
4. Push-up	50
5. Sit-up (fingers laced, knees bent)	40
6. Leg raiser (on extended arm)	20 each side
7. Prone arch (fingers laced)	30
Circulatory Activity (choose one per workout)	
Jog-run	3 miles
Rope (skip 2 min., rest 30 sec.)	3 series
Run in place (run 216, hop 30—2 cycles)	6 minutes
Water activity (see pages 493–494)	
Your progress record 1 2 3 4 5 6 7 8 9 10 11 12 13 14 15	
Step test (pulse)	Prove-out workouts

1. Toe Touch (Twist and Bend)

Starting position: Stand, feet shoulder-width apart, arms extended overhead, thumbs interlocked.

Action: Count 1. Twist trunk to right and touch floor inside right foot with fingers of both hands. Count 2. Touch floor outside toes of right foot. Count 3. Touch floor outside heel of right foot. Count 4. Return to starting position, sweeping trunk and arms upward in a wide arc. On the next four counts, repeat action to left side.

2. Sprinter

Starting position: Squat, hands on floor, fingers pointed forward, left leg fully extended to rear.

Action: Count 1. Reverse position of feet in bouncing movement, bringing left foot to hands and extending right leg backward—all in one motion. Count 2. Reverse feet again, returning to starting position.

3. Sitting Stretch (Alternate)

Starting position: Sit, legs spread apart, fingers laced behind neck, elbows back.

Action: Count 1. Bend forward to left, touching forehead to left knee. Count 2. Return to starting position. Counts 3 and 4. Repeat to right. Score one repetition each time you return to starting position. Knees may be bent if necessary.

4. Push-up

Starting position: Lie on floor, face down, legs together, hands on floor under shoulders with fingers pointing straight ahead.

Action: Count 1. Push body off floor by extending arms so that weight rests on hands and toes. Count 2. Lower body until chest touches floor.

Note: Body should be kept straight; buttocks should not be raised; abdomen should not sag.

5. Sit-up (Fingers Laced, Knees Bent)

Starting position: Lie on back, fingers laced behind neck, knees bent, feet flat on floor.

Action: Count 1. Sit up, turn trunk to right, touch left elbow to right knee. Count 2. Return to starting position. Count 3. Sit up, turn trunk to left, touch right elbow to left knee. Count 4. Return to starting position. Score one repetition each time you return to starting position.

6. Leg Raiser (On Extended Arm)

Starting position: Body rigidly supported by extended right arm and foot. Left arm is held behind head.

Action: Count 1. Raise left leg high. Count 2. Return to starting position slowly. Do required number of repetitions. Repeat on other side.

7. Prone Arch (Fingers Laced)

Starting position: Lie face down, fingers laced behind neck.

Action: Count 1. Arch back, legs, and chest off floor. Count 2. Extend arms forward. Count 3. Return hands to behind neck. Count 4. Flatten body to floor.

CIRCULATORY ACTIVITIES

JOG RUN—Alternately jog and run the specified distance. Attempt to increase the proportion of time spent running in each succeeding workout.

ROPE—Skip or jump rope continuously using any form for two minutes and then rest 30 seconds. Repeat three times.

RUN IN PLACE—Raise each foot at least 4 inches off floor and jog in place. Count one repetition each time left foot touches floor. Complete number of running steps called for in chart, then do specified number of straddle hops. Complete two cycles of alternate running and hopping for time specified on the chart.

STRADDLE HOP—*Starting position:* At attention.

Action: Count 1. Swing arms sideward and upward, touching hands above head (arms straight) while simultaneously moving feet sideward and apart in a single jumping motion. Count 2. Spring back to starting position. Two counts in one hop.

STAYING FIT

Once you have reached the level of conditioning you have chosen for yourself, you will want to maintain your fitness. To do this, continue the workouts at that level.

While it is possible to maintain fitness with three workouts a week, ideally, exercise should be a daily habit. If you can, by all means continue your workouts on a five-times-a-week basis.

If at any point—either after reaching your goal or in the process of doing so—your workouts are interrupted because of illness or other reason for more than a week, it will be best to begin again at a lower level. If you have had a serious illness or surgery, proceed under your physician's guidance.

BROADENING YOUR PROGRAM

The exercises and activities you have engaged in are basic and are designed to take you soundly and progressively up the ladder to physical fitness without need for special equipment or facilities.

There are many other activities and forms of exercise that you can use to supplement the basic program. They include a variety of sports; water exercises you can use if you have access to a pool; and isometrics—sometimes called exercises without movement—which take little time (6–8 seconds each).

Isometrics

Isometric contraction exercises take very little time and require no special equipment. They are excellent muscle strengtheners and, as such, valuable supplements.

The idea of isometrics is to work out a muscle by pushing or pulling against an immovable object such as a wall or by pitting it against the opposition of another muscle. The basis is the "overload" principle of exercise physiology, which holds that a muscle required to perform work beyond the usual intensity grows in strength. And research has indicated that one hard, 6- to 8-second isometric contraction per workout can, over a period of six months, produce a significant strength increase in a muscle.

The exercises described in the following pages cover major large muscle groups of the body. They can be performed almost anywhere and at almost any time. There is no set order for doing them, nor do all have to be completed at one time. You can do one or two in the morning and others at various times during the day whenever you have half a minute or even less to spare.

For each contraction, maintain tension no more than 8 seconds. Do little breathing during a contraction; breathe deeply between contractions.

And start easily. Do not apply maximum effort in the beginning. For the first three or four weeks, you should exert only about one half of what you think is your maximum force. Use the first 3 or 4 seconds to build up to this degree of force—and the remaining 4 or 5 seconds to hold it.

For the next two weeks, gradually increase force to more nearly approach maximum. After about six weeks, it is safe to exert maximum effort. Pain indicates that you're applying too much force; reduce the amount immediately. If pain continues to accompany any exercise, discontinue using that exercise for a week or two. Then try it again with about 50 percent of maximum effort and, if no pain occurs, you can go on to gradually build up toward maximum.

NECK

Starting position: Sit or stand, with interlaced fingers of hands on forehead.
Action: Forcibly exert a forward push of head while resisting equally hard with hands.
Starting position: Sit or stand, with interlaced fingers of hands behind head.
Action: Push head backward while exerting a forward pull with hands.
Starting position: Sit or stand, with palm of left hand on left side of head.
Action: Push with left hand while resisting with head and neck. Reverse using right hand on right side of head.

UPPER BODY

Starting position: Stand, back to wall, hands at sides, palms toward wall.
Action: Press hands backward against wall, keeping arms straight.
Starting position: Stand, facing wall, hands at sides, palms toward wall.
Action: Press hands forward against wall, keeping arms straight.
Starting position: Stand in doorway or with side against wall, arms at sides, palms toward legs.
Action: Press hand(s) outward against wall or doorframe, keeping arms straight.

ARMS

Starting position: Stand with feet slightly apart. Flex right elbow, close to body, palm up. Place left hand over right.
Action: Forcibly attempt to curl right arm upward, while giving equally strong resistance with the left hand. Repeat with left arm.

ARMS AND CHEST

Starting position: Stand with feet comfortably spaced, knees slightly bent. Clasp hands, palms together, close to chest.
Action: Press hands together and hold.
Starting position: Stand with feet slightly apart, knees slightly bent. Grip fingers, arms close to chest.
Action: Pull hard and hold.

ABDOMINAL

Starting position: Stand, knees slightly flexed, hands resting on knees.
Action: Contract abdominal muscles.

LOWER BACK, BUTTOCKS, AND BACK OF THIGHS

Starting position: Lie face down, arms at sides, palms up, legs placed under bed or other heavy object.

Action: With both hips flat on floor, raise one leg, keeping knee straight so that heel pushes hard against the resistance above. Repeat with opposite leg.

LEGS

Starting position: Sit in chair with left ankle crossed over right, feet resting on floor, legs bent at 90-degree angle.
Action: Forcibly attempt to straighten right leg while resisting with the left. Repeat with opposite leg.

INNER AND OUTER THIGHS

Starting position: Sit, legs extended with each ankle pressed against the outside of sturdy chair legs.
Action: Keep legs straight and pull toward one another firmly. For outer thigh muscles, place ankles inside chair legs and exert pressure outward.

Water Activities

Swimming is one of the best physical activities for people of all ages—and for many of the handicapped.
With the body submerged in water, blood circulation automatically increases to some extent. Pressure of water on the body also helps promote deeper ventilation of the lungs; with well-planned activity, both circulation and ventilation increase still more.
The water exercises described after the following chart can be used either as supplements to, or replacements for, the circulatory activities of the basic program. The goals for each of the five levels are shown in the chart below.

Women					
Level	1	2	3	4	5
Bobs	10	15	20	50	100
Swim	5 min	10 min	15 min	—	—
Interval swimming	—	—	—	25 yds. (Repeat 10 times.)	25 yds. (Repeat 20 times.)

Men					
Level	1	2	3	4	5
Bobs	10	15	25	75	125
Swim	5 min	10 min	15 min	—	—
Interval swimming	—	—	—	25 yds. (Repeat 20 times.)	50 yds. (Repeat 20 times.)

BOBBING

Starting position: Face out of water.
Action: Count 1. Take a breath. Count 2. Submerge while exhaling until feet touch bottom. Count 3. Push up from bottom to surface while continuing to exhale. Three counts to one bob.

SWIMMING

Use any type of stroke. Swim continuously for the time specified.

INTERVAL SWIMMING

Use any type of stroke. Swim moderately fast for distance specified. You can then either swim back slowly to starting point or get out of pool and walk back. Repeat specified number of times.

Weight Training

Weight training also is an excellent method of developing muscular strength—and muscular endurance. Where equipment is available, it can be used as a supplement to the seven conditioning exercises.

Because of the great variety of weight training exercises, we do not attempt to describe them here. Both barbells and weighted dumbbells—complete with instructions—are available at most sporting goods stores. A good rule to follow in deciding the maximum weight you should lift is to select a weight you can lift six times without strain.

Sports

Soccer, basketball, handball, squash, ice hockey, and other sports that require sustained effort can be valuable aids to building circulatory endurance. If you have been sedentary, it's important to pace yourself carefully in such sports, and it may even be advisable to avoid them until you are well along in your physical-conditioning program. That doesn't mean you should avoid all sports.

There are many excellent conditioning and circulatory activities in which the amount of exertion is easily controlled and in which you can progress at your own rate. Bicycling is one example. Others include hiking, skating, tennis, running, cross-country skiing, rowing, canoeing, water skiing, and skin diving.

You can engage in these sports at any point in the program, if you start slowly. Games should be played with full speed and vigor only when your conditioning permits doing so without undue fatigue. On days when you get a good workout in sports, you can skip part or all of your exercise program. Use your own judgment.

If you engage in a sport that exercises the legs and stimulates the heart and lungs—such as skating—you can skip the circulatory activity for that day, but you still should do some of the conditioning and stretching exercises for the upper body. On the other hand, weight lifting is an excellent conditioning activity, but it should be supplemented with running or one of the other circulatory exercises.

Whatever your favorite sport, you will find your enjoyment enhanced by improved fitness. Every weekend athlete should invest in frequent workouts.